THE WORLD AS IT IS

THE
WORLD
AS IT IS

---

*Inside the Obama
White House*

BEN RHODES

THE BODLEY HEAD
LONDON

1 3 5 7 9 10 8 6 4 2

The Bodley Head, an imprint of Vintage,
20 Vauxhall Bridge Road,
London SW1V 2SA

The Bodley Head is part of the Penguin Random House group of companies
whose addresses can be found at global.penguinrandomhouse.com.

Penguin
Random House
UK

First published in the United States by Random House in 2018
First published in the United Kingdom by The Bodley Head in 2018

www.penguin.co.uk/vintage

A CIP catalogue record for this book is available from the British Library

Hardback ISBN 9781847925176
Trade paperback ISBN 9781847925183

All photographs, unless otherwise indicated, are courtesy of the author
Title-page photo by Pete Souza
Book design by Barbara M. Bachman

Printed and bound by Clays Ltd, St Ives plc

Penguin Random House is committed to a sustainable future for
our business, our readers and our planet. This book is made
from Forest Stewardship Council® certified paper.

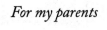

For my parents

"The clouds were building up now for the trade wind and he looked ahead and saw a flight of wild ducks etching themselves against the sky over the water, then blurring, then etching again and he knew no man was ever alone on the sea."

—ERNEST HEMINGWAY

CONTENTS

———

PART THREE   CHANGE: 2013–2014

PART FOUR
WHAT MAKES AMERICA GREAT: 2015–2017

PROLOGUE

———

OR THE FINAL TIME IN A FOREIGN COUNTRY AS PRESIDENT OF
the United States of America, Barack Hussein Obama eased into
his seat as a Secret Service agent shut the heavy door. "Let's go
home," he said.

Inside the presidential limousine—known as the Beast—the
world outside is silent and kept at a distance by inches of bulletproof glass and armored metal. There is an eerie familiarity to riding
in a motorcade, whether you are in an empty Saudi Arabian desert
or a crowded street in Hanoi. The front two seats are always occupied by Secret Service agents who never say a word; while they sit
there scanning the road ahead, you learn to talk as if they are not
present.

Obama glanced across at me and a light crept into his eyes. "Did
you see Ben forgot his socks?" he said to Susan Rice, peeling back a
wrapper and popping a piece of Nicorette into his mouth. He
laughed in anticipation of his own words. "I mean, come on, man.
Your socks!"

Each day that you travel abroad with the president, you place
your suitcase outside your hotel room door and someone picks it up
at a set time. This was part of the easy rhythm of travel that would
soon disappear. I began to explain that when I'd shoved my bag
outside my door at three in the morning, I thought I'd set aside a
pair . . .

He waved a hand at me. "I get it. It was a late night. I'm glad you guys had a good time while I was reading my APEC briefing book."

I looked out the window at one last stretch of crowds. The streets of Lima were littered with onlookers set against a backdrop of rising modern towers and older, more dilapidated buildings. They were watching, waving, and holding up smartphones—one more trickle of humanity among the millions of faces I had seen over the years through the window of a passing motorcade, straining for a glimpse of Barack Obama. Every now and then on these drives, Obama would glance out the window and offer a casual wave and I'd see someone's face freeze in a shock of recognition. Sometimes I would hold up my phone and take pictures of the crowds taking pictures of us, the only way to feel a connection with a mass of human beings whom I would never, could never, really know.

Normally, Obama would take out his iPad and scroll through the news or rejoin an endless game of Scrabble and ask us how we thought he did in the just-concluded press conference. I sat opposite him, just as I had on trips to dozens of countries over the last eight years. But—after the laughter at my socks faded away—he sat silently, chewing his Nicorette and staring out the window. This was the final trip, and despite the familiar rhythms, nothing about it felt normal. The whole world seemed to be passing us by.

I glanced across at the presidential seal affixed to the wood paneling next to the seat that Obama occupied—a seat that would be taken by Donald J. Trump in a couple of months.

AT OUR FIRST STOP, in Athens, we had planned to give a speech celebrating the resilience of democracy in its birthplace, with the Acropolis as the backdrop. As we'd sketched it out, we'd foreseen a defiant challenge to Russia and its revanchist leader, Vladimir Putin. Somehow, that setting no longer felt equal to America's moment. It was two weeks after the election of Donald Trump. We moved the speech indoors to an auditorium that could have been anyplace.

We ended up touring the Acropolis instead, on a pristine, warm morning. From its perch up on a hill, the world was lovely and calm—in the clear blue sky and sweeping view of Athens, there was no hint of the financial crisis gripping Greece, the flow of refugees crossing its borders, or the uncertainty that those forces had unleashed in the world beyond. I trailed Obama as he wandered through the collection of ancient pillars and scaffolding and tributes to the gods, a monument to the origins of democracy and the ruins left behind by lost empires and expired beliefs. When I saw him afterward, he repeated a maxim that he'd shared with me in the early morning hours after the election of Trump, a refrain that sought out perspective: "There are more stars in the sky," he said, "than grains of sand on the earth."

At our second stop, in Berlin, Angela Merkel asked to see Obama for dinner our first night there. Merkel has a kind of reverse charisma—stoic, self-possessed, with a slight smile that draws you in, a woman at ease in power and her own skin—and she greeted him with a hand on each arm. She was his closest partner in a world that offered few friends, and she had risked her political future by welcoming a million Syrian refugees to Germany. Obama admired her pragmatism, her unflappability, and her stubborn streak. Over the previous year, he had battled his own bureaucracy to increase the number of refugees that America would welcome, telling us again and again, "We can't leave Angela hanging."

The two of them sat alone at a small, simple table in the middle of a hotel conference room. They ate and talked for three hours, the longest time Obama had spent alone with a foreign leader in eight years. A few of us dined with her staff in an adjoining room. The Germans looked stricken; they spoke with unease about the new world coming, and the burdens on Merkel within it. "To the leader of the free world," I toasted, ruefully. One aide told me that Steve Bannon's appointment to the White House staff had been front-page news in Germany. "We know Bannon," he said, leaning toward me as if passing on a secret in confidence. Outside the window you could see the Brandenburg Gate in a gold light, and the Reichstag building, the replacement for the one that was set on fire as Hitler took power.

Later, Obama told us that Merkel had talked to him about her looming decision on whether to seek another term, something that she now felt more obliged to do because of Brexit and Trump. At the end of our time in Germany, when Obama bade her farewell at the door of the Beast, a single tear appeared in her eye—something that none of us had ever seen before. "Angela," he said, shaking his head. "She's all alone."

At this third and final stop, a summit of Pacific nations in Lima, Obama was pulled aside by leader after leader and asked what to expect from Donald Trump. Ever conscious of the norms of his office, Obama dutifully urged his counterparts to give the new administration a chance. "Wait and see," he told them. The leaders of eleven other countries who had painstakingly negotiated the Trans-Pacific Partnership (TPP) trade agreement met with Obama on the first day. If they were angry at having taken tough political decisions to bind their economic futures to the United States only to see the new president-elect commit to pulling out, they concealed it. Instead, they were almost apologetic in their suggestion that they'd probably just move forward with some form of the agreement without the United States.

For the first time in eight years, history felt out of our hands.

The Japanese prime minister, Shinzo Abe, apologized for having breached protocol by meeting with Trump at Trump Tower without telling Obama beforehand. The Japanese felt they had no choice but to strike up a relationship with a man who had threatened to charge Japan for the troops that we stationed there. Abe confirmed his plans to visit Pearl Harbor when Obama would be in Hawaii in December—a gesture of reconciliation that mirrored Obama's own visit to Hiroshima, and that suddenly seemed out of step with the times.

Obama met with the president of China, Xi Jinping, in a sterile hotel conference room, untouched cups of cooling tea and ice water before us. There was a long review of all the progress made over the last several years. Xi assured Obama, unprompted, that he would implement the Paris climate agreement even if Trump decided to pull out. "That's very wise of you," Obama replied. "I think you'll continue to see an investment in Paris in the United States, at least from states, cities, and the private sector." We were only two years removed from the time when Obama had flown to Beijing and secured an agreement to act in concert with China to combat climate change, the step that made the Paris agreement possible in the first place. Now China would lead that effort going forward.

Toward the end of the meeting, Xi asked about Trump. Again, Obama suggested that the Chinese wait and see what the new administration decided to do in office, but he noted that the president-elect had tapped into real concerns among Americans about the fairness of our economic relationship with China. Xi is a big man who moves slowly and deliberately, as if he wants people to notice his every motion. Sitting across the table from Obama, he pushed aside the binder of talking points that usually shape the words of a Chinese leader. *We prefer to have a good relationship with the United States,* he said, folding his hands in front of him. *That is good for the world. But every action will have a reaction. And if an immature leader throws the world into chaos, then the world will know whom to blame.*

On this final day, Obama held his last bilateral meeting with Prime Minister Justin Trudeau of Canada. In a back room at the convention center where the summit was held, the two sat in chairs next to each other with a few of us flanking them on either side. I avoided crossing my legs and instead kept my feet tucked under my backpack to hide my lack of socks. Obama—not usually an outwardly sentimental man—attempted to pass a torch of sorts. "Justin, your voice is going to be needed more," he said, leaning forward and putting his elbows on his knees. "You're going to have to speak out when certain values are threatened."

Trudeau said that he felt he had to, drawing on the example of his own father, who transcended his role as leader of Canada to become a global statesman. *I modeled my campaign on yours,* he added, referring to a brand of politics that now felt under threat.

In person, Trudeau's good looks tend to make him look younger than he is. Watching him, I thought about how much I had aged in my job; Trudeau looked younger than I did. *I will fight them*, he said, referring to the authoritarian trends in the world, *with a smile on my face. That is the only way to win.*

When they were done, we walked through the back passageways of the convention center, Obama clutching a Styrofoam cup of tea and waving to the maintenance staff as he made his way to a final foreign press conference. I didn't feel like watching. Instead, I sat alone on a bench in the fading light of dusk, fumbling through my BlackBerry, ensconced within a security perimeter guarded by men in suits with earpieces who folded their hands in front of them. When the press conference was over, I joined the pack around Obama walking out of the room, passing Trudeau and his team as they moved in the other direction.

ALONG THE STREETS OF Lima the crowds still waved as the president of the United States passed by.

"What if we were wrong?" Obama said, sitting opposite me in the Beast.

"Wrong about what?" I asked.

For days, we had been trying to deconstruct what had happened in the recent election. Obama had complained he couldn't believe that the election was lost, rattling off the indicators—"Five percent unemployment. Twenty million covered. Gas at two bucks a gallon. *We had it all teed up!*" Now he told me about a piece he had read in *The New York Times,* a column asserting that liberals had forgotten how important identity is to people, that we had embraced a message indistinguishable from John Lennon's "Imagine"—touting an empty, cosmopolitan globalism that could no longer reach people. *Imagine all the people, sharing all the world.*

"Maybe we pushed too far," he said. "Maybe people just want to fall back into their tribe."

His comment rested heavily as Susan and I made eye contact. Over the last couple of weeks, Obama was the one who had been putting on the bravest face. The night of the election, after he reminded me that there were more stars in the sky than grains of sand on the earth, I'd sent him a simple note, trying to cheer him up: "Progress doesn't move in a straight line." In private conversations with staff and in public interviews ever since, he'd been repeating a version of it: "History doesn't move in a straight line," he'd say, "it zigs and zags."

What if we were wrong?

Since I went to work for Obama in 2007, the one thing I never lost faith in was the confidence that I was a part of something that was *right* in some intangible way. Sure, we—the Obama White House—had gotten some things wrong. But the larger project— *that* was correct. The belief in America becoming a better place. The hope that if we can find strength in containing multitudes, then so can the world.

Something stung a bit in Obama's words, the suggestion that what he represented was, in the current moment, a lost cause. "But you would have won if you could have run," I said. Grasping for a different argument, I talked about the young people he had spoken to in a town hall meeting just the day before in Lima, as he had done in so many countries around the world. "They *get* it," I said. "They're more tolerant. They have more in common with young people in the United States than Trump does. Young people didn't vote for Trump, just like young people in the UK didn't vote for Brexit."

He didn't look up. "I don't know," he said. "Sometimes I wonder whether I was ten or twenty years too early."

The silence lingered. Over the past eight years, we'd had a thousand conversations that all felt like part of one running thread, talking about books we'd read and foreign leaders who frustrated us, about race and old movie lines, sports and theories of everything. My role in these conversations, and perhaps within his presidency, I had come to see, was to respond to what he said, to talk and fill quiet space—to test out the logic of his own ideas, or to offer a distraction—as he scrolled through his iPad or looked out the window, mind churning.

The motorcade reached the airport and pulled onto the tarmac before a waiting Air Force One. We stopped near the edge of a group of Peruvian and American "greeters" in a long, straight line to bid farewell.

As we waited for the agent to open the door, Obama leaned forward, elbows on his knees. "Maybe you're right," he said, returning to my comment about young people. "But we're about to find out just how resilient our institutions are, at home and around the world."

With that, he stepped out of the Beast and began to work his way down the receiving line. I got out and walked, my bare feet sticking against the worn leather of my shoes, to a spot under the wing of the plane where clusters of people stood, journalists recording the moment for posterity, staff posed for pictures with one another. The scene was entirely familiar to me after flying well over a million miles around the world on this plane, but it was about to disappear forever.

Barack Obama shook the last hand and made his way up the stairs. He always moved with ease, like an athlete playing a basketball game at slightly less than a hundred percent, holding some energy in reserve for the key moments of the fourth quarter. A man constantly in the public eye who hid important parts of himself. Over the last two years, I'd seen him become increasingly comfortable being both himself *and* the president—in individual moments, singing "Amazing Grace" in a black church that had been targeted by a white supremacist in Charleston; or in policies, ending an approach to Cuba that he had long told me he opposed. This evolution had made him more effective, more interesting, and ultimately more appreciated in these waning days of his time in office. This was one possible and painful answer to the question he had raised in the Beast: We were right, but all that progress depended upon him, and now he was out of time.

For the first time in eight years, there was no trip left to plan. Obama would board the plane as a successful two-term African American president and a vessel for the aspirations of billions of people around the world. But he was about to hand power over to a man who represented every political, economic, and social force that his own identity opposed. One joke that he told in the days after the election expressed his frustration at how this would impact the rest of his life: "I feel like Michael Corleone," he'd say. "I almost got out."

I was twenty-nine years old when I went to work for the Obama campaign. From the tarmac in Lima, I could no longer recognize the person who had moved out to Chicago to write speeches and live in a studio apartment with a few scattered Ikea items and a mattress on the floor. The catastrophes of 9/11 and the Iraq War had propelled me there, in search of a better story about America, and myself. I'd spent eight years pursuing it in a windowless West Wing office where I could hear rats scurrying in the ceiling above me and could walk into meetings where the fate of nations was discussed. I'd experienced highs I could never have anticipated, such as walking into the Vatican to tell a cardinal we were normalizing relations with Cuba. I'd suffered lows I couldn't yet understand, being demonized by the same forces that led to the rise of Donald Trump. Most of all, I'd subsumed my own story into the story of Barack Obama—his campaign, his presidency, the place where he was leading us.

Standing there, I struggled to find some feeling within myself that would sum up what it felt like to watch our country represented abroad for the last time by this man—decent and determined, at times reticent, at others bolder than any politician I'd seen. But watching him make his way up the stairs of the plane, all I could conjure up was a flood of disconnected images from trips past: a sea of humanity waiting to hear him speak in Berlin; a greeting party of drummers in the middle of the night in Ghana; millions of smiling people lining all the routes of our motorcade in Vietnam; the unlikely sight of Havana from the window of Air Force One. The sense of excitement that people had, all those people in all those places, all those faces looking back with hope. *That* is what I'd been looking for when I moved out to Chicago ten years before. And that, I realized, would no longer greet an American president abroad, so it was hard to feel anything other than tired and sad. I could not remember what I was like when the story began, and I had no idea what I—or the world—would be like after it was over.

There are more stars in the sky than grains of sand on the earth.

Obama reached the top of the stairs, and I thought he might stop for just an extra moment to take it all in, to offer himself some opportunity to mine the kind of thoughts that were racing through my head. But whatever memories were passing through his own head, however he felt about the hundreds of places he'd been as president and the millions of people he'd seen, despite the uncertainty that now awaited, he offered only a routine wave before disappearing through the doorway of the plane and into the journey home.

What if we were wrong?

PART ONE

HOPE

2007—2010

CHAPTER I

IN THE
BEGINNING

———

THE FIRST TIME I MET BARACK OBAMA, I DIDN'T WANT TO SAY a word.

It was a sleepy May afternoon in 2007, and I was sitting in my windowless office at the Woodrow Wilson International Center for Scholars, a D.C. think tank like dozens of others. I was underemployed and debating moving back home to New York when I got a call from Mark Lippert, who was Obama's top foreign policy aide in the Senate. Lippert was a young guy, like me, and I had come to expect phone calls from him every few days with random taskings; he was working for the most exciting politician to come along in years, and he clearly enjoyed the fact that anyone would take his call at any time.

"Ben," he said, "I was wondering if it's not too much trouble for you to come over and do debate prep with Obama?"

I gripped the phone a little more tightly. For the last few months I'd been doing everything I could to work my way onto the Obama campaign—writing floor statements on Iraq, drafting an op-ed on Ireland ("O'Bama"), editing speeches and debate memos. I had never gotten near the man, and I was starting to wonder if my volunteer work would ever turn into anything else.

"When is it?" I asked.

"It's right now."

The session was at a law firm a couple of blocks away, and I walked slowly, gathering my thoughts. Like all the work I'd done for the campaign, this felt like some sort of test, only no grade was issued at the end and no one would tell me if I'd passed. When I got there, I was directed to a set of glass doors that led into a large conference room. I could see at least fifteen people around a long table strewn with binders, stacks of paper, and soda cans. Obama was seated at the head of the table with his feet up. Lippert met me at the door, pulled me outside, and told me they were debating whether Obama should vote for a spending bill in Congress that would fund the so-called surge in Iraq. "I thought, why not call the Iraq guy?" he said.

A few months earlier, I had finished working for the Iraq Study Group, a collection of former officials and foreign policy experts who had been asked to come up with a strategy for the Iraq War. My boss at the time, Lee Hamilton, was cochair, along with James Baker. Hamilton was a throwback—a crew-cut Democrat from southern Indiana who had served thirty-four years in Congress. He wasn't just a moderate—he was a pragmatist who approached government without a trace of ideology. Baker was what the Republican Party used to be—a business-friendly operator who took governing as seriously as making money. Throughout our work, in meetings with members of the Bush administration that he'd helped put into power through his efforts on the Florida recount after the 2000 election, Baker's understanding of the scale of the mess that had been made in Iraq seemed to morph into a kind of paternal disappointment—he'd given the keys to his kids and they'd crashed the car.

For me, the project opened a window into a war that I'd watched unfold with swelling anger. As part of our work, we'd gone to Iraq in the summer of 2006, flying into Baghdad in a cargo plane with a group of servicemembers starting their tour, sitting in silence because the roar of the engine made it too difficult to be heard. I looked closely at the faces of these men and women who would soon be threatened by car bombs and improvised explosive devices, but they betrayed no emotion at all—just blank stares. The plane dropped sharply into Baghdad International Airport, making tight corkscrew turns to avoid antiaircraft fire. We flew in helicopters to the Green Zone. Down below, I could smell burning sewage and see the faces of children looking up at us with vacant expressions.

For several days, we stayed on the embassy compound in small trailers. At night, we went to a bar—the Camel's Back—where contractors got hammered and danced on tables. There were two beds in each trailer and a shared bathroom. A flak jacket was next to each bed in case of incoming mortar or rocket fire. I had the place to myself except for one night when I came back to find a bearded guy, perfectly fit and totally naked, standing in the bathroom. I noticed some neatly arranged Special Forces gear by his bed. We didn't say a word to each other. When I woke at dawn, he was gone. Years later, I would become familiar with the work that people like him did as I learned about it thousands of miles away in the basement of the White House.

During our stay, we were driven in armored vehicles to lavish compounds filled with gold-plated furniture and thick curtains left behind by Saddam Hussein. We met with Iraq's political leaders, American military officers, and a mix of diplomats, journalists, and clerics. We heard about violence between Sunni and Shia sects that was killing Iraqis just beyond the walls of the Green Zone—bodies in sewers, family members assassinated, nightmarish stories of group executions. We'd recap at night in James Baker's trailer, where he'd drink straight vodka in a tracksuit and just shake his head at how screwed up things were. The United States had nearly 150,000 troops supporting the Iraqi Security Forces, but everyone spoke of a series of militias as the main drivers of politics. One American general told us that unless the different sects reconciled, "all the troops in the world could not bring security to Iraq."

Each night, helicopters brought wounded Americans to a temporary hospital. When we visited, Hamilton spoke to a medic who gave us an overview of the work they did. "My job," he said, "is to keep these folks alive until we can get them up to surgery." He explained that our troops wear armor that covers your upper body well; what it does not cover is the lower extremities, nor does it guard against the force of the blasts that can cause trauma to the brain. Were it not for this armor, he said, the American dead in Iraq would be closer to the number of those killed in Vietnam; but for those who survive those wounds, life can become a permanent and painful struggle.

Just being there for a few days showed me how the most pivotal moment of my life had led to moral wreckage and strategic disaster. I moved to Washington in the spring of 2002, as the drumbeat for war in Iraq was sounding louder. I moved because I was a New Yorker and 9/11 upended everything I had been thinking about what I was going to do with my life. I had been teaching at a community college during the day, getting a master's in fiction writing at night, and working on a city council campaign. On September 11, 2001, I was handing out flyers at a polling site on a north Brooklyn street when I saw the second plane hit, stared at plumes of black smoke billowing in the sky, and then watched the first tower crumple to the ground. Mobile phone service was down and I didn't know if lower Manhattan had been destroyed. A man with some kind of European accent grabbed my arm and said, over and over, "This is sabotage." For days after, the air had the acrid smell of seared metal, melted wires, and death.

I wanted to be a part of what happened next, and I was repelled by the reflexive liberalism of my New York University surroundings—the professor who suggested that we sing "God Bless Afghanistan" to the tune of "God Bless America," the preemptive protests against American military intervention, the reflexive distrust of Bush. I visited an Army recruiter under the Queensboro Bridge. After leaving with a pile of materials and getting a few follow-up phone calls, I decided that I couldn't see myself in uniform. Instead, I would move to Washington to write about the events reshaping my world. I had never considered being a speechwriter, and I had never heard of Lee Hamilton, but one reference led to another and soon I found myself at the Wilson Center, one small cog in the vast machinery of people who think, talk, and write about American foreign policy. I was a liberal, skeptical of military adventurism in our history, and something seemed off about toppling Saddam Hussein because of something done by Osama bin Laden. But when you're putting on a tie and riding the D.C. metro with a bunch of other twenty-five-year-olds to a think tank a few blocks from the White House, angry about 9/11 and determined to be taken seriously, you listen to what the older, more experienced people say. The moment Colin Powell made his case for war to the United Nations, I was on board.

Now here I was, a few years later, seeing what that war had wrought. We began writing the Iraq Study Group report by committee, but after a few drafts, Baker's staff guy called me and asked me to take the lead. I'd stay up all night agonizing over sentence structure and whether the group was going far enough in calling for an end to the war. The first sentence of the report said "the situation in Iraq is grave and deteriorating," and the report called for a phased withdrawal of U.S. troops. Instead, Bush put more troops into the country. To me, the experience clarified two things: First, the people who were supposed to know better had gotten us into a moral and strategic disaster; second, you can't change things unless you change the people making the decisions. I had a decent policy job, but I wanted to get into politics. And I wanted to work for Barack Obama.

Lippert and I walked into the conference room, and I took a seat near the back end of the table farthest from Obama. From the moment I saw his speech at the Democratic convention in 2004, I had wanted him to run for president. He had been against the war when nearly everyone else went along with it. He used language that sounded authentic and moral at a time when our politics was anything but. There was also something else, something intangible. The events of my twenties felt historic, but the people involved did not. I wanted a hero—someone who could make sense of what was happening around me and in some way redeem it.

I was seated next to Tony Lake, who—along with Susan Rice—

was leading a network of foreign policy advisors for the campaign. Lake was a soft-spoken older guy with the smart but slightly scattered demeanor of a professor at a small liberal arts college, which he'd been for many years. He'd also been Bill Clinton's first national security advisor. Rice had also worked for Clinton, becoming the assistant secretary of state for Africa. Since then, she'd been a leading Democratic voice on foreign policy—unabashedly ambitious, well-spoken, and prolific—who risked her relationship with the Clintons to work for Obama. Still, over the last few months, I'd come to suspect that the network led by Lake and Rice was mostly about giving people a way to feel connected to a candidate they were unlikely to ever meet. Most of the work I'd done that actually reached Obama was coordinated by Lippert and another campaign staffer, Denis McDonough. It was Lippert, after all, who had brought me into this room.

David Axelrod was the principal strategist, and as I took my seat he was giving a long description of the political dilemma— Democratic primary voters would want any vote on the Iraq War to be a no, but if Obama voted no, a future Republican general election candidate would say that Obama failed to fund our troops in battle. The ghosts of the 2004 election, when Republicans painted John Kerry as soft on terrorism, lingered in the room. "I'm sure they're having the same discussion in the Clinton campaign," Axelrod said.

"Hillary will vote however I vote," Obama said. I was struck by his confidence; it could have seemed like arrogance, except he was so casual in his tone.

The conversation meandered around the room. Most everyone was neutral—describing the dilemma, as Axelrod did, but offering no clear recommendation. It felt as if the political advisors leaned no but didn't want to say so. When it got to Susan, she made the case for voting yes. Compact, permanently composed, and the only African American in the room other than Obama, she spoke in sharp, declarative language. "This is about the bullets that go in the weapons that defend our troops," she said. "This is a commander in chief moment."

As she spoke, I felt panic welling up inside me. I didn't want to be called on. At the time, I had a profound fear of public speaking. If a group was familiar to me, I didn't have a problem. But here, I wouldn't be able to conceal my nerves. I imagined myself staring blankly, then choking on my words. There, at the head of the table, was Barack Obama. What would he think if I couldn't get through a paragraph of advice?

To avoid having to speak in front of the group, I figured I'd give Lake my views. I leaned over and began to tell him why I thought Obama should vote no. Obama, a former law professor, has a trait that I would witness thousands of times in the years to come. He likes to call on just about everyone in a room. And he doesn't like it when people have side conversations. "Tony," he called out from the other end of the table. "You have a view you want to share?"

"Why don't we ask Ben?" Tony said.

"Who's Ben?" Obama asked.

"He helped write the Iraq Study Group report," Lippert said.

"Well, what do you think?" Obama looked at me. Nerves in my stomach became tightness in my chest, dryness in my throat. There was no way I could speak in paragraphs. So I had to do something different that would break up my speaking.

"Well," I said. "You oppose the surge, right?"

"Sure," Obama said. I took a deep breath.

"And you've introduced legislation to draw down our troops in Iraq and impose more conditions on the Iraqis to reconcile, right?" I asked.

"Yes," Obama said.

"And this legislation funds the surge and rejects your plan, right?"

"Yes."

Obama seemed to be getting irritated, so I got to the point. "Well, why would you vote to fund a policy that you oppose, that you don't think will resolve the situation in Iraq, and that contradicts the legislation that you've introduced? You should vote no."

The room was quiet for a moment. Obama leaned forward and tapped the table with his hand. "Okay, I think we've talked about this enough," he said. "I'll make a decision when I go up to the Hill."

When the meeting ended, people started to break into groups, and Obama got up to leave. After he reached the door, he stopped, turned around, and waded through a few people to come over to me. He extended a hand.

"Hey, I'm Barack," he said. "Glad you're with us."

I muttered something like "Thanks" as he turned away. Lippert asked me to walk with him to the Metro and told me something that he hadn't shared widely—as a Navy Reservist, he'd been called up to serve in Iraq. He'd be leaving in a little over a month, instead of going to Chicago to work in the campaign office as planned, and he was going to recommend they hire me. "No one out there knows anything about foreign policy," he said as he descended the escalator.

I stood at the entrance to a Metro station that I'd come in and out of for the last five years. Something had changed in my life, but I had no way of knowing the scale of that change. A couple of hours later, Obama—who valued, more than I knew, advice that draws on common sense to reject convention—walked onto the floor of the Senate. He voted no.

CHAPTER 2

TALK TO IRAN,
GET BIN LADEN

THE OBAMA CAMPAIGN NEEDED MORE THAN FOREIGN POLICY help—they needed a speechwriter, too, and asked me to move out to Chicago at the beginning of August to join a three-person speechwriting team while also being, essentially, the guy who knew something about foreign policy in the Chicago office. After I'd spent the last five years in the buttoned-up world of a D.C. think tank, where people lingered over lunch to talk about postconflict reconstruction, the communications department of an insurgent Democratic primary campaign was a revelation.

I reported to three people. The omnipresent strategist who weighed in on every issue was David Axelrod, a brilliant and disheveled former Chicago journalist known universally as Axe, who would call at all hours of the day to test out ideas—he saw, for instance, an article about how the Bush administration failed to take a shot at an al Qaeda leadership meeting in Pakistan in 2005 and wanted me to use that in an upcoming speech. The communications director was Robert Gibbs, a win-at-all-costs operative from Alabama who, shortly after my move, gave us all a football coach lecture about how the only time we were allowed to take off until the Iowa caucus was Sunday morning to go to church. The chief speechwriter was a charismatic twenty-five-year-old named Jon Favreau, the handsome leader of the under-thirty set on the campaign, who was known only as Favs. (Obama called him Fav, but no one ever corrected him.) When Favreau emailed me in July to tell me that I was going to have to write a "big terrorism speech," the subject line of the email was "Terror. It's Not Just for Terrorists Anymore."

I was hired at a time when foreign policy was increasingly important in the campaign. During a Democratic debate in July, Obama had been asked by a YouTube questioner if he'd be willing to meet, without preconditions, with a number of U.S. adversaries, including Iran and Cuba. "I would," Obama answered. "And the reason is this, that the notion that somehow not talking to countries is somehow punishment to them, which has been the guiding diplomatic principle of this administration, is ridiculous." Clinton disagreed, and—sensing an opening—later called Obama's position "irresponsible, and frankly naïve."

There usually aren't many differences on policy in a primary, and this one played into the narratives of both campaigns. Obama's message was that Clinton was too close to Bush because she voted for the Iraq War and couldn't be trusted to bring change; Clinton's message was that Obama wasn't experienced enough to be president. So this question about whether to pursue diplomacy with adversaries was about something bigger—about which criticism was right, and how the United States should conduct foreign policy after the Iraq War. I found myself in the middle of that debate, and I'd stay there for the next decade.

After I was offered the job, I gnawed on one question: How do you write a speech for someone you don't know? To capture Obama's voice, I studied his speeches, interview transcripts, and books, which I would end up rereading a dozen times. His first memoir, *Dreams from My Father*, is a kind of Rosetta Stone to Obama's life and worldview, and it offered up many eloquent turns of phrase that I would reuse again and again over the next ten years.

The goal for the "big terrorism speech" was to have Obama sound like someone who could be commander in chief, someone who could be a strident critic of the Iraq War and still be able to

wage war against the terrorists who attacked us on 9/11. This prem-
ise had the benefit of being true. One of the things that had drawn
me to Obama was a speech he'd given at an antiwar rally in 2002,
before the war in Iraq, when the people who knew better were saying it was bad politics and bad policy to oppose the war. "I know,"
he said, "that even a successful war against Iraq will require a U.S.
occupation of undetermined length, at undetermined cost, with undetermined consequences. I know that an invasion of Iraq without
a clear rationale and without strong international support will only
fan the flames of the Middle East, and encourage the worst, rather
than the best, impulses of the Arab world, and strengthen the re-
cruitment arm of al Qaeda. I am not opposed to all wars. I'm opposed to dumb wars."

The speech I was writing would bring that argument up to date.
Obama would lay out his drawdown plan for Iraq while calling for
two additional combat brigades in Afghanistan and a renewed
focus on al Qaeda. Beyond that, he would propose a counterterrorism strategy of strengthening other countries to go after terrorists;
closing the prison at Guantanamo Bay and ending torture; and expanding diplomacy and foreign assistance. It ended up being a re-
markably accurate blueprint for what Obama did as president,
especially on the two most controversial items: a renewed pledge to
pursue diplomacy with Iran over its nuclear program, and a promise
to go after Osama bin Laden in Pakistan.

The staffer who coordinated foreign policy for the campaign was
Denis McDonough, an earnest Minnesotan whose extreme polite-
ness concealed a steely ambition that would lead him to consolidate
national security decision making on the campaign and on the National Security Council and ultimately become White House chief
of staff. That July, bin Laden was back in the news because a U.S.
National Intelligence Estimate declared that al Qaeda had regener-
ated in Pakistan. Like Axe, Denis and I both thought that Obama's
position should include a commitment to go after bin Laden in
Pakistan.

Obama's external foreign policy advisors were wary. Several had already been uncomfortable with the call for diplomacy with Iran without preconditions. The day after the debate, the campaign couldn't find experts willing to go out and defend Obama's stance. The consensus in the foreign policy establishment was that Obama had made a blunder, and that was mirrored by a political class in Washington who felt that anything other than reflexive "toughness" on Iran was a losing proposition. Diplomacy, apparently, is "weak"; refusing to engage in diplomacy, by the inverse property, is "tough." Never mind that Iran was steadily advancing its nuclear program.

While the main office was in Chicago, the Obama campaign also had a small walk-up suite of rooms on Massachusetts Avenue near the Capitol. It was a place for Obama to have meetings and make fundraising calls, and for staff who happened to be in D.C. to get on a laptop. A few days before the speech, a group of policy advisors met there with Obama around a small conference table. As the speechwriter who had been hired by the campaign, I felt I had a new standing as I took my place at the small table with a few of the bigger foreign policy names on the campaign, including Susan Rice, Denis McDonough, Jeh Johnson—a lawyer from New York— and Richard Clarke.

Clarke was a former Bush administration counterterrorism official who had made a name for himself by blasting the Bush administration's failure to take the threat from al Qaeda seriously before 9/11. I remembered sitting in a charged Senate hearing room watching him testify before Hamilton and the other 9/11 commissioners, surprising the audience by apologizing to the 9/11 families present for failing to prevent the attacks. Now I listened as he voiced caution against a call to go after bin Laden in Pakistan. "Senator," Clarke said to Obama, "you have to get the tribes in the FATA to work with you"—referring to the tribal region of Pakistan along the Afghan border.

Others worried about blowback from President Pervez Musharraf of Pakistan, an American ally. After the external advisors left, Obama walked into another room, where Robert Gibbs was scanning press stories on a laptop screen. No one asked me to leave, so I followed Obama into the other room with Denis, hoping to get more insight into the person I was working for.

"Here's the man that won the straw poll," Gibbs said to me. The first speech I'd written for the campaign was for a Planned Parenthood conference, and Obama had won a straw poll of the attendees. "Congratulations, brother." I couldn't tell if he was being sincere or making fun of me, a foreign policy guy now writing constituency speeches.

Obama strolled over to read the screen over Gibbs's shoulder. The two of them had an easy familiarity that came from traveling together for years. "Senator," I asked, "how do you want to handle bin Laden in the speech?"

"I want to say we'd take him out," he replied.

"Do you want me to talk about Musharraf?" I asked.

He looked over his shoulder at me. "I don't care how we say it. I want to make clear that we'll get bin Laden."

Gibbs started reading aloud from the story they were looking at, in which Madeleine Albright was criticizing Obama for saying he'd talk to Iran. "What are these people talking about?" Obama said.

"Didn't she go to North Korea?" Denis asked.

Obama turned and laughed in a way that he does, leaning far forward and putting his whole body into it. "Right!" he said. "It. Is. Not. A. Reward. To. Talk. To. Folks." He pounded his open palm on the table as he spoke. "How is that working out with Iran? I want to double down on this. Put it in the speech. Robert, I want to do an interview. Can we get someone over here now?" This, I thought, was someone new, someone different.

Over the next few days I got a flurry of notes on each draft of the speech from a dozen policy advisors. Afraid of bucking people who were more experienced, I'd include their edits, only to get rebuked by Axe, Favreau, and ultimately Obama. Finally, I just started telling people no, Obama wanted to keep it the way it was. It's something I would keep doing for years.

On August 1, Obama was set to deliver the speech at the Wilson

Center. A few minutes before, this forty-five-year-old black man I was going to work for met with me and Lee Hamilton, the seventy-six-year-old white man who'd been my boss for more than five years. Later in the campaign, I'd spend a couple of days driving across southern Indiana with Hamilton as he campaigned for Obama—something he did for no favors, as he ended up turning down an offer to run the CIA. Southern Indiana once had a high concentration of KKK membership, and every audience was old and white. In diners adjacent to town squares, small college meeting rooms, and senior centers, Hamilton would plead for votes to skeptical groups of ten, twenty, and thirty, his voice raised an octave, his accent more folksy. "I know what you're thinking," he'd say. "He's different. He's young. He's *black*." Then he'd pause. "Well, I'm telling you, this guy is the future. And it's time for a change."

Hamilton and Obama chatted about Hamilton's latest project—a commission focused on the war powers of the president of the United States. "It's way too easy for any president to take us to war," Hamilton told Obama. Then we all took a picture together and Hamilton called me "a fine young man." I felt as if I was being sent off to summer camp.

A FEW DAYS LATER, I moved to Chicago. Until I could find a place to live, I slept on a cot in the guest room of a friend who lived out near Evanston, almost an hour by train.

My girlfriend, Ann, was not happy about the move. Ann and I had been dating for a few years and had recently moved in together. We were an unlikely pair. She was a tall, striking redhead from a big Catholic family in Huntington Beach—the heart of Orange County, California. She worked her way to Washington—from Orange Coast Community College, to UCLA, to the office of her local congresswoman, Loretta Sanchez, who talked her into giving D.C. a try. One of my best friends from high school, David Zetlin-Jones, worked for Loretta in Orange County and set us up. "What's he like?" Ann asked, open to the idea of a blind date because she knew no one in Washington. "He's a tall snowboarder," my friend replied, describing the kind of guys Ann dated.

I'm five foot seven and have never snowboarded in my life. When I asked him about this, he said, "I got you in the door. The rest is up to you."

Neither of us loved Washington, but we'd built something of a life there. By the time I went to work for Obama, she was a senior foreign policy advisor to the California senator Barbara Boxer. "At least you'll be back by February fifth," she said when I told her I was going to take the job in Chicago. That was the date when everyone expected Hillary to clinch the nomination. Ann wanted Obama to win, she just couldn't see America electing a black man named Barack Obama; he definitely wasn't going to carry Orange County.

Some of my friends warned me that I was making a mistake— "Richard Holbrooke's keeping a list of everyone who goes to work for Obama," one of them said, referring to Clinton's senior foreign policy advisor, who was presumed to be her lead candidate for secretary of state. Vernon Jordan, who had served on the Iraq Study Group, was slightly more generous. Over lunch at the Metropolitan Club, he said he was glad I was working for Obama. "Barack needs good staff," he said. "Still, we're going to whoop his ass."

Obama's opponents had pounced on our big terrorism speech. The bin Laden pledge was cast as a call to "invade Pakistan," and he was pilloried again for being naïve in wanting to talk to Iran. A couple of days later, Obama was asked if he would use nuclear weapons to take out terrorist camps in Pakistan, and he said no. The same people who attacked Obama for saying he'd take out bin Laden in Pakistan now said he was naïve for saying he wouldn't use nuclear weapons to do it. It all seemed like a stupid game in which sticking to a preapproved script was more important than being right; worse, the script hadn't changed because of Iraq.

MY FIRST NIGHT IN Chicago, I woke up around five in the morning and found several emails related to news that had broken overnight: Musharraf had condemned Obama's threat to get bin Laden, making headlines. I'd created an international incident. The first email was from Dan Pfeiffer, a generally unflappable strategist who was the campaign's deputy director of communications, forwarding a news story on Musharraf's comments to a group that included the senior leadership of the campaign and me, saying, "This may be the worst thing that's happened to us yet." I was alone in a city where I barely knew anyone, going into debt because of the pay cut I'd taken, and I thought I'd tanked the campaign. A knot formed in the pit of my stomach and tingled out into my arms, a sense of stress that stayed with me for the next decade. I rode to work that morning certain that I'd be ostracized. When I got to the square black office building where I would spend the next sixteen months, I sat on a bench outside for almost twenty minutes wondering what I was doing with my life. Then I got an email from Favreau asking me where I was.

When I got upstairs, I was promptly put to work drafting an op-ed about Pakistan in Obama's name—not for *The Washington Post*, but for the *Mason City Globe Gazette*. Iowa was what mattered, not Washington. A few days later, whatever doubts I had about our foreign policy fights went away when Obama did what I would see him do hundreds of times—turn defense into offense. Standing on a debate stage at Chicago's Soldier Field, he brushed off the repeated attacks by saying—in reference to the Iraq War—"I'm not going to be lectured by people who voted for the biggest foreign policy mistake of my generation."

My lifeline in this period was Samantha Power. If you had asked me who I wanted to become when I moved down to Washington, I probably would have said Samantha. She'd been a journalist in the Balkans and won a Pulitzer Prize in her early thirties for a book about America's failure to prevent genocide. To my generation of liberals, she offered an alternative to the neoconservative views that dominated the debate after 9/11: She supported an interventionist America that promoted human rights and prevented atrocities, yet she'd opposed the war in Iraq, standing apart from many liberal interventionists who were co-opted by the Bush crowd.

Like me, Samantha felt a sense of destiny about her work for Obama. She'd volunteered as a fellow in his Senate office, and she continued advising the campaign from Boston while she finished her second book. I would stay at the office late, because I had nowhere else to go, pacing in circles, talking to her. When he was being criticized for his positions on Pakistan and Iran, we wrote a memo that was released to reporters celebrating Obama's willingness to buck the "conventional thinking" that got us into war in Iraq—a routine campaign document that felt, to us, like a manifesto for a new epoch in American foreign policy. She never lost this enthusiasm—years later, before a meeting with Obama about whether the United States would join the global treaty banning the use of land mines, she sat in her office listening to Eminem's "Lose Yourself" on repeat to get ready. After a conversation with Samantha, I'd go home to my tiny studio apartment, in the kind of building populated by graduate students and service industry workers, thinking that I was part of a movement that would remake the world order.

Still, the campaign was grounded in those summer days by a series of bad narratives: Clinton would win because she was inevitable. Obama would lose because young people never turn out to vote. Clinton was racking up endorsements from the party elite. Obama wouldn't get black votes because he wasn't black enough ("I'm black enough when I try to get a cab," he told us). Clinton passed the commander in chief test. Obama was untested and, well, different.

None of that mattered to us. The office was filled with young people who spent all day staring at their laptops, communicating by Instant Messenger even when we were sitting next to each other. We spent our days acting as though we were in on a secret that nobody else knew—we were going to win the election, and the more people said we wouldn't, the more certain we were that we would. The campaign leadership sat in glass offices with open doors. The leader among equals was unmistakably David Plouffe, a short, intense forty-year-old man who spoke in staccato phrases and never showed any nerves. While the rest of us were looking at polls, he'd call all-staff meetings, with all the state offices dialing in by phone, and rattle off the number of caucusgoers that the campaign had reached in Iowa: the phone calls made, the number of doors knocked. In Iowa, he said, "we're going to drive a stake through the heart of the Clinton campaign."

Every few weekends, we were required to drive to Iowa and knock on doors. Most nights we'd go out to bars where no one knew who we were and no one but us talked about politics. We had all made this bet to work for the underdog campaign, so there was something essential that we shared, the belief that we were doing something both historic and right. It was unspoken that if you ever needed anything—a place for a visiting friend to stay, help with what you were working on, a person to talk to about something bothering you—someone would be there for you. We were down by 20 points in national polls. It was the happiest time of my professional life.

CHAPTER 3

A COMMUNITY
OF FATE

———

A COUPLE OF HOURS BEFORE BARACK OBAMA WAS SET TO address a crowd of two hundred thousand people in Berlin, I learned that our speech was going to echo Adolf Hitler.

The core contrasts with Clinton that we'd drawn in the summer of 2007 had been folded into a broader story—*change you can believe in*—that propelled us through a bruising primary campaign. Obama, the argument went, was different from the establishment that Clinton represented, and could therefore be trusted to bring change. The campaign had built like a wave, picking up people who aren't normally involved in politics, or who'd stopped believing that politics mattered. Now, at the onset of a general election campaign against John McCain, we were going to take that message around the world.

The Berlin speech was the heart of an audacious trip for a presidential candidate—a trip that would take Obama to Afghanistan, Kuwait, Iraq, Jordan, Israel, the West Bank, Germany, France, and the United Kingdom. Usually, the goal of any foreign policy effort on a general election campaign is to do no harm and check certain boxes—appealing to ethnic constituencies in key states; reassuring military base communities and veterans; and showing voters that you are, in some intangible way, tough enough to be commander in chief.

But the ethos of the Obama campaign was to do more than simply clear a bar, an ethos shaped by an African American candidate who lived the Jackie Robinson reality that black people had to do things better than white people to reach new heights. That's how we clinched the nomination—building a coalition of African Americans and young people, weathering a scandal about the inflammatory comments of Obama's pastor by having Obama give a starkly personal speech about race, and outmaneuvering the Clinton campaign by competing in every part of the country. Now, we set out to prove that Obama could handle visits to two war zones, negotiate the minefields of Middle East peace, and be welcomed in the capitals of Europe. The itinerary encapsulated our campaign's foreign policy message: After eight years of George W. Bush, we had to wind down the wars, reinvigorate diplomacy, and restore America's standing around the world. But we also clung to our share of defensiveness; a mistake abroad would be devastating in a campaign in which the only advantage for John McCain was experience, and we had internalized a siege mentality in the face of rumors that Obama was a Muslim, a Kenyan, a terrorist sympathizer, or all of the above.

I would be responsible for the words he spoke in public, and the Berlin speech was the center of my existence for a couple of weeks. As a thirty-year-old who had never written a speech delivered outside the United States, this was like being asked to ride your first race as a jockey on the favorite horse at the Kentucky Derby. It was, after all, Berlin. Kennedy: *Ich bin ein Berliner!* Reagan: *Tear down this wall!* The two most iconic speeches delivered by American presidents abroad both took place in Berlin. I read each of them dozens of times. I'd listen to recordings of them in my apartment late at night. I wanted, more than anything else, to help put Barack Obama in that continuum, to write words that someone like me might someday read. And to the campaign staff, this was precisely the objective—to put Obama visually in that continuum.

The one person who didn't seem enthusiastic about giving a

speech in Berlin was Obama. When Favreau and I talked to him about it, he didn't offer much beyond suggesting we use Berlin's story to talk about what we were proposing in our own foreign policy. Chancellor Angela Merkel rejected a request from the campaign for the speech to take place at the Brandenburg Gate, where Reagan had called on Gorbachev to tear down the wall, saying that the venue should be reserved for an actual president. When he learned about this, Obama was embarrassed and annoyed. "I never said I wanted to give a speech in front of the Brandenburg Gate," he snapped. It spoke to a larger dynamic in the campaign: While Obama was often blamed for the cult of personality growing up around him—arty posters, celebrity anthems, and lavish settings for his events—he was rarely responsible for it, and worried that we were raising expectations too high in a world that has a way of resisting change.

Before he left for Afghanistan, he read a draft of the speech and told us he was satisfied with it—"You could put this speech on the teleprompter and I'd be fine," he said—but I was hoping for more than that. I was hoping for edits that would elevate the speech and make it more than a summation of our worldview. The shift to a foreign audience hadn't been hard, as Obama's message about working across races and religions, his preference for diplomacy over war, his embrace of the science of climate change, and his recognition that the world needed to confront issues beyond terrorism were going to be well received in Germany. I kept looking for the phrase or two that might elevate that message, summarizing it in a way that could convey the same sense of common mission that Kennedy and Reagan had evoked.

On the flight from Israel to Berlin, the morning that he would give the speech, I told him that the venue we'd settled on—in front of the Victory Column at the end of a long boulevard—would allow him to speak to tens of thousands of people. "What if nobody shows up?" he asked, not kidding. When we landed in Berlin, it was clear that this was not going to be a problem. Crowds greeted our motorcade. Hundreds of people pressed against the barricades outside our hotel—cheering, holding signs, taking pictures, straining for a glimpse of Obama.

I had taken a step onto a much bigger canvas than a Chicago campaign office, one that had the immediacy of history. Here I was, thirty years old, traveling with a presidential candidate from Israel to Germany. My mother's family was Jewish, with roots in Poland and Germany. Those who didn't emigrate to the United States were killed in the Holocaust. They didn't leave, my mother always said, because they thought they were more German than Jewish. That decision always haunted me, in part because I understood it: I was raised outside the Jewish faith—in my father's casual churchgoing Episcopalianism—but aware of my Jewish identity, which was most acutely present through the family that I didn't have.

I first traveled to Germany when I was twenty years old on a train from Paris, where I was studying abroad. I still had the memory of falling asleep on the train in France and waking up to the sound of the German language being spoken over the loudspeaker, a conductor calling out the names of the next stops. Hearing these incomprehensible sounds evoked the secular New York Jewish education that I had received from my mother: The Holocaust was the central event of the twentieth century; you had family that was killed in the Holocaust; the Germans, the most civilized of people, *did* this. Still, on this trip, and on all the trips to come in the years ahead, there was little space for personal reflection. Instead, my energy—emotional and mental—would be channeled into the work I had to do.

I walked into my hotel room feeling a strange mix of adrenaline and crushing responsibility. Outside my window, I could see huge crowds massing. My room was full of antique furniture, and Secret Service agents guarded the floor. On my laptop was a Microsoft Word document that held the words that everyone was waiting to hear. There were still a few more hours until the speech. I opened my computer and stared at the text on the screen, which had become so familiar to me that the words seemed drained of meaning.

The heart of the speech, an echo of Reagan with a twist of Obama, was the one part I was confident about, so I read it over and over aloud—a ringing affirmation of globalism over crude nationalism: "The walls between old allies on either side of the Atlantic cannot stand. The walls between countries with the most and those with the least cannot stand. The walls between races and tribes; natives and immigrants; Christian and Muslim and Jew cannot stand. These now are the walls we must tear down."

Favreau had been reading a book about the "candy bombers"— American pilots who, during the Berlin airlift, helped win the hearts and minds of Berliners by air-dropping food, including candy for the children of the city. We used that story to frame the speech, as it seemed like the right anecdote to pay homage to history while conveying an idea central to Obama's worldview: that American leadership depended on our military but was rooted not just in our strength but also in our goodness. One anecdote from the book stood out: A German woman described it at the time, saying, "We are a community of fate!"

As a speechwriter, you are always looking for a new way to say something you've said before. This phrase echoed our campaign's message: *Yes we can. Our destiny is not written for us, it is written by us. We are the ones we've been waiting for.* But now—*community of fate*. This phrase said it just as well. Favreau and I wrote a big ending, building up to this line—"We are a community of fate!" It was the one thing in the speech that Obama loved the first time he read it. It offered a transition to conclude the speech by saying, in echoes of Kennedy, how that spirit had connected American pilots and a German woman in the street, and connected us still today; that we are all "citizens of Berlin." It worked so well that we included the single German word that translates to "community of fate" in the text of Obama's remarks: *Schicksalsgemeinschaft*.

Schicksalsgemeinschaft.

I stared at it on my screen. We would need a phonetic pronunciation, I thought. But something made me uneasy. Could a single word really mean "community of fate"? I Googled it. Paging through the results, I understood nothing except the Google translation, which confirmed the meaning. There were, embedded in dozens of links, a few Nazi references. It was German, after all. I emailed our lead Germany advisor and asked if there was anything to worry about in using that word. He checked with a couple of people and wrote back—all clear. I called Marc Levitt, our advance staffer, who was with the German man translating the speech so it could be posted online. I asked him if he would check about this one word— is there anything I should be worried about? There was a pause on the other end of the line: "He's relieved you asked," Marc said. "He says it's been bothering him all day."

He handed the phone to the man, who told me, "This is the title of one of Hitler's first speeches to the Reichstag."

I looked at the word on my screen and then out the window where the new Reichstag stood, a glass monument to transparency and the new German republic. "Are you sure?" I asked. "I didn't see that on the Internet."

"Yes, yes. Maybe not the title, but the Germans will know this."

I told Marc I would get back to them with a revised draft. I felt that tightness in my chest—how had I gotten so close to such a huge mistake? Was I not up to this job? I stared at the ending and tried to think of something that could replace it, but I couldn't. I emailed Reggie Love, Obama's all-purpose aide, to see if I could come see Obama. He told me they had just finished a workout and I should come by his suite. Not Obama's—Reggie's.

I went up a flight of stairs, showing my Secret Service pin to the agents who guarded the staircase, and found the door to Reggie's room. Reggie was six feet four and had been a basketball and foot- ball player at Duke; he exuded a casual charisma, as though no situ- ation that he found himself in was surprising or could lead him to alter his behavior in any way. He had become a mini-celebrity in his own right, an effect that would extend to other Obama staffers, often with as much baggage as benefits. Obama, wearing a gray shirt and black workout pants, was sitting at a small desk reviewing the speech on a laptop, smoking a Marlboro Red. Reggie was lying on the bed staring at his BlackBerry. The curtains were drawn to shield the room from any external audience. For a moment, I wondered how he could get away with smoking in a hotel room, then it occurred to me: He was a few months away from possibly being president of the United States, he could do whatever he wanted to do.

"I have some news," I said. "That line at the end—'community of fate.'" Obama looked up from the screen and nodded at me. "I spoke to the German guy translating the speech. He says that line was in one of Hitler's first speeches to the Reichstag."

There was a pause while I saw Obama process this new information about the key line that was currently on the computer screen in front of him, which was two hours away from being on the teleprompter as he spoke to hundreds of thousands of people. He held up one hand, signaling that he was about to say something important.

"Reggie," he said, "we have our employee of the month!" With this he leaned forward in what seemed like a cathartic full-body laugh. "Hitler? Really? 'Obama echoes Hitler in Berlin speech,'" he said, imagining the headline.

"Not what you're going for," Reggie said, without looking up from his BlackBerry.

"It's problematic," I said, volunteering myself as straight man.

"You think?" Obama said. Instead of being angry, the absurdity of the situation seemed to put him more at ease. "The Reichstag."

He reworked the ending himself while I stood there watching over his shoulder. For all my anxiety about this speech, it was only one piece of the much bigger and more surreal experience that he was going through. But my experience of this strange moment, like thousands of others that would accumulate in the years to come, drew me closer to a man who bore a responsibility that I could never fully imagine, but that I was a part of—as a witness and a participant, the guy who sent the speech to the teleprompter, not the guy who delivered it.

I went downstairs and loaded into a black SUV with Obama,

Axe, and Gibbs to make the trip to the speech site. The motorcade snaked through enormous crowds shouting and waving and covering their faces in shock at seeing this person riding in the seat opposite me. "Why are there so many people here?" Obama asked.

We sat there not knowing what to say. We could tell that Obama was nervous—there was a jerkiness to his usually smooth movements as he intermittently waved or sat back in his seat. How do you put someone at ease who is about to speak to two hundred thousand Germans? They were cheering and pressing against barricades as we drew closer to the stage. Then Axe, who is Jewish, broke the silence. "Boy, the Germans are a lot nicer than my grandparents made them out to be."

The car let us out backstage where Obama was briefed by a young advance staffer on what, exactly, he would do. Stand on this piece of masking tape. Wait for this signal. Walk up this flight of stairs. Turn and walk this number of paces. The crowd will be in front of you. Wave. Walk up to the lectern. Prompter screens to the right and left. I went around to get a look at the crowd—an ocean of humanity that went on as far as you could see.

By the time he jogged up the stairs, the nervous man I'd seen in the car was gone, replaced by a charismatic leader who moved with ease, smiling, waving casually to the crowd as if it was the most normal place in the world for him to be, standing there in front of people who were ready to love whatever he said. I stood off to the side watching him. As he started into his speech, I realized that the words he spoke would not be as powerful as the image of him, an African American, standing on these stages. This was the gift and the struggle of working for Obama.

I walked behind the large structure that had been set up to hold the journalists covering the speech so that I wouldn't have to watch. I was confident in the speech I'd written, but couldn't bear to watch it delivered. Any extended silence would make me think the audience didn't like it. Any wind-up to an important point would feel too long. Over the next eight years, I almost never saw a speech that I wrote being delivered to a crowd; instead, I would choose the detached experience of pacing backstage, occasionally glancing at my BlackBerry and reading the initial reactions to the speech as it was being given.

When you are a speechwriter and the speech that you have written is finished, you go from being the most indispensable member of the staff to being temporarily irrelevant. Afterward, I lingered at the site, and then followed the trail of humanity back to the hotel, people clutching signs and cameras as if they had been to a rock concert. Returning to my room was like going back in time. Everything was still in the same place—the open laptop; cups of coffee; a half-drunk glass of wine; printed-out copies of an almost finished draft—but the anxiety and adrenaline were gone. Taking in this scene, I realized that I was developing an addiction to this life—the moments I craved were not the grand crowd scenes when speeches are delivered, but rather the accumulating pressure that leads up to them; the moments when everyone is waiting to hear the words there on your laptop, as if you know a secret that has yet to be whispered to the world.

THAT NIGHT, OBAMA LOOKED relieved to be over the hump of the speech as he joined the staff in a local restaurant for drinks with the traveling press. He ordered a martini and seemed at ease amid a cluster of people all straining to hear the casual conversation he was making at one end of the table. I was seated next to Maureen Dowd, a columnist from *The New York Times* whom I'd read for years. I was excited, a little nervous. "Who are you?" she asked. "The speechwriter," I said. She gave me a level stare and then complained that she wasn't seated next to someone more important.

Even as the coverage of the trip was glowing, there was a trickle of columns that were somewhat critical of the Berlin speech, lamenting that it didn't lay out a clear enough foreign policy vision, that it was a missed opportunity. I got some emails suggesting that the main reason for this was that I hadn't shared the speech with enough people. "People are never going to say anything nice about a speech that they didn't work on," one person said to me. It fore-shadowed a problem we'd confront going forward—we were winning without the people who were the arbiters of opinion in Washington, people who were going to withhold a measure of praise so long as they weren't occupying the constellation of positions around Obama.

In an insurgent campaign, you go through every day with a chip on your shoulder. As we reached new heights, I only seemed to find reasons for the chip on my shoulder to grow—nursing small slights and remembering who opposed us; navigating new surroundings and craving acceptance from people who were more established, even as I was the one drawing closer to a future president. We had defeated Clinton, were about to defeat McCain, but we had done so by challenging the assumptions of the same establishment that we were about to join—the media that would cover us, the Congress that would have to pass laws, the commentators who would sit in judgment of us after the voters.

On the flight home, Obama loosened his tie and came and put his arm around each of us, a look of satisfied exhaustion on his face. "We got that done," he said. "Now we can go win an election." A few days later, the McCain campaign put out an ad showing Obama waving to the throngs in Berlin, a picture of Paris Hilton popping up on the screen, and a voice saying, "He's the biggest celebrity in the world, but is he ready to lead?" It seemed childish and a little insulting to compare a man who had been a U.S. senator, a constitutional law professor, and the first African American to lead the *Harvard Law Review* to a vapid celebrity. But it turned what we accomplished on the trip inside out. Whereas I had envisioned Obama in the continuum with Kennedy and Reagan, the ad used his very success abroad to delegitimize him. It was impossible to imagine a similar ad being run against a white senator from Illinois.

The effort to delegitimize Obama would get its first messenger when Sarah Palin was announced as McCain's running mate a few weeks later. I learned of the announcement when I woke up the morning after Obama delivered his acceptance speech at the Democratic National Convention. *Who is that?* I thought, staring at the television screen. But as much as she became a punch line, Palin's ascendance broke a seal on a Pandora's box: The innuendo and conspiracy theories that existed in forwarded emails and fringe right-wing websites now had a mainstream voice, and for the next eight years the trend would only grow. We had shown that Obama could fill the role of leader of the free world, and his success had only made a whole slice of the country that much angrier.

CHAPTER 4

THE PRESIDENT IS
ON BOARD
THE AIRCRAFT

———

O N SEPTEMBER 15, 2008, THE LOFTY PROMISE THAT CHARAC-
terized much of Obama's campaign was met by a harsh reality that
both ensured Obama's victory in the election and imposed limits on
his upcoming presidency. Lehman Brothers filed for bankruptcy,
triggering fears of a catastrophic recession, and John McCain uttered one of those phrases from which presidential candidates never
recover: "The fundamentals of the economy," he said, "are strong."

That night, I joined a conference call with Obama and a group
of his advisors, sitting in an office with my BlackBerry on speaker-
phone, typing up what was said in case it would be useful for remarks the next day. Things had changed a lot since March, when I'd
written a speech that attacked the deregulation that took place
under Bill Clinton. Now one of the architects of that policy—Larry
Summers—was speaking at length about what we needed to say to
calm the markets. At the end of the call, Obama asked me to take
the policies from the March speech and drop them into a new
speech that he would give the following day in Colorado. "Make it
the final verdict on a certain approach," he said, referring to the mix
of trickle-down economics and deregulation that had dominated
American political discourse since Reagan. "But make sure you run
the language by these guys first."

It was a good time to start smoking again. I had quit for most of my twenties, but as the pressure of the campaign built, I found myself standing in the plaza outside our office building in an ever-growing circle of people falling back on bad habits. That night, I was down there every hour or so. A group of economic advisors who had picked up food for the night passed by on their way back to work. Brian Deese, a brilliant young guy with the beard of an indie rock lead singer, who would end up helping to design the plan that saved the American auto industry, stopped to talk. "The Japanese markets are opening," he said, "so pretty soon we'll know whether or not the entire global economy is going to fall into a great depression."

"What are the odds of that?" I asked, hanging on to my cigarette.

"I'd say a little less than fifty percent," he said.

I finished the speech at home, sending a few paragraphs at a time to a team of economic advisors who did shifts through the night to vet my language for accuracy and market anxieties. "Jobs have disappeared, and people's life savings have been put at risk. Millions of families face foreclosure, and millions more have seen their home values plummet," I wrote, addressing topics far afield from my foreign policy background. "So let's be clear: What we've seen the last few days is nothing less than the final verdict on an economic philosophy that has completely failed." Here I was, in my tiny studio, sitting on a mattress pushed against the wall, laptop open on my knees, wondering what kind of world we would be taking leadership of after November. I was already going into debt because of the two rents I was paying, and now the value of my mutual fund was about to be cut in half. I had thought the Iraq War would be the inheritance that shaped an Obama presidency. I was wrong.

Meanwhile, a group of us were asked to fill out the forms necessary to get an interim security clearance so that we could access classified information as soon as the election was over. On page after page, I had to list every place I had lived, who I had worked for, everyone I had lived with, every drug I'd taken, every foreign contact I'd had, everything of potential suspicion that I'd done for ten years—a process that is not easy for a thirty-year-old closer to a life of part-time work, shared apartments, and partying than my middle-aged counterparts, decades into respectability.

The night before Election Day, as people were making plans for the parties they'd be attending, I got a call from Cassandra Butts, an old friend of Obama's who was helping to run the transition. She told me my interim clearance had been denied because of past marijuana use. I could still get a clearance, she assured me—the FBI would just have to do a full investigation of my background first.

This uncertainty hung over me on Election Day, the first time in eighteen months that I had nothing to do. As soon as the polls closed, Obama was declared the victor, and a group of staff was herded into vans that would take us the short drive to Grant Park. It was our first entry into an eight-year bubble. Tens of thousands of people filled the park, but we were in an area up front, near the stage, guarded by Secret Service and police, where they'd set up tents for different clusters of VIP politicians, celebrities, campaign donors, and staff. I found myself hugging people I barely knew, being introduced to people who'd barely been involved in the campaign, posing for pictures with Democratic senators, and gravitating toward the core of young staffers who'd been together since before Iowa. And then there they were: Barack, Michelle, Malia, and Sasha Obama, striding onto a stage in front of many thousands, our first black First Family—instantly recognizable, but seemingly further removed by their own new status.

When the speech was over, the Obamas made the rounds to each of the tents, surrounded by Secret Service, offering versions of the same thank-you message. Obama passed by me in one crowded tent, leaning forward to take a picture. "Now it's time to get to work," he said in my ear before moving on to the next tent.

AFTER THE HIGH OF the election, my lack of a clearance shadowed me like an asterisk. Every day, I'd go to work in the transition office—a government building in downtown D.C. where the lobby was thronged with people I'd never seen before, seeking jobs—and I'd be reminded of my diminished status because of documents I couldn't read, meetings I couldn't attend, rooms I couldn't enter. I took a job as deputy director of White House speechwriting; if I was kept out of national security, I could write more speeches about financial regulation. Finally, a few weeks later, Butts called me up to her office. The background investigation was completed, and I would get my clearance. She smiled, a soft-spoken, genial African American woman with close-cropped hair. "You're not the only one who had a problem," she said, "but you're the first fish who has made it upstream." Late in our administration, Cassandra Butts died two years after she was nominated to serve as ambassador to the Bahamas, her nomination held up by a Republican senator, Tom Cotton, because she was friends with Barack Obama.

Our administration was filled with many of the people who we had run against. Larry Summers would be Obama's top economic advisor. Bob Gates, the secretary of defense through Bush's surge, was asked to stay on at the Pentagon. Hillary Clinton was named secretary of state. For each hire, I could see the rationale—in a time of crisis, bring in the most experienced people; in a potential second Great Depression, have continuity in national security; in a city where you're an outsider, keep your political adversaries close. But cumulatively, it felt like a punch in the gut. To those of us who worked on the campaign, it made us feel as if our searing criticisms of the establishment may have been just politics after all.

I soon found myself in the awkward position of being Obama's representative to the team preparing Hillary Clinton for her confirmation hearings. I wrote her a memo summarizing our foreign policy, some of which had been framed as an argument against her. The first time we met, I was told to come to Whitehaven—the shorthand name for her house in Washington, which was the name of the street where she lived. When I arrived, she was flanked by many of the people who had been senior aides on her campaign. But she was unfailingly polite, complimenting my memo, putting me at ease, and earnestly soliciting my views throughout a session in which she prepared for her congressional hearing. "What would the president-elect think about this, Ben?" she would ask me. Still, I had the sense that the real meeting would take place after I left.

Our speechwriting team spent those days working on the inaugural address, occasionally recapturing the camaraderie of the campaign in group writing sessions that went on for hours. But we also had the strange experience of watching Jon Favreau become a celebrity. Newspapers reported on who he was dating or the apartment he bought. I was uncertain about my place. I knew the president personally and had a job and now a clearance. But I was below the cutoff line of senior staff and celebrity that had picked up people like Gibbs, McDonough, and Favreau like a sudden gust of wind. Did I need to choose between national security and speechwriting? Who was going to tell me what to do? How long was I going to do this, anyway? I missed the campaign.

Inauguration Day only deepened my unease. My parents came down from New York and were more excited than I was. My father had grown up in the segregated South and attended Robert E. Lee High School in Baytown, Texas—a refinery town where his own father spent a lifetime working for Exxon. There, he liked to say, he was taught Texas history, Southern history, American history, and world history, in that order. His vote for Obama marked the first time during my life that he had supported a Democrat for president. He had gone door to door, with bad knees, in New Hampshire, Pennsylvania, and Texas, trying to explain to people like himself why they should vote for a black man named Barack Hussein Obama. He poured himself into the campaign as if it was a form of personal redemption, an unspoken acknowledgment that he'd been an unwitting beneficiary of an unjust system. The only two times I cried during the campaign were when I called him— the day Obama was nominated, and the day before he was elected.

To my parents, Obama brought together the twin threads of the civil rights movement and the Kennedy brothers that formed the heroic narrative of their youth. They met in Washington in the 1960s—my father was a young, tall, blond, conservative attorney who worked in Lyndon Johnson's Department of Justice; my mother was a young, dark-haired, liberal staffer at the newly created Department of Housing and Urban Development. She had been friends with people who were close to Andrew Goodman, a civil rights worker who was killed in Mississippi. Even though my father was a Republican, he and my mother spoke about "Jack" and "Bobby" as if they were departed family. When they came to Washington for Obama's inauguration, they revisited the Georgetown neighborhood where they'd fallen in love, going to bars where John F. Kennedy had taken Jackie. My father would call me to keep me abreast of their movements, speaking excitedly about the opportunity to see "Barack" get sworn in as the forty-fourth president.

I had six tickets—two for my parents, two for me and Ann, and two for Ann's sister and her boyfriend. They were for the "purple zone"—a standing room area one ring out from the good seats. It was bitterly cold. As the hours passed, we never moved forward to a place where we could even be close to seeing the ceremony. There were frightening moments when bodies surged forward and pressed together. My parents asked if there was another way through, but I had no answers. When people passed out, it got worse because the ambulances that inched through the crowd only packed us in tighter. As I stood there, helpless, I felt a profound embarrassment as I saw a creeping disappointment on the faces of my family.

We ended up backing out of the scrum and going to Ann's office to watch the speech. Senator Barbara Boxer gave my parents their one sense of special access when she briefly appeared on her way to the inauguration platform. "Welcome, welcome," she said. "We have cookies and coffee. We are so proud of Ann and Ben!"

We stood there clutching paper coffee cups, still bundled against the cold, and watched on a small television set in the office. I sensed a conspiracy among my guests to conceal their disappointment at missing the historic moment that they had traveled to see. My father awkwardly patted me on the back a couple of times, saying, "He looks great." My mother insisted, over and over, that it was better to watch inside, where it was warm.

THE NEXT DAY, I reported for the first of 2,920 days of work at the White House. I had two formal jobs—one as the deputy director of White House speechwriting, and one as the senior director for speechwriting for the National Security Council. Because the bureaucracy that processed my employment is not accustomed to this, I also got two offices. One was in the cavernous Eisenhower Executive Office Building, with a door that was opened by a code that you spun out on a dial like an old-fashioned safe. The EEOB, as it was called, is located across from the White House and houses the vast majority of the White House staff in a grand setting with wood-paneled offices, winding staircases, and frescoed ceilings. My other office was in the West Wing of the White House on the ground floor, just down the hallway from the Situation Room. That first day, as I walked in, I couldn't quite believe that I was allowed to be there.

To get to my office, I had to walk through Favreau's. It seemed strange to see him in a suit—on the campaign, we wore T-shirts to work. He told me, excitedly, that you could call the White House mess and order a coffee to go, and they'd give it to you in a cup with the presidential seal. I walked into my office and took in the quiet of the place. It had the feel of an underground bunker. The ceiling was dropped down low. (I would later learn that that was because it was underneath the Oval Office, and the wires that provided the encryption for the president's communications needed extra space.) An old wooden desk had two computers on it—one for unclassified information, and one marked Top Secret. I hung my coat on a hanger in the small closet, feeling, in some new way, grown up.

My blue White House staff badge gave me access to the entire complex. I kept expecting to get stopped by one of the uniformed Secret Service agents or Marines who stand or sit at a series of different checkpoints, but instead, I was allowed to wander. I walked down the colonnade next to the Rose Garden, where I'd seen old photographs of Jack and Bobby Kennedy huddled, arms crossed. I lingered on the ground floor of the White House itself, my movements followed by the eyes of official portraits of former First Ladies. I went into rooms that were featured in movies depicting the lives of fictional presidents: the Map Room, with old military maps that showed the movements of our troops into Europe during World War II; the China Room, where I stared at Mary Lincoln's selection of plates. I walked by the Oval Office, the Cabinet Room, and the Roosevelt Room, the three places where a president spends most of his days. The overwhelming impression I got was of the smallness of the place. There are a few dozen people who work in the West Wing. You realize quickly that there are no other people who occupy some position of higher authority. It's just you.

ON A CAMPAIGN, EVERYTHING you do is focused on one objective: getting elected. Every utterance is part of one argument: Vote for this person. The actual presidency floats somewhere beyond Election Day—a blank slate to be filled in by the power of your candidate's ideals, the rightness of his proposals. My first foreign trip drove home the extent to which the state of the world would shape the Obama presidency as much as our own ideas did.

A foreign trip begins in a series of black vans that take you the ten miles from the entrance of the West Wing to Andrews Air Force Base and drop you off at the staircase to Air Force One. Your name is checked off a list held by a uniformed airman as you board the plane, and then you have a while to get settled before the president arrives by helicopter. The plane is both unlike any other you will ever be on and not as nice as you think. It's nearly thirty years old, and the interior has the feeling of 1980s luxury: large light brown leather seats; wood paneling; beige carpeting. Bowls of fruit and M&M's line the shelves that run along the side of the plane. The president's office is up front, a spare room with a desk and a couch that runs along the wall; adjacent to it are a bedroom and a shower. A senior staff cabin holds four people in large chairs that swivel around, with a phone at each seat so that you can place calls that require you to push a button to be heard while you talk. A long hallway takes you past a conference room where Obama would spend so much of his time over the next eight years, sitting at a table playing spades with a handful of aides while ESPN played on a muted television. Past the conference room, there is a larger staff cabin with a couple of four-tops and a workspace where two enormous old computers are bolted to a table. When I turned one on for the first time, it coughed and moaned and took a while to boot; when it finally did come to, the emergency remarks that George W. Bush delivered when Russia invaded Georgia in 2008 were still on the desktop—a reminder that we are all temporary employees and have to respond to whatever cards the world deals us. Beyond that, there's a guest cabin, seating for the Secret Service, and then—in the very back—a cluster of seats for the traveling White House press pool, a select group of print and television reporters who are with a president wherever he goes.

After taking my seat, a voice piped in over a speaker with updates: "The president is fifteen minutes out"; "The president is five minutes out"; "The president has arrived"; "The president is on board the aircraft." Not "President Obama." In the machinery that moves the president around, he is described as more of an object than a human being. As I sat in my large beige chair reading printed drafts of the many sets of remarks he'd give over the course of the next several days, I felt myself sinking into the comfortable embrace of a machinery that would feed me, fly me, carry my bags, and move me around cities so that I could perform my function for "the president."

Our first stop was in London for the G20—a gathering of the leaders of the world's largest economies—who were meeting to coordinate a response to the financial crisis. The awkward fact for us is that we were asking other countries to spend money to stimulate the global economy in order to fix a crisis that the United States created.

In London, we managed to secure commitments that tallied up to over $1 trillion, which would bring comfort to the markets while putting enough people back to work to stimulate demand. But the American pressure grated on the Europeans, touching off a multi-year debate about whether Europe should go along with the kind of spending we were pursuing. Obama knew that he had leaned hard on other countries to follow our lead, so he expressed some humility in his closing press conference when he was asked whether he believed in American exceptionalism. "I believe," he said, "in American exceptionalism, just as I suspect that the Brits believe in British exceptionalism and the Greeks believe in Greek exceptionalism." It was a quote that would be used for the next eight years to cast Obama as less than sufficiently adamant in his belief in America's primacy among nations.

At our next stop—a NATO summit in Strasbourg, France—Obama found himself asking countries to increase their troop commitments in Afghanistan. Almost none of the leaders wanted to do this—the Afghan war had become increasingly unpopular. It seemed that we were squandering his popularity to address the circumstances we'd inherited instead of being able to invest it in the new initiatives we envisioned. Obama echoed this frustration when I saw him the first night in France. "I'm spending all of my political capital," he said, "just to keep things going."

In Prague, we aimed to break out of simply reacting to our inheritance, with a speech that called for a new arms control agreement with Russia; an effort to secure nuclear materials around the world; and diplomacy with Iran to prevent it from obtaining a nuclear weapon. The words spoken by a U.S. president, I knew, can prompt action in a way that a candidate's words never could. As with the speech in Berlin, Obama spent little time on the draft, given all of the other things he had to do, so I found myself alone in a hotel room the night before the speech, staring at the words on the computer screen and wondering if we were setting the bar too high: *"We will seek the peace and security of a world without nuclear weapons."*

In the middle of the night, a ringing phone woke me up and I was asked to come to an urgent meeting in the traveling National Security office. The North Koreans, who had tested a nuclear weapon a couple of years earlier, had just tested a ballistic missile. Temporary NSC offices on the road are unpleasant places. Blue tarp is put up along the walls of a hotel room to prevent video surveillance; a constant mind-scrambling mix of pop songs plays to block efforts to eavesdrop. Obama came into the middle of the cramped room, surrounded by a handful of aides, and said, "Being president isn't as glamorous as they make it sound."

He sat listening to a series of advisors brief him about this missile test. In a few hours he would speak to tens of thousands of Czechs. As I sat there listening, I realized that our speeches had many different audiences now, among them the leadership of North Korea. "I'm going to get a little sleep," Obama told me. "You better add something on this."

I had barely slept myself for the last several days. I sat at my computer inserting a strongly worded warning to the North Koreans about the isolation they'd face for continued nuclear and missile tests. It was sobering to think that our decision to schedule a speech on nuclear weapons could have set in motion a series of decisions in Pyongyang that led to a missile being fired into the sea. I felt worn down by days spent in traveling staff offices, offstage from the action. When we got back to the plane, I fell into a deep sleep, only to be awoken by Obama shaking me. For a moment I had no idea where I was, until I came to the realization that the president of the United States was standing over me. "Ladies and gentlemen," he said, "Ben Rhodes!" Everyone broke into a round of applause, as the speech had created the most affirmative moment of the trip. Obama rarely gave positive feedback, but—like a coach who knows how to get the most out of his players—he chose the right moments.

He brought me up to his office at the front of the plane. Turkey was up next, and he'd be speaking to the parliament there. I could see circles under his eyes and a heaviness in his face—he had been working a lot harder than I had. "I don't know how much I'm going to be able to put into this one," he said.

"It's in good shape," I replied. "There's just this question of how far to lean in on the genocide." During the campaign, we had promised to recognize the fact of the 1915 Armenian genocide, and Samantha Power had been emailing me steadily to argue for some reference to it in the speech. All of the other advisors, less invested in the purity of our campaign positions and more focused on the need for Turkish cooperation, wanted to avoid it altogether.

"I don't think I should stand there and do that in their parliament," Obama said.

"You'll have another chance when you make a statement on the anniversary in April," I said.

There was also the matter of Turkey's treatment of minority religious and ethnic groups. Obama thought for a moment. "Let's get into it," he said, "by talking about how we've been able to overcome similar issues. It's not like we're without sin. I mean, what happened to the Indians? Or black folks? Let's make the point that democracy is the way we deal with those problems, all right?"

Obama went to play cards and I walked back to my seat and typed up some language that set up the point Obama wanted to make, running through a list of areas where Turkey needed to improve its human rights record and ending with "I say this as the president of a country that not very long ago made it hard for somebody who looks like me to vote, much less be president of the United States. But it is precisely that capacity to change that enriches our countries." The references to America's own historical sins—to people like Obama and me—reflected a positive, patriotic, and progressive view of American history; the capacity for self-correction *is* what makes us exceptional.

This first, long journey ended with a visit to Iraq. As we landed we got word that sandstorms were going to make it impossible for our group to helicopter into the Green Zone. Instead, a heavily ar-

mored motorcade drove us from the tarmac to Camp Victory—
a large sandstone palace close to the airport that was once one of
Saddam Hussein's preferred stomping grounds and now served as
the headquarters for U.S. forces in Iraq. While Obama spoke with
Iraq's prime minister, I wandered around the palace, which still had
on display gifts that Saddam had received from admirers like Yasser
Arafat and Muammar Gaddafi. More than a thousand troops
cheered when Obama said it was time to turn things over to the
Iraqis and bring them home. I stood there watching, thinking that
Obama would never have become president without the mistake
America had made in Iraq, nor would I have ended up working for
a president.

When we got back on the plane, the crew served a dinner of
steak and potatoes. Sealed in the white noise of an aircraft that already felt like a second home, I felt that I had proved myself, that I
belonged, that what we were doing was not only interesting but
important. In addition to working to stabilize the global economy,
increase commitments to the Afghan war, and put forward an
agenda to roll back the threat of nuclear weapons, Obama had told
a different story about what America was and how we would engage other nations and peoples. But on-the-fly decisions we had
made about the words Obama spoke inflamed the spreading attacks and innuendo, from Fox News to the halls of Congress:
Obama doesn't believe in American exceptionalism, he's not patriotic, he's not like Us, he might even be Muslim. I had become the
coauthor of "Obama's Apology Tour."

CHAPTER 5

CAIRO

————

W HAT IS AMERICAN FOREIGN POLICY?

Day in and day out, it's a trillion-dollar annual enterprise that plows forward like an ocean liner, shaping the lives of people in its wake whether they know it or not. The embassy in New Delhi tries to help U.S. businesses get into the Indian market. The USAID mission in Nairobi meets with the Kenyan Ministry of Health to help the fight against HIV/AIDS. A scholarship student from Indonesia boards a plane bound for an American university. The U.S. military conducts a joint exercise with the South Koreans to deter North Korea. Our intelligence community shares information about a terrorist plot with Europeans. A Special Operator leaves a Baghdad trailer at dawn to capture or kill a terrorist. A taxpayer-funded F-16 fighter aircraft is delivered to the Egyptian military.

These actions take place on their own momentum—rooted in a vast complex of deployments, alliances, international agreements, and budget decisions that could have been made a month, a year, or decades ago. This reality contributes to occasional schizophrenia, because our foreign policy represents a particular view of U.S. interests at the time that particular decisions were made. And so our Treasury Department enforces an embargo on trade with Cuba that was established in the 1960s even as USAID tries to deliver phones and printers to dissidents there that would be more readily available without an embargo. Our troops fight a war on terrorism in Afghanistan in the early 2000s against jihadists who in the 1980s were armed by the United States and praised as frontline fighters in the war on Communism. Our diplomats try to broker an Israeli-Palestinian peace agreement while our foreign assistance finances the Israeli military that enforces the occupation of an increasing amount of Palestinian land.

We sustain these investments because, on balance, we believe the return is worth it even if we occasionally suffer losses, embarrassments, and moral compromises. Our network of military alliances has enabled the growth of prosperous democracies in Europe and Asia and averted another global war between major powers since the end of World War II, even as it antagonizes countries like Russia and China and causes them to align against us. Our foreign assistance and trade agreements have facilitated rapid improvements in how people live in many parts of the world, including the United States, even as globalization has also eliminated jobs and entire American industries and encroached on people's sense of tribe, faith, and nation. Our military and intelligence services make it harder for dictators to acquire nuclear weapons or terrorist networks to maintain safe havens, even as our actions sometimes fuel the grievances that dictators and terrorists thrive upon. So for any president, the conduct of foreign policy represents a strange mix of managing the circumstances you've inherited, responding to the crises that take place on your watch, and being opportunistic about where you want to launch the new initiatives that will leave an imprint on the world.

Obama was unique in that the mere fact of his own identity was going to leave an imprint on people abroad. In addition to being the American president, he was a symbol for the aspirations of billions of people—particularly ethnic minorities in the developed world and young people in the developing world. It's why we carved out time for him to engage populations who wouldn't normally meet an American president—playing soccer in a favela in Brazil, meeting Dalits in India, or visiting a refugee center in Malaysia. It's why we established programs for him to engage young people, particularly in the two regions most associated with his background, Africa and Southeast Asia. And it's one reason why he focused so much on the words that he spoke abroad. "We're telling a story," he told me early that first year, "about who we are."

Over the years, much of my authority within the White House was tied to the perception that Obama and I had some kind of "mind meld"—that I could anticipate what he would want to say or do on a particular issue, or that he trusted me to speak for him. There were, of course, enormous differences in our backgrounds, and there was a yawning gulf in our responsibilities. But I did come to see some similarities in our personalities. We both have large groups of friends but maintain a sense of privacy that can lead people to see us as aloof. We're both trying to prove something to our fathers and were nurtured and encouraged by our mothers. We both think of ourselves as outsiders, even when we were in the White House. We're both stubborn—a trait that allows us to take risks but can tip into arrogance. We both act as if we don't care what other people think about us, but we do. Yet these similarities form only a small part of a broader picture—a reality in which I was a junior partner who worked hard to understand what my boss wanted to say and do in the world.

Barack Obama came to office with a different worldview from those of his predecessors and the type of (largely white male) people who serve in elevated national security positions—one that encompasses the complexities of U.S. foreign policy. He was born in Hawaii, a former U.S. colony that hosts America's Pacific fleet, nurtures a diverse citizenry, and serves as a bridge between the Americanized Pacific and East Asia. His grandfather served in Europe during World War II, and his great-uncle helped liberate the concentration camp at Buchenwald. He lived in Indonesia as a child, just years after a U.S.-supported coup initiated bloodletting that killed hundreds of thousands of people—the kind of event that barely registers in the United States but shapes the psyche of a foreign country. His mother worked to help women make a living from weaving clothes or baskets beyond the borders of the developed world. His father came of age during Kenya's liberation from British imperialism and was educated at some of America's finest universities; when he returned to Nairobi, he ended up marginalized as a member of the minority Luo tribe, a technocrat whose Western ideas clashed with a culture of corruption and patronage—ultimately broken, unemployed, and alcoholic, he died in a car crash. And, of course, Obama became centered in his own identity as an African American, joining a continuum of those who had suffered oppression but managed to achieve change through nonviolent mobilization.

So just about every aspect of American power and its role in people's lives since World War II lurks somewhere in Obama's background—our capacity to keep the peace abroad and to disrupt it; our capacity to transform individual lives through both our generosity and our callousness; the allure of our democratic values and our imperfection in realizing them. Yet the strangeness of this background to many Americans left plenty of space for people to misunderstand or misrepresent how it impacted his view of American foreign policy.

To some on the right, it was a sign that he must nurture a reflexive opposition to American power—he must be a Kenyan anticolonialist, a fellow traveler of the likes of Fidel Castro and Yasser Arafat. But the experience of Obama's own family showed that liberation without mature institutions is its own form of oppression, as corruption and tribalism can overwhelm the individual. Yes, Obama believes in the liberation of peoples, but he is at his core an institutionalist, someone who believes progress is more sustainable if it is husbanded by laws, institutions, and—if need be—force.

To some on the left, there was a mirror image—an expectation that Obama would be hostile to America's national security state. Yes, he harbored a deeper concern about overreach—how our policies affect people in places like Indonesia; the casual manner in which, from Vietnam to Iraq, we failed to consider the consequences of our actions; the dangers of unchecked executive power. But

Obama believed in a competent, stabilizing force: the necessity of taking military action against certain terrorist networks, the benefits of globalization in lifting people out of poverty, the indispensability of the United States to international order. He wanted to redirect the ocean liner of American foreign policy, not sink it.

And to many in government, the president's worldview doesn't really matter. Every agency has its own interests, which don't change with the presidency. The military wants more freedom of action. The State Department wants to sustain existing relationships and arrangements. The intelligence community wants more capabilities. Everyone wants more—more money, more people, more support from the White House. Usually, a president presses his agenda through the leadership of these institutions. Yet Obama took office without an established set of relationships with the type of people who take those jobs, because he had been in Washington for a total of only four years. Most of the people who filled the top positions at Obama's State Department or Pentagon were people he had never actually met.

In Obama's first year, I was in a smaller circle of White House aides who knew Obama, had internalized his worldview, and had no personal or institutional interest beyond helping him articulate his foreign policy. Because he was spending most of his time trying to rescue the economy, he turned to speeches as a vehicle to reorient American foreign policy, to communicate a new direction not just to the American people and audiences abroad but to his own government. And because of how much he cared about words—and trusted me—I often got an uncurtained window into his thinking, one that made me a bridge between his speeches and his actions.

This became clear to me with two speeches in May. For weeks, Obama had made a series of decisions about national security issues related to the rule of law. His plan for closing Gitmo had been complicated by congressional opposition; he decided to release the Bush administration memos justifying torture but not to prosecute those responsible; he chose not to release photos showing U.S. troops abusing prisoners abroad. But the ad hoc nature of these decisions grated on him, as he felt there was no context to these announcements we were making, no guiding vision. So there was talk of him giving a big speech laying out his approach to all of these issues. His personal assistant, Katie Johnson, called me up to the Oval Office with a simple "POTUS wants to see you."

When I got there, he had a legal pad in front of him with what looked like a lengthy outline on it. "Here's what I want to say," he said.

"Do you want me to get anyone else?" I asked.

"Why don't I just give this to you—you can fill in the others."

With that, he proceeded to pace slowly around the Oval Office for nearly an hour, pausing every so often over the pad on his desk, dictating his outline. Within it he had embedded a series of policy decisions and how he wanted them framed—about how to categorize detainees at Gitmo, about how to balance transparency and secrecy in government. When he was finished, he told me to scrub it with the rest of the staff and get him a draft in a few days. And so I had the awkward responsibility—as, essentially, a midlevel staffer—of calling a meeting the following day with the senior White House staff so that I could tell them what the president wanted to do.

As I was working on this speech, it became clear to me how agencies form their own antibodies against a president's desire to move in a particular direction. A practice of having the intelligence community review speech drafts had been put in place after George W. Bush overhyped Saddam Hussein's efforts to acquire nuclear material in his 2003 State of the Union address. Now Obama wanted to assert that tactics like waterboarding amounted to torture; the intelligence community struck that formulation, preferring the more antiseptic "enhanced interrogation techniques." Obama wanted to call Gitmo a danger to American national security; the intelligence community wanted to strike that. Obama wanted to say that the 240 Muslim detainees in Gitmo had spent years "in a legal black hole"—a relatively noncontroversial statement, since no one at Gitmo had been convicted of a crime; the intelligence community wanted to delete that sentence as well, offering instead this justification: "The detainees at Guantanamo have more legal representation and have been afforded more process than any enemy combatants in the history of the world."

Sitting in my windowless office and reading those comments, I felt the gap between working on a campaign and working in the White House. The person I was working for was president of the United States, and a figure uniquely revered by people around the world; but his views did not necessarily reflect those of the U.S. government.

ON A LATE SATURDAY morning after the speech, I was back in the Oval Office to get Obama's initial thoughts on another speech that he was going to give two weeks later in Cairo. The fact that he was giving it at all was rooted in a relatively obscure line in the first major campaign speech I'd drafted for him almost two years ago. Sifting through a list of proposals submitted by different advisors, I'd found the idea of "addressing the Muslim world during my first hundred days in office." In August 2007, it had seemed a distant enough idea, and one that captured Obama's potential to change America's image abroad. Over time, it took on a life of its own among Muslim populations, who had high expectations for an American president named Barack Hussein Obama with Muslim relatives. As we took office, it was referred to inside the White House as simply "the Muslim speech."

After the inauguration, there was some debate about whether the speech should be given at all—there was enough to do without having Obama fly somewhere to speak to a global faith community that most Americans viewed with suspicion. But the anticipation around the speech, from Muslims and the media, raised the cost of walking away from the idea, and we ended up presenting Obama with two choices for where he could deliver the speech: Jakarta, the place where he had lived as a boy, which offered a venue for him to talk about a more tolerant brand of Islam; or Cairo, which was the center of a region that had been the source of so much extremism and instability in recent decades. Jakarta was the safer choice, far from the wars, conflicts, and autocrats of the Middle East. And that's precisely why Obama chose Cairo. "Let's be honest," he told a group of us. "The problems are in the Arab world, not Indonesia."

In the weeks leading up to our Oval Office session, I cast a wide net for what to include, reaching out to academics, religious leaders, and prominent Muslim Americans. Within the government, even as bureaucracies can be rigid, there are deep reservoirs of talent, and the people who spent their days thinking about how to engage Muslims around the world seemed relieved at the chance to have their ideas heard at the White House. Much of the advice focused on what the United States had done wrong. The "Global War on Terrorism" had made many Muslims think that all we cared about was terrorism, and that we viewed them all as potential terrorists. As one Muslim colleague said to me, the phrase "radical Islam" is heard by many Muslims as a characterization of Islam itself and not of a faction within it. Meanwhile, the polling that had been done showed that what most Muslims actually cared about was poverty, corruption, and unemployment. If you asked them what they wanted to work with America on, the answers were education and entrepreneurship, science and technology. If you asked them what U.S. policy was focused on, they said oil, Israel, and weakening the Muslim world.

"We should begin," Obama said on that Saturday, "with the history of colonialism." He asked me to come alone to these sessions, but this time I brought McDonough along. There was going to be a lot that Obama wanted to say, I knew, that might be unpopular with other advisors. I wanted a witness so I wouldn't be fighting these battles by myself. "We need to name the sources of tension." He was walking slowly in a circle around where I was sitting on the couch, scribbling down what he was saying on my notepad. "Then go to the Cold War, and how there was a tendency to see the Middle East as peripheral to the world's concerns, and that has to change."

He wanted to describe a new framework for how we could co-

operate with the Muslim world. "The West," he said, "has to reedu-
cate itself about Islam and the contributions that it has made to the
world, and Islam has to recognize the contributions that the West
has made to articulate certain principles that are universal." He
ticked through Islam's contributions to art, science, and mathemat-
ics when "we were a backwater"—including himself in what would
have been, at the time, Europe. Then, "we need to talk about the
contributions that America has made." The goal, he said, could be
shorthanded as "We have to know each other better." He talked
about how religious absolutism ultimately fails as a means of governing, just as imperialism does. He stopped walking when he
landed on some language that he wanted to use in the speech: "Any
world order that elevates one group of people over another will fail."
He sat down in the chair facing us. "Then I want to talk about how
I benefited from experience in both worlds."

"Some of the language about how you've had Muslims in your
family and learned to appreciate Islam in Indonesia?" I asked.

"Some of that," he said. "I'd say I appreciate the differences, but
I've also learned that there are things that all people aspire to. More
opportunity for their children. Family. Faith. These things we share."
He summed up what would be the wind-up portion of the speech,
and then a transition to more difficult issues. "We can't ignore the
basis for tensions; those are genuine. We won't ignore them or brush
them under the rug. We need to face them squarely."

Sometimes Obama has a way of talking that feels as though he's
trying out ideas—testing whether they sound right spoken out
loud, wanting people to argue with him. Other times he has a clear
sense of what he wants to say, formulated in his mind while he sat
in meetings, watched ESPN, played cards, worked out, or lay awake
at night. This felt like one of those moments.

He ticked through a list of issues he wanted to address. The need
to wipe out terrorist networks without compromising our values.
Iraq, and our plans to draw down our troops. Israel and Palestine.
The pursuit of a nuclear agreement with Iran. Then we went into
the social issues—democracy, opportunity, gender equality. Each of

these questions, he said, deals with "how we interact with Islamic countries, and how modernity interacts with Islam." Occasionally my eyes would drift to the family photos behind the Oval Office desk, and beyond that—out the windows—to the playground set he'd installed for his daughters. In the Rose Garden, his mother-in-law sat on a small bench talking to a visiting friend.

He said we had to find a way to reach Muslims who "didn't think it was such a great thing to have a McDonald's down the street and American pop culture on their television." All people, he said, want to maintain their identity in the modern world. "We should acknowledge that not everything we see is positive—there's a mindless violence, a crude sexuality, a lack of reverence for life, a glorification of materialism." That said, he wanted to make several statements of belief in human progress—that countries succeed when they are tolerant of different religious beliefs; that governments that give voice to their people and respect the rule of law are more stable and satisfying; and that countries where women are empowered are more successful. "When I was a kid in Indonesia," he said, "I remember seeing girls swimming outside all the time. No one covered their hair. That was before the Saudis started building madrassas." This was a theme he'd come back to again and again. He told a story about how his mother once worked in Pakistan. She was riding on an elevator. Her hair was uncovered and her ankles were showing. Yet even though she was older, "this guy in the elevator with her couldn't stand to be in that type of space with a woman who was uncovered. By the time the door opened he was sweating." He paused for effect. "When men are that repressed, they do some crazy shit."

When he was done, we talked through a few issues. One was democracy. I pointed out that the challenge wasn't just the sensitivity of addressing the issue in a repressive country; it was the fact that if there was ever a real election in Egypt, the Islamist party— the Muslim Brotherhood—would probably win. America tended to express support for the type of democratic activists who would get only a small percentage of the vote, and it made us less credible.

Obama paused on this, then offered a formulation: The United States should welcome the legitimacy of all political movements, even those we disagree with, but we will also judge any political movement by whether they choose to act and govern in a way that is consistent with democratic principles. Little did we know how that position would be tested at the height of the Arab Spring.

I spent several days working on the speech, often hiding out in my second—unused—office in the EEOB where nobody could find me—sanding down harder-edged points, filling out the policy sections with inputs from the rest of the government. I worked with a devout Muslim on the White House staff, Rashad Hussain, to sprinkle in references from the Koran. To personalize it as much as I could, I ended up lifting, almost verbatim, a line from the culmination of *Dreams from My Father* describing Obama's thoughts as he sought a connection with his absent father in Kenya, which spoke to a search for something universal in people no matter where they came from or what they believed: "It's a belief that pulsed in the cradle of civilization, and that still beats in the heart of billions. It's a faith in other people, and it's what brought me here today."

Given the high profile of the speech, we also tried to nudge forward different policies. A few weeks before the speech, Obama had written a secret letter to the Supreme Leader of Iran indicating an openness to dialogue on the nuclear program. In response, we'd received a secret letter back—a long and obstinate recitation of the perceived crimes of the United States, particularly the U.S. role in a coup that overthrew the Iranian government in the 1950s and installed the repressive shah. The letter indicated that relations between nations had to be approached with "courage, rectitude, and resolve."

Since letters weren't going to set a new tone, in the speech we tried to set a new tone for dialogue with Iran by acknowledging the past—thinking it necessary to name the difficult history in order to move beyond it: "In the middle of the Cold War," Obama would say, "the United States played a role in the overthrow of a democratically elected Iranian government. Since the Islamic Revolution, Iran has played a role in acts of hostage taking and violence against U.S. troops and civilians. This history is well known. Rather than remain trapped in the past, I have made it clear to Iran's leaders and people that my country is prepared to move forward." To send a message to those watching carefully in Iran, we inserted the Supreme Leader's own words, turning them back at him: "It will be hard to overcome decades of mistrust, but we will proceed with courage, rectitude, and resolve."

The most heavily scrutinized section was about Israel and the Palestinians—an issue that also drew on the varied aspects of Obama's background. On the one hand, he had deep roots in the Chicago Jewish community, which has been historically close to Israel; on the other hand, he had empathy for the Palestinian predicament (during a campaign debate prep, he snapped at me when I suggested going easy on Israeli settlements—"If we can't criticize settlements, then we might as well go home"). In Israel, Benjamin (Bibi) Netanyahu had just been elected prime minister, and his government—along with its supporters in Washington—were expressing concerns that Obama would use the speech to lay out a peace plan. White House advisors like Chief of Staff Rahm Emanuel and Tom Donilon, who was deputy national security advisor, shared those concerns. The speech should not be seen as about the Israeli-Palestinian conflict, they said, because that would validate the view that all the problems in the Middle East were rooted in Israel's occupation of Palestinian land.

The caricature of Rahm is that he swore all the time, and he did. But a lot of the time he seemed to do it to live up to his caricature ("the secretary of fucking agriculture") rather than to put people down. More than being profane, he was constantly in motion: The first time he called me with edits to a speech, he was swimming. He was avowedly pro-Israel and pro-peace, and he kept a careful eye on the politics of Israel. He argued that it was going to be hard—if not impossible—for a center-left government in the United States to make peace with a center-right government in Israel. But he felt that trying was important. When he got tired of hearing me argue that Obama had to show empathy to the Palestinians, he started calling me Hamas. "Hamas over here," he'd say, "is going to make it impossible for my kid to have his fucking bar mitzvah in Israel."

Rather than put forward a peace plan, Obama accepted a recommendation to call for a halt to Israeli settlements that were encroaching further into the land necessary for a Palestinian state. Rahm and Axe were occasionally smeared as "self-hating Jews" for any pressure we put on Israel, but instead of pushing back on the smear, we usually responded by reciting all the ways in which we were supporting Israel. In Washington, the American Israel Public Affairs Committee (AIPAC) and other organizations friendly to Netanyahu had established themselves as the adjudicators of what was pro-Israel, and they had zero tolerance for any pressure on the Israeli government, and enormous influence with Congress. Most Americans, of course, also felt a natural affinity for Israel.

As we got closer to the date of the speech, the lobbying grew more intense. I was asked to sit down with Lee Rosenberg, one of the leaders of AIPAC, who had been a fundraiser for Obama's campaign. Rosy, as he was called, wanted to make sure we weren't breaking new ground in our support for the Palestinians, or indicating that the Israeli-Palestinian conflict was the root of all problems in the Middle East. He then implored me to call on the Muslim world to recognize Israel "as a Jewish state." This was a formal position that the United States had not yet taken, as it would be a signal that millions of Palestinian refugees will not have the right to return to Israel as part of a peace agreement. I sat there and took his request on board, assuring him that we were breaking no new ground in our support for the Palestinians. The Israelis were by far the stronger party in the conflict, but we were acting as if it was the reverse.

One final decision was whether Obama should travel to Israel after going to Cairo. Given the concern about not wanting the speech to be seen solely through the prism of the Arab-Israeli conflict, we decided not to go. Ironically, we would be criticized for years by Netanyahu's supporters for that decision, even though it was responsive to their concerns. Indeed, this established a pattern—a post facto criticism of Obama for not being sufficiently pro-Israel, which ignored the fact that he wasn't doing anything tangible for the Palestinians and which absolved Israel's own government for its failure to take any meaningful steps toward peace.

By the time we took off for Saudi Arabia, the stop that came before Cairo, Obama had given me a speech draft that was covered in handwritten edits—in the margins, on the backs of pages, on torn-off pages from a legal pad. He was frustrated by the flood of edits that watered down points he wanted to make. "I'm not going to fly all the way to Cairo to give this speech and then whiff," he told me tersely. Axe worried that the speech didn't have a headline and was too theoretical for an American audience. While my colleagues slept all around me on the overnight flight, I stayed up, the glow from my laptop illuminating the small handwriting on Obama's marked-up pages in front of me. The anxiety I felt at working on a speech that would be carefully parsed around the world was eclipsed by a confidence that Obama was making the speech better, and that his heavy editing could serve as a justification to ignore the stream of notes that continued to flood my in-box.

When we landed, we went to one of the many compounds owned by Saudi Arabia's King Abdullah. It was laid out like an Arizona subdivision, complete with golf carts that transported you to identical housing units amid the rolling desert. When I opened the door to my unit, I found a large suitcase. Inside were jewels. In my sleep-deprived state, I thought that maybe this gift represented some kind of bribe to the person writing the Cairo speech, until I heard from others who had received the same suitcase. You're not allowed to keep these gifts unless you are willing to reimburse their cost, which ran into the tens of thousands of dollars. I took a nap while Obama met with the king. Later that night, I joined him as he recapped the day. He was irritated. The Saudis had let him down, refusing to take Gitmo detainees and holding back on a peace gesture with Israel. He passed me some more edits to the speech and I stayed up late working through them in a staff office that was in a large, ornate room with heavy curtains and thronelike chairs.

Obama came in shortly before midnight to talk through a few sections with me and Denis McDonough.

"There's a lot of discomfort with using the word 'occupation,'" I said, referring to the edits to the Israel section that continued to come through.

"What else are we supposed to call it?" he asked.

We ended up affirming our "unbreakable" bond with Israel, calling Holocaust denial "baseless, ignorant, and hateful," and declaring that "threatening Israel with destruction—or repeating vile stereotypes about Jews—is deeply wrong." We tried to balance this with language that spoke to "the daily humiliations—large and small—that come with occupation," and saying "the situation for the Palestinian people is intolerable."

THE NEXT MORNING WE flew into Cairo, descending over a sprawl of low-rise housing and empty roads. On the way in from the airport, Egyptian security forces stood with their backs to the motorcade, uniformed men only a few paces from each other for miles. There were no people on the street in one of the most crowded cities in the world. Thousands of uniformed personnel had been ordered to face away from the cars, looking out into the distance, searching for anyone who might pose a threat.

The speech was being given at Cairo University, and I waited with Obama in a nondescript hold room as the audience was seated. "This speech is going to raise expectations," he said.

"I think we were pretty careful in saying that a speech isn't going to solve all these problems," I replied.

"Yes." He paused. "You know, Bush's second inaugural is a great speech, but you can't just promise to 'end tyranny' in the world." He let the thought hang in the air; he'd just met with Mubarak, a tyrant who had ruled Egypt for decades. "The language is great," he added. "It's probably Bush's best speech."

"I think we landed in a good place," I said.

"I hope nobody throws a shoe at me," he said.

I felt imprisoned in my chair, which was on a balcony along the wall. But as soon as Obama opened with *"Assalamu alaikum,"* the audience erupted in cheers, and I felt the tension recede. We had selected a crowd that mixed secular activists, intellectuals, political leaders, clerics, women's rights activists, and members of the Muslim Brotherhood. All of the factions who would fight it out in the streets of Cairo a few years later were represented in one room, cheering for the parts of the speech they liked—the clerics applauding Obama's defense of a woman's right to wear a hijab in the United States; activists yelling "We love you" when he spoke about democracy; women cheering when he talked about a society needing to unleash the potential of its girls.

After the speech was over, we flew by helicopter to the Pyramids. "I think that went okay," Obama told me. For an hour, we got a private tour of the ancient monuments that dot the desert on the outskirts of Cairo's sprawl—crawling through small chambers, squinting at ancient words chiseled into the walls, looking at the sarcophagi of pharaohs. As we posed for pictures, we had a remarkable sense of privacy; there were no other people in sight. Mubarak had set a broad security perimeter, a gesture that spoke to his power—one authoritarian leader inviting his American patron to tour the tombs of his long-dead authoritarian predecessors, structures with far more permanence than words.

In the years to come, I'd get asked again and again how I felt about the Cairo speech, especially as Islam and the West—and Islam and modernity—continued to be in tension. Touring the Pyramids that day, though, I knew that it wasn't the kind of speech that could be measured against the state of the world at any one particular moment. It expressed what Obama believed and where he wanted to go, the world that *should be.* In writing the speech, and over the course of the trip, we'd seen the forces aligned against that outcome: the contradictions of American foreign policy; the corruption of Saudi Arabia; the repression in Egypt; the extremist forces lurking just out of sight; the intractability of the Israeli-Palestinian conflict.

Years later, after Obama left office, I ran into a Palestinian-born woman whom I knew casually. She said she'd never forgotten the Cairo speech, which she connected to the initial protests of the Arab Spring. I said that that was assigning too much responsibility to a speech. "It wasn't the speech," she said. "It was *him*. The young people saw him, a black man as president of America, someone who looked like them. And they thought, why not me?"

CHAPTER 6

OBAMA'S WAR

WHEN OBAMA TOOK OFFICE, WE HAD BEEN AT WAR IN Afghanistan for seven years—longer than our engagement in the Revolution, the Civil War, World War I, or World War II. And yet, because he had supported the war in Afghanistan and called for "two additional combat brigades" during the campaign, the media started calling Afghanistan "Obama's War" shortly after he became president. The phrase always bothered me. It struck me as a prime example of how Washington looked at something as morally consequential as a war and turned it into a political drama.

During his first year in office, there was an inexorable demand for Obama to pour more troops into Afghanistan. The stage had been set during the transition. The commander in Afghanistan, General David McKiernan, had requested more than ten thousand additional troops in order to blunt the growing momentum of the Taliban insurgency—a request that the Bush administration left for Obama to fulfill. Obama approved McKiernan's request in February, effectively fulfilling his campaign commitment. He had also ordered an initial review of our policy, resulting in the March 27 announcement, which emphasized that Afghanistan and Pakistan needed to be approached with a common strategy so that we could root out the terrorist sanctuaries on the Pakistani side of the border. But that review deferred a decision about whether to embrace a counterinsurgency (COIN) strategy, one that would require many more U.S. troops for a much longer time.

Within the government—and the group of people who think, write, and talk about foreign policy—the debate about what to do in Afghanistan was becoming a proxy for a debate about what had gone wrong in Iraq. To Obama, the failure of the Iraq War was the decision to invade in the first place. To some supporters of the war, the results generated by a counterinsurgency strategy that involved putting more U.S. troops into the fight to secure the Iraqi population demonstrated that the problem in Iraq had been the strategy for fighting the war, not the war itself. But while dissatisfaction with the war in Iraq allowed Obama to become president, during his first year in office, our Afghanistan policy would be shaped in large part by people who embraced the indispensability of COIN.

Bob Gates was exactly the right mix of competent, diligent, calculating, and occasionally hypocritical to thrive in Washington for decades. Throughout the 1980s and '90s, he held a series of high-level positions at the CIA and on the NSC. When I worked with him on the Iraq Study Group, he was comfortably installed as president of Texas A&M University, home to the George H. W. Bush Presidential Library, which had been significantly funded by wealthy Saudis and Kuwaitis grateful for America's help during the Gulf War. In his trips to Washington, Gates arrived nearly thirty minutes early for each meeting—a habit that sent a message about his discipline. He would draw a cup of coffee into a Styrofoam cup, sit at an empty table, and flip through documents as he waited.

As secretary of defense for the last two years of the Bush administration, Gates succeeded as an effective manager of the massive Pentagon apparatus. He also forged a close partnership with the commander in Iraq, General David Petraeus, who became a rock star within the Republican Party because of his willingness to be the public face of the war at a time when George W. Bush was an increasingly unpopular figure. Obama got along well with Gates, whose calm demeanor and clinical manner of speaking earned him the nickname Yoda. Obama felt he needed continuity at the Pentagon at a time when he was going to remove 150,000 American troops from Iraq and spend much of his early presidency averting a Great Depression. He also kept Petraeus, who had been promoted to head of Central Command (CENTCOM), the sprawling military region that included the Middle East and South Asia.

Petraeus was a smart man who chose his words carefully. In 2009, he was at the height of his influence over the thinking that guided the wars in Iraq and Afghanistan. He was so popular in some circles that he was mentioned as a potential Republican presidential candidate, though he volunteered to me more than once on the sidelines of Situation Room meetings that he had no interest in politics. In demeanor, he came across more as an academic than a politician, with carefully parted brown hair and a habit of delivering his advice in studious paragraphs that created word clouds around the PowerPoint slides in front of him.

Hillary Clinton proved to be an effective manager of the State Department, combining tenacious support for her Foreign Service officers with an alert political antenna. She made a point of demonstrating her preparedness for meetings, showing up with thick binders of briefing materials that she would page through intermittently during discussions. Her curiosity led her in eclectic directions—on our first foreign trip together, she started a lengthy discussion with me about the need for the United States to pursue a more nuanced foreign policy toward the Arctic region, describing how thawing ice caps were initiating a competition for resources and affecting the movement of ships. On the wars, she often sided with the military— throughout 2009, she rarely took a position in an internal discussion about Iraq or Afghanistan that differed from Gates's.

Within the State Department, Richard Holbrooke had been named her Special Representative for Afghanistan and Pakistan (SRAP)—a position she created just for him. Holbrooke was a towering figure in the Democratic Party's foreign policy establishment. He had forged a heroic narrative around his diplomatic prowess over three decades—from his time as a young Foreign Service officer in Vietnam to his negotiation of the Dayton Accords, which ended the war in Bosnia. While SRAP wasn't the level of appointment he sought—he harbored a lifelong ambition to be secretary of state—he turned the office into an empire within the State Department, hiring a mix of accomplished academics and talented young acolytes who served as a deeply loyal cohort and kind of mini think tank.

Having reached the pinnacle of his power in the 1990s—a high-water mark for American influence in the world—Holbrooke retained a persistent belief in the ability of the United States to shape events abroad, even in a region as war-torn, complex, and foreign as Afghanistan and Pakistan. He also reveled in the theater of being a leading diplomat. After one meeting, he guided me out of the State Department by the arm and—as if on cue—the mayor of Karachi stepped out of a car and the three of us huddled conspiratorially, Holbrooke reciting statistics about the city's water supply as if it held the key to success in the AfPak region.

The only senior official who consistently opposed sending more troops to Afghanistan was Joe Biden. As vice president, Biden floated in a unique space, somewhere above everyone else and below Obama, but without an agency like State or Defense to give him an independent power base in the government. At sixty-six, he was two decades older than Obama, and also embraced a more old-fashioned brand of politics—he'd walk through the hallways of the West Wing, stopping to talk to people, gripping your forearm and holding on to it while he spoke. Obama liked that Biden had an instinct for this brand of politics, and came to love him with the almost protective sense of devotion to an older family member.

In the Situation Room, Biden could be something of an un-guided missile. Whereas Gates was stealthy in his bureaucratic maneuvering, Biden would go on long discourses about why it was foolish to think we could do anything more than kill terrorists in Afghanistan, and he solicited military advice outside the chain of command that prepared requests for more troops that would work their way up to Gates and, ultimately, Obama. He would pepper his comments with anecdotes from his long career in the Senate, repeatedly declaring that experience had taught him that "all foreign policy is an extension of personal relationships." He learned the names of all the grandsons of the Iraqi Kurdish leader, Masoud Barzani. He detested Afghanistan's president, Hamid Karzai, and thought the U.S. military was jamming Obama.

Amid this outsized cast of characters, the man who did the most to frame Obama's Afghanistan decision in 2009 was General Stanley McChrystal, whom Gates installed as the war's top general that May. The fifty-four-year-old McChrystal had a mythical reputation in the military. He helped to build America's Special Operations capability in Iraq and Afghanistan—the elite troops who kicked down doors, captured or killed terrorists, and mapped insurgencies like doctors tracing the spread of cancer within a patient's body. He was surrounded by a tight cohort of loyal officers, including General Michael Flynn, who were more comfortable in the distant headquarters of a war zone than in Washington. If Petraeus was the polished, intellectual architect of a strategy that sought to secure Iraqi and Afghan neighborhoods, McChrystal was the fit field soldier who unwound by drinking Bud Light Lime and had spent years sharpening the tip of the spear.

On September 21, 2009, I woke up to a *Washington Post* story by Bob Woodward that began, "The top U.S. and NATO commander in Afghanistan warns in an urgent confidential assessment of the war that he needs more forces within the next year, and bluntly states that without them the eight-year conflict 'will likely result in failure,' according to a copy of the 66-page document obtained by the *Washington Post*." A flurry of other leaks revealed that McChrystal was seeking forty thousand to eighty thousand additional U.S. troops. All of us in the White House, including Obama, read about these things in the newspaper before the recommendations reached his desk. The brazen nature of the leaks left me feeling a bit overwhelmed. They were boxing Obama into sending troops into Afghanistan and setting him up to take the blame for any bad outcomes that followed if he didn't—even though those outcomes were likely to happen anyway.

Over the past several weeks, the pressure on Obama had already been building. The troops he'd sent into Afghanistan hadn't made much difference, and the August elections led to credible allegations of massive voter fraud by the incumbent president, Hamid Karzai. Influential Republicans like John McCain were already calling for more resources to replicate the success of the surge in Iraq. A cult of personality was emerging around McChrystal, who had received a series of glowing profiles after his appointment—he was the savior who was going to salvage Afghanistan, just as Petraeus had done in Iraq. The stage was set for a Washington drama: Would the young antiwar president back or buck the advice of these wise and experienced advisors?

A WEEK AFTER THE McChrystal report was leaked to the *Washington Post*, I was formally promoted to deputy national security advisor for strategic communications and speechwriting—an absurdly long title that I would hold until the end of the Obama presidency.

Up to that point, the leadership of the NSC had been split among four people. At the top of the pyramid was Jim Jones, a four-star general and former commandant of the Marine Corps who looked like a tall, square-jawed, handsome actor playing the role of a four-star general and former commandant of the Marine Corps. Jones never quite took to the role of staffer. He tended to float above the NSC like a monarch—serving as an effective envoy with foreign governments and offering advice on issues that interested him. He had a strange habit of giving this advice to Obama while looking at someone else in the room, which sometimes put me in the awkward position of holding eye contact with him while he spoke to the president. He had no problem letting others around him brief Obama, which allowed the deputy national security advisor, Tom Donilon, to carve out an influential role.

Donilon was the kind of guy widely known inside Washington and nearly anonymous outside it. As a young man, he'd been a sharp-elbowed political operative working for Jimmy Carter in the White House. While his brother, Mike, never left the role of political consigliere for Joe Biden, Tom worked hard to make a turn from politics to foreign policy. He spent the Clinton years in State Department roles, and the early 2000s credentialing himself through the types of establishment organizations that function as a farm system for future national security officials: the Aspen Strategy Group, the Council on Foreign Relations, the Atlantic Council. His closeness to Rahm—together with Jones's hands-off style—allowed him to take control of the levers of national security decision making: the coordination of different agencies that prepare options and recommendations that go up to the president.

Then there was a bottleneck. After the election, both Mark Lippert and Denis McDonough wanted to come to the White House to be—essentially—Obama's guy on the NSC. Lippert had served in Iraq until the summer of 2008, and during that time Denis had taken his place as Obama's lead national security staffer. The two of them were friends—former Hill staffers in their thirties. They shared an office meant for one person, and each kept changes of clothes there to account for endless hours. They were both capable of performing the role of multipurpose aide and gatekeeper—being the decision maker on issues related to Obama's schedule; controlling the paper flow; working with the White House on communications strategy; helping staff the government; making sure Obama's personal priorities were addressed. But they both couldn't keep doing the same job. Ultimately, Lippert would be the one to leave. I liked Lippert, and always thought he missed the days of being Obama's Senate aide, without all the politics of working in the White House. He had loved serving in the military, and that summer he arranged to have himself redeployed overseas.

As this played out, Denis told me that he was going to take the job of NSC chief of staff, and he wanted to know if I would take his position as deputy national security advisor for strategic communications. I'd have a standing invitation to Deputies Committee and cabinet-level Principals Committee meetings, he said, and NSC meetings with Obama. I would be in charge of communications on national security—preparing Obama for his press conferences and interviews and Robert Gibbs for his press briefings, running a staff of about ten people at the NSC, and coordinating the spokespeople for State, Defense, and other agencies. I would also be in charge of the sprawling ways that the United States reaches foreign publics— from exchange programs to information operations.

I said I needed some time to think it over. I couldn't imagine saying no, but something made me uneasy. I liked the idea of having more of a voice on policy and more stature in the White House. I didn't like dealing with the press that much, but was assured (falsely) that that could be delegated. My one demand was to keep writing the major national security speeches. I was also able to hire another national security speechwriter, Terry Szuplat, who proved to be a rock of intelligence and stability for the next seven years.

The source of my unease didn't become clear to me until I delayed telling Ann about this new opportunity as we were driving back to D.C. from a weekend in New York, shortly before our wedding. I mentioned that Denis had floated the prospect of this job. She went quiet and looked out at the road. "So that's a deputy national security advisor position?" she asked.

"Yes," I said.

Her response was neither negative nor enthusiastic. "We're going to be in Washington for a while, aren't we?"

"Not necessarily," I said. But in that moment, I knew what had been churning inside me since Denis first broached the job. I'd made a choice, back in 2007, to go work for Obama to see if I could help get him elected. Since then, I had never really thought about what my job would be other than writing speeches. Now I was being offered the kind of position that carries more responsibility than writing another man's words; that puts you in charge of other people; that begins to define you to the wider world; and yes, that keeps you in Washington for a while.

"You know we will," Ann said. "But it's an unbelievable opportunity."

I looked out at the passing darkness of southern New Jersey, the exits getting farther apart as we approached Delaware. I'd made the drive to and from New York dozens of times since I'd moved down to D.C. as a twenty-four-year-old who figured I'd be there for a few years and do some interesting things before moving back to fulfill my true calling writing for a magazine or churning out books. My best friends, who I almost never had any time to speak to anymore, all lived there. My brother had just recently welcomed his second son.

Ann and I were about to get married, and this promotion was going to ensure that I wasn't going to move to New York or any-where else for the foreseeable future. I wasn't going to go to happy hours after work, or watch live music, or keep in touch with old friends, or go to movies and read books as they came out, or see a lot of my parents before they got older, or see my nephews grow up. Instead, I was going to be a deputy national security advisor.

Here is how I was officially elevated to this position: I talked to Gibbs, who described how he liked to be prepared for his briefing while checking his fantasy football team on the computer in front of him, concluding with "This will be fun." Then Axe came down to my office and closed the door. He worried aloud about whether I had the stomach for the day-to-day grind of dealing with the press—"I can see you doing well with the thoughtful people like David Ignatius," he said, citing the *Washington Post* columnist, man-aging in his own unique way to praise and put me down at the same time, but that was it. There were, as far as I could tell, no other can-didates, and no one considered that I might say no. Obama told me, in passing, "I want you in the room more," something he'd tell me more and more over the years until I was in the room all the time.

A few weeks before the change became official, Ann and I were married. We held the ceremony in Los Angeles. Orange County was out of the question for a New Yorker; New York was too expen-sive and out of the question for a Californian; Washington didn't feel like home to either of us—it felt like a place where we worked. So we chose a venue in a Los Angeles park, behind the striking Art Deco public library—Southern California enough for Ann and her family, urban enough for me and mine. It was a spectacular spot—the skyscrapers surrounding us, the weather just right. To me, it also suggested that we were people—at that moment—who weren't really from anywhere; we didn't live at home, but we also weren't ready to go back home, wherever that was.

The biggest contingent at our wedding were Obama people—the late twenties and early thirties set, people who'd bonded on the campaign and become something of a family. For one night, we set aside the stress of our jobs and had a party. The deejay played a hip-hop playlist. A conga line danced on the walls of a fountain. I sang George Michael's "Freedom 90" into the deejay's microphone standing on a wall. It felt like the period on a stretch of time when we all hadn't quite been promoted to positions of higher responsibility—before people took over departments of government, joined the cabinet, had kids, got divorced, succeeded in (or failed out of) government, or went off to make money. At the end of the night, Samantha Power was carried dramatically out of the wedding party by her husband. Denis McDonough and his wife flew back to Washington on a red-eye. Favreau stayed up most of the night to draft a speech that Obama would give to a joint session of Congress urging that they pass healthcare reform.

We took only a couple of days off after getting married. Instead, Ann and I delayed our honeymoon by over a year because I had to get back to Washington to prepare for the United Nations General Assembly and the looming Afghan review. After I moved into my new job, the U.S. government installed a communications system in our small two-bedroom apartment. Ann called it the Command Center. It took up a chunk of our living room and occasionally made strange noises during the night as a system of fans turned on to cool the devices. Sometimes it was so loud that it woke us up. When I complained about this to people at work, I learned that these noises were not uncommon—I was just the only person with one of these installations who lived in a small apartment, a place where it could not be stored in a more distant room, out of earshot. I still lived in a young person's home.

CHAPTER 7

WAR AND A
PEACE PRIZE

———

THE AFGHAN REVIEW WAS ONE OF THOSE DRAMAS THAT WASH-
ington loves while it is happening and then moves on from as soon
as it's over.

The meetings usually ran two to three hours. Obama sat at the
head of table, flanked by officials in descending rank order, with
others joining by Secure Video Conference, including McChrystal
and Karl Eikenberry, our ambassador in Afghanistan. In the early
meetings, Obama said he didn't even want to discuss the "resource
request" before we established what was achievable. But it was always the unspoken presence in the room.

Obama wanted to show his government how he went about
making decisions, so we needed to understand what was happening
in Afghanistan and Pakistan, define our interests, test what resources were necessary, weigh those needs against all of our other
priorities at home and around the world, and then make a decision.

Obama wasn't against sending in more troops, but he wanted to
make sure we didn't define their mission in overly broad terms. He
would sit there taking his own notes while different principals
talked. Then he would offer his own summation at the end of the
meeting. In painstaking detail, he worked to establish a few base-
lines: al Qaeda and the Taliban were allied but distinct—the former
a terrorist group trying to attack the United States, the latter a do-

mestic political actor inside Afghanistan; the Taliban could not be defeated so long as it had political support in Afghanistan and a safe haven in Pakistan; Pakistan would not abandon its support for groups like the Taliban so long as their primary concern was having proxies against neighboring India. It was clear he wanted to focus on defeating al Qaeda, not on remaking Afghanistan. That, in turn, would mean fewer troops for a shorter period of time.

For me, it was a time of transition into a new job where I'd be involved in the closed-door meetings and be responsible for shaping the public view of what was taking place in them. I felt a small thrill at being with such well-known people, sitting in a row of chairs along the back bench of the Situation Room, taking notes. But I rarely spoke, unsure of when to weigh in, deferential to more experienced people who largely saw my role as putting out generic statements that did more to obfuscate our deliberations than illuminate them (*"Today, the president and his national security team met to discuss the situation in Afghanistan . . ."*). Meanwhile, people steadily leaked information that all pointed toward Obama's sending in forty thousand troops, and it felt as though I had little ability to control anything other than the inevitable speech that Obama would give when the three-month review was over.

Early in the process, we made an effort to steer the public debate. Gibbs had me invite a couple of *New York Times* reporters to the White House to speak to John Brennan, who was Obama's top counterterrorism advisor. This is the kind of thing you do when you want to signal that you're communicating something important: arrange for an interview with someone who rarely grants them, tell the reporters that you want to offer a sense of our thinking. Brennan was a career CIA guy who appeared to do nothing but work. He once had a hip replacement and came to the office the next day. His experience in the Middle East made him skeptical that the United States could shape events inside the countries there, even as he was adamant about the need to take out terrorist networks. He spoke sparingly, but with a precision and gravitas that made you stop and listen closely. He used to complain when people used the word "fulsome" as a synonym for "robust," because it actually is a synonym for "noxious"—he'd look at me whenever the word was used incorrectly in a meeting, an eyebrow slightly raised.

Sitting down with the reporters, Brennan made the case that the Taliban and al Qaeda had to be viewed separately, arguing that "when the two are aligned, it's mainly on the tactical front." He stressed that we needed to destroy al Qaeda but that it wasn't necessary to destroy the Taliban to accomplish this goal. The Taliban had to be pushed back to give us the capacity to go after al Qaeda, but we couldn't destroy a movement indigenous to Afghanistan's tribes with local agendas that did not include launching attacks against the United States beyond Afghanistan's borders.

When the session was over, I felt we were finally beginning to get our message out, laying a predicate for a less ambitious commitment in Afghanistan. But when the story came out, with the headline AFGHAN WAR DEBATE NOW LEANS TO FOCUS ON AL QAEDA, I felt I was playing out of my league. Going to the press, especially the *Times,* was a blunt instrument, and the story could have come only from the White House, given the view it reflected. The Pentagon was a large building, staffed with thousands of people, so leaks could be blamed on an anonymous multitude. The White House was small, and the number of people who knew what was going on in the Afghan review numbered fewer than twenty. I knew people were unlikely to blame Obama, or even more senior aides like Brennan. It's always easier to blame the younger guy.

I got a chilly phone call from Gates's press secretary, counseling me that people in his building were upset with the story. Gates met privately with Obama to say that he was furious—this was no way to conduct a review. Obama expressed no concern to me about the story, but he wanted to keep Gates happy, so in the next meeting he made a point of saying that he didn't want to read any more about the deliberations in the newspaper. To me, the hypocrisy was stinging. The whole review had been shaped by leaks from the military designed to box Obama into sending more troops into Afghanistan. I kept reading anecdotes in the press about how much Gates hated leaks, when nearly all of them emanated from his department. I knew that Admiral Mike Mullen, chair of the Joint Chiefs of Staff, and General Petraeus shared an independent communications advisor who seemed to spend much of the day in casual conversations, meals, and drinks with reporters—something that I didn't have the time to do. I thought about Axe's comment—maybe I wasn't up for this kind of thing.

In meeting after meeting, the principals seemed to calibrate their arguments to align with Obama's views without changing their position on troops. Gates argued that he wasn't for a CT strategy or a full COIN strategy—he was for something in between, something that promoted a strong, effective government that delivers services to the people. When the shortcomings of the Afghan government were pointed out, Gates said that we should not give "one dollar or soldier" for a corrupt government—even though that's exactly what we were doing. Petraeus said our goal was not to defeat the Taliban but to deny them population centers. Mullen talked about the psychological piece—the need to create the impression that the Taliban will lose. For the same reason, Clinton said that putting in troops wouldn't work but you still need to put in troops. It seemed to sum things up perfectly: We had created political pressure on ourselves to send in troops based on a theory of COIN; the review was determining that COIN couldn't succeed; but all of the arguments still pointed to sending in the same number of troops. *We are not going to defeat the Taliban,* Obama kept saying. *We need to knock them back to give us space to go after al Qaeda.*

As the review ground on, the public pressure on Obama shifted from making the case for more troops to something more primal, a criticism that would persist for seven years: He was, Washington concluded, dithering. Nothing bothered Obama more than one column by David Brooks in *The New York Times.* Brooks, a temperamentally moderate guy, announced that he had spoken to the nation's "smartest military experts," people "who follow the war for a living, who spend their days in military circles both here and in Afghanistan." These people, according to Brooks, "are not worried about his policy choices. Their first concerns are more fundamental. They are worried about his determination." As if that wasn't clear enough: "Their concerns are about Obama the man." Brooks gave the assurance that "most of them, like most people who have spent a lot of time in Afghanistan, believe this war is winnable"—though he didn't describe what winning looked like. He concluded that for Obama, "the most important meeting isn't with the Joint Chiefs and cabinet secretaries. It's the one with the mirror."

"Why is this whole thing being framed around whether I have any balls?" Obama asked a small group of us in the Oval.

He had begun to call us up there every now and then to recap what had gone on in the meetings downstairs. "I think it's clear I care about Afghanistan, because I'm spending all this time trying to get it right." We nodded in agreement.

As would often be the case, he vented about things that he could not really change, the structural dynamic in Washington that sees politics as a game and foreign policy as an extension of politics. Turning serious, he reiterated that he was willing to send in more troops, he told us, but he was worried about sustainability. The chart that the military used to plot the troop requests showed our commitment to Afghanistan going up to about a hundred thousand troops over the next two years—and then staying there indefinitely. McChrystal assessed that we would need a substantial force for four years, until the Afghan Security Forces would be able to take the lead. Meanwhile, Eikenberry was arguing that the Afghan government would never get its act together if it felt as if we were going to be staying forever.

"This is going to cost a lot of money and a lot of lives," Obama said, kicking off one of the final Situation Room meetings. "Am I going to see kids who had their legs blown off at Walter Reed and Bethesda in eight years?" The room was quiet. He held up the chart showing the forty thousand troops sent into Afghanistan and staying there, a line that hit a plateau, a line that represented lives forever changed. "You keep giving me the same option," he said. "I can't sell this. It will be six years until we're essentially back to where we are now." Speaking as the only one who had to think about everything the U.S. government has to do around the world, he said, "A six-to-eight-year war at over fifty billion dollars a year is not in the national interest. The Petraeus surge [in Iraq] was much quicker than that. This has to be a surge like that."

Biden chimed in, "That's goddamn right." He argued that we should put in no more than the smallest force necessary to do counterterrorism—no more than ten thousand troops.

Obama asked each of the principals for their final recommendation, and one by one they endorsed McChrystal's troop request. Clinton said we needed to show resolve and "act like we're going to win." Gates supported the recommendation, while agreeing with Obama that the military would need clear timelines—a concession to Obama's view. Mullen gave his strong endorsement, adding that by mid-2011 we'd either be "winning or losing." Petraeus, the intellectual architect of the approach, simply said that he agreed with Gates, Clinton, and Mullen. Brennan gave the best summary of what we ended up doing. He noted that we'd have to sustain our ability to go after al Qaeda in Afghanistan and Pakistan and train Afghan Security Forces, all of which required more troops for some time. But he noted that it would take "at least a generation" to transform Afghanistan, and that we needed to stick to more modest goals. I said nothing.

Obama said he'd think about it. He told me to get started on the outline of a speech. On Thanksgiving, I sat in my dad's home office—which had once been my childhood bedroom—and started to work on it as my family watched football in the other room. While my parents were filled with pride at my new position, giving toasts over dinner to the health of the president of the United States, my mind was far away, on the computer screen that held a barely begun speech, and I had no idea how to explain to them what it was I'd been doing. Instead, I wanted to talk about anything else. The next day I was back at work.

Obama called me up to the Oval Office. It was just the two of us, standing near the door, and he asked me what I thought he should do. In the short silence that followed, I felt the full weight of his question—for weeks, I'd sat along the back bench, filled with opinions about what was being said. Now, a man with the authority to send troops to fight a war was asking me what I thought. I was hesitant—I was too new at this; I had a sense of which arguments held together best, but I didn't feel it was possible for me to predict what was going to take place in Afghanistan.

"I agree with Brennan," I finally said. "You need a surge to push back the Taliban. But the goal should be to target al Qaeda, train the Afghans, and then have a transition." I was describing how we would articulate the strategy more than I was making a recommendation. I then started to make arguments back to Obama that he'd made downstairs. I wasn't adding a lot of value.

"Target, train, transfer," Obama said. I could tell that he was trying out a catchphrase, one he might use to sell the escalation of this war as something less than the COIN strategy that he had rejected in his mind.

Ultimately, Obama decided to send thirty thousand American troops to Afghanistan, with NATO getting us the rest of the way to forty thousand. We would announce it as a temporary surge—in eighteen months, the troops would start to draw down. We'd secure Afghanistan's major population centers, then shift to training and counterterrorism—essentially endorsing the Petraeus-McChrystal approach for two years, and then shifting to the Biden-Brennan approach sooner than the military wanted. At Biden's suggestion, Obama had all the principals memorialize their agreement with the plan in writing. It felt like a bit much, but this was the lesson from Vietnam: Limit escalation.

The next day we met to go over his speech. The tone, he said, should be "sober and adult—not depressing." He sat next to me on the couch and began to talk, not so much about the speech, but about the kind of president he wanted to be. "The American people are idealists," he said, "but their leaders have to be realistic and hard-headed." At the beginning and end of the speech, he wanted to draw upon American idealism—Roosevelt's belief that we "carry special burdens" in the world. In between, he wanted to acknowledge that in disorderly places there is a limit to what we can achieve. When he was finished he went back behind his desk and sat down.

I stood there an extra moment. I'd watched him get pushed into a corner that fall and stay there. I'd seen him try to slow the momentum that was leading inexorably to more troops, more war; I'd watched as that process became, essentially, a negotiation between the far-reaching recommendations of his advisors and his own sense of realism. At the same time, the economy was teetering on a ledge between depression and slow recovery, and an overhaul of American healthcare was creeping through Congress. The American public was exhausted by nearly a decade of war. In a way, we'd failed him by making him spend so much time on this review. He'd reshaped what had come to him and turned it into something that he felt was necessary, something worthy of sacrifice, something with limits. But I could still sense his unease at sending young people to die.

"I'm proud to work for you," I said. It felt a bit awkward—as though I was overstepping a boundary with a man who tended to keep his emotions at a distance. "I just wanted to say that."

I was trying to sum up something, to convey that I saw how lonely his job must be, and perhaps to say something about how this experience was changing me, how I'd try to do better. It would be the only time I ever told him that. He looked up at me. "I appreciate you," he said. "Get to work."

In the coming days, he consistently took out of the speech any language that spoke of winning or victory. He would pay tribute to the troops, but not overpromise. "We should glorify their service," he told me, "but we should not glorify war." Years later, Gates—the most important advisor in the process—would say that Obama's strategy was right, but he was not sufficiently committed to the mission (a convenient way for Gates to argue that *he* was right, and any problems in Afghanistan were Obama's). But that was wrong. Obama was committed to taking out al Qaeda; that was just not as ambitious a mission as what the military had in mind.

He gave the speech on December 1 at West Point. I stood backstage with him as rows and rows of uniformed soldiers awaited his
words. Some of them would end up dying as a result of the decision
Obama was announcing. Before going out, Obama fidgeted a bit
backstage, waiting as a large clock ticked down to the moment
when he would stride out onto the stage to deliver the address.
"They're so young," he said.

A WEEK AFTER ESCALATING the war in Afghanistan, Obama flew
to Oslo to receive the Nobel Peace Prize. To help him prepare the
remarks he'd give at the ceremony, Obama had asked Jon Favreau
and me to give him a selection of speeches and essays about war—
John F. Kennedy speaking about the nature of peace and calling for
a nuclear test ban treaty; Churchill, Roosevelt, and Lincoln at war;
Mahatma Gandhi, Martin Luther King, Jr., and Reinhold Niebuhr.
The two of us sat together and drafted a speech that mainly dealt
with the tension of his getting the award at the beginning of his
presidency. We sent it in to Obama and heard nothing back until
ten on the morning we were going to board the plane for Oslo.

He called us up to the Oval Office, along with Samantha Power.
Without our knowing, she'd sent Obama a memo laying out sweeping ambitions for the speech, which she saw as a chance to address
fundamental issues of war and peace. He looked tired and a little
annoyed. "I had to stay up all night writing this," he said, handing
us seven pages torn from a yellow legal pad, each filled with his tiny,
neat handwriting. The only other time he had written a speech from
scratch was during the campaign, when he delivered his address on
race.

For the next several hours, I sat at my desk typing up his writing,
polishing it in places, dividing up sections with Favreau. Obama
had turned the entire speech into an effort to deal with the tension
of getting the award right after he had decided to send thirty thousand troops to fight in a war. Samantha's memo, together with the
Afghan review, had stirred something inside him. I started to circu-

late the draft, which was dotted with quotes from Niebuhr; medita-
tions on the meaning of war; and personal language reconciling his
current position with his political heritage: "As someone who stands
here as a direct consequence of Dr. King's life work, I am living
testimony to the moral force of nonviolence. I know there's nothing
weak—nothing passive—nothing naïve—in the creed of the lives
of Gandhi and King. But as a head of state sworn to protect and
defend my nation, I cannot be guided by their examples alone."

For the first time, I boarded Marine One with him and Michelle
Obama because I needed extra time to work on the draft. The helicopter flew over downtown D.C. at dusk. There was the Washington Monument from above, the Lincoln Memorial in the distance.
I tried to disappear into the couch that faced the two of them, while
Michelle chided me a bit. "He was up most of the night," she said,
in what felt a little like a rebuke.

"I know, I know," I said.

We flew all night and none of us slept. Obama read over revisions a page at a time in his office; I worked on the oversized computer in the back; Favreau and Power made edits in the conference
room. The speech broke down into a simple structure that anticipated so many of the debates we'd have in the years to come: the
first part a description of when war is just, the second a description
of how we must pursue peace, including a commitment to diplomacy: "I know engagement with repressive regimes lacks the satisfying purity of indignation. But I also know that sanctions without
outreach—condemnation without discussion—can carry forward
only a crippling status quo." Finally, we told him to get an hour of
sleep before we landed.

When we got to the hotel, we went to a makeshift staff office to
finish the speech. Samantha had been focused on the section that
laid out the case for when it is just to fight a war. Obama had defended the traditional concept of the use of force in self-defense; in
other cases, he said, war had to meet certain international standards
such as the enforcement of international law. These were the cases
in which, Obama had written, eerily foreshadowing Syria, "More

and more, we all confront difficult questions about how to prevent the slaughter of civilians by their own government, or to stop a civil war whose violence and suffering can engulf an entire region." Samantha wanted to insert the concept of nations having a "responsibility to protect," saying that if governments commit atrocities, nations were justified—if not obliged—to intervene. This would have represented a significant new policy for the United States, which Samantha knew. "Think of the message this will send," she kept saying.

I didn't know if Obama wanted to go that far. He was in his hotel room getting ready. It was morning in Oslo—the middle of the night in D.C.—and Samantha and I sat there arguing this point while I squinted at Obama's last edits. I felt I needed to get another opinion so I wouldn't be the only one making this decision. I called Denis McDonough, who never seemed to sleep. He felt strongly that we couldn't include a commitment of that significance without running it through a formal process in the government. I went to meet Obama outside his suite, where he had some final edits. I summarized the debate I'd been having with Samantha, and he looked at me with exasperation. "I'm on my way to deliver the speech," he said. "This isn't the time to be making policy." Jon and I made his final edits—language that spoke of the tension between "the world as it is" and our effort to strive for "the world that ought to be."

In March 2010, Obama made his first visit to Afghanistan as president. We had to travel in secret. On our descent, all the lights on Air Force One were shut off to avoid offering a target. We boarded helicopters at Bagram Airfield and flew into Kabul. All I saw was a scattering of lights in the rolling hills beyond, like reflections of moonlight on a rippling lake. The presidential palace was a tranquil complex of buildings with internal courtyards, full of fountains and winding pathways. While Obama met with Karzai, I smoked and made small talk with some of the guys who formed McChrystal's inner circle.

Like so many of the troops I met in government, they represented the ethos of a post-9/11 generation that had been asked to bear so many more responsibilities than the rest of the American people, while being given complex missions in challenging places. They were smart, tough, and mission-oriented, without the luxury of questioning the mission.

We flew back to Bagram and Obama spoke to a cheering throng of uniformed servicemembers. All told, we were on the ground for only a few hours, VIP visitors escorted within a security bubble in Kabul, far from where the fighting was taking place, out in the sprawling darkness.

A FEW WEEKS LATER, Karzai came to Washington, and McChrystal's team invited me out to his house at Fort McNair, a handsome multistory home with a backyard. We stood drinking Bud Light Limes out of a trash can filled with ice. McChrystal had an easy camaraderie with the people around him. They struck me as decent guys doing their best in a difficult spot, as confused at how to navigate Washington as I had been when I took my job. I was surprised at how openly they complained about the Pentagon, which I hadn't yet heard from servicemembers. Each agency, I was learning, had its own layer of bureaucracy and rivalry. Later that night, Ann and I went out to dinner with one of McChrystal's closest aides, Dave Silverman. We were at a tapas restaurant in downtown D.C., about as far away from Afghanistan as you can get. We agreed to keep in touch, and Ann and I talked on the way home about how we could see ourselves striking up a lasting friendship.

It wasn't to be. Not much later, a story came out in *Rolling Stone* that depicted McChrystal and his team as an out-of-control boys' club, speaking crudely of just about everyone involved in Afghanistan policy. Littered with quotable put-downs of everyone from

Biden ("Are you asking about Vice President Biden? Who's that?")
to Holbrooke ("Oh, not another email from Holbrooke. I don't
even want to open it"), it ignited a firestorm. I had to reach out to
Silverman that night and tell him that Obama wanted McChrystal
to come home for consultations. He was surprised—they knew it
was bad, but from the distance of Afghanistan, where McChrystal
was the most powerful human being, it seemed to them like a passing storm.

That night, I met Obama on the patio outside the Oval Office.
He asked me to write two speeches for the next day—one in which
he'd decided to keep McChrystal for the sake of continuity, and one
in which he'd decided to fire him to enforce the principle of civilian
control of the military. He didn't tell me what his decision would be,
but he tipped his hand when he spent a lot more time giving guidance for a decision to get rid of McChrystal. He seemed more sad
than angry. "Stan's a good guy," he said.

I woke to emails from Silverman about how contrite the team
was and about how McChrystal was an honorable man who had
learned his lesson. I didn't doubt him. McChrystal believed deeply
in what he was doing, even if I had my doubts about the wisdom of
COIN in Afghanistan. But no private could talk about a captain
the way McChrystal and his team talked about their chain of command in the story, and why was a general even talking to *Rolling
Stone* in the first place? It was a sign of how out of whack things had
gotten in the post-9/11 wars, in which the glorification of Petraeus
suggested that the way for a general to get ahead was to have independent lines to Congress and the media. It was also an outgrowth
of how the entire Afghan review had unfolded, with Obama's views
being secondary to those of the military officers who reported to
him.

That morning, Obama called a few of us into the Oval Office.
He said he was reluctant to fire McChrystal, but he would never be
able to exert civilian control over the military if he didn't. After I
left the meeting, I walked down the hallway and passed the Roosevelt Room. I saw McChrystal standing there, waiting for his

meeting with Obama, looking nervous and somewhat diminished—
not the commanding figure who had seized control over the debate
about Afghanistan policy back in the fall.

After the announcement, Obama convened his national security
team—the same personalities who had proved so hard to manage
during the Afghan review. It was a brief meeting, and he raised his
voice, which almost never happened. "If people can't pull together
as a team, then other people are going to go. I mean it." As he
walked down the hallway afterward, he turned to me. "It's too bad,"
he said. "I really did like Stan." A year later, he would announce the
beginning of a drawdown of American troops from Afghanistan,
on schedule.

CHAPTER 8

THE END OF
THE BEGINNING

———

H ERE IS WHAT MY LIFE WAS LIKE DURING THE FIRST YEAR after I took my new job.

Sometimes the phone would ring in the middle of the night. Two in the morning, three in the morning. I'd pick it up and hear "This is the White House Situation Room calling for Mr. Rhodes," followed by news of some calamity—a natural disaster, an attempted coup, a car bombing in Afghanistan. I'd stare at my Black-Berry, waiting to see if any more news emerged. Ann would ask me what was going on, and I'd tell her. "What do they want you to do about it at two in the morning?" she'd say. I'd email people I knew who worked at the embassy in the affected area to make sure they were all right. If I felt we needed to release a statement, I'd email a few people to get a draft started. Then I'd lie in bed, imagining what it was like to be there—where the protest was massing or the truck bomb went off—to get the same phone call I got, only it was to tell you your wife or brother had been killed. I knew the bad news before everyone else. I'd lie awake for as long as it took for my mind to shut back down so I could drift to sleep.

I'd wake up between six and seven. Each morning, an appointed White House "media monitor" would send a list of news stories to a large group of staff, anything having to do with Obama or, to a smaller list, national security. *The New York Times, The Washington*

Post, The Wall Street Journal, the wires (AP, Reuters, Bloomberg, AFP), then *Politico, USA Today,* the *Los Angeles Times,* the *Chicago Tribune,* the congressional dailies (*The Hill, Roll Call*), an assortment of right-wing media (Fox News, the *New York Post, The Daily Caller, Breitbart*), transcripts from the various television morning shows, longer magazine pieces, and—in later years—notable tweets. This is how I got my news for ten years—by scrolling through my BlackBerry, reading different versions of the same story, looking for a shift in the narrative about Obama or our foreign policy, for what might raise an international issue that was escaping attention, for what lines of attack Republican critics were repeating in ways that might signal a new, coordinated effort—to keep Gitmo open, to bomb somebody, to portray Obama as un-American. I could tell they were getting traction if I also got emails from reporters, cutting and pasting a quote from a Republican critic and asking if I had a response. This was Washington presenting a constant choice: Ignore something and let it stand, or feed it oxygen by hitting back.

I'd shower and shave listening to NPR, the calmest minutes of my day, and head out the door around eight, walking to the bus stop on Connecticut Avenue. I'd stand on the bus for the ten-minute ride, scanning the last of the clips on my BlackBerry and seeing what emails from my colleagues might set the tone for the day. I'd get off the bus at Seventeenth and I, where armies of lawyers and lobbyists made their way to soulless eight-story office buildings, and walk south among a dwindling group of people making their way to the White House. I'd flash my blue White House badge at a Secret Service gate where foreign tourists sometimes argued with agents in broken English because they thought they could enter there for a White House tour.

Entering the West Wing, I'd grab a coffee from the White House Mess carryout window and be trailed back to my office by a "briefer," someone from the intelligence community who would sit across my desk and walk me through the President's Daily Briefing (PDB). In those days before we switched to iPads, the PDB was a mahogany leather binder with the seal of the president on it. The first few items—referred to as "articles"—were one- or two-page summaries of key topics or developments that would also go to Obama. Usually, they dealt with whatever bad thing around the world merited his attention: terrorism, a worrisome trend in the Middle East, a new development with China or Russia. I was always struck by the exclusion of large global trends—climate, governance, food, health—in favor of an intricate level of detail about terrorist plots. After 9/11, the intelligence community was going to let any president know anything it knew about a potential plot, even if there was little he could do about it.

The briefer watched me as I read the material while offering additional color. These people had been up all night. They would meet in the early morning hours with the analysts who drafted the PDB articles to get additional context so they'd be ready for queries from people like me. I always felt compelled to ask questions, even when I didn't have any, because they worked so hard to be prepared. In addition to the PDB articles, they'd include a packet of intelligence reports—a tiny sample of the enormous volume of information collected by the U.S. government—that were relevant to topics that were a focus for the White House. They called this "traffic."

When I finished this briefing, I'd open my email and usually find *Politico Playbook* there, a "tipsheet" emailed to a few thousand people in media and government. I never subscribed to it, I just started getting it in my in-box one morning around the election. It attempted to distill the news into what people needed to know—what were the storylines driving political coverage and debate; what D.C. insider had a birthday ("Ari Fleischer is 57!"); who was out the previous night (spotted at Bobby Van's!). It portrayed American politics as a game played by a few thousand insiders who mainly cared about who was up and who was down in the daily narrative, yet to fulfill my responsibilities as a national security *and* communications official, I had to be familiar with the contents of both the PDB and *Playbook*.

This hit home for me over Christmas in 2009. We were sitting around the tree in my parents' living room when I got a call: "This is the White House Situation Room calling for Mr. Rhodes ..." A young Nigerian named Umar Farouk Abdulmutallab had tried to set his underwear on fire on a flight to Detroit. His underwear contained explosives. They didn't ignite. When the plane landed, he was arrested, taken into custody, and questioned. Was anyone hurt? I asked. No. Was this part of a broader plot? No. Was there a claim of responsibility from a terrorist group? Not yet.

Then American politics and media took over.

A few days later, I'd open my *Playbook* to this headline: "Briefs bomber may disrupt plans to empty Gitmo—Test of leadership for Hawaiian White House: cerebral, or slow?—GOP plans to keep hitting Dems on terrorism—Invasion of the body scanners." And then this analysis:

> Good Tuesday morning. The White House gets harsh reviews for its handling of the briefs-bomber aftermath, with the lead headline of The New York Times saying of the president's remarks yesterday: "MOVES TO QUELL CRITICS." Peter Baker's Honolulu dispatch begins: "President Obama emerged from Hawaiian seclusion." A Yunji de Nies piece on "GMA" showed clip after clip of the White House response being attacked on cable news (mostly by Republicans) and made a big deal of the president's golfing and "even playing a game of tennis before his public address."

I spent a few days earnestly telling reporters that we didn't want to overreact, but this approach was dismissed as cerebral. After a few days of hysteria, al Qaeda's affiliate in Yemen claimed responsibility for the attack and grew in prestige because they had successfully terrorized America. Democratic support for closing Gitmo plummeted simply because Republicans were on television asserting that Obama was weak and terrorists like Abdulmutallab should be sent to a military prison. Part of me wanted to ignore this side of

my job—I wanted to read intelligence reports, go to policy meetings, write speeches that I hoped the world understood. But that
wasn't an option.

Later in the morning, I'd prepare for the daily press briefings out
of the State Department, the Pentagon, and the White House.
We'd hold conference calls with the spokespeople at different agencies to go over the key news items of the day and what we were
going to say about them. Then I'd join the several staffers in the
NSC press office—most of them Foreign Service officers (FSOs)
who worked for a year or two at the NSC—to walk Robert Gibbs
through the questions he was likely to get in his White House press
briefings. These FSOs were around my age, people who'd signed up
after 9/11 and served at embassies across the Middle East and
around the world. They were acutely aware of how foreign publics
consumed the words that came out of the United States government, of where we could make an impact and where we couldn't.

When the briefings were done, I'd eat lunch at my desk and
catch up on emails. The early afternoon was usually filled with a
Deputies Committee meeting, in which the deputy-level officials
from various agencies—State, Defense, the intelligence community,
and Treasury—come together to make policy on different issues.
These meetings were always in the Situation Room and usually ran
a couple of hours. Each agency would present its view, the meeting
evolving toward some kind of consensus that could make its way up
to the cabinet-level officials and—if necessary—Obama. At first, I
felt intimidated at being included in these groups. But I had a clear
equity—how would these policies be received publicly at home and
abroad, how would we explain them, and how should we take that
into account as we made policy. I also came to see that people assumed I knew, or could anticipate, what Obama would think on an
issue. In the absence of international crises throughout 2010, these
meetings—and our foreign policy—focused largely on methodically
advancing a few issues. Implementing the Afghanistan strategy.
Withdrawing troops from Iraq. Negotiating a New START arms
control treaty with Russia. Imposing sanctions on Iran. But 2010

would be the last year when foreign policy felt somewhat routine; those meetings would become far more consequential soon enough.

In many ways, my job that year was to help keep things calm on our accounts while Obama pursued his domestic agenda, particularly healthcare. The night that the Affordable Care Act passed Congress, Obama had a small group of us up to the White House residence to celebrate. He looked as if a weight had been lifted off his shoulders as he hoisted a martini glass on the Truman Balcony and told us, "This is what we all came here to do—this." Standing there, I realized everyone in the White House supported the totality of his agenda—not just our pieces.

In the late afternoon, between five and seven, I would usually focus on planning for whatever the next big item was on the calendar—the next speech, the next major policy rollout, the next foreign trip. This part of my job grew in the fall, when Donilon replaced Jones as national security advisor, with Denis McDonough moving up to the lead deputy national security advisor role. This left the role of NSC chief of staff vacant for several months, leaving me the responsibility of planning Obama's schedule—what foreign countries he'd visit, who he'd meet with there—a responsibility I'd hold for the rest of the administration.

Foreign trips were my favorite part of the job. You got to immerse yourself in a different place for a period of time—its politics, how it fit into U.S. foreign policy, what its people cared about. Strange things happened—in Russia, I came back to my room from the staff office to find a cleaning woman standing next to the bed and three men in suits going through my things; they put everything down and walked out without a word. You saw the impact Obama had on certain audiences—in Ghana, it seemed every television channel was playing a documentary about his life, and the radio was filled with people singing his name—"Barack *Obama,* you are our *Obama.*" Speeches that he gave abroad got little attention at home but would be carefully consumed in the places where he gave them for years.

At the end of the day, between eight and nine, I'd come home and eat dinner with Ann and watch some television. Before going to sleep, I'd check a last round of emails close to midnight; there was always some loose end to be tied up, some question to answer. Then I'd drift to sleep, playing over the day in my head, thinking about what I had to do when I woke up.

THAT NOVEMBER, AS WE WERE preparing to go to Asia, an enormous electoral wave gave the Republican Party control of the House of Representatives—a stinging repudiation of a two-year period in which Obama saved the global economy, passed a $1 trillion stimulus, reformed financial regulations, and passed healthcare legislation. We expected to lose, but not as badly as we did; our people had stayed home, and Palin's had turned out. In the days after the election, I had come into the Oval Office and caught the tail end of conversations in which Obama was calling a member of Congress who'd lost the election because of their healthcare vote, thanking them for making a difference.

When you show up as Barack Obama in India or Indonesia, no one there cares about the midterm results. This created a strange discordance between the somber bubble we traveled within and the enthusiasm outside it. I packed the schedule—Barack and Michelle Obama dancing with schoolchildren in Mumbai; Obama holding a town hall meeting with students; the first African American president paying tribute to Mahatma Gandhi in Delhi; Obama, the man who lived in Indonesia as a child, delighting a crowd with phrases in Indonesian. Those were always my favorite moments on trips—moments that connect a president to people in other countries, when people didn't just see Obama but felt seen by him.

I thought the trip was going great, but he was tired and increasingly cranky; much of our press was waiting to write that the world was souring on Obama just like the electorate back home. Things started to fall apart in Seoul on the fifth day, when we attended the G20. We missed a deadline to complete the renegotiation of a free trade agreement with South Korea, and the trip quickly turned into a story about Obama's diminished star.

Before a press conference, Gibbs, Jen Psaki, and I walked into a conference room to brief him. Psaki was kind, curious, and unflappable, with bright red hair, a permanent smile, and a maternal instinct for her colleagues. She had started in Chicago around the same time as I did, and over the years she became like a sister within our surrogate Obama family. Obama was sitting with his top economic advisors, and they had been complaining about the lack of credit they were getting for rescuing the global economy from a depression. Gibbs, Psaki, and I quickly became the object of blame for how the press covered foreign policy and, by extension, our politics back home. "Does anyone in the press even care that we're responsible for every word in this communiqué?" Obama said, holding up a sheet of paper—the carefully negotiated text that the G20 would issue upon completion of the summit. In reality, the answer was no; it was hard for *me* to care about the communiqué. I avoided making eye contact with Psaki because I would have laughed.

His G20 frustration was clearly a proxy for everything else—the midterms, the press, the sense that he'd been handed as bad an inheritance as any president since Roosevelt and no one cared. By this point, I'd learned that Obama got mad only at the people closest to him—with everyone else, he was unfailingly polite. By the time we got to Japan, I was the only one around when he wanted someone to complain at. He called me up to his suite, one of dozens of such rooms that I'd see him in over the years, all eerily familiar in their uncomfortable opulence. He had all the newspapers laid out on a table by the door, their headlines a Greek chorus of ridicule. He gestured at them, a scowl on his face, sarcasm in his voice: "Isn't there something we can do about this?"

Feeling tired myself, I snapped back, "No, not when we don't actually reach a trade agreement."

He moved on to the next thing, preparing for the APEC summit, as if that very fact encapsulated the absurdity of being president and never getting a break. "Remind me why this organization even exists?"

With that, I started to laugh, and so did he, as a group of APEC policy experts walked into the room looking confused. I felt the same frustration he did at the venal politics at home. But I was also upset at him. I'd spent months planning a trip that would appeal to each of these countries—India, Indonesia, South Korea, and Japan—countries that accounted for a billion and a half people, with distinctive governments, interests, and populations. India, the home of his hero, Gandhi; Indonesia, his home as a boy. Often, I felt as though I cared more about the global progressive icon Barack Obama than Barack Obama did.

The next and final day, we went to see a giant Japanese Buddha that Obama had visited as a child. We'd picked the site knowing that it would strike a chord in a Japanese culture that loved Obama and this type of recognition. He was quiet on the ride out as the helicopter flew over brilliant green hills and a winding coastline. The motorcade then drove for miles on twisting roads, through small fishing villages lined with people—thousands of people, smiling and waving. Even for Obama, the crowds were extraordinary. A kindly older Japanese woman then showed Obama around the twelfth-century Buddha, an austere stone monument that put midterm elections in perspective.

When we got back to the helicopter, he looked out the window for a few minutes. Then he looked at me and said, "That was good to do."

"It will be the biggest story here in Japan," I said.

"I know. I know why you make me do all of this stuff on trips," he said. "It matters to a lot of people." We rode on in silence.

THAT DECEMBER, I TRAVELED with Obama to Hawaii as the lone NSC staffer who would be there during his Christmas vacation. As soon as Air Force One took off, I felt a sense of relief. We'd been through two years of the campaign, then two years in the White House. We'd proved to ourselves that we belonged, suffered a drubbing in the midterms, and then bounced back—ramming the repeal of Don't Ask, Don't Tell and the ratification of the New START treaty through Congress. Gay people could now serve openly in the military, and the United States and Russia would be pointing fewer nuclear weapons at each other. We had learned that a White House on its back foot can still accomplish more than just about any other institution in the world.

The staff was put up at a hotel in Waikiki, and I had a balcony that looked out over the Pacific Ocean. There was a soothing rhythm to the days—waking up at five to put together a memo for Obama on what was happening around the world; reading books not related to work; driving to the northern shore of Oahu, taking in the surfers, shrimp trucks, and small bungalows and coming to understand why someone could find his own little piece of the world here and never go back. But there was a lonesome tinge to the experience. Ann was with her family in California before flying out to Hawaii for the second half of the trip. So on Christmas Day, I walked through groups of people on the beach, away from friends and family for the first time in my life.

That night, one of the advance staffers put together a small party in one of the basement conference rooms of the hotel. I went for a little bit, mingling with an odd assortment of staffers, and then left to sit up on my balcony. Another hotel, one of hundreds. I had gained a new life that brought me to this beautiful place with a president, but I'd lost my old one as well. I called Ann, and then my parents, and could hear the background noise of more familiar holiday experiences that were now distant. As the sun set into the Pacific, I listened to the voices of strangers wafting up to the balcony and thought about my family and friends. I'd become somebody they watched from afar—whose quotes they might read in the newspaper more often than they spoke to me—someone whose experiences were unknowable to them.

A few days later, Obama invited a few of us to go snorkeling at Hanauma Bay. I drove there with Ann in a rental car, parked, and then we walked over a hill. Down below lay a curving, pristine beach that opens out onto the bay, a reef glistening in the sun. Normally thousands of people might pass through here on a given day, but one day a week it's closed, and they let the Obamas use it. The Secret Service had shut down a perimeter surrounding the beach, and casually dressed agents stood on the tops of the tall rock formations that overlooked us. The beach was dotted with only the Obama family, their friends, and a handful of staff. I'd never snorkeled before, and after I got over the awkwardness of it, I allowed myself to forget the world beyond whatever was in the water beneath me. When I walked back up onto the beach I saw Obama headed toward me, looking even thinner than usual without a shirt on. He stood next to me and we looked out at the water. "This doesn't suck," I said.

He pointed up to a place at the top of the hill that looked over the scene. "You see that spot up there?" he said. "My mom used to come here every day and sit there looking out at the bay when she was pregnant with me." I could hear waves lapping at the shore. "I've always thought that's one of the reasons why I have a certain calm." For a moment, the entire world seemed to quiet.

This calm belied a gathering storm. Just a few days earlier, a small story had popped up on my BlackBerry, one of millions of stories that happen every day, most of which lead to nothing beyond the confines of their community. A fruit cart vendor in Tunisia, Mohamed Bouazizi, had grown frustrated by the harassment he faced from corrupt officials and set himself on fire, initiating protests in the small North African nation on the other side of the world.

PART TWO

SPRING

2011–2012

CHAPTER 9

EGYPT

*The Transition Must
Begin Now*

———

A
FTER WE GOT BACK FROM HAWAII, OBAMA HAD A CALL
with Hosni Mubarak. Over the previous three weeks, the protests
in Tunisia had spread like a brushfire. On January 11, Zine El-
Abidine Ben Ali, the dictator who had ruled Tunisia for decades,
fled power. People in Cairo had begun to mimic Bouazizi, setting
themselves on fire to protest corruption, repression, and Mubarak.
Despite these tremors, the intelligence community did not initially
think that the protests were likely to topple other governments.
Men like Mubarak and Bashar al-Assad of Syria were too entrenched, able to count on the loyalty of security services and the
backing of foreign powers. In the case of Egypt, that power was the
United States, which had provided decades of military assistance
following the Camp David Accords and forged deep relationships
between the Egyptian state and our own national security establishment.

I was part of a cohort of younger staffers in the government who
shared a distaste for the corrupt way in which the Middle East was
ruled. Most of the Foreign Service officers had served there and had
friends there who felt no connection to their own governments—
the mix of monarchies and autocracies whose legitimacy rested on

a family's claim to a piece of land, or militaries who insisted upon a tight-fisted rule to keep an enemy at bay—Islamists, terrorists, Iran. These younger staffers were much more certain of spreading unrest than the more senior people. Meanwhile, a patchwork of aides was pressing for more support for the protesters across the region: Gayle Smith, the NSC's senior director for democracy, a flamboyant, white-haired former journalist who had served as an Africa expert under Clinton. Mike McFaul, the NSC's senior director for Russia, who had spent most of his life thinking and writing about democratic movements. And, of course, Samantha Power. *Egypt is next,* they'd say, and will be a test of whether we'd stand on the side of the people in the streets or the autocrats trying to put them down.

Obama's call with Mubarak was focused on Middle East peace, but he used it to discuss the protests in Tunisia. "We think it is best if Ben Ali does not return to Tunisia," Obama said. "We hope the Tunisian government will hold free and fair elections in the future."

I think he will not be able to return again, Mubarak responded with confidence. *You will not succeed unless the people are very fair and want you. I told the same thing to Gaddafi.*

In the days that followed, every television in the West Wing showed silent images of protest—young men running in the streets; masses gathering in Tahrir Square; people the same age as me chanting together and then being dispersed by the same security forces who had guarded our motorcade route in Cairo. Meanwhile, Hillary had insisted the Egyptian government was stable. Biden said in an interview that no, Mubarak wasn't a dictator. We issued mild calls for the government to show restraint in suppressing the protests. We were, it seemed, a step and a half behind the people in the streets, implicitly siding with a dictator in the country where Obama had talked about how democracy was compatible with Islam and the Arab world.

Privately, Obama was telling people that his sympathies were with the people. If it were up to him, he told McFaul, he'd prefer that "the Google guy" run Egypt, referring to Wael Ghonim, a prominent activist who was helping to lead the protest movement.

He didn't mean it literally; he was indicating solidarity with the younger protesters trying to bring about change. But his senior team was in a different place. Gates and our military favored stability in Egypt, and they felt that stability came with Mubarak. The Clintons had a long-standing relationship with Mubarak, dating back to the Middle East peace process of the Clinton years. The intelligence community was wary of extremists taking advantage of the unrest.

The main driver of opinion seemed to be generational, with the younger staff pressing for change. Mubarak no longer represented stability, we'd say—his dictatorship was the source of instability. This was a once-in-a-generation chance to achieve meaningful reform in the Arab world. We had a moral responsibility to be on the right side of history. It would be a betrayal of what Obama stood for, of what his own election represented, if we weren't.

This divide was starkly illustrated for me when Obama gave his first statement on Egypt on the twenty-eighth. The protests were now boiling over, and Egypt seemed poised on the precipice between a brutal crackdown and some kind of radical change. The statement I drafted spoke about the universal rights of the protesters and called on the government to respect those rights, refrain from violence, and pursue "a path of political change." Tom Donilon and Denis McDonough asked me to give a copy to each of the principals. The edits that came back took out almost all of this language. One draft illustrated the resistance to change so starkly that I saved it and kept it in my desk for the next six years: Every word about human rights and the grievances of the protesters was removed—all that remained were the calls on the protesters to be peaceful, and expressions of support for the Egyptian government. Written in the margins was, simply, the word "balance." Obama ended up using the draft I'd written, largely intact.

THE RHYTHM OF THOSE days was unlike anything I'd experienced before. Ann was traveling, so I'd go home every night around ten, eat on the couch while drinking something stiff, watching cable news, and falling asleep to the scene of crowds swelling. I'd wake and go to work, get my briefing—dominated by stories of unrest in Egypt and surrounding countries—and then attend a standing eight-thirty Deputies meeting to review what was happening. Before every briefing, Gibbs would complain that we weren't embracing the protests, arguing that our calls on the government to show restraint risked looking ridiculous. One day, as I sat in Gibbs's office, the large, mounted television screen showed government-associated goons on horseback with machetes trying to clear Tahrir Square. "How the fuck am I supposed to call that restraint?" he said.

Every meeting seemed consequential; every statement felt pivotal. People would forward me reports that had been sent to them by their friends who had taken up living in Tahrir Square, quoting verbatim from things that Obama had said, lamenting that he wasn't taking their side; on the other hand, our military and diplomats were getting calls from Egyptian officials expressing anger that Obama was abandoning them. The only thing they had in common is that they seemed to care, deeply, about what we were saying. And to me, it seemed, there were clear-cut choices—between right and wrong, boldness and caution, the past and the future.

To those of us who were pushing for change, it was clear that the cabinet-level principals were not. Time and again, Bob Gates, Hillary Clinton, and Mike Mullen would put forward the Egyptian government's view—that the protests would die down; that things could be channeled into a "national dialogue"; that our policy should aim to revert to the status quo. This approach was being pushed hard by the Gulf States, chiefly Saudi Arabia and the United Arab Emirates (UAE), who feared this kind of unrest coming to their capitals.

On January 29, Obama got a call from King Abdullah of Saudi Arabia, who complained that our statements were too forward-leaning. In a sign of how closely our words were being watched, he took exception to statements Gibbs had made in his briefings supporting the protesters. He dismissed the people in the street as nothing more than the Muslim Brotherhood, Hizbollah, al Qaeda, and Hamas. This was their view of who was protesting in Egypt: terrorists. But that is not what the rest of us could see with our own eyes. The protesters weren't just Islamists, they were secular activists, young people, Coptic Christians.

Obama sensed this, too. He called me up to the Oval Office. I stood in front of his desk and we discussed the administration's current public line on Egypt. "You're in all of these meetings, right?" he asked.

"Yes," I said, realizing he had little idea how I spent my days when I wasn't with him.

"I want you to speak up," he said. "Don't hold back just because it's the principals. You know where I'm coming from. And we're younger."

I took that as license to raise my voice. Gone were the days of the Afghan review when I'd hold back my views for fear of overstepping some boundary. In one meeting, where there was broad agreement at a senior level that we should invite the leaders of key Arab countries to Washington as soon as possible to reassure them of our support, I couldn't contain myself. "Maybe if we're going to have all the corrupt autocrats over, we could think about actually inviting some of these young people, too . . . for balance." The people at the table sat there grimly; the young people on the back bench loved it. I was inspired by the moment; I was also making enemies.

Things came to a head in the Situation Room on February 1, in a meeting where the principals were debating whether we should counsel Mubarak to step aside. Obama took the unusual step of coming down to join a meeting he wasn't scheduled to attend. We'd gone around and around, with Clinton, Gates, and others recommending that we stand by Mubarak, and the more junior people urging that we press him harder.

Shortly after Obama came downstairs, Mubarak went on television to address the Egyptian people. We stopped the meeting and turned on the televisions that lined the walls. We all sat there in silence watching Mubarak standing at a lectern, an Egyptian flag beside him, a man who had held office since 1981—just four years after I was born. Occasionally I looked at Obama, but he betrayed no emotion. Mubarak announced that he would not seek another term as president. But he was combative in pledging to serve out his existing term, warning of a choice between "chaos and stability" and pledging to die on Egyptian soil.

When the speech was over, Obama spoke. "That's not going to cut it," he said. "Those people are not going to go home." He effectively ended the debate by saying that he was going to call Mubarak and tell him that it was his judgment that he needed to step down. The call was set up for an hour later. Staff left to go draft Obama's talking points. I went to my office to draft a statement that he would give afterward. Then I ran up to the Oval Office for the call.

"I want to share my honest assessment about what I think will accomplish your goals," Obama told Mubarak. A few of us stood there, scattered across the office, farther away from the desk than normal, as if we didn't want to crowd him. Obama cradled the phone against his ear while a speaker played for the benefit of the others in the room. A translator turned Obama's words into Arabic, creating pregnant pauses and giving Mubarak extra time to digest the words, since he spoke English quite well. "I say this with the greatest respect," Obama continued. "I'm extraordinarily proud of my friendship with you. It is my belief that if the transition process drags out for several months and you continue in your office, that the protests will continue. It will make [the situation] harder to control, and I think your role and the role of the Army will be made much more difficult. I think now is the time to present Egypt to its next government. I think now it is time for you to move in a timely fashion in not allowing the Muslim Brotherhood to take advantage of the situation."

You don't understand the culture of the Egyptian people, Mubarak shot back. He had stopped waiting for translation at certain points. *Egypt is not Tunisia,* he said. *These protests will be over soon.*

The conversation went on like that, back and forth, for another ten minutes. I stood next to Donilon and McDonough, who leaned

over and asked when was the last time that an American president
had had a conversation like this with a foreign leader. "Marcos, I
think," Donilon offered, speaking of Reagan's break with our ally in
the Philippines.

Obama began to wrap up the conversation, speaking off the cuff,
no longer even glancing at the talking points. "Mr. President," he
said, leaning forward, elbow on his desk, "I always respect my el-
ders. You've been in politics for a very long time. There are moments
in history—just because things have been the same way in the past
doesn't mean they will be the same way in the future." When he
hung up, Obama looked at us and shrugged, as if to signal that he
didn't think he'd gotten through. It was the last time they spoke.

During the call, there had been some churn about the statement.
The key line read, "It is my belief that an orderly transition must be
meaningful, it must be peaceful, and it must begin now." After the
draft was circulated, calls and emails were lobbed in to Donilon and
McDonough to take out the line altogether, with Gates and Clinton insisting that we at least take out "it must begin now." As
Obama was about to walk out to deliver his remarks, I asked him
what he wanted to do. "Leave it in," he said. The following day,
when Gibbs was asked what Obama had meant by "now," he replied: "Now started yesterday."

ON FEBRUARY 5, OBAMA got a call from David Cameron, the
prime minister of the United Kingdom, who was worried that we
weren't being aggressive enough in pressing Mubarak to step down.
Cameron said he was confused by what Frank Wisner had said that
day.

"Wisner?" Obama replied. "I have not seen that."

Frank Wisner came from one of the families that defined America's role in the world after World War II. His father had been one
of the top people at the CIA. Wisner had had a long career at the
State Department, serving as ambassador four times, including five
years in Egypt at the end of the Cold War. As the protests picked

up, Obama accepted a recommendation from Hillary to send Wisner to Cairo as a special envoy. He was someone whom Mubarak trusted, a reminder of a better time when our countries were in lockstep during the dissolution of the Soviet Union. Wisner's difficult task was to counsel Mubarak to initiate a transition in Egypt. The last words I heard Obama say to him as he set out on his mission were straightforward: "Be bold."

Wisner succeeded in securing Mubarak's promise not to seek another term as president, but that wasn't enough for the people in the streets, or for Obama. A few days after Obama's statement calling for a transition, unbeknownst to any of us in the White House, Wisner videoconferenced into an international security conference in Munich. Because he had just completed a stint as a presidential envoy, people assumed he was speaking for the administration when he said, "You need to get a national consensus around the preconditions of the next step forward, and the president must stay in office in order to steer those changes through." This was the remark that had caught Cameron's attention. Clinton, who also attended the conference, had made comments that seemed to reinforce Wisner's.

Obama was incredulous when he hung up the phone with Cameron, and he called a group of us into the Oval Office. "What is going on here?" He asked me to call the people traveling with Clinton while he called her himself. Later, after the call, Donilon told me he'd never seen him that upset, voice raised, standing at his desk. He'd already taken the unprecedented step of telling Mubarak he needed to step aside—something that was going to hurt his relationships with some powerful interests in the Gulf and Israel; now his own administration appeared to be walking that back.

There were other voices of caution. Brennan had spent much of his career working on issues related to the Middle East. Unlike some of the other principals, he knew Mubarak couldn't weather the storm. But he warned that Egypt wasn't ready for democracy, that the population had no experience of a politics that wasn't zero-sum. The same Saturday, as I was working to clarify Wisner's statement in the press, Brennan gave me a note: "It is a truism to say that there is a far greater unity among the masses in Egypt on what and who they want to see gone than there is on what and who they want in its/their place."

The next several days felt like an inevitable conclusion to a drama whose main acts had already taken place. Nothing that Mubarak said mollified the protesters, and the Egyptian military began to distance itself from him. Our media, focused on the Washington angle, was filled with stories of mixed messages coming out of the U.S. government—a dynamic that ensured we were making everyone unhappy: the people in the streets, who thought Obama had been slow and uncertain, and the people in power, in Cairo and the Gulf, who thought that Obama betrayed an ally—a belief shared by many in Washington.

I was increasingly frustrated. The president I worked for had taken a bold step to embrace a social movement that was demanding change, and yet the ambivalence within his administration was going to ensure that he was seen as behind the curve. Meanwhile, I heard that the ambassadors from Saudi Arabia and the UAE, two of the most powerful envoys in Washington, were telling people in the press and the foreign policy establishment that Obama had been badly advised by younger people like me who were more interested in preserving Obama's brand than listening to the wise hands who understood that democracy couldn't work in the Middle East. It was the beginning of a multiyear effort by those two countries to restore a dictatorship in Egypt, and it would ultimately succeed.

The one thing that seemed to be on our side, however, was the reality on the streets of Egypt. Day after day, the protests spread and Mubarak's regime seemed to crumble around him. On February 11, I woke to the news that Mubarak had fled to the resort town of Sharm el Sheikh and resigned.

It was, it seemed, a happy ending. Jubilant crowds celebrated in the streets of Cairo. I drafted a statement for Obama that drew comparisons between what had just taken place and some of the iconic movements of the past several decades—Germans tearing down a wall, Indonesians upending a dictatorship, Indians marching nonviolently for independence.

I went up to the Oval Office that morning to review the statement with Obama. "You should feel good about this," he said.

"I do," I replied. "Though I'm not sure all of the principals do."

"You know," he said, "one of the things that made it easier for me is that I didn't really know Mubarak." He mentioned that George H. W. Bush had called Mubarak at the height of the protests to express his support. "But it's not just Bush. The Clintons, Gates, Biden—they've known Mubarak for decades." I thought of Biden's perennial line: *All foreign policy is an extension of personal relationships.* "If it had been King Abdullah," Obama said, referring to the young Jordanian monarch with whom he'd struck up a friendship, "I don't know if I could have done the same thing."

As Obama delivered a statement to a smattering of press, it seemed that history might at last be breaking in a positive direction in the Middle East. His tribute to the protests was unabashed. Yet our own government was still wired to defer to the Egyptian military, and ill equipped to support a transition to democracy once the president had spoken.

When the statement was over, we walked back to the Oval Office. It was a bright winter day, sun splashing on the Rose Garden, as we walked down the colonnade. Obama had several calls scheduled with Arab leaders, including Mohammed bin Zayed, the powerful crown prince of Abu Dhabi who was known by his initials. "MBZ, ABZ, MBN," he said, citing a few of the Gulf Arab leaders who were similarly known by their initials and who had been lobbying on behalf of Mubarak.

"Who are these guys?" Gibbs said.

"I don't know," I said to Obama, "but they're not going to be paying for your presidential library."

CHAPTER 10

LIBYA

———

ONE OF MY EARLIEST MEMORIES OF AMERICAN FOREIGN
policy is of Ronald Reagan sitting behind the desk in the Oval Office and explaining, in his grandfatherly way, that we were bombing
Libya. I was eight years old. My father loved Reagan, so to me he
could do no wrong. If Reagan said we had to teach Gaddafi a lesson
for sponsoring terrorist attacks, then surely he was right. Gaddafi
was a villain, and our president was a hero who rode horses with the
queen of England. I never imagined that Gaddafi would be at the
center of events that would shape the Obama presidency and my
own role in it.

Early in the administration, Gaddafi seemed more of a punch
line than an adversary. In 2009, at our first United Nations General
Assembly, he made waves when he was accompanied by a squad of
female bodyguards and gave a rambling hundred-minute speech
that called for an investigation into the assassination of John F.
Kennedy. On the other hand, he had improved his international
standing by giving up Libya's nuclear weapons program. Gaddafi
had turned into another aging and erratic dictator, with rich children who liked to hang out in London and intelligence services
who fought al Qaeda.

A few days after Mubarak stepped down, the protests in neighboring Libya escalated sharply. There were new calls for Gaddafi to go. Security forces used live ammunition to fire into the crowds. Rebels seized control of parts of the country, including the second-largest city—Benghazi. Instead of Egypt, it was now Libya on every television screen in the West Wing, dominating the questions at press briefings, and forcing its way onto the agenda of the president of the United States. On February 22, we reached one of those turning points that became familiar in the Arab Spring—the moment when a dictator gives a big speech that indicates how he's going to respond to the calls for him to step down. A group of us sat in my cramped office watching the television as Gaddafi—dressed in burnt-orange robes—stood in front of the remains of a building that had been bombed by Reagan, an English translation scrolling across the bottom of the screen. Defiant, he vowed to "purify Libya inch by inch, house by house, home by home, street by street, person by person, until the country is clean of the dirt and impurities."

For me, this was a time when every moment had the electric charge of history. I would host meetings with Libyan Americans who came to the White House to share stories of their besieged families who were fighting for their lives, showing us photographs of children half a world away, imploring us to do something, anything, to help. Journalists who moved from one protest to another called me—not to seek comment, but to share stories, as they were experiencing their first glimmer of hopefulness in a war-torn Middle East and wanted to talk about it. Experts sent us papers trying to place the unfolding events in the Arab world in historical context: Was this analogous to the fall of the Berlin Wall, when the nations of Eastern Europe transitioned to democracy like flowers blooming; or was this like Hungary in 1956, or Tiananmen Square in 1989, popular movements that would be trampled by strongmen? I'd lie awake in bed, my mind racing. A few weeks ago, it seemed that helping to pass the New START treaty was the biggest thing I'd be a part of in government; now, every statement we made, every meeting I was in, every decision Obama had to make, felt like the most important thing I'd ever been a part of—and I wanted us to do something, to shape events instead of observing them.

We exhausted the available options within days—freezing Gaddafi's assets, putting in place travel bans for him and his family, working through the United Nations to impose an arms embargo, referring him to the International Criminal Court for potential crimes against humanity. People with ties to the Gaddafi family were sent messages that he should leave, take up residence somewhere else, let the country avoid a civil war—to no avail. On February 26, in the most routine kind of press statement—the "readout" of a call between Obama and Angela Merkel—we decided to call for Gaddafi to go. "The president stated that when a leader's only means of staying in power is to use mass violence against his own people, he has lost the legitimacy to rule and needs to do what is right for his country by leaving now." Gaddafi was the second Arab leader whose departure we had sought in as many months. He would not be the last.

And yet even as it felt as if things were moving at an accelerated pace, the world outside the White House pressed in upon us, insisting that we were moving too slowly, doing too little too late. In 2011, it wasn't just television images that brought the conflict home; in social media feeds, Gaddafi's crackdown was narrated in text messages and Twitter posts. Because the world could now digest the brutal advance of Gaddafi's forces in real time, whatever happened was on our watch. Members of Congress started to call for a no-fly zone over Libya, so that Gaddafi's planes would be grounded. Reporters asked us how many more people had to die before Barack Obama did something.

Most people in government didn't want to do anything. The military made it clear that Libya wasn't a priority—they had two wars to deal with and little desire for a third. A no-fly zone wasn't just a talking point, it was a complex undertaking that involved eliminating all of Gaddafi's air defenses and patrolling the skies over Libya indefinitely. Others in the White House wondered why, with the economy foremost on the minds of Americans, the Arab

Spring consumed so much of Obama's time. No one had voted for Obama so that he'd do something about Libya. When the U.S. government wants to avoid doing something, it avoids producing the options to do something. And so as the days went by, no option for a no-fly zone made its way to Obama, even though it was being debated across Washington and other capitals around the world.

Arab leaders told Hillary Clinton that they were prepared to be part of an effort to punish Gaddafi. In Europe, the spotlight-loving French president Nicolas Sarkozy signaled that he was going to push for a United Nations Security Council resolution calling for a no-fly zone. Soon we would have to take a position one way or another, so Obama convened a meeting of his National Security Council on March 15 to decide where we would stand at the UN.

The meeting was in the Situation Room and started with an assessment of the situation in Libya. Each of us had a map in front of us that showed Gaddafi's methodical progress in taking back pieces of the country. His army had reached a place called Ajdabiya, a town of about eighty thousand people in the middle of the desert. Ajdabiya, the briefers explained, was the last stop on the way to Benghazi, a city of more than six hundred thousand and the center of anti-Gaddafi resistance for decades. From Ajdabiya, Gaddafi's forces could effectively cut off access to power and water for the people of Benghazi. This was the type of siege that foreshadows a massacre.

Samantha—who lived with the permanent tagline "Samantha Power, Pulitzer Prize–winning author of *'A Problem from Hell': America in the Age of Genocide*"—passed me a note saying that this was going to be the first mass atrocity that took place on our watch. I looked at the names of towns and cities written on the map in front of me, most of which I was unfamiliar with just a few weeks ago. And here we were, debating whether the people in those places would live or die. I looked at Obama, leaning back in his chair and holding the piece of paper, eyeing the same map, the same places.

Clinton had dialed in by phone from Paris. It was late there and she sounded tired. She had been on a long trip throughout the

Middle East and Europe and, she said, the leaders there were ready to pledge diplomatic and military support for a no-fly zone, and she supported it.

Obama went around the table to get everyone's views. Biden said that intervention was, essentially, madness—why should we get involved in another war in a Muslim-majority country? Gates and Mullen also argued against doing anything—the military already had its hands full in Iraq and Afghanistan. Bill Daley, a bald, Chicago-accented centrist who'd recently been hired as chief of staff to make deals with Republicans and stabilize relations between Obama and the business community—seemed incredulous that we were debating the issue at all, given everything we had to do at home. Susan Rice argued for more assertive action. *This is like Rwanda,* she said, citing a genocide that had been a stain on her own conscience—she was a midlevel staffer in the Clinton White House when hundreds of thousands of people were killed there in only a few months, many with machetes. She'd been a minor character in Samantha's book, and not one of the good guys. "We have a moral responsibility to act," she said.

And then Obama diverged from his usual script: Having heard the views of his principals, the people sitting around the table, he started to call on people who occupied the seats along the walls. He wanted, I could tell, different views. One by one, the more junior staffers argued for action, highlighting the generational chasm that had opened up over the last several weeks. When it got to Samantha, she talked in humanitarian terms, pointing out that we knew what Gaddafi had done in the past when his rule was threatened. "He massacres civilians," she said. "He told us what he was going to do in Benghazi—he'd go house to house, killing people."

Obama turned his chair to face me. "Ben?"

I repeated some of the other arguments that had been made—the humanitarian risk, the danger of signaling that dictators could stay in power if they killed but would fall if they didn't. As I spoke, I could sense Obama's ambivalence. I realized that my job—my responsibility for communications—offered me an argument that might resonate: the fact that we would have to stand up and explain to the world why we *weren't* acting in Libya if we chose not to.

"The international community is prepared to do this," I said. "We know there's going to be a debate at the United Nations. We know there's support for action. We know the French are going to move forward. So the one thing I'd also say, I guess, is that we'd have to consider what we would say if we choose not to do something." I paused to let that scenario sink in. "We'd have to explain to the American people and the world why we're choosing not to join the international community in doing something."

Bob Gates and Mike Mullen sat stoically at the table, looking as if they'd rather be discussing just about anything else, noting that no other country had the capacity to establish a no-fly zone without our support, reminding us that when we'd done so in the past—over northern Iraq or the Balkans—we had to bear the burden ourselves. Obama asked what impact a no-fly zone would have on the scenario we'd heard about from the briefers, an assault on Benghazi by Gaddafi's ground forces. None, they said. Even if our planes were securing the skies above Libya, Gaddafi's troops could still advance on the ground.

"So we're debating an option that won't even solve this problem," Obama said. There was an edge of anger in his voice. It was quiet for a moment. "What time is it?" he asked, looking over at the clocks on the wall. He had a dinner scheduled that night with Gates, Mullen, and all the U.S. military combatant commanders and their wives—an annual social event at the White House. "I'm going to go have dinner with the CoComms, and I want us to get back together afterward and look at some real options."

Over the next few hours, pop-up meetings were held throughout the White House, options papers written, UN Security Council resolutions drafted, military plans sent over from the Pentagon— the types of contingency plans that remain buried in the enormous bureaucracy until they're called up by the White House. And then, around seven thirty, we all returned to our seats in the Situation

Room, a new set of maps and papers in front of us, a stark menu of options in front of Obama: Bomb Gaddafi's forces on the ground to stop their advance on Benghazi; put a no-fly zone in place; or do nothing, leaving any action to others.

We reconvened for a second meeting, taking the same seats we'd occupied a couple of hours ago. Obama was briefed on the new options, which included a no-fly zone and a more aggressive option to go after Gaddafi's forces on the ground. At the end of the meeting, Obama told us he'd made a decision. We wouldn't support the French resolution for a no-fly zone. Instead, Susan would put forward a U.S. resolution that went beyond a no-fly zone, calling for "all necessary measures" to protect civilians on the ground, a euphemism for war. To put the military at ease, he'd call Cameron and Sarkozy himself and make clear to them that we'd lead the effort to take out Gaddafi's air defenses and ground forces at the beginning of the operation, but we'd expect the Europeans to move into the lead after a period of days. He turned to me. "Days, not weeks," he said. That would be our public posture.

With that, things were set in motion. Within two days, after frantic work by Susan, a resolution passed the UN Security Council authorizing the use of force to protect civilians in Libya. Military plans accelerated and Obama secured commitments from the French and British. At the same time, a defiant letter from Gaddafi to Obama reached the White House. "We in Libya are confronting the terrorists of al Qaeda," it read. "In Libya there are no political and administrative demands, nor are there any disputes.... If you decide that terrorism need not be fought, then let's negotiate with bin Laden." This was not a man who was going to meet our demands.

BRASÍLIA WAS AN UNLIKELY place to start a war—a planned capital city, built for government business, dotted with 1960s and '70s-style concrete office buildings. It could not have been farther from the Middle East. While Obama met with Dilma Rousseff, the for-

mer Marxist guerrilla and political prisoner who had become president, I worked in a staff office at the Palacio do Planalto, the
Brazilian equivalent of the White House. Our expectation was that
military operations would start in Libya the next day. But at the
same time that Obama was holding his meeting, Sarkozy was hosting a conference on Libya in Paris. With Gaddafi still advancing on
Benghazi, Clinton reported that Sarkozy was pressing for military
operations to begin that day. This could only work if the United
States began taking out Gaddafi's air defenses immediately.

While Obama wrapped up his meeting, we started to assemble
his top national security team for a conference call. After some
tense moments when the call kept dropping, Obama was patched
through and I watched him listen intently. The military was ready
to go now, they just needed his order. "You have my authorization,"
he said, with formality. Brazil prides itself on not interfering in the
affairs of other countries, and not going to war. Its president was a
woman of the left, persecuted by Brazil's former military government because of her politics. This was probably the first war ever
launched from the offices of the Brazilian president, and it was
being done by a foreigner.

We moved on to a luncheon for prominent Americans and Bra-
zilians that was being hosted at the Foreign Ministry. I sat nervously eyeing my BlackBerry for news reports while the man next
to me, a Brazilian businessman, quizzed me on the positions that
Obama had taken on ethanol subsidies during the 2008 campaign.
The whole scene spoke to an absurdity in the office of the American
presidency—Obama sat at the head table, carrying out his duties,
promoting American business in a country of more than two hundred million people, while the vast machinery of the U.S. government, on Obama's order, was preparing to rain down bombs on a
country of seven million.

The next event was a CEO forum at a convention center. Obama
would have to say something public about the war he'd just started;
otherwise, the first picture taken of him after giving this authorization would be sitting at a conference room table flanked by a bunch

of CEOs. Everywhere a U.S. president goes, a venue is identified where he can give an emergency statement to a group of assembled press from behind a lectern bearing the seal of the president of the United States. When we got to the convention center, we delayed the start of the CEO forum, and I set to work writing a statement while the advance team set up the room.

"Today," I wrote, "I authorized the Armed Forces of the United States to begin a military action in Libya in support of an international effort to protect Libyan civilians. That action has now begun." I paused and looked around the room, a large empty space with a scattering of tables. Obama, Bill Daley, Tom Donilon, and a few other aides chatted on the other side of the room, giving me some space. Somewhere over Libya, American planes and missiles were making their way toward Gaddafi's forces. But there was no time to process any of it. There was a statement to finish, a day's schedule to complete. I wrote as strong a statement as I could in less than half an hour. Obama read it quickly but carefully. As with the Afghanistan speech, he dialed it down—gone was the invocation of "never again," the reference to the Holocaust, the seminal massacre that prompted generations to consider going to war to stop human beings from killing other human beings. Even in that moment, Obama didn't want to overpromise.

The next day we were in Rio. We drove into the City of God, a sprawling favela. As the motorcade snaked through streets of patchwork housing—corrugated roofs, colorful windowpanes, cratered sidewalks, thousands of Afro-Brazilians straining to get a glimpse of Obama—I thought about how to measure the impact of Obama and his presidency on this anonymous multitude, how to weigh the impact he had on people like those lining our motorcade route against the practical reality of a war that we had joined on the other side of the world. I watched him kicking a soccer ball with a handful of excited kids in a community center, wondering what was churning through his mind.

The rest of the trip, Obama existed within the bubble of his schedule—meetings, speeches on Latin America, state dinners—

while the rest of us were on calls or in press briefings related to Libya. For the first time in my life, I was the spokesperson for a government that had just gone to war—I did press briefings on camera, or on the phone pacing next to a parked motorcade. Somewhere along the way, I lost my razor, and our last night in San Salvador, Obama snapped at me.

"What, you can't even bother to shave?" he said.

At first I thought that he was kidding. "I think my razor is somewhere in Brazil," I said.

"Pull yourself together," he said. "We have to be professional here." There was an edge to his voice; he wasn't joking.

I felt like exploding. *I haven't slept more than three hours in days. I'm doing three jobs out there defending this war for hours each day.* Obama seemed oblivious to the work I was doing out of his sight, work that left me no time to buy a razor. But as I calmed down, I realized that these little flashes were how he relieved some of the stress that he had to be feeling, and that being composed and professional—*doing the job*—was how he managed to take everything in stride. I hadn't just failed to shave; I'd deviated from his ethos of unflappability.

On the flight back to Washington, I headed to the back of Air Force One to brief the journalists who were traveling with us. All of the pressure on us to act in Libya had taken a 180-degree turn the moment we did. Before, we had been getting questions about how many people had to die before we acted; now we were getting questions about how we could avoid mission creep, whether we could transition to a European command, and whether we were "at war" in Libya. I had been told by our lawyers that I was not supposed to use the word "war"—we hadn't sought congressional authorization, and were arguing that it was a limited military operation, and therefore within the president's constitutional authority. That legalistic position, of course, was why I was being asked the question.

"If it's not a war," a journalist from Fox News asked, "what's the right way to characterize this operation?"

I'd answered dozens of questions about Libya over the last few days. I was exhausted, leaning against a wall with a bunch of tape recorders in my face. I didn't have a good answer. "I think," I said, "that what we are doing is enforcing a resolution that has a very clear set of goals, which is protecting the Libyan people, averting a humanitarian crisis, and setting up a no-fly zone." I was giving a stock response, which felt unsatisfactory—phony—so I went a step further. "Obviously that involves kinetic military action, particularly on the front end." "Kinetic military action" was the type of language used in the Situation Room, a euphemism for dropping bombs and blowing things up. In this context, it sounded like a dodge, a way to call a war something other than a war.

When we got back to D.C., it was apparent—in a way that you miss when you're traveling—that we were not receiving the same benefit of the doubt that had greeted Reagan's "kinetic military action" twenty-five years earlier. The Republicans who had demanded that we put a no-fly zone in place now shifted the goalposts, demanding that we do more to "win" in Libya. The left was nervous about another war in the Middle East. Critics on both sides were bemoaning the fact that we weren't seeking congressional authorization, even though there was no way that a Republican House would pass it if we did. In short, there was little constituency for what we were doing in Libya.

This hit home for me one night when I was sitting on the couch watching Jon Stewart, the ubiquitous comic voice of authority for my demographic. He was running a series of segments on *The Daily Show* titled "America at Not-War." He started to mock my phrase—"kinetic military action"—while a photo of me looking about twelve years old flashed on the screen. My stomach started to churn and I turned the television off. My own worldview had been shaped, in part, by reading books like Samantha's and watching liberals go on shows like Stewart's to promote movies like *Hotel Rwanda*. Sure, I'd said something that sounded a bit Orwellian, and I was a spokesperson for the U.S. government—whose military actions overseas prompt skepticism from large chunks of the population at home. But in my mind, I was part of a group of people acting to implement a humanitarian principle. Now it felt as if I was being punished for it, and as if I had argued for Obama to do something that his own base recoiled against. My skin would have to get thicker.

EVERY MORNING THOSE FIRST few days back in Washington, Obama convened a small meeting in the Situation Room to get briefed on the progress we were making in Libya—a much more hands-on approach than he ever took to daily operations in Iraq or Afghanistan. Gaddafi's air defenses were destroyed. His forces were stopped on the outskirts of Benghazi, perhaps saving tens of thousands of lives. Not a single American had been injured. After a few days of American pilots being in the lead, we transferred the operation to a NATO command, with French and British pilots taking on the bulk of the bombing. It was what Obama wanted: multilateral, no ground forces, limited objectives.

One common criticism emerged from Congress and the media: Obama had not formally addressed the nation since authorizing military action. So, on March 28, two weeks after the Situation Room meeting that had set everything in motion, he gave a speech at the National Defense University in Washington. The television networks said they wouldn't carry it in prime time, so it was scheduled for the second-tier window of 7:30 P.M., an apt metaphor for the Libyan operation—cable, not network; evening, not prime time; kinetic military operation, not war. The speech was on a Monday, and I spent a weekend writing it. Obama was defensive. Everything had gone as planned, and yet the public and political response kept shifting—from demanding action to second-guessing it, from saying he was dithering to saying he wasn't doing enough. Even while he outlined the reasons for action in Libya, he stepped back to discuss the question that would continue to define his foreign policy: the choice of when to use military force. Unlike other wartime addresses, he went out of his way to stress the limits of what we were trying to achieve in Libya—saving lives and giving Libyans a chance to determine their future, not installing a new regime or building a democracy. He said that we would use force "swiftly, decisively, and unilaterally" to defend the United States, but he emphasized that when confronted with other international crises, we should proceed with caution and not act alone.

I stood backstage watching the words roll on the teleprompter. In just two months, the world had turned upside down. We'd seen a regime fall in Tunisia, broken from a longtime U.S. ally in Egypt, and intervened in Libya. History, it seemed, was turning in the direction of young people in the streets, and we had placed the United States of America on their side. Where this drama would turn next was uncertain—protests were already rattling a monarch in Bahrain, a corrupt leader in Yemen, a strongman in Syria.

After the speech, as we began to disperse to the motorcade, I got word that Obama wanted me to ride with him back to the White House. I slid into the seat opposite him, just the two of us in the limousine as it pulled out of the loading zone and onto the darkened streets of Washington.

"That turned out well," he said.

"I think so," I said.

"We still need to give a speech that puts all of this in context," he said. "That steps back a little bit."

"I was working on that a couple of weeks ago. Then Libya happened." I started to talk about how we could frame all of these different countries by talking about a set of principles that would guide the United States, the opportunity that was emerging for change.

Obama's eyes drifted out the window to the passing scenery, the National Mall, monuments to leaders and wars past. "It's hard to get a grasp on what's happening," he said.

"It's playing out pretty fast," I said.

"We could spend all of our time on it," he said. He'd spent a lot of time recently on foreign policy. There was still an unsettled economy, a looming debate with Republicans over raising the debt ceiling, a reelection campaign that was just gathering steam. "I just wish I had some more bandwidth," he said as the limousine turned in to the south driveway of the White House.

I HAD NEVER HEARD the phrase "lead from behind" until it appeared in a *New Yorker* article about Obama's foreign policy in April 2011. The article was typical of a Washington genre: the step-back review of a particular policy—in this case, foreign policy—in which a writer interviews a mix of administration officials and outside critics to make sense of things. Most of these pieces disappear without much notice, adding to an accumulating conventional wisdom. But on occasion, a particular turn of phrase can become a bumper sticker that is affixed to a presidency. I knew we might be faced with that scenario when I sat in my office late one afternoon reading this long *New Yorker* piece by Ryan Lizza, and reached the end: "Obama may be moving toward something resembling a doctrine. One of his advisors described the president's actions as 'leading from behind.'"

I had no idea who the unnamed advisor was, but a lot of people thought it was me—one of the hazards of my job was that many people assumed that just about every quote attributed to an "unnamed advisor" on foreign policy was me. We were constantly asked about what the "Obama doctrine" was, and we usually rejected the question. The world was too complicated to sum up in a doctrine, and the only recent effort that a president made to declare a doctrine was George W. Bush's regrettable assertion that we'd preemptively go to war to prevent countries from acquiring weapons of mass destruction. We were going to be damned if we did declare a doctrine and damned if we didn't; looking at the risks of overpromising or oversimplifying, we decided to avoid the question.

Predictably, there was an explosion of criticism on the right, which branded "leading from behind" as "the Obama doctrine" and used it to cast him as weak, indecisive, and un-American. The more mainstream response concerned why Obama had chosen "leading from behind" as a doctrine, even though he hadn't. It was all nonsense—Obama had never uttered the phrase, and he wouldn't have used it to describe his own foreign policy; it was a show, designed to distill complicated international issues into a debate that could take place on cable news.

At the same time, the real estate developer and reality television show celebrity Donald Trump began flirting publicly with his own presidential run. Like anyone who grew up in 1980s New York City, I knew Trump as a tabloid punch line, more famous for his mistresses than his politics. But instead of protests in Arab cities, it was now Trump's face popping up on the television screens throughout the West Wing, the cable news networks shadowing his every move. The thing that drew the most attention was his nakedly racist demand for Obama to release his birth certificate—a subject of derision, at first, within the White House, but as the days went on and the attention stayed on Trump, that derision turned to anger over the outright racism of the attack, and the ceaseless, credulous attention it was getting. Obama was more annoyed at the media than anything else—"I can't believe they're giving this airtime," he said.

Personally, I recoiled at another part of Trump's interviews and stock speech. Time and again, he talked about all the Americans getting killed in Libya, and the assertion would go unchallenged. I'd call reporters to demand a fact check—no Americans were getting killed in Libya, and Americans watching at home shouldn't be misled to believe that they were. In response, they'd deflect any responsibility to fact-check everything Trump said—after all, who would take him seriously?

I took all of the criticism of Obama too personally because I felt helpless in the face of what seemed to be the insanity of it all. *No Americans are being killed in Libya! Barack Obama never said "leading from behind"!* More profoundly, I thought a bar was being set that we could never clear. The same people who had been demanding a no-fly zone were now attacking Obama for being "weak" on Libya.

Donald Trump was simultaneously criticizing Obama for not taking Libya's oil and for getting Americans killed. The Arab Spring
was upending a rotted, corrupt, authoritarian order in the Middle
East, and yet the debate about these seismic events in Washington
was an extension of our own partisan, diminished discourse.

CHAPTER 11

BIN LADEN

Life Inside a Secret

———

ONE APRIL MORNING, I NOTICED MULTIPLE MISSED CALLS from the blocked number that normally signaled that it was the Situation Room calling. When I called back, I was told to come to work immediately. John Brennan and Denis McDonough wanted to see me.

When I got to Brennan's office, they asked me to close the door, which was unusual. Brennan's office was across the hall from me at the back of a suite of rooms designed to house classified information. It was a somewhat unpleasant place, with a mini-fridge, a single-cup coffee maker, a dropped ceiling, piles of intelligence reports, multiple computer screens at different levels of classification, different-colored phones, and shelves half-filled with books, most of which appeared to be unread gifts. During one semirenovation, they found dead rats in the walls. Yet in the global war against al Qaeda—the mix of surveillance, drone strikes, and special operations that take place in some of the most remote parts of the world—Brennan's office was the nerve center. Any decision that Obama had to make about whether to launch an operation to kill or capture someone came through here.

"This is very sensitive," Brennan said, folding his hands in front of him. "We may have a lead on bin Laden."

They described a scenario that seemed implausible no matter how much I wanted it to be true. Working through our knowledge of a network of couriers associated with bin Laden, we'd identified a compound in Abbottabad, deep inside Pakistan and close to a Pakistani military academy. We weren't certain that bin Laden was there, but it was the best lead we'd had since he'd slipped across the Afghan border in December 2001. Obama had been meeting for some weeks with a tight-knit circle of advisors, and he was nearing a decision about whether to target the compound—through a Special Forces raid or some kind of strike. I was now going to be brought into that circle, because someone needed to plan for how any action would be explained to the wider world if Obama decided to move forward.

With this, my entire life narrowed to this one thing, this secret, which I could not talk about with anyone else. I had noticed for the past few weeks that there were occasionally meetings in the Situation Room that were not announced. The assistants of senior national security officials had camera feeds on their computers that could show you what was happening in each of the three conference rooms; for some meetings, those cameras were turned off. I'd felt a little miffed at being excluded from whatever was going on, though I knew better than to ask about it. Now I was being initiated into this secret society.

I started to attend endless daily meetings, cochaired by Brennan and McDonough, at which every aspect of this matter was discussed. They'd start with a review of the "intelligence case," usually presented by Michael Morell, the deputy director of the CIA. Morell spoke with frightening precision, numbering his points, leaning forward a bit as he spoke as if bringing you into a conspiracy, and then sitting back in his chair, hands folded, when he was finished. The points were often the same: the nature of the compound, larger and more secluded than other homes in the area, and surrounded by a high wall; the number of people in the compound, their suspected ages and genders, and how they matched up with those of bin Laden's family; their "pattern of life"—the fact that they almost never came and went, wore Pashtun clothing, and burned their trash; the presence of a tall man who paced occasionally in the courtyard. *The pacer*, they called him.

A team of operatives was being deployed to Afghanistan in the event that a mission to capture or kill the pacer was set in motion. Another option was to just take out the compound with a precision strike. Beyond that were many questions: *Who would call the Pakistanis and when? Who would call the Saudis and when? What happens if we capture him alive? If he's dead, how can we verify that it's bin Laden? How should he be buried? What happens if it's not him? What happens if it all goes wrong?*

Late on a Thursday afternoon, Obama chaired a meeting that would be his final one before making a decision. The timing was being driven by an almost impossibly cinematic concern: The absence of moonlight over Abbottabad that weekend offered the best window to launch an operation. The meeting kicked off with a briefing on the latest intelligence, and Obama asked questions which suggested that he had spent many hours thinking about it— he knew how tall the people were who lived in this compound, how many families lived there, that they burned their trash. I watched Obama digest this information, wondering how much he'd been turning it over in his head while I'd been with him in other meetings over the last few weeks. Along with me, there were a few other newcomers, including a "red team" of intelligence analysts who had been brought on to review the case that it was bin Laden at the compound. They had a lower degree of confidence—40 to 60 percent, they said. The conversation went down a rabbit hole, people debating percentages, until Obama lost patience with the exercise.

"That's enough," he said. "Ultimately, this is a fifty-fifty call."

The conversation then turned to the ways that we could get this pacer. Admiral Bill McRaven was overseeing the special operations team that had deployed to Afghanistan. He spoke with confidence, conveying a sense that this is the type of thing that he and his men did for a living, but that they were also taking extra care in preparing for this circumstance. I'm confident we can get in and out, he said. There was another option—to simply take out the compound—but Obama seemed less interested in that, as it would deny us the certainty that the pacer was indeed bin Laden, and whatever intelligence could be gathered from the compound.

Obama moved methodically around the table asking for people's recommendations. For the first time, Gates was in a different place from the uniformed military. He was firmly against a raid. Too risky, he said. He referenced Desert One, Jimmy Carter's botched effort to rescue the Americans who had been taken hostage by Iran. Like that operation, this one would involve covertly sending American helicopters deep inside another country. Desert One had resulted in eight dead Americans, a humiliated United States, and a stinging electoral defeat for a first-term Democratic president. I was deflated that Gates spoke the words out loud.

Mullen and McRaven, on the other hand, were strongly supportive. So were Brennan and Leon Panetta, the director of the CIA. Biden was opposed, and he went on at length about the catastrophe that could ensue with Pakistan—a firefight at the scene, threats to our embassy, a break in our relations. Clinton described it, repeatedly, as a 51–49 call. Ultimately, though, it was too risky not to go—what if people learned that we had the chance and we failed to act? To her, the risk of not going outweighed the risk of going. She voted yes.

It was obvious to me that Obama was going to do this. He had a way of looking straight ahead when he was listening at the same time that his mind was elsewhere. I could tell that he had turned the intelligence over and over in his mind ("this is a fifty-fifty call"), that he understood the risks with Pakistan. When he asked me what I thought, I simply said, "You always said you were going to do this." Because I'd lived through the debate on the campaign, I knew he had meant what he said about going into Pakistan. He asked me to prepare for four scenarios: (1) bin Laden is at the compound and it's a success; (2) bin Laden is at the compound and it's messy—people killed, Pakistani security services, instability; (3) bin Laden's not there but we get in and out cleanly; (4) bin Laden's not there and it's a mess.

At the end of the meeting, Obama didn't tip his hand, he just said he'd make his decision overnight. As people filed out of the room, Biden pulled Denis and me into a smaller, adjacent room and closed the door. He looked genuinely pained. "You fellas really think he should do this?"

"I do," Denis said.

I agreed, and repeated my point about Obama's always having said he would go into Pakistan to get bin Laden.

"Well," Biden said, "I'm just trying to give him a little space." I believed that—Biden sometimes took strident positions in meetings to widen the spectrum of views and options available to Obama. He also worked hard to understand Obama's mind.

"You've always got his back," McDonough said.

"You better believe it," Biden replied. "But we're also going to need to say some prayers."

I started to prepare all the materials we'd need. I had no one else to work with in the White House, so I sat alone at my classified computer, putting together the playbook for each scenario. I edited declassified points that had been prepared by the CIA laying out the intelligence basis for action—particularly if bin Laden wasn't there, we'd have to explain why we thought it might have been him. I compiled all of bin Laden's declarations of war on the United States and his celebrations of the 9/11 attacks. I pulled together statements by Bush and Obama pledging to get bin Laden. Sitting there alone, late into the night, I felt I was revisiting the events that had led me down to Washington and into the Obama campaign—events that had been eclipsed, in some ways, by the turmoil of the Iraq War and the tumult of the Arab Spring. *This,* I thought, *is what we were supposed to do after 9/11.*

I opened a new document, titled it "Remarks of President Barack Obama," and began drafting the speeches he might give along with the different scenarios—but the words didn't come. The negative scenarios were too nightmarish to contemplate, let alone put into words, and the positive scenario seemed as if it should not be jinxed by this kind of preparatory work. I knew that I wouldn't have a lot of time to write something if the operation went forward, but I left undisturbed the history that had yet to happen.

The next morning, a Friday, Obama relayed his decision to move forward with the raid, which opened up a three-day window during which the operation could take place. On Saturday, I came to work in the morning to finalize my preparations along with George Little, who was in charge of public affairs at the CIA. The White House Correspondents' Dinner was that night, the annual black-tie affair hosted by the White House press corps, a giant party to which the president and members of his staff and administration are invited and at which the president tries to make a funny speech. As I walked by the Oval Office, I saw Jon Favreau huddling with Jon Lovett, a former speechwriter; they were working on the remarks for the dinner, and they were excited about a series of jokes that would mock Donald Trump, who was going to be in attendance.

I left work that afternoon to meet my brother, David, for an afternoon run. The awkward fact for me was that David is president of CBS News, and he would be staying at my apartment over the weekend with his wife, Emma. Over the years, the two of us had studiously learned to avoid talking to each other about work. Some of that was due to the risk that each of us could benefit from the other's professional position; some of it was rooted in a general aversion to talking politics. Growing up, we'd been close—because we were each other's only sibling, but also because we had different interests and points of view in a way that ensured we weren't competitors. I was into baseball and underage drinking and books; David was less conventional—memorizing maps, skiing, and agitating to skip the inconvenience of being a teenager in order to get to work. In high school, he worked on Ross Perot's first presidential campaign; in college, he worked for a Houston city councilman and interned for a libertarian magazine; after graduating, he spent twelve years rising through the ranks at Fox News until he became vice president in charge of news gathering.

My revulsion at Fox News in those years was surpassed by pride in my brother for rising so quickly. And he wasn't particularly ideological—he was somewhat cynical about politics in general and a savant about the news business. During the 2008 campaign, David came out to Chicago to visit the Obama campaign offices a couple of times, trying to repair relations with the senior leadership after someone on Fox had said something particularly offensive about Obama. I rarely had advance notice of his meetings, so I was sometimes surprised to see him walk by my workspace on his way to see Axe or David Plouffe.

During one of these visits to Chicago, my brother came over to my apartment after dinner and we took some beers up to the rooftop of my building, which offered views of the Sears Tower in the distance. He was, he told me, leaving Fox. I didn't press him on the reasons, but knew that it had become an increasingly ideological and unpleasant place with the rise of Obama. Unspoken also was the possibility that the emerging unhinged anti-Obama milieu driven by Fox's leader, Roger Ailes, might make life uncomfortable for a member of the leadership team who was closely related to someone working in the Obama White House. He'd gotten an offer to run Bloomberg Television, and he thought he could manage leaving without putting himself on Ailes's enemies list. I was relieved, and we hugged awkwardly—as brothers do—two guys whose careers were about to take off in ways that we never would have predicted when he was giving me his old IDs to use so I could buy beer.

That Saturday, we ran a few miles along the Georgetown Canal together, not talking about work—he in better shape and thus better able to talk, going on about the details of parenthood while my mind raced with every possible scenario that could take place the next day. At thirty-eight, he was the youngest president in the history of network news, but I couldn't talk to him about what would be the biggest story of the year.

———

LIKE A THIRD-TIER AWARDS SHOW, the White House Correspondents' Dinner is the kind of ritual that you complain about
while desperately seeking an invitation. Washington people pretend to be glamorous in the basement of a characterless hotel,
drinking bad wine, avoiding one another, and craning their necks to
catch a glimpse of passing celebrities. That night, I walked through
the cramped, carpeted hallways of the Washington Hilton surrounded by a black-tie crowd of political and media elite, people
I never felt entirely comfortable around. Every now and then, I
would spot someone who *knew*—there's Michael Morell across the
room—and we'd make eye contact and nod at each other, as if we
were giving a signal: Yes, see you at ten tomorrow. Somewhere in
the early morning hours of Abbottabad, Osama bin Laden was
waking up, perhaps for the last morning of his life.

The drama at the dinner was the presence of Donald Trump.
After months of dealing with Trump's invidious "birther" innuendo,
Obama took the unprecedented step—just a few days earlier—of
publicly releasing his long-form birth certificate. He was not happy.
The decision to release the document had been his alone, made with
his personal attorney—he knew, in ways that perhaps his white staff
didn't, that the issue wasn't going to go away otherwise.

When Obama walked to the microphone, all I could think of
was how his mind must have been on the men who were preparing
to fly deep into Pakistan on his orders, and how the already absurd
scene in front of him must have been even more oppressively trivial.
But he betrayed no trace of distraction. Reeling the audience in
with his unique approach to comedy—he'd sometimes laugh at
jokes he read, as if he was surprised to hear how funny they were
when spoken aloud—he slowly worked his way around to Trump:
"Donald Trump is here tonight!" Just saying the words brought
laughter and applause. "No one is happier, no one is prouder to put
this birth certificate matter to rest than the Donald. And that's because he can finally get back to focusing on the issues that matter—

like, did we fake the moon landing." The whole room seemed to exhale at the chance to laugh about it; it was funny, but in a way, Obama was letting the largely white elite laugh about their failure to contain the birtherism in our politics. Some of their networks, after all, had given Trump a platform to peddle racist lies, and few Republicans condemned it. "We all know about your credentials and breadth of experience. For example—no, seriously, just recently in an episode of *Celebrity Apprentice* at the steakhouse, the men's cooking team did not impress the judges from Omaha Steaks. And there was a lot of blame to go around. But you, Mr. Trump, recognized that the real problem was a lack of leadership. And so ultimately, you didn't blame Lil Jon or Meat Loaf. You fired Gary Busey." The room exploded in laughter.

THE NEXT MORNING, a Sunday, while everyone was still sleeping, I showered and dressed. Around ten, as people were beginning to stir and wander into the kitchen for coffee, I announced that I had to go to work. David asked if I'd be back soon and I said no, offering no further detail, and we said nothing more.

The Deputies and Principals met in the Situation Room, where we'd spend the next twelve hours or so. We went through the motions as if it was any other meeting—getting the latest update on the compound; going through all of the various things that had to get done; reading in all of the officials who needed to know that they might be unexpectedly busy later that day. I had to ask Pete Souza, the president's photographer, to come in to work so he could capture the scene, however it played out. We made Starbucks runs and sat silently waiting for our coffee orders, unable to talk about what we were thinking. Then, back in the secure confines of the Situation Room, we waited, chatting nervously.

Obama came down around two o'clock to get updated just as the operation was set to begin. Leon Panetta was on a screen from CIA headquarters and McRaven was on from Jalalabad, the Afghan town near the border where the team was taking off for the long helicopter ride to Abbottabad. Once they were in the air for the ninety-minute flight, Obama went back up to the Oval Office to sit and play cards, a more relaxing way to kill time than sitting with us. With nothing to do, we started telling one another the stories of where we were on 9/11 to pass the time. I thought of the view from a helicopter flying through a moonless night in Pakistan.

Obama came back down a few minutes before the team was supposed to land at the compound. We all took our seats and McRaven began narrating the operation, like a play-by-play announcer giving you the highlights of a baseball game on the radio. All we could see was McRaven's face, wearing a headset, on a split screen in front of us with Panetta. At one point, a helicopter clipped the side of one of the high walls of the compound as it was coming down, and McRaven told us they'd had to make an improvised crash landing. We still didn't know if bin Laden was at the compound and already it seemed that the worst-case scenario was playing out. People avoided making eye contact. McRaven sounded unconcerned, as if he was relaying that a light rain shower was passing. *The pilot will handle it,* he said.

In the small conference room across the hall, a general sat hunched over a laptop with a video feed in front of him that allowed him to monitor the raid in real time. When Obama figured out that there was a better seat in the next room, he walked over there, trailed by most of his principals. I didn't go. I was nervous, and felt I shouldn't intrude. So I was still sitting in the large conference room when both McRaven and Panetta said that "Geronimo" had been identified. I didn't know what that meant and had to ask someone. That was the code name for bin Laden. To me, this was the key moment—we wouldn't have to tell the world why U.S. ground forces had flown all that way into Pakistan for no reason. I shot out of my chair and out into the hallway behind the small conference room, which was filled with the most senior people in government. I peered in around them and saw Obama eyeing the screen. Mullen fingered his rosary beads. Suddenly, the phrase "Geronimo EKIA" was being repeated. I heard Obama say, "We got him." Some people clapped awkwardly. Everyone started smiling at one another silently. *Could it really be this easy?* the smiles seemed to say. Pete crouched in the corner, taking pictures. I decided to get some air.

I walked outside to the area adjacent to the press briefing room, where a driveway curves down from the entrance to the West Wing to the bowels of the White House residence. It's among the least scenic places on the complex: a slab of gray concrete between a sloping lawn and the white walls of the structure where the press sits. But you could smoke there, and that's what I did, pacing back and forth. The whole operation was playing out thousands of miles away, and the people I worked for were still monitoring it inside the quiet of the West Wing, behind the closed doors of the Situation Room. There was work ahead—meetings, to-do lists, notifications to foreign governments, calls to former presidents and congressional leaders, a speech to be written and delivered. But I needed these minutes alone.

The balcony of my Queens apartment used to have no view of Manhattan except for the tops of those towers, something I didn't even realize until a few days after the attacks. I was one of millions of people whose lives had been altered in some way by 9/11, I thought. A twenty-four-year-old graduate student, handing out city council campaign flyers outside a polling site, preparing for a life of . . . *what?* I'd never know. I lost that life and was now a thirty-three-year-old government official pacing outside his workplace. Normally, at important moments in our lives, we call the people we love. I could call no one.

In that moment, it was as if none of the events of the last decade had taken place—no wars, no Great Recession, no political discord, no experience of my own. It was as though I had just turned away from the sight of the first tower collapsing into ash. Osama bin Laden was dead. I was one of a few dozen people in the world who possessed that knowledge. It was midafternoon and the Sunday sun was high in the sky. A couple of cameramen doing weekend duty walked by. I stood there, hesitant to go back inside because that would set time back in motion, the purity of the event polluted by what came next. Nothing would ever feel this right.

I WALKED BACK INTO an unchanged scene in the Situation Room. Then Obama stood up and announced that he wanted to be notified as soon as the Special Operations team was out of Pakistani air space. There were muted congratulations, but things could still go wrong; there was much to do.

Once the team was safely back in Jalalabad, Obama returned to the meeting. Admiral Mullen left the room to call the chief of Pakistan's army, General Kayani, to tell him we'd launched this military operation in his country. The question became how certain we could be that it was bin Laden. Apparently, some of the women in the compound had identified him at the scene—Sheikh Osama. The intelligence community had done a facial recognition test that confirmed it was him, but these tests had only a 95 percent confidence rate. DNA evidence would take another day or two. McRaven reported that one of his men, someone who—at six foot four—was the same height as bin Laden, had lain down next to the corpse to confirm that the height was a match. Obama leaned forward. "You guys need to get a tape measure."

There was a debate about whether to make a statement that night or the next morning. The consensus in the room was the next morning, as we'd want to get the highest confidence that it was bin Laden, and we had a number of notifications to make. I was worried that the Pakistanis or al Qaeda could get out in front of us. There was, after all, the smoldering wreckage of a helicopter in the middle of a compound deep inside Pakistan. I had the Situation Room monitoring media from the region. One story posted with the headline ARMY CHOPPER CRASHES IN ABBOTTABAD. "The chopper," the story read, "was on its routine flight when it crashed. . . . Witnesses disclosed that there were two helicopters, one of which crashed to the ground. The cause of the crash is as yet unknown."

Twitter users in the area were beginning to post about a crash. When Mullen returned, he said that Kayani wanted us to put the news out right away so that it would be clear we were going after bin Laden—the only potential justification for going so deep into Pakistan.

With that, Obama decided to announce the operation that night. It was approaching eight o'clock already. We'd have to notify the television networks, read in all of the spokespeople for the government, and I'd have to draft remarks. As Obama was walking out of the room—on his way to call former U.S. presidents and the leaders of Pakistan and the United Kingdom—I stood up and called out from across the room, "Hey, I'm going to have to grab you for a few minutes." Everyone turned and looked at me with a bit of surprise—it was a presumptuous way to talk to the commander in chief in front of a room full of people. He gestured for me to follow him.

We sat down in the chief of staff's office to go over what he wanted to say. "Let's keep it straightforward," he said: "Tell the story of how we got here, starting on 9/11; announce the operation; underscore the need to remain vigilant."

"I was thinking of that speech you gave during the campaign," I said.

He looked at me and smiled. "Me, too," he said. "I've been thinking about that a lot lately."

He wanted to end on the note that "America can do big things." He wanted to remind the country, he said, that we once came together around 9/11; that for all the pain and polarization of the last decade, we stuck with it, and we got bin Laden. "No other country in the world," he said, "could have done that."

One by one, I had to call people—Dan Pfeiffer, David Plouffe, Jay Carney, our press secretary—and ask them to assemble in the White House immediately. When I told the NSC spokesman, Tommy Vietor—one of my closest friends—he said, "Fuck yes, I've been waiting three years to get this call." I was frantic, needing to write a speech while these guys were scheduling an address to the nation and fending off leaks.

I sat at my desk and drafted the statement, ignoring the steady flood of emails that started to come in once the news began to trickle out. We told the networks to plan for a statement from Obama a little after ten, but that time started to slip. As I was writing, I was feeling that the remarks reflected my own journey—the images of 9/11 that I'd seen (*"hijacked planes cutting through a cloudless September sky"*); the stories of 9/11 families whom I'd come to know during my work with the 9/11 Commission (*"parents who would never know the feeling of their child's embrace"*); the steady counterterrorism work that I'd witnessed in government (*"around the globe, we worked with our friends and allies to capture or kill scores of al Qaeda terrorists"*); the necessity of not making this a war of religion, which had been central to our message in Cairo (*"the United States is not—and never will be—at war with Islam"*). Sitting there, as much as I wished I had a draft to work from, I realized another reason why I had been unable to write anything in advance: Inhabiting the moment of bin Laden's demise allowed the full experience of the last ten years to reemerge.

When I went upstairs, Obama was talking to the Pakistani president who had succeeded Pervez Musharraf, Asif Ali Zardari, a man who was thrust into a leading role when his wife, Benazir Bhutto, Pakistan's prime minister, was assassinated by extremists—a politician who was sure to face a backlash at home over America's violation of Pakistani sovereignty. But he wasn't upset. Whatever the fallout, he told Obama, it's very good news. *It's been a long time. God be with you and the people of America.*

Obama was calm, focused on the next thing he needed to do. I waited outside the Oval Office for him to finish his calls, then sat at the desk of his personal assistant, Anita Decker Breckenridge, who had been with Obama since his days in the Illinois State Senate, making a few rounds of edits, his appearance drifting later and later. Around eleven thirty, he handed me the final pages, and I ran ahead of him, down the colonnade and up to the East Room, where he'd make the remarks, so I could insert the last changes into the teleprompter before he made the long walk down the red-carpeted hallway to address the American people.

It is strange to watch a president speak to an empty room, especially when you know that tens of millions of people are watching. Clinton, Gates, Mullen, and a few others sat in scattered chairs while Obama spoke into a camera. I stood against the back wall, watching him speak phrases that would take on their own life—"Justice has been done," which would be a headline in newspapers around the world; "We must—and will—remain vigilant," an exhortation that I would see flashing, time and again, in the opening credits to the Showtime series *Homeland*. John Brennan stood next to me, a rare look of satisfaction on his face. I leaned over and asked him, "How long have you been trying to get this guy?"

"Fifteen years," he answered, saying nothing more.

When the speech was over, we all gathered around Obama, unsure what to do next. He thanked everyone for all the work we'd done, then said he was heading upstairs to be with his family and go to bed. The cabinet members made their way to the black cars that would take them where they needed to go. I had to go back to the West Wing to lead a conference call for reporters, making use of the talking points we'd prepared in advance. When I walked outside into the spring night on the colonnade, I could hear raucous cheering and chants of "U.S.A.!" drifting over the White House.

I left work some thirteen hours after I'd arrived guarding the secret of why I was there. Now the entire world knew. The only exit that was open was the southeast gate, down on Seventeenth Street, and the streets were full of people. I saw college students piled into cars, driving slowly, honking horns, waving flags, two guys standing on top of a slow-moving car as though they'd conquered the world, and it occurred to me that they were only ten years old when 9/11 happened. They'd grown up in this reality and now they were reveling in the closest thing that the United States of America would ever get to a "victory" in the post-9/11 wars.

When I got home, Ann was up with the television on. "I'm proud of you guys," she said. We shared a long hug. "Do you think he told Michelle?" she asked.

THE NEXT DAY, we asked Brennan to do the regular White House briefing to respond to the deluge of inquiries that we were getting. In his straight, authoritative style, he relayed what we'd heard back about the raid from the military, including the fact that bin Laden had been killed in a firefight and may have used women as human shields. Republicans pounced on this, accusing us of leaking details about the raid to make Obama look good. In fact, Brennan was trying to denigrate bin Laden—a man he hated, the leader of a terrorist organization that he wanted to shame. When the information changed as all the participants in the raid were debriefed, we updated our answers, which led to more questions from the press and more criticism from Republicans. The high of the raid, the ability to just feel good about something, dissipated quickly. If the country's politics couldn't even allow us to enjoy *this,* then literally nothing would bring the country together.

Obama had one final decision to make: whether to release photographs of bin Laden's body. I argued in favor. My concern was that al Qaeda would use the absence of photos to suggest that bin Laden was still alive, creating a conspiracy theory that we'd have to deal with for years to come. I was totally wrong, as al Qaeda ended up confirming bin Laden's death within days.

Someone in the military compiled, literally, a photo album of those several hours between the operation and the burial, and we met in the Chief of Staff's Office to flip through the photos in silence. There is the bloodied corpse of bin Laden. There he is laid out on the floor. There he is being prepared for an Islamic burial. There is the tall, shrouded body being lifted, tilted, and then slipped into the sea. A final photo showed the last visible end of the corpse disappearing beneath the water.

Obama, a man who had publicly released his own birth certificate a few days ago, told us in the Oval Office that no—there was no way that we would release the photos. "We're not going to spike the football," he said.

CHAPTER 12

GATHERING CLOUDS

———

EVERY PRESIDENCY IS A STORY WITH ONE PERSON AT THE CENter of it. This is how America organizes its political life and history books. This is how the world consumes the disparate elements of American democracy in an age of American dominance. The president as hero or villain; the president as the person who decides, consoles, commemorates, and reacts; the president as temporary royalty, in command and at the mercy of events that share this time with him.

In the spring of 2011, Barack Obama's story was gaining a certain momentum. A hundred thousand troops had left Iraq. The economy had stabilized. Healthcare reform was law. Bin Laden was dead. Obama had largely done the most important things that he said he was going to do. The United States could pivot from saving our economy to assembling the pieces of a new foundation. The war in Afghanistan was about to turn to deescalation. The Arab Spring held out the promise that positive change could be forced upon the world by the frustrated masses.

But something was missing—the supporting characters, in Congress and around the world.

With the kinds of opposition parties that Johnson or Reagan had, Obama would have been reforming the tax code and rebuilding American infrastructure. But at home, the Republican Party had embraced a strategy of virulent and brazen opposition that led healthy majorities of its own voters to believe that Obama was born in Kenya. Mitch McConnell, the Republicans' leader in the Senate, abandoned any pretense of cooperation, saying that his top priority was to make Obama a one-term president. The decorum that usually shielded national security from politics was tossed aside. The hard truth was that Republicans had been rewarded for this behavior by winning the House of Representatives, aided in part by the constant echo chamber of Fox News and the flood of unregulated money released into American politics by the Citizens United Supreme Court decision. With this Congress, even just basic business like funding the government and confirming nominees for political appointments was going to be a struggle. Ambitious legislative activity was out of the question.

Abroad, the forces of tribalism and nationalism were building, like tremors before an earthquake. As autocrats were threatened in the Arab world, they responded with escalating violence and sectarianism. Globalization had pushed up against people's sense of their own unique identity. In Russia, Vladimir Putin was planning his own return to the presidency, watching warily as popular movements upended Mubarak and Gaddafi. In Europe, the undertow of the financial crisis had spread an economic malaise that was beginning to eat away at public confidence in the European Union. Conflict, a changing climate, and the spread of smartphones and smuggling networks were increasing the flow of refugees from South Asia, the Middle East, and North Africa. In Israel, where Obama had wanted to pursue peace, he did not have a partner.

ONE FRIDAY NIGHT IN MAY, Ann and I were out having drinks when I got a call from the White House operator asking me to come meet Obama around ten. "There's not someone else who can go?" Ann said, only half-kidding.

When I got there, Obama came down to the Usher's Office, just downstairs from his residence, wearing a blue short-sleeved shirt— the only sign that he was into a weekend. He'd been working. We had all been working nonstop since Egypt caught fire.

That week, in a speech at the State Department, Obama had taken positions on two of the four "final status issues" related to Middle East peace, the questions that must form the basis of any two-state solution between Israel and the Palestinians. On behalf of Israel, he called for it to be recognized as a "Jewish state" (the step we didn't take in Cairo), and he endorsed an Israeli security presence within a Palestinian state that would end only after a negotiated transition. He also called for borders "based on the 1967 lines with mutually agreed swaps"—a euphemism known to anyone who has worked on the peace process, which meant a Palestine that is roughly the same size as the one at the end of the 1967 war, with exchanges of land to account for Israeli settlements that have been established since.

In a way, there was nothing remarkable about Obama's stating public positions: It was one of those oddities of foreign policy that everyone who worked on Middle East peace knew what positions the United States had taken privately in negotiations dating back to the Clinton administration. The border and security arrangements that Obama described were the first two final status issues. The other two, thornier ones were refugees and Jerusalem. Palestinian refugees would not be allowed to return to Israel, but would be resettled within the new Palestinian state. Jerusalem would be the capital of both countries, with East Jerusalem going to the Palestinians. Yet these positions were never stated publicly, because neither the Israelis nor the Palestinians were prepared to accept them.

We had reached an impasse. The peace process of 2010 had collapsed when the Israeli government refused to extend a partial freeze on new settlement construction, and the Palestinians refused to negotiate without one. In February 2011, Obama had vetoed a resolution at the UN Security Council that condemned Israeli settlement construction using words taken from Obama's speeches. Now the Palestinians were threatening to seek formal recognition at the United Nations. Prime Minister Netanyahu had been similarly recalcitrant, talking about peace and doing nothing to pursue it. The question was what we should do about all of this.

Clinton and Gates recommended that Obama publicly embrace all four positions, and so did I. It would lay down a marker for whenever an actual peace process resumed, and it would align our public positions with our private ones. It might also forestall the Palestinian push for recognition at the UN, which was certain to isolate the United States and Israel. But taking a public position, particularly on Jerusalem, would have been politically explosive at home, drawing fierce opposition from AIPAC and others who opposed recognition of a Palestinian capital in East Jerusalem. I saw Obama labor over the issue, not wanting to risk a fight with Israel when it was unlikely to lead to a peace agreement. With the speech approaching, a compromise option had been floated by Tom Donilon and Dennis Ross, the lead staffer on the Middle East: Obama could take public positions on two of the issues, borders and security, and leave Jerusalem and refugees for later.

"If this doesn't work," Obama told me, "then I can always take positions on all four issues at the UN in September." But it felt as if we were caught in between—doing enough to have a fight with Netanyahu, but not enough to make any real difference.

And that's exactly what happened. The day after Obama's speech, Netanyahu sat in the Oval Office and lectured Obama in front of the press while lying about the position that Obama had taken. "Israel cannot go back to the 1967 lines," he said, even though Obama had not called for that. "These lines are indefensible.... Remember that before 1967, Israel was all of nine miles wide. It was half the width of the Washington Beltway. And these were not the boundaries of peace; they were the boundaries of repeated wars because the attack on Israel was so attractive."

It was the perfect way to mobilize opposition to Obama among the leadership of the American Jewish community, which had internalized the vision of Israel constantly under attack. I was familiar with the emotions. As secular Jews in postwar New York City, my mother's family maintained its sense of Jewishness in part through support for Israel. Some of this was rooted in guilt—they'd emigrated to Brooklyn, not Tel Aviv; and some was rooted in the heroic

Israel of the 1960s and '70s, Jews building a nation in the desert, fighting off Arab armies, led by towering figures like Golda Meir, who seemed both indefatigable and profoundly just. But as the demographics of Israel changed throughout the 1990s and 2000s, and invading Arab armies were replaced by occasional acts of terror, the Israel that my mother's generation idealized was increasingly eclipsed by an Israel driven by the settler movement and ultraorthodox émigrés. That was Netanyahu's political base, and he knew how to play in American politics on their behalf.

Netanyahu's smack at Obama came just as the 2012 presidential campaign cycle was cranking up, and it succeeded in igniting a firestorm of criticism. Mitt Romney said Obama had "thrown Israel under the bus." A number of congressional Democrats distanced themselves from the speech. I was given a list of leading Jewish donors to call, to reassure them of Obama's pro-Israel bona fides. It was far too painful to wade into these waters with no prospect of success. Netanyahu had mastered a certain kind of leverage: using political pressure within the United States to demoralize any meaningful push for peace, just as he used settlements as a means of demoralizing the Palestinians. The Israel that I felt love and admiration for had a government that seemed determined to make us a foil.

This was my mindset as I walked into the White House at ten o'clock that Friday night. Obama was slated to speak in front of AIPAC that weekend, and it would be his chance to rebut Netanyahu. I didn't draft the speech, but he wanted to give me the edits. He also wanted to vent. He sat down next to me on a bench, holding pages of handwritten notes.

"This is as annoyed as I've been as president," he said. He was tired, and I could tell by the edits he was holding that he'd been working on them for several hours.

"It's not on the level," I said. This is a phrase that we used, repeatedly, to describe the dishonesty we often felt surrounded by.

"It's not on the level," he repeated. "Dealing with Bibi is like dealing with the Republicans."

"You know," I said, "I used to be a member of AIPAC." I explained my family's history, how support for Israel was a kind of secular religion. "So this is all frustrating for me on a personal level."

"Me, too. I came out of the Jewish community in Chicago," he said. "I'm basically a liberal Jew."

With that, he walked me through the additions he'd made to the speech—a careful explanation of the positions he'd taken, coupled with concern about Israel's growing isolation, and a blunt assessment of the demographics in Israel and the West Bank that were making it impossible for Israel to endure as both a Jewish state and a democracy if the occupation endured. But we both knew that nothing he said was going to move this ball forward. This is where we'd find ourselves throughout the administration: unable to nudge Israel in the direction of peace, and left holding up a mirror that showed the necessity of doing so.

A COUPLE OF DAYS LATER, we left for a weeklong trip to Europe. We started in Ireland, where Obama had a distant relative in the small town of Moneygall. He was welcomed as a favorite son, traveling to a pub in his "ancestral home" and then giving a speech to tens of thousands of people in Dublin. David Plouffe had replaced David Axelrod as a senior advisor at the White House by this point, bringing the same sense of discipline and hard-edged focus that guided us through the campaign. As I watched Plouffe smiling at the sight of the Irish prime minister endorsing Obama, I had the first sense that a reelection campaign was under way. The following day, Obama had a London schedule dominated by meetings with the royal family, and I grew concerned that the trip was beginning with too little substance. When I shared this concern with Plouffe, he looked at me as if I was crazy. "Are you kidding?" he joked. "This is perfect. The queen will be a great validator for us with white people."

I laughed, realizing that it was true. Plouffe was able to recognize the absurdity of our politics without being dragged down by it. I was less sanguine. I was starting to feel the adrenaline that had propelled me through the last several months disappearing, and I couldn't reconcile how much doing the right thing didn't seem to matter. I thought it was right to break from Mubarak when he was preparing to crack down on his people, but that decision had badly divided our own government, which was falling back into the habit of deference to the Egyptian military. I thought it was right to save thousands of Libyans from Gaddafi, but we were now being second-guessed, as the averted massacre in Benghazi gave way to a lengthy air campaign. I thought it was right to pursue peace between Israelis and Palestinians, but doing so only invited political pain. Perhaps we'd be better off just visiting Irish pubs and English royals.

The Obamas were staying at Buckingham Palace, and a group of us were invited to attend a state dinner. I had to rent a white-tie tuxedo for the event, and when we arrived we were escorted into a room with furniture that looked as if it belonged behind a velvet rope in a museum—delicate armchairs, lavishly embroidered couches—as members of the royal family circulated, making sure you were never by yourself, expertly making five minutes of conversation that put you at ease before moving on. The women wore diamond tiaras; some of the men, military uniforms. One of these ladies, after telling me about her various hobbies, looked at me quizzically—"You do know who I am, don't you?" she said. *Of course,* I assured her. When she walked away, Plouffe asked me who she was and I told him I didn't have the slightest idea.

Obama stood next to the queen, a stoic yet kindly-looking woman adorned in jewels. Standing there, you got the sense of the impermanence of your own importance—this woman had met everyone there was to know over the last fifty years. We ate at a huge horseshoe-shaped table, a team of waiters in red coats bringing out each course in perfectly synchronized formality. Obama sat at the head of the table, chatting amicably with the queen. When the dinner was over, we were moved to another room, where they served after-dinner drinks. I found myself in a conversation with David Cameron about the HBO show *Entourage,* which we both apparently enjoyed—in a room full of royals, the prime minister is oddly diminished, just another staffer.

When the delegation was getting ready to leave, Obama asked Favreau and me to come back to his room to go over edits to a speech. The next day, he was being given the honor of becoming the first U.S. president to speak to the British Parliament in the historic Palace of Westminster. Obama wanted to offer a broad defense of Western values, but first he—like anyone who has just had dinner at Buckingham Palace—wanted to talk about his evening.

"I really love the queen," he told us. "She's just like Toot, my grandmother. Courteous. Straightforward. All about what she thinks. She doesn't suffer fools."

"She doesn't have to," Favreau said.

We were sitting in a large, ornate room where there was one small table set up with a laptop computer on it. These were guest quarters, and Michelle Obama was getting ready for bed in the adjacent bedroom. At this point, a butler came in. "Mr. President, pardon me," he said. We stopped talking and looked at him. "There's a mouse."

Obama responded immediately, "Don't tell the First Lady."

"We'll try to catch it, sir."

"Just don't tell the First Lady," Obama repeated.

After the man left, I said, "Maybe it really is a dying empire."

Obama laughed. "No, they've still got a lot going on. Did you see the bling on the queen?" He was right—her whole dress had glittered. Obama looked at us. "You guys clean up pretty well."

The walls were covered with giant portraits of kings and queens past, a room full of ghosts. "I'm just a few years away from being in the State Senate and living in a condo," he said, looking around. We were almost whispering; I didn't know whether it was out of deference to the First Lady in the next room or the surroundings. With that, he turned to the words on the page, a soaring endorsement of Western values.

Westminster Hall resembled a cathedral, the pews filled with Members of Parliament and honored guests. The White House staff were seated on a stage opposite a group of British luminaries, the first row made up of former prime ministers—John Major, Tony

Blair, Gordon Brown—who sat with stoic, even gloomy, expressions. As we waited for Obama to come out, the only thing that felt stranger than being in such a grand setting was the fact that—more than two years into the job, with all the things that had taken place—it did not feel unusual to be there.

When Obama came out, he was greeted with a thunderous ovation. Then the conservative Speaker of the House of Commons delivered a soaring introduction: "It is my honor, Mr. President, to welcome you as our friend and as a statesman.... It has fallen to you to tackle economic turbulence at home, to protect the health of those without wealth, and to seek that precious balance between security which is too often threatened, and human rights which are too often denied." It was striking to hear the story of the Obama presidency articulated by a conservative British politician in words that a Republican politician would never dare to use at home.

As my mind wandered over the events of the last few months, Obama's speech built to its climax, a ringing defense of human progress from someone whose own family had been oppressed from the seat of this empire in the past: "In a world which will only grow smaller and more interconnected," he said, "the example of our two nations says it is possible for people to be united by their ideals instead of divided by their differences; that it's possible for hearts to change and old hatreds to pass; that it's possible for the sons and daughters of former colonies to sit here as members of this great Parliament, and for the grandson of a Kenyan who served as a cook in the British Army to stand before you as president of the United States."

THE NEXT MORNING, I had a terrible hangover. There had been a party in the queen's honor, then Cameron's staff invited us to a club across the street from our hotel, where our whole team stayed out way too late. When I forced myself out of bed, I'd slept less than two hours, my last recollection being Favreau teaching admiring Brits how to speak with a South Boston accent. We boarded the smaller Air Force One for the short flight across the Channel, and I willed myself to sleep as soon as we took off. A few minutes later, I woke up to find Obama standing over my seat, poking me, a huge smile on his face. He was clearly egged on by Pfeiffer, who was grinning behind him. "Can't a guy get a little peace?" I yelled instinctively.

When we got to the hotel, we went straight into a bilateral meeting with the Russian president, Dmitry Medvedev. The room was hot and windowless. Obama and Medvedev sat side by side, and a few Russians were lined up opposite the U.S. delegation; a couple of them looked as if they'd had a night similar to mine.

Medvedev had always gotten along well with Obama. Together, they had improved relations between the United States and Russia from the low point of 2008, when Russia invaded Georgia. We'd completed the New START treaty, reached an agreement to resupply U.S. troops in Afghanistan through Russia, and cooperated to enforce stronger sanctions on Iran. We assumed that Vladimir Putin, who was then serving as prime minister, supported this orientation, since he was widely seen as the real power in Moscow. But recently, it seemed that we had gone too far for Putin in pulling Medvedev toward an American position on the UN Security Council resolution on Libya. Russia was historically aligned with Libya and opposed to U.S.-led efforts to impose regime change on other countries, and Putin had publicly criticized Medvedev over Libya. Russia was heading into a presidential election, and it still was not clear whether Putin would run to reclaim the office that he had handed off to Medvedev.

The impact of Putin's criticism was apparent immediately. Medvedev began the meeting with a long complaint about our policy in Libya. He's a short, compact man with wide-knotted ties and charismatic body language—crossing and recrossing legs, making dismissive gestures with his hands. He brushed aside the question of Gaddafi at first. *I never gave him kisses like the Europeans,* he said. But he went on a rant about how we'd started the war in Libya to protect civilians but were now trying to install a new regime. He was right, of course, although it was hard to see how civilians could ever be protected in Libya while Gaddafi was in power and trying to slaughter them. His rant seemed as much for the benefit of the hard-liners on his side in the room, men who were close to Putin.

After the opening talking points had been delivered and the conversation became more casual, Medvedev surprised us when he said, *Gaddafi has to go. He is messianic.* It was a pattern that we'd seen—Medvedev breaking somewhat from the Russian hard line and saying what he seemed to truly believe. You got the sense that he was further out in front of Putin than we knew. Later in the meeting, when Obama explained to him that he couldn't just demand that the WTO grant membership to Russia because he wasn't all-powerful, Medvedev agreed and came back to Gaddafi. No one is all-powerful, he said, except the man with the little green book. It was a reference to the bizarre book of political propaganda that Gaddafi had published in 1975. Among other things, it instructed people on how to breast-feed, dress, and design sporting venues. Medvedev, it seemed, had a hard time feigning support for the more extreme thugs aligned with Russian interests.

Toward the end of the meeting, Obama said the reset in relations between the United States and Russia had to be strong enough to outlast their personal relationship. In the back of his mind was the looming Russian election and the possibility of Putin's returning to power. Sasha and Malia, Obama joked, could someday get elected and try to start a new Cold War. He was trying to make light of the very real sense of drift that had taken hold in the relationship—a sense that the opening of 2009 and 2010 was soon to be eclipsed by the darker forces within Russia, the cruder nationalism that Putin represented. Medvedev joked about this himself, pointing to a particularly grim member of his delegation and suggesting, *He is like Palin.* This would be our final meeting with Medvedev before Putin announced his intention to run for the presidency.

After the meeting, I went to my room. It was in the corner of the resort hotel where we were staying, and the windows overlooked the long red carpet where G8 leaders walked in to shake hands with

Sarkozy. I watched as Obama and Sarkozy greeted each other and walked over to a rope line to shake hands with a group of people. Then I went into the bathroom, got on my knees, and threw up.

At that moment, the absurdity of it all seemed to close in around me. Two days ago, I'd eaten dinner in Buckingham Palace. Now I was about a hundred feet from my boss, the president of the United States, getting sick. Sure, I'd had too much to drink and too little sleep. But more than that, it was the accumulated stress of several months of responding to constant, world-changing events. Those months had changed me. Maybe it was the huge decisions that had been made; maybe it was the harsh criticism of people on opposing sides of debates, or the warm embrace of people like the British elite; maybe it was the increasing proximity to Obama. But whatever it was, I was no longer nervous about raising my voice in meetings, speaking in front of others, or standing up on camera and briefing the press. Somehow it had become second nature to do those things—whatever anxiety I felt was no longer on the surface, but it was there, buried deeper within me, emerging in moments like this.

WE FLEW TO POLAND and I shuddered a bit while they played "Taps" at the memorial for the Warsaw Ghetto. Part of my family had been Polish Jews. During my first trip to Poland in 2001, just a few months before 9/11, I'd come to Warsaw as a twenty-three-year-old backpacker and took a bus out to the town where they'd been from. Working off a guide book, I found a boarded-up synagogue and then a Jewish cemetery. Some of the headstones had been defaced with swastikas and excrement, along with the names of death camps. A few empty vodka bottles were smashed, suggesting it was the kind of place where far-right young men came to get drunk and make themselves feel empowered, the counterpoint to the story of human progress that Obama had just told in London.

I was scheduled to break off the trip a day early the next morning. A year and a half after our wedding, I was going to meet Ann for our honeymoon—a few days in Vienna, Salzburg, and Prague. That night, I lay down in my room for the kind of fitful night where you never really feel like you're asleep, but occasionally look at the clock and find that it has skipped forward by an hour or two. I got up around six and stuffed my remaining clothes into my bag. While the rest of the traveling staff slept, I wheeled my things out of the security bubble of the Secret Service–guarded floor, and out into the anonymous Warsaw street.

The train station was a short walk away, and when I got there I was filled with dread that I would miss the train or get on the wrong one, as there was little English on the big board in front of me. Here I was, able to plan and execute a trip for the president of the United States, and yet I couldn't trust myself to catch a train. When I finally did board the right train, I was so strung out I couldn't close my eyes. I stared out at the green Polish countryside rushing by, at the tracts of blooming farmland, but my mind was still racing around. I fidgeted with my BlackBerry, worried that there was something I'd forgotten to do for Obama's final day in Poland. When I finally fell asleep, I dreamed I was with people from work.

I arrived in Vienna and took a taxi to a small, pleasant hotel room overlooking the Stephansplatz—the giant cathedral and square in the heart of the city. Thirteen years ago, I'd come here on my first long train ride in Europe as a student and met an ex-girlfriend in front of the cathedral. I had no cellphone or GPS maps in those days, so it felt like an achievement to find another human being in the middle of a foreign country based on a plan that had been made on the phone a few days earlier. I was back here now, completely drained, waiting for my wife, who was still a couple of hours out, having waited eighteen months for a honeymoon.

For the first time since I went to work for the Obama campaign in 2007, Ann and I would have more than a week away from work or family. I sat on the bed and thought about where Obama was on his schedule in Warsaw. I felt a sense of emptiness and detachment from the events that had taken place over the last several months; it was as if another person had lived that experience—arguing with people in meetings, writing speeches whose every word would be scrutinized, delivering the views of the United States government in front of cameras. I looked out the window at the cathedral, with its soaring spires and perching gargoyles built by generations of workers who never saw the end result of their labors. I lay down on the bed, feeling like a character in a Cold War movie hiding out in a safe house, and finally drifted off to sleep.

CHAPTER 13

REACTION
AND ACTION

———

As we moved deeper into 2011, I became increasingly conscious of a divide between those issues where we were reacting to events and those where we were acting to shape them. This divide had always existed—the tension between what a president wants to get done and what the world forces him to respond to—but with the outbreak of the Arab Spring, the balance had shifted dramatically in the direction of reaction.

That summer, a sense of crisis was escalating in Syria. It began with young people gathering in the streets, scrawling graffiti on the walls: THE PEOPLE WANT THE REGIME TO FALL. The forty-five-year-old dictator, Bashar al-Assad, responded with mass arrests and torture. We deployed the now familiar tools: public condemnation and targeted sanctions. But this was not Egypt—Syria was an adversary that could tune out the United States and count on the support of Iran and Russia, which were determined to prop Assad up. Over the summer, in response to attacks from the Syrian military, the protests turned violent, and members of the government and military started to defect. In July, the Free Syrian Army was formed to resist the Assad regime.

Syria, in those days, was one more tableau on a sprawling canvas of crisis. We were fighting a war in Libya and trying to midwife a transition in Egypt. We were trapped in an awkward mix of criticism and support for a repressive government in Bahrain, and fight-ing al Qaeda in Yemen while the president there faced his own protest movement. Obama was locked in a political crisis at home, as congressional Republicans refused to lift the debt ceiling, prompting palpable fears that Congress could destroy the Ameri-can economy. Two days before the money was scheduled to run out, Republicans agreed to lift the debt ceiling in exchange for deep spending cuts. The experience left us all feeling diminished—the accomplishments of the last two years were behind us, and now we were in a war of attrition with Republicans that we had not sought, and that no one could win.

By August, Assad was moving beyond mass arrests to bombard-ments of neighborhoods. There was not yet any consideration of a military response by the United States. There was no Benghazi to be saved from an advancing army, no international coalition or United Nations mandate. The most immediate question was whether—or when—to call publicly for Assad to step down as the leader of Syria. We knew that he wasn't going to heed our com-mand, but we had issued similar calls regarding Mubarak and Gad-dafi. There was a moral stance to be taken, and a political message to be sent that Assad was irredeemable in the eyes of the free world.

Given my communications role, the Syria staffers on the NSC came to me and said they thought it was time to make the state-ment. Our diplomats thought it could lead to the closure of the embassy, but we were on that path anyway. Clinton supported it, and the Treasury Department had a stronger package of sanctions ready to go. Obama said he was open to doing so, provided that we acted in concert with our allies. A diplomatic strategy was prepared to maximize Assad's isolation. I drafted a statement in Obama's name, which included these sentences: "We have consistently said that President Assad must lead a democratic transition or get out of the way. He has not led. For the sake of the Syrian people, the time has come for President Assad to step aside." On the morning of August 18, I emailed Obama to make sure he was good with the text of the statement, and he replied yes. And so it was sent out to the world, with Cameron, Sarkozy, and Merkel issuing their own joint statement echoing Obama and saying Assad should "face the reality of the complete rejection of his regime by the Syrian people."

Looking back, while the focus has always been on whether we should have taken military action, I am haunted by the question of whether some more assertive diplomatic initiative could have avoided some of the violence to come, even if it didn't require Assad's immediate ouster. We were counting on the building pressure on Assad from within to be met with growing isolation from abroad in a way that would cause his regime to crumble. Meetings were held to plan for what would happen after he left power; openings pursued to test whether he would leave peacefully; evaluations done on which figures within his government could participate in a transition. Whereas U.S. government assessments had downplayed the potential for Mubarak to step down before February 2011, they now veered in the other direction, anticipating Assad's ouster. Most analysts seemed to think his days were numbered, and so did I. Yet I detected a greater degree of skepticism from Obama, who cautioned us: "Syria could be a longer slog than we think." He was, I think, turning over in his head the point he'd posed to me in the limo ride back from his speech on Libya: whether we had enough bandwidth to shape the Arab Spring. Later, I would come to see he was also debating something else: whether it was shapable at all.

In late August, while Obama was on vacation on Martha's Vineyard, I went up to New York City. I needed a quiet few days, a chance to get away by myself and visit old friends before flying out to California to meet Ann and her parents. Every time I arrive in the city, emerging from the escalators at Penn Station, I feel a release as soon as I disappear into the crowd. Some people relax in the country or on the beach; for me, it is a crowded subway car or a cramped Chinatown street. I walked for miles, emptying my head, looking at the Freedom Tower going up—sun beating off the glass, cranes bent in the sky. I checked my phone and noticed social media reports of Libyan rebels closing in on Tripoli. Sitting in Battery Park, I started getting emails from young staffers at the NSC and State—people who knew which social media accounts to follow. This is how the White House learned that Tripoli was about to fall: on Twitter.

It had been five months since the first American bombs fell over Libya. Without putting a single soldier on the ground or suffering a single American casualty, we'd helped save thousands of lives, and now Gaddafi's government was collapsing. It felt as though maybe, just maybe, the tide was turning against the strongmen of the Middle East. A friend of mine on the NSC sent me her favorite Gandhi quote: "In the end, tyrants fall. Think of it. Always." It seemed possible to believe that.

A few weeks later, Gaddafi was killed in his hometown of Sirte. A coalition drone struck his convoy; Gaddafi fled the vehicle and tried to hide in a drain pipe; a group of rebels dragged him out and killed him. It was an apt metaphor for the entire war: us in the air, Libyans on the ground. As Brennan told me, "a fitting end for one of the biggest rats of the twentieth century."

THAT FALL ALSO SAW the end of Obama's first-term push for Middle East peace. Every September, we would head up to New York for a few days at the United Nations General Assembly (UNGA), where the world descended for an intense period of diplomacy. Life at UNGA revolved around the Waldorf-Astoria, a grand old hotel on Park Avenue that seemed to revel in the fact that its best days were in the past—the hallway carpets slightly stained and faded; the walls filled with black-and-white photos of celebrities hanging out with one another in the 1950s, portraits of Harry Truman and Dwight Eisenhower. Every year around UNGA, the hotel would fill with diplomats, African and Middle Eastern delegations, journalists, spies, and a gigantic American contingent. The whole thing was tinged with nostalgia, including for another time in American foreign policy—the post–World War II years when the world came to us.

The first night at UNGA, Obama and his top advisors always met in the penthouse suite at the Waldorf, which doubled as the residence for the American ambassador to the United Nations. Susan Rice had taken well to the job. She has a mind that can wrap itself around minutiae, and she had mastered the intricacies of the UN—how to navigate the various bureaucracies and procedures, how to craft a resolution, how to cajole votes. Her direct manner served her well in an environment that values strong personalities, and her relationship with Obama gave her that intangible asset that foreign governments value most: closeness to the president. We'd done some of our biggest business through Security Council resolutions on Iran sanctions and Libya, and she'd delivered. The position of UN ambassador is one of the stepping stones to secretary of state, and Susan was in a strong position if Obama was reelected.

Susan had also stayed in close touch with me—reviewing drafts of speeches, popping in to see me when she was in the West Wing, greeting me with a hug and slap on the back. Alone among people of cabinet rank, she'd taken the same forward-leaning positions as Samantha and me on Egypt and Libya. If she couldn't quite read what was going on at the White House, she'd give me a call. If she thought I said something stupid, she'd respond with a bemused "What you talkin' about, Willis?" There was a sense that those of us who had gone through the campaign together were family and, implicitly, had one another's backs.

She had altered the stodgy feel of the penthouse by hanging large canvases of modern art, and as we sunk into well-worn chairs and couches, a waiter served drinks and hors d'oeuvres.

Susan painted a grim picture on Middle East peace. We were working to secure a majority of votes on the Security Council against recognizing the Palestinians—that way, they would be less likely to force the issue to a vote. With everything else going on in the world, we had a play to run to ensure we won Gabon's vote to block Palestinian statehood. I found the whole thing depressing— we weren't doing anything other than averting even worse outcomes.

This became clear in our meetings with foreign leaders, who all seemed to be playing roles in a drama that they knew would end in the same way: with the United States blocking the Palestinians at the United Nations, Israel isolated, the Palestinians frustrated. In a meeting with Recep Tayyip Erdogan, the Turkish prime minister, Erdogan read back the words from Obama's speech at the previous year's UNGA with a thin smile—imploring everyone to work for the goal of being back at the UNGA the following year with a peace deal, one that could welcome Palestine to the General Assembly. Obama and Erdogan had forged a working relationship, albeit one that took up a lot of time. Erdogan liked to debate matters at length. With each passing year he grew more stubborn—as he consolidated power at home, he seemed less accustomed to dissent of any kind. Obama argued that it was untenable for the Palestinians to achieve statehood at the UN—it had to be negotiated with Israel. Look at South Sudan, he said—it took many years and a negotiated settlement for the world's newest country to be born.

And it took years of sanctions on the north, Erdogan shot back. *Are you suggesting the same for Israel?*

After the meeting, Obama called me up to his suite to go over the speech he would give to the UNGA the next morning. We went through edits, and then he paused on the Middle East section, in which we were fully embracing Israel's position. "I hate it when Erdogan has arguments to make," he said.

"The Sudan one was pretty good," I said.

"The thing is," Obama said, "I really don't think the Palestinians should go to the UN. I just can't make Bibi want peace."

"Have you seen *Jerry Maguire*?" I asked.

"Of course," he answered.

"Dealing with Netanyahu is like that," I said. *"Help me help you."*

Obama laughed. It would become something we'd repeat over the years when Bibi inevitably rejected any effort at peace. I stayed up until two finishing the speech, toughening the language to make it stronger in support of Israel. I had no problem summoning the words to defend Israel in front of a group of delegates that included a lot of hypocrites and outright anti-Semites. The Palestinians did need to achieve statehood through a negotiation with Israel, but it was also obvious that Netanyahu wasn't going to negotiate seriously.

After the speech, I wandered back to the Waldorf for Obama's meeting with Sarkozy, who had surprised us that morning by declaring his support for Palestinian recognition by the General Assembly. Obama was annoyed; we are not usually surprised like that by allies on such a sensitive matter. Sarkozy breezed into the conference room followed by his entourage, a short, elegantly dressed man in constant motion, and sat down next to Obama. The press came in and Sarkozy lavished praise on Obama. As soon as they were gone, Obama got serious. "Nicolas," he said, "you've got to give us a heads-up on things."

Sarkozy cut him off. *Barack*, he said, *you are absolutely right. Let me tell you why I did what I did. I despise this man Netanyahu. He humiliated you in the Oval Office. He lied to me.* He went on and on—grabbing his lapels, pounding the table for emphasis.

Obama smiled throughout, and tried to lighten the mood. "Nicolas," he said, "I've already got my Nobel Prize. I'd be happy to see you get yours."

Our last meeting of the day was with Mahmoud Abbas, the Palestinian president. They met alone, with only one staffer for each side, so I stood waiting in the hallway outside the room. When the door opened, I saw Obama guiding Abbas by the elbow out of the room. An older man, slow and deliberate in his movements, he shook Obama's hand and left to walk down the hall. He looked deflated, a man playing a role leading nowhere, buffeted by forces stronger than himself from all around: Israel, the United States, the Arab states. I had no way of knowing whether he truly wanted to make peace, but I knew that he was finding little more than rhetorical support from us.

Obama signaled for me to come in and eat dinner with him: his usual plate of salmon, brown rice, and steamed broccoli. The simplicity of his meals always said something about his discipline—food was something that sustained his health and energy in this job, not something to be enjoyed.

"How do you want me to read this meeting out?" I asked.

"Here's how you should read it out," he said. "I've decided to be a one-term president. I'm going to support the Palestinian bid at the United Nations."

He was tweaking me—knowing that I was disappointed at where things had ended up, but also knowing that I had no better ideas. He was unable to push Israel to stop its settlement of Palestinian land, and despite Netanyahu's intransigence, he would always side with Israel when push came to shove. It felt as though the Israeli-Palestinian conflict was something we had to manage, not solve—keep the two sides talking; persuade the Palestinians not to give up on the prospect of a state altogether; block the United Nations from piling on Israel. Reaction, not action.

As we struggled to keep a lid on the various crises boiling over across the Middle East—where autocracy, tribalism, and sectarianism seemed more powerful than any external force, even the United States of America—I looked for other regions and issues to devote my time to, places where we could do something affirmative in the world.

That November, we were scheduled to go to Asia. A few weeks before we left, Jake Sullivan, Kurt Campbell, and Danny Russel asked to meet me at the White House. Jake was Hillary's deputy chief of staff and director of policy planning. In reality, he did a little bit of everything, and did it better than anyone else. He was my age, a Minnesotan with straight, parted sandy brown hair who had followed the kind of career arc that leads to the top of America's foreign policy establishment: impeccable academic credentials, Supreme Court clerk, top aide on Hillary's presidential campaign.

Kurt was the assistant secretary of state; a large man with a larger personality, he was equally passionate about grand strategy and a quixotic personal quest to find the remains of Amelia Earhart. Danny was more understated, a Foreign Service officer who had spent decades immersed in the intricacies of Asian politics and had been elevated to the job of top Asia staffer at the White House by a president who shared his personal affinity for the region.

They pitched me an idea: The time was right to pursue an opening with Burma. For nearly fifty years, it had been ruled by a reclusive military junta. Like many Americans, my awareness of Burma was through the story of Aung San Suu Kyi, the Nobel Peace Prize–winning daughter of Burma's independence hero who had been imprisoned—largely in her own home—for most of two decades after she swept to victory in a 1990 election. By the fall of 2011, there were signs that things were changing. The military had adopted a new constitution that transitioned to a civilian-led government. Suu Kyi had been released from house arrest and was reentering politics. They suggested that Obama should use his Asia trip to announce that we would reengage the Burmese government and that Hillary would visit the country. I agreed to do what I could to get this done.

For the last two years, we had worked to elevate the importance of the Asia Pacific region. Many of the issues that motivated Obama—growing the American economy, combating climate change, forging new rules to govern trade and commerce among nations—depended upon cooperation in Asia. While the Middle East represented the past—its religious wars, American-backed autocrats, Iranian revolutionaries, terrorist threats—Asia seemed to represent the future. It helped that the people and governments in Asia wanted to deepen relations with the United States, in part because of their concerns about the largest emerging power in their neighborhood: China. Our November trip would be pivotal, shaping our Asia policy for the rest of the administration.

We started in Hawaii, where the United States would be hosting APEC, a summit of Pacific countries. We spent two days there, signaling a tougher stance on China and a more assertive posture in Asia. With a nod from Obama, we took the ongoing negotiations over a trade agreement with a large bloc of Pacific nations—the Trans-Pacific Partnership, or TPP—and played it up as the center-piece of our broader regional strategy, one in which the United States, and not China, would write the rules of international trade. We were preparing to announce a deployment of Marines to a new base in Australia. And we finalized plans for Obama to call Aung San Suu Kyi and make his announcement that we were opening up relations with Burma.

On our last night there, Tom Donilon, Jay Carney, and I got a message that Obama wanted to have a drink. That was unusual; Obama usually passed his nights playing cards or doing work. We went up to his suite, which had a huge deck overlooking the Pacific, and settled in while Obama explained that he wanted us to see the view. He switched from mindless banter to contemplative conversation while a valet brought us drinks and bowls of snacks. "You know," he said, "everything is just better in Hawaii."

"It helps that there are no snakes," I said, a piece of trivia I had learned.

"We have a lot of mongoose for that purpose," he said, once again fulfilling his role as the guy with an answer for everything. Then he started talking about Asia more broadly—the mix of cultures, religions, and races he found so familiar. "Hawaii has a lot in common with Jakarta," he said. "There's a certain communal spirit. Americans are more individualistic." He sipped his drink and looked out at the endless ocean. "When you spend time growing up in Jakarta like I did, and see the masses of humanity in a place like that, it makes it harder for you to think purely of yourself."

We sat there in a moment of pregnant silence, and I tried to imagine what it was like to grow up on crowded Indonesian streets in the 1960s. Then Obama started to complain that people in Washington liked to say that he was aloof. "Few things irritate me more," he said, mimicking the line of criticism. "'He's aloof, he doesn't have friends.' That could not be more wrong. I'm almost always around people. I just have a different group of friends than people who've been running for office since they were twenty-two."

Donilon pointed out that people like Clinton and Bush had been coming to Washington long before they ran for president, but Obama didn't want to dwell on other presidents. "The thing is," he said, "I was a fully formed person before I went into politics. And I didn't have any money until my book started to sell after the [2004] convention. It took me twelve years to sell fourteen thousand books."

Obama recalled how he'd finished *Dreams from My Father* in Bali, writing in longhand because it helped him think. I looked around at this terrace, with its endless view of the Pacific, and it occurred to me how far away this suite was from some backpacking destination in Bali. This part of the world, which had shaped Obama, was going to be more important to the future than the familiar battlefields of the Middle East, but it was distant from the debates that dominated in Washington. "This really is a great view," he said.

Obama got up to go to bed, and I walked down a flight of stairs to my room. It was my thirty-fifth birthday.

AFTER A STOP in Australia, we flew to Bali for the East Asia summit, the first time that the United States attended this forum for Asian nations, a signal of our increased focus on the region. On the flight, Obama called Aung San Suu Kyi. With her agreement, he would announce that we'd be opening engagement with the Burmese government and sending Hillary Clinton to visit. I sat opposite him, listening in as they talked.

They discussed the trends in Burma, with Suu Kyi running through a list of issues—the democratic reform process, the release of political prisoners, the process of reconciling with over a dozen ethnic armed groups in the country. She spoke more as a politician than an icon of democracy, referencing her outreach to the military that imprisoned her all those years. We want them to understand that we will work with them if they work with us, she said. The United States should be very clear in talking to them about rewards, not punishments. We don't need to be talking about punishments—they know all about punishments.

Obama told her that he was going to announce the visit from Hillary. Suu Kyi agreed, and then spoke about the need to reconcile the warring ethnic groups in the country. *I hope you can come to Burma yourself before too long,* she said. *We have many admirers of you here. Many NLD wear T-shirts with you on them,* she said, referring to her political party.

In Bali, we stayed at a hotel with balconies that looked out on a pond full of giant lizards. We met up with Hillary, who was joining us for the summit. Our press was always eager to get access to her, and she agreed to do a series of interviews, but lamented the fact that they would likely focus more on her own political future than the issues she'd been working on. "How many questions do you think I'll get on Asia?" she said. "Maybe one?"

So far, the trip had gone exactly as planned. We'd signaled a pivot to the Asia Pacific nations—with large commercial sales and TPP representing our economic strategy; the deployment of Marines to Australia representing a deepening security commitment; and the opening to Burma representing a commitment to promote democracy and expand relations in Southeast Asia. It was widely and rightly interpreted as a challenge to China.

The last night of the trip was the gala dinner for the East Asia summit. We sat in a cavernous convention center.

There were three hours of entertainment—a Filipino girl band singing pop standards such as "Fly Me to the Moon"; a large video screen showed statistics about Southeast Asian countries on a loop—their GDP, their population growth—then the MC improbably invited Quincy Jones to the stage. He lumbered up from some corner of the room, talked about being asked to do this the night before, and mentioned having just come from Morocco, where he'd produced an album called *Voices of the Arab Spring* for the king. Like us, Quincy was making his own pivot to Asia. Then he announced that he was going to sing "We Are the World" and invited "my President Obama and Premier Wen" to come up on stage to sing with him, hands clasped. I stopped chewing ice. Jay Carney and I began to launch from our chairs, prepared to use physical violence if necessary to stop this photo op from taking place heading into an election year. But before we had to do anything, Obama was waving Quincy down from his seat. Wen sat frozen in his chair. A large group of children joined Quincy on stage instead. *There comes a time when we heed a certain call.* Advance staff asked us to load the motorcade, since the dinner was ending and the U.S. president leaves first, which led to the unfortunate visual of the entire U.S. delegation walking out to "We Are the World."

Back at the hotel, Obama called me to the villa where he was staying. Standing there in the giant batik shirt that leaders had been made to wear, he complained about getting jammed with another China meeting the next day. "How many times do I need to tell you that I'm getting overscheduled on these trips?"

"At least you didn't have to sing with the guy," I said.

Obama laughed. "SBY definitely paid Quincy to be there," he said, referring to the president of Indonesia.

"Not as much as the king of Morocco," I said.

"All right, that's good. Get out of here," he said.

That night I sat staring at the lizards off my balcony. I thought about Obama. He was like a subject I'd studied for years—reading his books, analyzing his comments, internalizing his speech edits, channeling his worldview into written words and policy. But still I wrestled with the constant concern that I was losing myself inside the experience, transformed into a cipher for the needs of this other person who, after all, was a politician, playing the role of U.S. president.

There is always something sad about the last night of these trips. They consume you for weeks, they move you around—without sleep—for days. You stay in beautiful places, see strange things, meet famous people, and develop an intense camaraderie with the people you are with. But I felt like it was impossible to explain these things to people back home—my wife, my parents, my old friends. It was like you inhabited two parallel lives—one that made you who you were, and the other that was consuming that person, and transforming you into someone else.

CHAPTER 14

LIFE, DEATH,
AND BENGHAZI

———

THE DAYS PASS, PASSING TRIPS, PASSING CRISES, PASSING CER-emonies, meetings that bleed into one another, windowless rooms, lunch from the carryout window on the ground floor of the West Wing guarded by dozens of Secret Service officers at a variety of outposts, snipers watching from on top of the White House, looking out at the perimeter gates ringing the complex and the tourists, D.C. residents, the occasional protester or crazy person who wants to stand as close as they can to this nerve center for the application of power in the world, all of it running on an endless loop. There is, always, a relentless flow of information: intelligence reports, casualty reports, notifications of natural disasters, and economic data finding their way to the right people in the right offices—reports that offer bits of information about billions of individual lives, about the manner in which things might or might not be changing.

The days are long, the weeks are long, the months are long, but the years are short—one day you look up and realize you're on the precipice of the final year of a presidential term. You see the world in a different way, as if you could open a window and catch a glimpse of anything that is touched by the reach of the United States government. You can be a part of actions that shape these events—your voice in a meeting, your intervention on a budget line item, your role in crafting the words that a president speaks. You are also a bystander to crises that elude intervention, buffeted by the constant and contradictory demands made on an American president—by other American politicians; by the media; by advocacy organizations; by people around the world. You never know what is the one meeting, the one decision, the one word or phrase that will matter.

On December 18, 2011, one large piece of business was finally completed as the last convoy of U.S. troops left Iraq. Ironically, the timing had been determined by an agreement between the Bush administration and the Iraqi government, reached shortly before Obama took office. For many months, Obama considered leaving a small presence of troops there, and even signed off on a force of ten thousand that would continue to train Iraqi Security Forces. But this was predicated on the Iraqi government's agreeing to give American troops immunity from criminal prosecution, something America demands for our troops around the world and that seemed particularly necessary in the unpredictable currents of Iraqi politics. The Iraqi government, conscious of its sovereignty, refused. So on October 21, Obama held a videoconference with the prime minister of Iraq, Nouri al-Maliki. The two leaders determined that the removal of U.S. troops would be completed on schedule.

Ending a war in which there is no clear victory is an anticlimactic thing. The flag-draped coffins and funerals were over, as was the $10 billion a month price tag. But by the time we finished pulling out, the focus on Iraq had faded—it was a marker of a different era, the defining event of a different presidency. The only thing that wouldn't fade was the effort to shape the perception of what had happened there. For years to come, the war's supporters would blame the further tragedies that would take place in Iraq on the fact that we didn't keep those ten thousand troops there, rather than on the decision to invade the country in the first place.

What does it mean to invade a country, topple its leader, face a raging insurgency, open a Pandora's box of sectarian conflict across a region, spend trillions of dollars, kill hundreds of thousands of people, and permanently alter hundreds of thousands of American lives? Something in the character of post-9/11 America seemed unable, or unwilling, to process the scale of the catastrophic decision, and the spillover effects it had—an emboldened Iran, embattled Gulf states, a Syrian dictator who didn't want to be next, a Russian strongman who resented American dominance, a terrorist organization that would turn itself into an Islamic State, and all the individual human beings caught in between.

I WENT TO CALIFORNIA for Christmas. My father-in-law, Roger Norris, had recently been diagnosed with Stage IV lung cancer, a private tragedy amid the global ones that consumed most of my days. It was unlikely, the doctors said, that he would live more than a year.

Roger was a quiet man. Born in Ohio, raised in Michigan, he made his way to California and worked his whole life as an engineer—first for Douglas Aircraft, which then became part of McDonnell Douglas, which then became part of Boeing. He helped to build the airplanes and spacecraft that became the ballast of America's postwar power. He raised seven kids and settled in Huntington Beach, with its wide beaches, two-car garages, and good public schools.

On my first trips to Huntington Beach, I'd felt out of place— a New Yorker wandering the few sidewalks, searching in vain for a *New York Times*. The household was always bustling, but it could be a raucous place. Roger was an island of calm, tinkering at some project outside in the garage, reading the L.A. *Times,* lending money to his children when they needed it. He allowed himself few indulgences. On one of his visits, I took him to a baseball game, and as we ordered a third beer he told me he hadn't had a few beers at the ballpark in decades.

After his diagnosis, we began a project of checking things off his bucket list. His interests seemed frozen in the 1950s, like the photographs on the walls of the Waldorf. We saw Bing Crosby's *White Christmas* and ate New Year's dinner at Lawry's, a classic Beverly Hills prime rib joint. We went to New York and saw *Jersey Boys* on

Broadway. Ann, the family organizer, planned additional trips to Santa Barbara and Hawaii. She idolized her father, who had been the one who took her to book fairs and talked politics against the backdrop of Huntington Beach's surfing culture.

With a death approaching, I watched as the wider world shrinks to a family circle, and ultimately becomes inconsequential. Yet my time was limited, the pull of pressing events never farther away than my BlackBerry. My own experience was improbable and exciting to the people around me—people like my father, the son of an engineer from Baytown, Texas, or Roger Norris, an engineer from Michigan who had gotten in his car and driven west. At the same time, the things my job offered seemed symbolically important but impersonal. Prominently displayed in the Norris household was a picture of Barack Obama with Ann at a state dinner, with the president's inscription, TO ROGER, THANKS FOR DOING SUCH A GREAT JOB WITH ANN. I represented how far Ann had come from Roger's simple Michigan roots, but it was always hard for me to explain what I did—something more easily captured in that framed photograph.

For big chunks of 2012, I'd be alone in D.C. while Ann took leaves of absence to be with her family out in California. At the White House, the world continued to spin on its axis, even as the reelection campaign started to envelop all that we did. You had to do the things that were in front of you without knowing whether you would be around to see where the story would go.

IN THE EARLY MONTHS of 2012, there was real concern that there was going to be a war between Israel and Iran. The Iranian nuclear program continued to advance, the threats out of Israel were becoming more bellicose, and there were signs that a strike on Iran's nuclear facilities could be imminent. A steady stream of U.S. officials traveled to Jerusalem to counsel against an attack. In the White House, we prepared for scenarios in which a strike took place and the United States was drawn into a wider regional war with Iran—

a country much larger, more sophisticated, and more powerful than Saddam Hussein's Iraq.

To obtain leverage on Iran, we were steadily expanding sanctions. This required the cooperation of other countries, which needed to help us reduce the revenue that Iran could get from selling oil. Throughout 2011 and 2012, in meetings with China, Japan, South Korea, India, and European countries, Iran sanctions topped the agenda, as Obama convinced leaders to do something against their own economic interest. But still Netanyahu complained he wasn't doing enough.

When Netanyahu visited Washington to address AIPAC in early March, I spent several days leading a public campaign to make the case that there was *time:* time to let tougher sanctions sink in, time to test whether diplomacy could make a difference. We prepared a set of talking points that rebutted the arguments for war. We had meetings with groups of prominent columnists and journalists to make our case. We held briefings for members of Congress who were nervous about being out of step with Israel. Obama sat down for a lengthy interview in which he made it clear that he would strike Iran's nuclear facilities if he thought it necessary to do so, but that we were not yet at that point. He gave a speech restating those positions, and he said the same things to Netanyahu in private. At some point that spring, Netanyahu blinked, and we were spared the consequences of another war.

But on many issues, it felt as if the looming election sidelined more ambitious foreign policy initiatives; that politics was crowding out any capacity for risk. I worried that we were becoming so conservative that we were losing touch with what we had set out to do. We had done a lengthy review of the cuts that we could make to the U.S. nuclear arsenal after the conclusion of the New START treaty, a key pillar of the affirmative agenda that Obama announced in Prague. We settled for the most modest option.

On Egypt, I'd grown frustrated at how our government had largely reverted to deference to the Egyptian military, which was playing a double game—mouthing words of support for democracy while taking steps to undermine civil society at home. I'd raise this, but Obama would lose patience. "Our priority has to be stability and supporting the SCAF [Egyptian Military Council]," he snapped at me. "Even if we get criticized. I'm not interested in the crowd in Tahrir Square and Nick Kristof," he said, referring to a columnist who'd been critical of our Egypt policy. He rationalized this because the military had to ensure that elections took place, but he also seemed to be talking himself into the rightness of more incremental change. Burdened by a reelection campaign, buffeted by the stridency of his opposition at home, divisions among his own team, and a sense that he lacked good partners abroad, Obama seemed at times to be using his powerful mind to find justifications for more modest ambitions. Another time, at a meeting on what he was aiming to accomplish in his first term, I pointed to the potential for a democratic opening in Burma. "Ben," he said, "no one cares about Burma in Ohio."

These comments stuck with me. For the first time, I felt out of step with my boss. In the quiet of my empty apartment, I began to wrestle with bigger questions. How would I see myself in five years if I couldn't remember what I was like five years ago? How do you establish your own voice when your entire reputation is founded on someone else's? How much can you compromise your own positions in service of a larger good before you sacrifice them? I felt we had gradually trimmed our sails and lowered our sights—a year after the heady days of the Libya intervention and bin Laden operation, it felt as if we were becoming technocratic, competent managers of things amid a world roiling with change. Drone strikes to take out terrorists. Reducing the population at Gitmo but unable to close it. Averting a war with Iran while imposing sanctions.

I was advocating proposals that weren't expedient or politically popular. More pressure on the Egyptian military. More action in Syria. More time spent on places like Burma. And yet I also saw how little those issues mattered in the campaign that was taking place. We needed to designate one White House official who worked on national security to be able to coordinate with the reelection campaign on messaging. I was the only option. I'd been responsible for the public messaging around Obama's national security policies for five years. I'd have to shift—from being an employee of the NSC to an employee of the White House—a small bureaucratic move that seemed designed to protect those institutions more than me.

I looked, increasingly, for smaller things that I could work on—if I had outlets on issues where I could make a difference, it could add a layer to my experience at work separate from the grind of politics and the intractability of some of the larger issues on our agenda. One issue was education in Libya. With the country struggling to put itself back together, there were plans for the United States to help Libyans restore a system of higher education.

Late that spring, I met with our ambassador, Chris Stevens, who had served in Benghazi throughout the revolution. He had a reputation for being the kind of envoy who worked with people as well as governments—knowing the language, the food, the culture of the place he was posted. He had a calm demeanor, sandy brown hair, and an easy smile. "We already have the attention of the government on this, and we need areas where we can cooperate," he said. "It'd be great if you could give this a push out of here."

We talked about where to find money in the budget; what partners to enlist; how this fit into the broader picture of our Libya policy. "I think we can get the diaspora involved in this," I said, referring to a number of the Libyans I'd met.

"They already are," Stevens said. A number had returned to the country.

As we wrapped up, I said, "I'd like to visit."

"That would be great," he said. I thought I'd go sometime after the election.

THAT AUGUST, MY FATHER-IN-LAW took a turn for the worse and I flew out to California again. When I arrived, he had just come home from the hospital. He was frail, his body weakening, as he hadn't been responding to treatment and couldn't really eat. He thanked me for coming, as if it was an inconvenience. The next day, he slipped into a different place, unable to speak, and a twenty-four-hour hospice nurse was dispatched to the house. Ann and I slept upstairs in the room where she lived as a child as her father lay dying in the living room downstairs. People took turns saying goodbye. Ann's twelve-year-old niece, Emma, played the piano. She had become the center of Roger's life.

He died two days later, surrounded by family, in the house where he raised seven children. Making myself useful, I took Emma to In-N-Out Burger. In the blur of days that followed, funeral arrangements were made, stories were told, friends of Roger's came and went. He was the type of person who had quietly made a larger impact on people's lives than anyone knew.

In the days leading up to the funeral, we went through some of Roger's old things—the small amount of stuff that he'd saved or put aside. I found a folder stashed away in the closet filled with newspaper clippings that traced some key moments in my career—an article in the *Los Angeles Times* about my role in the Cairo speech, yellowing just a bit around the edges, a flattering piece about the young group of Obama White House aides trying to find a different way to communicate with the Muslim world. He had never told anyone about this habit of his, nor asked me much about my work. Whenever it came up, he seemed to keep a respectful distance, not wanting to probe. I tried to picture him, alone with a scissors, cutting up his morning paper with an engineer's precision and putting the clippings away neatly in the closet to be found later, at another time, by another person.

ON THE AFTERNOON OF TUESDAY, September 11, 2012, we started to get alarming reports out of Cairo. Hundreds of chanting protesters had gathered at the walls of our embassy. Apparently, a video entitled *Innocence of Muslims*, a crude and seemingly obscure movie intended to humiliate the Prophet Muhammad, had generated this backlash. A fourteen-minute trailer had been posted on YouTube earlier in the summer. An Egyptian Coptic Christian who lived in California was promoting the video, and it started to get picked up in Egypt. Part of it was then dubbed into Arabic, and a short segment was shown on Egyptian TV. Islamist clerics condemned the movie, fueling a sense of grievance that brought thousands of Egyptians into the streets.

The immediate concern was security at our embassy. In an effort to calm the protests, our embassy spokesman had put out a statement saying "the Embassy of the United States in Cairo condemns the continuing efforts by misguided individuals to hurt the religious feelings of Muslims." I sat at my desk watching the video—a low-budget Internet movie that portrayed Muhammad as a decadent character, the protagonist in a knock-off of bad late-night Cinemax. Meanwhile, as the day turned into evening in Cairo, the crowd scaled the walls of our compound and raised a black flag used by militants across the Middle East, with an insignia that read, in Arabic, THERE IS NO GOD BUT GOD AND MUHAMMAD IS HIS PROPHET. I spent much of the afternoon in meetings about what needed to be done to secure our embassy and stanch the swelling uproar.

Late in the afternoon, as I sat in Denis McDonough's office recapping our public messaging plan, I learned that the crisis wasn't limited to Cairo—something had also happened at our diplomatic compound in Benghazi. In a meeting with his secretary of defense, Obama had directed that the military do what was necessary to secure U.S. facilities in Libya and across the region. There was a sense of crisis escalating.

Unlike Cairo, there was not a large contingent of American journalists in Benghazi, so there were no TV cameras and little reliable information about what was happening. Information trickled in. Chris Stevens was apparently at the compound when it came under attack, and he was unaccounted for. I thought about the man who had just recently sat in my office, earnestly discussing how to improve higher education in Libya, and hoped he wasn't hurt. At one point, there was a positive report—Stevens's cellphone had called a senior State Department official. But over the course of the evening, the reports grew darker—the call had been placed from a hospital; Stevens was badly injured; and, then, as evening settled in Washington, the word came: Stevens was dead. Another American was also reportedly killed. Suddenly we were faced with this terrible news, the thing you fear the most, the death of Americans overseas.

I sat in my office, feeling numb, remembering when the genial, dogged, and optimistic Stevens had sat—full of life—across from my desk a few months ago. It is a reality of twenty-first-century communications that you have to address totally different audiences at the same time, because anything you say will be consumed by the entire world. We now had several pressing communications challenges. First, the United States government had to confirm the death of Chris Stevens and another American, a thirty-four-year-old named Sean Smith; to condemn the violence that killed them; and to mourn their loss. Second, U.S. embassies in the Middle East, worried about further protests, were asking for statements that distanced the U.S. government from this video and condemned its attacks on the Prophet Muhammad. Third, we needed to deal with a right-wing American media that had already started to attack the statement put out by the U.S. embassy in Cairo for blaming the violence on the video rather than the protesters.

Given that an ambassador had been killed and diplomatic facilities were under assault, our initial statement would come from Clinton. Jake Sullivan took the lead on it, and I reviewed different drafts and signed off for the White House. The language was straightforward—"I condemn in the strongest terms the attack on our mission in Benghazi. . . . We are heartbroken by this terrible loss." Later in the statement, we addressed the concerns expressed by our embassies overseas without suggesting that any violence was justified: "The United States deplores any intentional effort to denigrate the religious beliefs of others. . . . But let me be clear: There is never any justification for violent acts of this kind." More than three years later, I'd have to go over the language of this statement in careful detail before a congressional committee.

I stayed at work until there was nothing left to do. Around nine or ten, I walked home, feeling a mix of sadness and anger. Egypt and Libya—the two places that, a year ago, had represented so much hope, were now roiling with protests by people who had nothing to offer except hate. Two Americans were dead.

When I got home, I poured a large glass of Scotch and opened up my laptop to see if there was any other news. Around midnight, I saw a statement that had been put out by Mitt Romney: "It's disgraceful that the Obama administration's first response was not to condemn the attacks on our diplomatic missions, but to sympathize with those who waged the attacks."

I stood in my bedroom processing the words as waves of anger washed over me. For a moment, I couldn't even understand which statement Romney meant; then I realized that he was referring to the statement that the embassy in Cairo put out earlier in the day, before anything had happened in Benghazi. I had grown accustomed to ugly Republican attacks, but this felt different. Some threshold had been crossed. They were slamming us in the crudest possible way in the middle of a crisis. They were attacking career Foreign Service people who had issued a statement while their embassy was under siege. They were ignoring the fact that the video *was* offensive. They were making it harder for us to say things that could help protect American lives abroad. They would say anything if it could cast Obama as somehow anti-American. It wasn't just politics, it was sickening in its cynicism.

We were now in some new, uglier reality. I could never have guessed just how ugly it would become: that for the next four years, "Benghazi" would be transformed from the name of a city in Libya where American intervention had saved tens of thousands of lives into something entirely different: a word that represented the sentiment in that statement of Romney's, an expression of an ugly conspiracy theory to delegitimize Obama and Clinton, destroy any concern for facts that didn't fit the theory, and dehumanize a small group of people, including me. *Benghazi.*

The next morning, I woke in the predawn hours to learn that two more Americans had been killed overnight in some kind of firefight. The details were sparse. I got to the White House early, where there was a meeting to review security measures for our embassies across the Middle East. I locked myself in my office to write a statement that Obama would give just a couple of hours later in the Rose Garden, working off situation reports from the State Department and some limited biographical information on the men who died, and suggesting language to distance ourselves from the video. I wrote many statements like this, locked in my office with the door closed, acutely aware that a lot of people—including the president of the United States—were waiting for me to get the thing done. Ben Fishman, the Libya staffer on the NSC who had been close to Ambassador Stevens, came by to ask that we add something to the remarks about how much Stevens meant to young people across the government. Fishman looked like hell.

Obama ended up giving the statement a little before eleven, with Clinton by his side. He condemned the "outrageous and shocking attack" and pledged "to bring to justice the killers who attacked our people." He echoed Hillary's words from the night before: "There is absolutely no justification to this type of senseless violence. None." He paid tribute to Stevens, noting that he was a "role model to all who worked for him." Then, in the type of language we'd always include after a terrorist attack, he said, "No acts of terror will ever shake the resolve of this great nation." After the statement, he lingered in the area outside the Oval Office, where a bank of television screens showed the different cable television networks responding to what he'd said. He watched for a minute or so while the commentators focused on what Romney had said the night before. "That should be disqualifying," he said, shaking his head.

The rest of the week, protests over the offensive video continued to grow in dozens of cities around the world—from Islamabad to

Sana'a to Tunis. The overwhelming fear was that Friday would be a bloodbath, Fridays being the biggest protest days in Muslim communities, as it's the weekend and people attend Friday prayers, where imams can stir up a crowd and extremists can take advantage of the chaos. A crisis response team started meeting regularly about what we could do to mitigate the situation. We reached out to all alumni of U.S. exchange programs in the Middle East, hoping to draw from whatever reservoir of goodwill had been built up. We contacted Google and YouTube to try to get the offensive video taken down. We disseminated talking points condemning the denigration of Islam in the video while affirming that there is never any justification for violence. While we were doing this, other parts of the government were ramping up security at embassies, consulates, and military facilities across the Arab world.

At home, the right-wing outrage about our criticism of the Internet video continued to build as Republicans worked hard to make Benghazi into a political problem for Obama. It was as though I was inhabiting two entirely different worlds: I'd spend most of my day trying to convey messages to people outside the United States who were offended by the video; then I'd spend an hour or two helping Jay Carney prepare for questions about whether we were apologizing for the video, or whether Obama's foreign policy was a failure. When I focused on the audience outside the United States, I opened myself up to criticism for being tone-deaf, politically correct; when I focused on figuring out how to respond to Republican critics, I opened myself up to criticism for being political. It was like dealing with mirror images of insanity.

One night that week, as I walked out of work, I saw a candlelight vigil taking place in front of the White House. I recognized a few of the people—Libyan Americans I'd met with at the White House when we intervened to save Benghazi. They were honoring the memory of Chris Stevens. A small circle formed around me. One of them had tears in his eyes, thanking me for the role I'd played in supporting President Obama's intervention in Libya and saying that he feared for the future of the people there.

"Do you think this means the United States will have to leave Benghazi?" he asked.

"I hope not," I said, but I knew that it did.

ON FRIDAY, EVERY TIME I walked into my office and saw the television playing another video of protest, I felt a sense of chaos, as though something was unraveling that could never be reassembled. A steady stream of reports was delivered to my office detailing how American diplomats in different places were being told to shelter in place. Ten thousand people protesting in Khartoum. In Lebanon, young men set fire to American fast food restaurants. In Tunis, four people were killed at the U.S. embassy when an angry mob climbed the walls and raised a black flag. In Cairo, hundreds were arrested in Tahrir Square. In Afghanistan, the Taliban launched an attack that killed two Marines. Meanwhile, the caskets of the four Americans killed in Benghazi were returned to Andrews Air Force Base. I felt I was watching the Arab Spring turn dark in real time.

That afternoon, I got called up to the press secretary's office. Jen Palmieri, the White House communications director, was sitting with a handful of staff. They looked at me a little sheepishly. "We need someone out on the shows," Jen said. All five Sunday shows were asking.

"Really?" I asked. She knew I thought those shows were a Washington ritual that accomplished little for us other than ruining people's weekends. None of our national security principals liked to do them, but she made a credible argument.

"The world is on fire," she said, gesturing up at the images on television. She thought we needed someone to convey that we were on top of it. Also: Netanyahu was going to be on, and he was surely going to take shots at Obama; it'd be useful to have someone ready with a response. "Do you mind reaching out to Hillary?" she asked.

I emailed Philippe Reines, Clinton's communications advisor, and asked if she'd be up for doing the shows. I got no response. Next, I asked Tom Donilon. He looked at me as if I were crazy. The only person left was Susan Rice. She was a diplomat. She could pay tribute to the people lost and in danger, talk about our approach in the Middle East, and respond to whatever Netanyahu said about our Iran policy. I had an initial conversation in which Susan told me she was planning to go away that weekend with her kids, but said she'd be willing to do it if Clinton could not. I called back later, when I still hadn't heard from Clinton.

"People think we need someone out there," I said.

There was a pause. "What about Hillary?"

"She doesn't want to do it," I said.

She laughed. "So I'm it?"

"Looks that way."

"Okay," she said. "I'll do it, if you do my prep."

I sat at my desk and put together a document to help her prepare. It took only a few minutes—I merged the different Q&As that our press team already prepared for Jay Carney's daily briefings, since she'd be getting the same questions, and I listed some objectives up top to make the document feel like more than a repurposed set of press guidance. One of the questions we'd been getting was whether the protests across the Middle East showed that our foreign policy was a failure, so one of the objectives I listed was to show that the protests were rooted in the Internet video, not a failure of U.S. policy. I never could have guessed how these few hurried minutes at my desk would become one crucial link in the chain of a massive conspiracy theory.

I went home. Ann, still reeling from the death of her father, was frustrated with me for being absent. She was taking things out of cabinets and cleaning them, the kind of thing she did when she wanted to distract her mind and keep me at a distance. I stared at my BlackBerry, catching up on things I'd missed in the crush of events. There was an email chain about what talking points people should be using to describe what happened in the Benghazi attack. There was a Deputies Committee meeting the next morning, as there had been every morning that week, about how to deal with the various issues—embassy security, the Internet video, the collapsing world. We'd also have to give Susan updated points for her to use on the Sunday shows. I wrote back and said that we could just deal with this at the meeting. I was standing in the closet so Ann wouldn't snap at me for being on my BlackBerry. This was the last thing I wanted to be doing.

At the Deputies meeting, we spent most of our time on updates to our security posture at embassies, one country after another. Mike Morell was on via videoconference from CIA headquarters. When the issue of the talking points on the Benghazi attacks came up, he cut off the discussion, saying that he would rework them and send them around for use. I was grateful—one less thing to do. A little while later, we got an email from Morell with the revised points. I made one edit, changing a reference to our "consulate" in Benghazi, since it was not a consulate.

After the meeting, I left to do some errands with Ann, who was now barely speaking to me because of my long hours. We got the car washed and then went to the Calvert-Woodley liquor store on Connecticut Avenue. While she was inside, I sat in the car and joined a phone call to prep Susan for her Sunday show appearances. At first, the campaign staff was dialed in, but I kicked them off the call before Susan could dial in—we couldn't have them brief a national security cabinet official. I walked Susan through the likely criticisms from Netanyahu that she'd have to respond to, mostly demands that we be tougher on Iran, tougher on the Palestinians. We went through all the security measures that we were taking at our diplomatic facilities, and then went through the various criticisms of our foreign policy that she'd be asked about. On the question of what happened in Benghazi, I told her we were lucky—the CIA had prepared points for this purpose, and I'd send them to her to use. Later, after I got home, I forwarded the points to her press aide to pass on. That was that.

Sunday morning, I had to go back in to work for more meetings. Protests had spread to places as far-flung as Paris and Sydney. The crisis prompted by this Internet video was going to be with us for a while. Susan taped her Sunday shows, but I was in the Situation Room at the time. I never did see a single one of those appearances, though I read the transcripts that were sent around by our media monitor on my BlackBerry and thought that—all things considered—she'd done a good job. I left work early that afternoon, hoping to have a few quiet hours.

CHAPTER 15

A SECOND TERM

D EBATE PREPARATION TOOK PLACE AT A RESORT IN HEN-
derson, Nevada. As the motorcade made its way farther out from
Las Vegas, past where people actually lived, we went by a strip mall
that sat empty like a twenty-first-century ghost town, a relic of the
financial crisis. Even though this first debate was on domestic issues, I was the national security staffer assigned to the trip. I passed
up the opportunity to sit in on the prep sessions, choosing instead
to go on long runs on the surrounding golf courses, emptying my
head while jogging down fairways baked brown by the desert sun.
The hotel where we were staying had a Middle Eastern theme, with
an "Arabesque" lounge, Moroccan patterns, and a signature cocktail
called "the Casablanca." I'd sit in the air-conditioned, empty lobby,
sedated by this American creation of an idealized Arab world.

Each night, Jon Favreau would emerge from the debate prep sessions more and more nervous. Obama was flat, irritable, and long-
winded. Favreau was notoriously anxious in campaign seasons—
riding what he called a "poller-coaster" of emotions, checking the
daily tracking polls, always anticipating the worst. But he also knew
Obama in a way that only a handful of us did, and it turned out he
was right. After three days in Nevada, we flew to Denver, where
Obama was thoroughly beaten in a debate with Mitt Romney. A
group of us watched backstage on a television screen as Obama came

across as somehow diminished and annoyed by criticisms that he found unfair. He had been cruising to reelection, so the debate offered a turn in the media narrative: Suddenly, Obama was on the ropes.

In the days that followed, Obama had small groups of us into the Oval Office. "That one was entirely on me," he said. "It won't happen again."

To buck up Obama's spirits, I made a list of ten other times that things looked terrible over the last six years: when we were down by 20 points to Hillary; Reverend Wright; Palin's high point; Scott Brown's election; the 2010 midterms; the debt ceiling. He loved this, and called me up to the Oval to go over it.

"I wasn't really that stressed about Palin," he said. "I don't remember that. Maybe she got to *you*."

"That hockey mom thing worked for a little while," I said. "What was the worst?"

"The debt ceiling," he said, and looked momentarily pained by the memory. "Because that one wasn't just about me. A lot of people could have been hurt."

The second debate would be a "town hall" format, in which selected audience members ask screened questions after they're called on by a moderator. An exact replica of the debate stage was built at a golf resort in Williamsburg, Virginia, right down to the color scheme: red carpet, star-spangled flourishes along the curved exterior. For three days, we sat in the audience seating that circled the debate stage, pretending to be real people asking questions of Obama and John Kerry, who was playing Mitt Romney. Obama would practice an answer, and then we'd critique his performance.

"Get into it faster."

"Look at the person who asked the question."

"Don't forget your home base."

At some point, Obama, who liked to name the absurdities of politics, snapped. "I get it," he said. "So this isn't really a debate at all, it's just a performance." He asked that we just write up the best

answers he could give on key questions, drawing on the best answers he gave in debate prep.

One of the questions was on Benghazi. In practicing an answer,
we had to tell him about all the conspiracy theories gaining traction
on the right. Obama had been on a news blackout, so he didn't believe it.

"Do people really think this?" he asked.

"It's all over Fox," I said.

"This is some real tin hat stuff." One of the theories was that
we'd refused to call what happened in Benghazi "terrorism" and had
invented the connection to the Internet video to make his record on
terrorism look better.

"I'm telling you, it's all over Fox," I said. I explained how he'd
called it an act of terror the day after the attack, then Susan Rice
had said the attack developed out of protests over the video, then
the director of the National Counter-Terrorism Center had testi-
fied that it was carried out by al Qaeda–affiliated extremists. Susan's
reference to protests, which had been a part of the intelligence
community's talking points, had been seized on by the right.

"How exactly is it a cover-up if we're the ones who told people
that it was terrorism?" he asked. "Just explain that to me. And what
were we covering up?" It was something he did, acting as if you
believed the crazy things that you were telling him.

"Don't think too much about it. It will make your head hurt."

He practiced his answer on Benghazi, and kept saying, "I stood
in the Rose Garden the next day and called it terrorism." When he
finished, I spoke first. "No," I said, "remember, you called it an *act of
terror*."

"What's the difference?" he asked, annoyed.

"Trust me," I said.

"Act of terror," Favreau repeated.

He got better as practice went on, more comfortable in approaching the debate as a performance. We flew up to Hofstra and
did one more practice run at a pair of lecterns in the lobby of a hotel

where we had a few hours to kill. "I stood in the Rose Garden and called it an act of terror," he said, looking at me and Favreau, over-enunciating the word "terror" to make the point that he got it and thought it was ridiculous, this distinction between terror and terrorism. Then he went up to his room to eat dinner and I went to the bar and drank bourbon. We were nervous. A good debate, and he'd be on a path to victory; a repeat of Denver, and he'd be in trouble.

As the debate got under way, Obama was clearly stronger. About halfway through, the Benghazi question came, and Obama launched into a version of the answer he'd practiced. Romney pounced: "I think it's interesting the president just said something which is that on the day after the attack he went into the Rose Garden and said that this was an act of terror."

"That's what I said," Obama responded.

Romney looked surprised, even shocked, at his good fortune. "You said in the Rose Garden the day after the attack, it was an act of terror? It was not a spontaneous demonstration, is that what you're saying?"

Obama was now the one who looked pleased. "Please proceed, Governor," Obama said.

"I want to make sure we get that for the record," Romney said, "because it took the president fourteen days before he called the attack in Benghazi an act of terror."

"Get the transcript," Obama said.

"What an idiot," Favreau said, as we watched this unfold on a television backstage. Candy Crowley, the moderator, confirmed that Obama was right. Romney looked indignant, then deflated—he just *knew* that Obama had not called it an act of terror. Sitting there, half-drunk and delighted, it nonetheless unsettled me a bit that Romney—an intelligent man—really did seem to believe something that wasn't true. You could almost see how his debate prep had gone, a group of aides who'd been feeding on a steady diet of Fox News preparing him to pounce on Obama for refusing to call it terrorism, for inventing a story about an Internet video. I assumed they were just cynical; what if they actually believed this stuff?

ON ELECTION DAY, A small group of us were invited to the Obama suite at the Hyatt as it became clear that he would win: me, Jon Favreau, Dan Pfeiffer, and Cody Keenan, who was slated to take over as chief speechwriter after Favreau left. We clustered a tactful distance across the room from where the Obamas were gathered with a group of family and close friends, watching the results on television.

Because the election was called earlier than anticipated, the room had the feeling of a low-key party. There was a spread of appetizers, wine and beer, thirty or forty people scattered about. Obama made the rounds, talking to the different clusters of guests like the groom at a wedding. Michelle Obama presided over the family area, offering hugs to all who approached her. When Obama came over to us, he looked more relaxed than I'd seen him in a long time. "In some ways this one is sweeter than 2008," he said.

"Two thousand eight was pretty good," Pfeiffer responded.

"This one feels better," he said. "Folks know you pretty well after four years."

As I looked over at Malia and Sasha, now grown into teenagers, it occurred to me that the anxiety any president feels about being rejected by voters must have been magnified for Obama because he was the first African American president; you don't want to be the first and be deemed a failure. I wondered how much some of the occasional irritability that had flared up over the last few months was tied to this. As the night dragged on, Romney refused to call and concede, even though it was obvious that he had lost badly. Finally, as it was getting closer to midnight, Obama stepped out of the room to take the call. When he came back in, he had a look of both amusement and surprise. "He kept talking about how many urban voters turned out," he told us. "Urban voters."

——

FROM THE WINDOW OF Air Force One, Burma unfolded below, a mysterious expanse of river, rice paddies, and unspoiled green dotted with the occasional small village. It was less than two weeks after the election, and Obama was about to become the first American president to set foot in this distant country.

We landed at a small, dilapidated airport in Yangon. Air Force One felt too large for the surroundings. As the motorcade turned onto the airport access roads, we were greeted by row after row of schoolchildren waving flags. At first, the sight of these smiling young faces was reassuring, but as their identical uniforms stretched on, the authoritarian choreography felt a little chilling. *Where were we?* Then we reached the main road, and the crowds swelled into the tens of thousands, most in T-shirts or wrapped in Buddhist robes, mothers and fathers with their children, people as far as you could see. The crowds pressed in against the motorcade whenever it slowed, people smiling, cheering, staring in wonder at something they never believed they would see. A few years before, people weren't allowed to gather like this in public. It felt as if the place we were visiting was changing in some intangible way just through the fact of these crowds, isolation ended, an expression of hope.

We drove to Aung San Suu Kyi's home, a white house nestled against a lake where she'd been imprisoned for nearly two decades. We parked the limousine in a driveway adjacent to her front veranda, where she stood waiting for us. She showed us into a small room filled with trinkets that she'd received over the years. A picture of Gandhi rested on the shelves alongside well-worn paperbacks. She had a striking face with deep, dark eyes, and black hair with streaks of gray and a flower in it. I sat in a chair along the wall, while Obama, Hillary, and Suu Kyi sat around a round table, each of them still icons in their own way.

We've made progress, but this is still a country with many problems, Suu Kyi said. *The young people have very high expectations, and of course we don't want to let them down.* She spoke at great length without interruption, winding around points, describing relatively obscure parliamentary maneuvers. Hillary had told us that she takes pride in being a politician now, and that was clear. Obama rested his cheek on his hand and listened. While offering support to the democratic opening, he asked her about the troubling situation facing the Rohingya people in Rakhine State, an ethnic minority that was confined in part to displaced persons camps. *This will be very difficult*, she said, referring to efforts to improve conditions there. *Of course we believe the human rights of all people in Burma must be respected.*

Later that day, Obama gave a speech at the University of Yangon. The university, once a center of opposition to the military junta, had seen scores of students beaten and killed in the protests that followed Suu Kyi's victory in the 1990 elections, which were annulled. The school had been shut down for many years and was being reopened for the speech. While Obama spoke, I roamed the corridors, examining the dilapidated building. Inside, the crowd, unaccustomed to watching political speeches, sat in silence until some tentative applause started to build at certain points toward the end, when Obama talked about the need for reconciliation. Obama also affirmed the dignity of the Rohingya, a name that was rarely spoken aloud in a country where a large majority of people denied that the Muslim ethnic group even existed.

Afterward, as the flight to Cambodia gained altitude, Obama came to see me. "That was worth doing," he said. He looked out the window. "It's interesting how the place feels frozen in time. It reminds me of what Jakarta looked like when I lived there. Now it's just high-rises. They'd be smart to preserve some of what makes this part of the world different."

Our time in Cambodia would be dominated by the Middle East. For the second time in the immediate aftermath of an Obama election, Israel was at war in Gaza, and we were working to secure a cease-fire. I had to pull Obama from a gala dinner in Phnom Penh so that he could talk to Mohamed Morsi, the recently elected Egyptian president. Morsi was the leader of the Muslim Brotherhood, which had close ties to Hamas. Obama was pressing him to use his influence to get Hamas to stop firing rockets into Israel, and Morsi was eager to show that he could deliver. Back at the hotel, before going to bed, Obama told us that we should wake him if Morsi wanted to talk again. The Situation Room called me after midnight to say that Morsi was asking to speak to Obama. Tom Donilon was asleep, so for the first time, I had to go into Obama's suite to wake him up. Wearing sweatpants and a T-shirt, he gave me a strong shove on the way to the phone, feigning anger. He sat there cradling the phone, taking notes and coaching Morsi through the assurances that were necessary from Hamas in order to get a cease-fire. When he hung up, he asked me to set up a meeting with Hillary first thing the next morning—he was going to send her to Israel and Egypt to conclude a cease-fire.

It was after two. I went to my room and lay in bed staring at the ceiling. I was entering a new role as one of the only constants in the second term, the kind of person who could wake him up to take a call from the Egyptian president. The trip to Burma represented the opportunity to make our own priorities, and yet, because of my communications responsibilities, I would always find myself pulled, as if by gravity, to crises. Could I really handle two or four more years of this storm chasing? I closed my eyes to find a little sleep but kept getting woken up by the whine of a mosquito flying in circles around me. I swatted at the air as the minutes turned into hours, drifting into and out of a fitful sleep, not remembering whether Morsi had called, whether I'd have to get up again to do something—what, I could not remember—until I woke at the first light of dawn to find the mosquito exploded in a pool of my own blood on the pillow next to me.

ON THE FLIGHT HOME, Obama was calling different aides up to the front of the plane to talk about what they wanted to do in a second term. Samantha, who would become ambassador to the

United Nations. Mike Froman, who would become U.S. trade representative. White House colleagues who were poised to become cabinet members. Obama was in his office, having changed into casual clothes, and asked me to sit next to him on the couch.

"So, have you thought at all about the second term?" he asked.

"Not really," I said.

"Is there anything else you want to do?"

"No," I said. "But I don't want to be miserable in the job I have." I didn't know if I was referring to the frustration with the lack of ambition in our policies, or the sense of fatigue at the mix of responsibilities—some large, some mundane—that I carried with me: planning the schedule, writing the speeches, briefing the press on the worst event happening in the world.

The white noise of the plane hummed in the background. "I feel like we're just too afraid of our own shadow sometimes," I said.

"We have to be." Referring to Donilon, he said, "Tom has to worry about a car bomb going off in Times Square or an ambassador getting killed."

I started to complain about the process. We weren't pressing an affirmative agenda, taking on issues like Cuba that I knew Obama wanted to get to. It began to feel as though I was complaining about Donilon and McDonough, which wasn't my point. "I'm tired of just being the guy who defends drones."

Obama read me quickly. "So, more Cuba, less killing," he said. "Look, I feel you. We've got four more years now. We've got a lot to get done. Why don't you think about a couple of projects you'd like to take on, issues where you can take the lead?"

"That sounds good," I said.

"We can keep talking about this. But I'd like you to stay where you are." He paused. "You're not just an advisor, you're a friend."

"Thanks," I said. I wasn't sure what to say. He started to talk about other staff changes that he was mulling, how to replace Favreau and a few other key people, and then he went back to the conference room to play cards. I returned to my seat and closed my eyes. Back when I worked for Lee Hamilton, one of his longtime staffers had warned me always to remember: In Washington, when you work for someone, you're staff, no matter how close you get to your boss. I had begun to drift asleep when a hand shook me awake—Obama had spoken to Morsi again and I'd have to brief the press at the back of the plane. Even friends, after all, are staff.

CHAPTER 16

YOUNG MEN WAGE WAR, OLD MEN MAKE PEACE

IN THE FALL OF 2012, A PROPOSAL MADE ITS WAY TO OBAMA recommending that he provide military support to the Syrian opposition. In the years that followed, this proposal would take on mythical status as a road not taken that could have led to a different outcome. The reality is that it was a small-scale recommendation to engage a portion of the opposition, providing them with a fraction of the support that Russia and Iran were providing to the Assad regime. David Petraeus, by that time the director of the CIA, pushed for it. He was also honest about what it was and wasn't: *This won't change the direction of the war,* he'd say; *it will allow us to build relationships with the opposition.*

I was ambivalent. Over the course of the fall, I'd fought a losing battle against those who wanted to designate part of the Syrian opposition—al Nusrah—as a terrorist organization. Al Nusrah was probably the strongest fighting force within the opposition, and while there were extremist elements in the group, it was also clear that the more moderate opposition was fighting side by side with al Nusrah. I argued that labeling al Nusrah as terrorists would alienate the same people we wanted to help, while giving al Nusrah less incentive to avoid extremist affiliations. It spoke to the schizophrenia in American foreign policy that we were simultaneously debating whether to designate the Syrian opposition as terrorists and whether to provide military support to the Syrian opposition. And it spoke to the hubris in American foreign policy to think that we could engineer the Syrian opposition whom we barely knew—and who were fighting for their lives—through terrorist designations and some modest military support.

I also argued that if we were going to intervene in Syria's civil war, we should do so with our own military. From Central America to Afghanistan, America didn't have a great track record with arming proxies. If we thought it was worth tipping the balance against Assad, we should be debating whether to strike his regime directly. I pressed this point in a few meetings in late 2012 and early 2013, but I was usually the only person doing so other than Jake and Samantha.

In one meeting early in the second term, Obama went around the room as he normally did when he wanted to test the status quo of his policies. Jake and I were sitting together on the back bench, and when it got to us, we made versions of the same argument. If things keep deteriorating, I said, we should "consider bombing Assad's runways" or we should "consider limited strikes against some regime infrastructure."

I spoke the words, but they felt hollow. Obama seemed to listen passively, not making eye contact, rubbing his forehead as I spoke. It was wrenching to read about the brutality of Assad every morning, to see images of family homes reduced to rubble. I felt we had to do *something* in Syria. I'd aligned myself, in 2011, with a bet on the people in the streets—from Tunis to Cairo, from Tripoli to Damascus. But by early 2013, I felt I was playing a part, the advocate for action, and couldn't muster the same passion that I had during the Libya debate. What difference would it make to bomb runways? That was a point I'd picked up from other advocates for action, but I couldn't answer the question Obama posed in response. "And what happens after we bomb the runways and Russia, Iran, and Assad rebuild them?" After the meeting, McDonough took to calling Jake and me Cheney and Rumsfeld.

———

ONE MORNING EARLY IN the second term, Obama sat in the Roosevelt Room to meet with a small group of journalists that I'd assembled. It is not unusual to invite a handful of columnists or commentators in to meet the president, usually off the record. This time, though, was different, as I invited a handful of people who weren't usually included in these sessions—people who spent most of their time reporting in the Middle East and who were largely sympathetic to the protesters who were pushing for change. Instead of aiming to influence them, I was hoping their stories could have some impact on Obama, pressing him to be more assertive in Syria and across the region.

One after another, they offered an unvarnished view of the chaos engulfing the region, and Syria in particular. The trends were not good—opposition movements were becoming more extremist, Iran was doubling down on its support for Assad in Syria, Gulf countries were funding groups in Syria and Libya that were more militant than the United States wanted. Most of them argued that the United States was failing to shape events, though I noticed that the most senior correspondent lacked any hope that events *could* be shaped. Obama listened intently, asking questions as much as he offered his own opinions. When the session was over, I followed him into the Oval Office, where I quickly realized that the session had had the opposite of the effect I intended— where I heard a call to action, Obama had heard a cautionary tale. How could the United States fix a part of the world that was that broken, and that decades of U.S. foreign policy had helped to break?

Sensing my unease, he asked me what I thought. "We're sixty percent pregnant across the region," I said, and ticked off a list of complaints that I'd been keeping in my head over the last year. "We're half in on Middle East peace, on Syria, on Egypt, on the pursuit of a nuclear agreement with Iran. We have to go big."

He asked me to follow him back to his private dining room, where we could continue the conversation while he ate lunch. There on the wall was a painting of Lincoln, deep in thought, consulting Grant at the height of the Civil War; a photo of Obama meeting Nelson Mandela; a pair of boxing gloves used by Muhammad Ali. Obama sat at the table while I remained standing. I worried that I was overstepping my bounds.

On Middle East peace, he told me, he had tried repeatedly, but Bibi wouldn't make a deal. On Syria, he kept asking for them, but there were no good options. "And on Iran," he said, "what do you want me to do? Give a speech offering to recognize their right to enrich [uranium]" in return for easing sanctions?

"It's not so much one thing," I said. "We just need to be more opportunistic, to go big when we can." I reminded him of the limo ride back from the Libya speech, when he'd said he wished he had the bandwidth to focus on the Arab Spring. "What would we do with that bandwidth?" I asked. "Sir," I continued, with unusual formality, "this is a seismic geopolitical shift and social movement. It's taking place up here"—I held my hand up by my head—"but our actions are down here." I lowered my hand to my waist.

"Maybe that's right," he said, "but we can't fool ourselves into thinking that we can fix the Middle East." He paused, chewing. "I love that you care this much. But what's the line from *Lawrence of Arabia*?" he said. It was a movie we frequently quoted to each other. "'Young men make wars. . . . Then old men make the peace.'"

DESPITE HIS MISGIVINGS, OBAMA decided that the first foreign trip of his second term would be to Israel and Jordan. Throughout his first term, we had waited to make our first visit to Israel, thinking that we would go when there was an opening in the peace process. Four years in, it was clear that an opening might never come. Obama had been criticized repeatedly throughout the election for not having visited Israel. Now, he decided, it was time to go.

I spent weeks preparing an itinerary, one that might encompass the full breadth of Israeli history—the Israel Museum, to demon-strate the historical Jewish connection to the land; Herzl's tomb, to pay tribute to Zionism; Yad Vashem, the Holocaust Museum; Rabin's grave, to honor Israel's martyred peacemaker; an exposition on entrepreneurship, to showcase Israel's burgeoning start-up cul-ture. I worked on the schedule with Israel's ambassador to the United States, Michael Oren, who had been a harsh critic of Obama but wanted the visit to go well and seemed reconciled to four more years of a Democratic White House. In multiple conversations, he encouraged me to have Obama visit a village of Ethiopian Jews. I demurred, a little put off by this persistent suggestion that Obama would want to see black Jews more than others.

In the receiving line in front of Air Force One, Bibi told Obama that he was familiar with me from "cables." Obama told him that my brother ran CBS News. "Ben has a proud Jewish mother," he said.

Bibi chose to focus on my connection to CBS, not Judaism. "Sounds incestuous," he said.

"Not if you watch CBS News," Obama replied.

For me, the trip was filled with conflicting emotions. Working on Obama's speech, I felt a bit like a bystander, aware of my own half heritage, neither full Jew nor non-Jew. Israel's history is in no way normal, and its security concerns are rooted in a history of anti-Semitism that continues to the current day. At the same time, I had to confront the intractability of the Palestinian predicament as I wrote the latest appeal for peace, knowing it would likely fall on deaf ears.

The morning of the speech, we flew by helicopter to Ramallah to meet with Mahmoud Abbas. I looked out at rolling hills and could see where Israeli settlements were splitting the West Bank in two. We were in the air for less than ten minutes, but the contrast could not have been starker: Israel from the air resembles southern Eu-rope; the settlements looked like subdivisions in the Nevada desert; the Palestinian towns looked shabby and choked off.

After a long meeting with Abbas, Obama met with a group of

young Palestinians in a small classroom. Each took turns speaking and had a wrenching story of occupation. I noticed one boy, about eighteen, who looked the most agitated throughout the meeting, staring at his hands while the others spoke. He was last to speak, and when his turn came he told similar stories of friends imprisoned, freedom of movement restricted. Finally, he built up to a line that he had clearly practiced. "Mr. President, we are treated the same way the black people were treated in your country. Here, in this century." He paused, and let a pregnant silence hang over the table. "Funded by your government, Mr. President."

Obama looked drained. He had no good answer for the kid, so he didn't bother faking it. He talked about how much promise they had, how he hoped young Palestinians could get a higher profile in the United States. He defended Israel, saying that the Jewish people had a right to be concerned about their security. He ended on the most optimistic note he could find—how young people gave him hope, how they reminded him of his own daughters, how Israeli mothers should be able to see them and hear their stories because they would understand. Often, when Obama was frustrated by governments, he'd talk about their people.

We took the helicopter back to Jerusalem and I sent the final draft of the speech to the teleprompter from my BlackBerry. Backstage at the convention center, he started talking about how tough the meeting had been.

"That last kid seemed like he got his courage up," I said.

"Yes," Obama said. "It took a lot of guts for him to do that." He told me a story that the former Palestinian prime minister Salman Fayad had told him, about how the Israelis parked a car in front of his office every few days and sat there, watching him. "It's not about security," Fayad had said. "It's about power."

"Well," I said, "that makes our theory more necessary: Show the Israelis you love them but also challenge them."

"That's your theory," he said. "The Ben Rhodes theory." Obama—who was often accused of putting too much stock in speeches—was more cynical than I about the capacity for a speech to change entrenched attitudes, particularly a conflict as intractable as the Israeli-Palestinian one.

I watched the speech backstage on the teleprompter. Obama paused for a moment, and I saw the text freeze. "I'm going off script here for a second," he said, "but before I came here I met with a group of young Palestinians from the age of fifteen to twenty-two. And talking to them, they weren't that different from my daughters. They weren't that different from your daughters or sons. I honestly believe that if any Israeli parent sat down with those kids, they'd say, I want these kids to succeed; I want them to prosper. I want them to have opportunities just like my kids do. I believe that's what Israeli parents would want for these kids if they had a chance to listen to them and talk to them. I believe that." His comments were met with rolling applause, and when he dived back into the prepared text it occurred to me that this tribute—this imploring of Israelis to see Palestinians as human beings no different from themselves— might be the most he would be able to do to keep a promise to those Palestinian kids.

That night, at a dinner hosted by Shimon Peres, I sat next to his daughter—an older woman who spoke accented English and could have fit in at the seders I went to as a kid. She recounted the story of how her family had hid throughout the Holocaust, the pride they felt upon reaching Israel, the imperative of bringing the nearly dead language of Hebrew back to life. It evoked in me a sense of pride at what Israelis had accomplished over the last seventy years, but it was also hard to reconcile that sense of history, generosity, and justice with those Palestinian kids. Obama's vision—so readily accepted by young people everywhere, including the young Israelis in the convention center—seemed to clash with the harder edges of politics, the world in which one side needs to win and another needs to lose.

THE HOPEFUL CHAPTER THAT began with the spread of the Arab Spring to Egypt in 2011 came to an end during a trip that we took to Africa in June 2013. In Tanzania, Obama called Mohamed Morsi from a secure room in his hotel, as protests against the Egyptian government were again building in the streets. This time, we had indications that the Egyptian military—backed by the Saudi and Emirati governments—was stoking the unrest, preparing the over-throw of the deeply flawed yet democratically elected government. They were also sponsoring an information campaign against the U.S. ambassador, Anne Patterson, casting her as an accomplice of the Muslim Brotherhood. It was a way to apply pressure on us, to demonstrate that this time they weren't going to yield in their in-tention to see the type of government they wanted in Cairo just because of America's views. In one of the more brazen acts that I'd experienced in my job, the Emirati ambassador to the United States, Yousef Al Otaiba—a man treated as a leading voice on the affairs of the region in the corridors of power in Washington—sent me a photo of a poster that cast Patterson in this light with no other message attached.

Morsi sounded tired but defiant as Obama spoke to him from the makeshift NSC office. Obama urged him to do something to reach out to his growing opposition, some gesture at a unity gov-ernment that could hold the country together. "You know," he said, "I just left South Africa, where Nelson Mandela is in the hospital and is very sick. You know when he came to power he could have gone to the white minority in South Africa and said, 'We are now the majority and we're going to do what we want. We'll follow the rules but you are a small minority in this country.' But he didn't do this. He went out of his way to reach out to the minority. He even put his former prison guard, the man who had been the warden of the prison where he had been held, in charge of the security ser-vices. It was those gestures that showed he was about bringing the country together and sending the message that in fact everyone is part of this thing. . . . You are not just the head of the Muslim Brotherhood, you are the president of Egypt. You need to listen to everyone, and your cabinet needs to be reflective of everyone, and the rules and the constitution include everyone."

Morsi kept reiterating his democratic legitimacy, the fact that he'd won an election. But he also grew reflective, a man who knew his time might be running out. *My background was in physics,* he told Obama, *but I also know Egypt very well.* In contrast to the un-democratic steps he'd taken to try to alter Egypt's constitution, Morsi said, *I'm doing my best to write history for a new Egypt that is really democratic, and what I want to see in my life is that power is transferred in elections to another candidate.*

A few days later, Morsi was toppled in a military takeover of the government and put into prison, where he remains to this day. A general, Abdel Fattah el-Sisi, took power, casting himself as a savior of Egypt from Islamists with the full backing of Saudi Arabia and the UAE—two U.S. allies that had actively subverted democracy and worked against U.S. policy. In Washington, a tortured debate ensued about whether to label what had been clearly a coup, a coup—which would entail restrictions on the type of assistance that we provide to the Egyptian government. In meetings, once again, I was in a small minority of people arguing on behalf of de-mocracy in Egypt, saying that we should label it a coup for the sake of our credibility; I lost the argument, and I didn't press the point. As with intervention in Syria, my heart wasn't entirely in it any-more. I could tell which way the argument was going to go, and which way events were going.

Obama was the most powerful man in the world, but that didn't mean he could control the forces at play in the Middle East. There was no Nelson Mandela who could lead a country to absolution for its sins and ours. Extremist forces were exploiting the Arab Spring. Reactionary forces—with deep reservoirs of political support in the United States—were intent on clinging to power. Bashar al-Assad was going to fight to the death, backed by his Russian and Iranian sponsors. Factions were going to fight it out in the streets of Libya. The Saudis and Emiratis were going to stamp out political dissent in Egypt before it could come to their kingdoms. A Likud prime minister was going to mouth words about peace while building settlements that made peace impossible. Meanwhile, innocent peo-ple were going to suffer, some of them were going to be killed, and there didn't seem to be anything I could do about it. Obama had reached that conclusion before I had. History had opened up a doorway in 2011 that, by the middle of 2013, had been slammed shut. There would be more war, more conflict, and more suffering, until—someday—old men would make peace.

PART THREE

CHANGE

2013–2014

CHAPTER 17

CLENCHED FISTS

———

AFTER MY CONVERSATION WITH OBAMA ON AIR FORCE ONE, I'd thought about the question he had posed: *Why don't you think about a couple of projects you'd like to take on?* I began to keep a file in my head of what I called the "affirmative agenda," issues where we could be doing more. Cuba. Colombia. Burma. Exchange programs. Development in Africa. Places where a little investment from the United States might make a positive difference. I told McDonough, who was poised to become chief of staff. Then we had a meeting with Obama before the inauguration where we went through a thick briefing that reviewed all of the things that we might do in a second term. Obama stopped on Cuba. "Let's see what we can do here," he said. "But we'll have to get Alan Gross out of prison."

Alan Gross was a sixty-three-year-old American USAID sub-contractor who had already spent three years in a Cuban prison. He was arrested in December 2009 while delivering satellite and com-munications equipment to Cuba's small Jewish community, and accused of spying. Before Gross's arrest, we had made some incre-mental changes in our Cuba policy, such as expanding the capacity for Cuban Americans to travel and send remittances to the island. The Cuban government had also initiated some reforms, including allowing for the emergence of a small private sector so that people could own their own shops, restaurants, and taxis. This created an opening for American travel and money to flow directly to Cubans, without getting caught in the net of the U.S. embargo. But Gross's unjust arrest made it impossible to press forward with further changes.

As the State Department pursued Gross's release, the Cubans insisted that he be exchanged for four Cubans imprisoned in the United States. These prisoners were part of the so-called Cuban Five—or Wasp Network—a ring of spies arrested after Cuba shot down two small airplanes that were dropping leaflets into Cuba in the 1990s, killing four people.

The only way to get Gross out of prison and set the stage for broader changes was through sustained diplomacy, but we had no formal diplomatic relations with Cuba. The U.S. Congress had a handful of well-placed hard-liners who were dead set against improving relations, including Cuban Americans Bob Menendez—the Democratic chairman of the Senate Foreign Relations Committee—and Republican Marco Rubio. Meanwhile, the Cubans did not trust the State Department, which had spent decades trying to isolate Cuba and channel assistance to opponents of the Cuban government. If we were going to talk, it was going to have to be done secretly.

I was largely a bystander on Cuba issues in the first term, but I had grown frustrated by the status quo. Every time we traveled to Latin America, our summits were dominated by complaints about our Cuba policy. There was zero evidence that our hard-line approach was doing anything to advance human rights. Obama himself told me repeatedly that he was unhappy with our Cuba policy and wanted to change it. U.S. interests, common sense, and honesty suggested this was something we should change. In Obama's first inaugural address, he had said, "To those who cling to power through corruption and deceit and the silencing of dissent, know that you are on the wrong side of history, but that we will extend a hand if you are willing to unclench your fist." I wanted to test whether we could make that connection with Cuba.

The lead staffer on Latin America at the White House was Ricardo Zuniga, a forty-two-year-old Foreign Service officer who was a leading Cuba expert in the government. Born in Honduras to a politically prominent family, he moved to the United States amid the upheaval that plagued Central America. After his father was murdered in Honduras in 1985, Ricardo's family stayed in the United States. He had served as the human rights officer in Havana from 2002 to 2004 and spent much of his time trying to meet with opponents of the Castro government. Later, he was on the Cuba Desk at State when Gross was arrested in 2009. Ricardo also found himself the consistent target of Cuban government propaganda, derided on state television and trailed by Cuban agents. Unbeknownst to me, he'd been developing a plan to pursue a secret channel with the Cuban government and shake up the status quo.

Shortly after the Situation Room meeting in which Obama signaled an interest in doing something on Cuba, McDonough asked me to go for a walk, which he often did when he wanted to have a conversation that touched upon something personal. His looming promotion to chief of staff felt as though it could open a bit of a chasm in our friendship. We'd known each other since 2002. He was my oldest friend in the White House. But soon he would be among the most powerful people in the country. In the future, when we'd go for walks, we'd be trailed by Secret Service agents.

The southwest gate of the White House clanged, and we started to walk around the ellipse that curves around the south side of the White House grounds, tourists snapping pictures of themselves with the long, sloping lawn in the background. He began to explain that he thought it would probably be too much for me to take on everything in my "affirmative agenda" file. Before I could say anything in response, he said, "Why don't you do Cuba?"

"I want to do Cuba," I said in response.

"No, I mean why don't you actually *do* Cuba," he said. "Someone is going to have to open up a channel with the Cubans and negotiate Alan Gross's release. Ricardo's been working up a plan, but we need someone senior to lead it."

"You mean do the negotiation myself?" I asked. I had just

thought about running some meetings on Cuba policy. "I haven't done anything like that."

"We're going to need someone close to the president to do this," he said.

I started to feel some nerves in my stomach. I couldn't say no, but it wasn't what I thought I'd be saying yes to, and I couldn't even envision what this would be—diplomacy with whom, when, where? "Okay," I said. "Yes."

"Great," he said. "You should mention it to POTUS next time you talk to him and then get with Ricardo."

McDonough had a style like this, a way of rewarding you while challenging you. Obama was doing the same thing with him—he was about to become chief of staff, the man in charge of the president's domestic policy agenda, and he'd held only national security jobs. *Why don't you do Cuba?* I didn't want to betray that I was nervous, that I might not know how to do this; the only thing I knew for sure about Cuba was that every effort to improve relations so far had failed.

My conversation with Obama was brief, and came in the context of his asking me if I'd figured out what my wish list for a second term was. "Denis talked to me about leading Cuba policy, and doing the negotiations," I said.

"I know," he said. "It's a good idea. Our man in Havana."

Over the next few weeks, I started to meet with Ricardo, who had a straightforward plan: We'd propose a dialogue with the Cubans on Alan Gross and counterterrorism. That way, if the effort leaked, no one could object. But our hope was that we'd get traction and gradually expand the dialogue to address deeper issues in the relationship. In May 2013, we sent a short message to the Cubans proposing a meeting. It was the first test of whether the Cubans wanted to pursue engagement, and we didn't know what we'd get in response. "Who shows up for them is what really matters," Ricardo said.

It wasn't a foregone conclusion that they'd respond favorably. For decades, the Cuban government had built its legitimacy in part on opposition to the United States—it was a guiding principle of Cuba's foreign policy, and a justification for cracking down on dissent at home. Improved relations with the United States would undercut that narrative. Advocates for engagement weren't subtle in arguing that more travel, more commerce, and more connections between the United States and Cuba would help the Cuban people while also catalyzing reforms on the island. It would also dramatically improve the standing of the United States in Latin America.

A few days after we sent the message, Ricardo came to see me—he liked to do everything in person. "We got a message back and it's serious," he said. Alejandro Castro, Raúl Castro's son, would lead the delegation, which agreed to meet with us in Canada. Up to that point, Alejandro had been a bit of a mystery in the United States. His titles were colonel and chair of something called the Cuban National Security and Defense Commission—a relatively new creation, modeled in part on the American NSC. By all accounts, he was playing a larger role in the Cuban system, but nobody knew exactly what that meant. Most analysts thought he was the most powerful man in Cuba after Raúl and Fidel. I could speak for Obama and there was no doubt that he would speak for his father.

THE CANADIANS HAD GRACIOUSLY agreed to host us, and when Ricardo and I landed in Ottawa we were met at the gate by a pudgy man who made sure we got through immigration with no problem and escorted us to a waiting van. We asked no questions and were driven through a sun-splashed June day into the surrounding countryside, with empty roads rolling through dense forest—the Canadians had taken our request for discretion seriously. In a flat Canadian accent, the driver peppered us with trivia about Ottawa and the vacationing habits of people in this region, as if we were visiting tourists, before driving through a gate and up a winding driveway to a house with a large wraparound porch, which looked out over a lake dotted with the occasional kayak or fisherman.

We were shown into a room with a long table that looked as if it could seat at least twenty people. I took my things out of a backpack—a spiral notebook, a binder with talking points that anticipated the several hours of discussion. I was anxious, tired from waking before dawn to make the flight, and nervous because I had no idea where this was leading. I sipped from a water bottle and waited there to begin the highest-level negotiations between the governments of the United States and Cuba in decades.

Alejandro breezed into the room, trailed by three other Cubans, and took my hand with both of his, greeting me like an old friend. He was a big man who spoke and laughed loudly. Befitting the sense of mystery that comes with all things Cuban, he had apparently lost vision in one eye in a training accident while serving in Angola. With slightly thinning hair and black wire-rimmed glasses, he looked more like an academic than a colonel; in fact, he'd spent the previous years publishing works of history, including screeds against American imperialism and full-throated defenses of the Cuban Revolution.

He introduced the rest of his party, but the other two men barely spoke. One of them was older, with a permanent frown, the look of a man who had done many things on behalf of the Cuban security services over the years. The other was younger, spoke good English, and seemed to have a boundless curiosity about us. The interpreter was an elegant older woman named Juana who conveyed an air of having seen everything. And she had: She'd been Fidel's translator for more than thirty years.

Alejandro began by saying that Cuba wanted this to be an open channel of communication. He gestured at the stoic older man sitting next to him who had participated in back-channel conversations with Americans in the 1990s, saying they'd learned from the past. He noted that Obama was respected in Cuba and in Latin America and emphasized that Raúl did not want to "damage Obama's political capital"; instead, he wanted to offer him "political space" to improve the relationship. I responded in kind, saying that we wanted to maintain the channel as well, and we hoped we could make progress on securing the release of Alan Gross, deepening counterterrorism cooperation, and improving the U.S.-Cuba relationship.

We had a somewhat forced discussion about terrorism—Cuba wasn't exactly an al Qaeda target, and Cuban security services weren't exactly lax. Then the history lesson began, as Alejandro offered a review of "U.S.-based terrorism" against Cuba. In a methodical tone—almost matter-of-fact, as if it was a common dinner table topic in Cuba—we heard a detailed review of the last sixty years: the Bay of Pigs invasion; the CIA's attempts to assassinate Fidel (more than six hundred, by their count); rumors of Cuban American complicity in the assassination of John F. Kennedy; how Luis Posada Carilles, Cuban-born and CIA-trained, had bombed a Cuban airplane, killing seventy-three people, and was now living freely in the United States ("He is Cuba's bin Laden"); Iran-Contra and Central American death squads; how Cuban exiles in the United States planned bombings in Cuba, and on and on.

I sat calmly listening to this recitation for well over an hour, gazing neutrally at Alejandro while he spoke in a Spanish that I barely understood, waiting for translation. I knew I could respond with a similar list of Cuban transgressions. Ricardo, who sat next to me silently, had warned that something like this was coming. I looked down at my talking points, which did not cover this expanse of history. I realized that my relative youth could be an advantage.

"I understand that this history is important to you," I said when he was finished. "But I wasn't even born when a lot of this happened." I folded my hands in front of me and looked at Alejandro while the words were translated. "President Obama wasn't even born when the Bay of Pigs invasion took place. He sent me here to look forward, and that's what I want to do." I talked about how we'd recently opened relations with Burma, how we'd worked to move beyond history in the Americas. "You mentioned Iran-Contra," I said. "President Obama just recently shared a dinner table with Danny Ortega [the Sandinista leader whom the U.S.-backed Contras had fought against]. So we can overcome the past, all of us, even if it's important to us."

During the lunch break, we broke from our roles. I went downstairs for a few minutes to gather my thoughts, and when I came back up, standing over a tray of sandwich wraps and sodas, Ricardo was talking about fishing in the waters off Cuba and the Florida Keys.

"It's sad," I said, "that Cuba is only ninety miles from Florida, yet so few Americans have been able to travel there."

"Jay-Z and Beyoncé just visited," Alejandro said.

"People-to-people exchange," I joked.

Alejandro laughed loudly, holding a sandwich in one hand. Then he turned serious. "The Cuban people," he said, "were very respectful of them. They admired how they carried themselves with dignity and humility."

"At least they were able to go," I said. "But it didn't make our lives easier in the White House."

"I am surprised," he said, "at how you treat us here with respect. We can tell that you are treating us as equals." We stood chewing our food, pondering this observation.

The rest of the day we circled around our agenda. There was the occasional tense moment—when they attacked our democracy programs, and when we defended the right of people in Cuba to protest. But just the fact that we sat there for six hours talking, back and forth, without descending into argument felt like an achievement. We'd accomplished our minimal objectives for the meeting— establishing a channel, building a relationship, agreeing that we would meet again in a few weeks.

At the airport, Ricardo and I settled in at the bar, which looked like just about every airport bar I've ever been to in my life, just two guys grabbing a couple of beers before catching a flight back to Dulles. Ricardo made careful notes about next steps, yet we both knew that the real achievement was the meeting itself. The right Cubans had shown up, and they seemed determined to build a relationship that could lead somewhere. Ricardo closed his notebook and settled into his beer. He was the kind of guy who seemed to indulge in any small privilege that life offered up—the song that comes on the radio; the view of a lake from the house where we'd met the Cubans; the memory of some fishing spot off the coast of Cuba. He'd spent nearly fifteen years working on Cuba, which meant he'd spent nearly fifteen years being frustrated.

"I think these guys are serious," he said as we stared at a television on mute. "This could be the real deal."

SOUTHEAST ASIA BECAME THE other region I took on, as it pulled together the different threads of what interested me the most in our foreign policy: the burden of history, and the wars in Vietnam, Cambodia, and Laos; the strategic importance of a region that was increasingly important to our position vis-à-vis China; an essential part of any effort to combat climate change; a sprawling place populated by people of different religions and ethnicities. A place of opportunity.

Burma was at the beginning of what was going to be a long and uncertain transition. Aung San Suu Kyi was now a member of parliament, leading her National League for Democracy (NLD), the largest opposition party to the military. Political prisoners who had spent decades in jail were being released. Generals were trying to reinvent themselves as politicians. Western corporations were debating whether to invest. Ethnic insurgencies continued to rage in the periphery. In Rakhine State, along Burma's border with Bangladesh, a Rohingya Muslim minority was persecuted by the Burmese military and a Buddhist majority.

In July, I set off to Burma for the first time without Obama. Our envoy there was Derek Mitchell, an expert on Asia and democracy who had helped design our Burma policy. He was, as far as I could tell, one of the busiest men in the country. "The Burmese are drowning in work," he told me as we drove into Naypyidaw, Burma's planned capital city, on an empty ten-lane highway. He explained that a main driver of reform was the success of other Southeast Asian countries: Burma's generals had gotten tired of traveling to places like Singapore and feeling left behind. Another was China: The corruption that came with living under Chinese influence was sparking a backlash among the people. Finally, there was Suu Kyi, an icon popular enough to hold together a potent opposition but struggling to adapt to life as a politician. "She's focused almost entirely on reforming the constitution," he said.

"So she can become president?" I asked.

"Yes, but she'd say also to end military rule." The military still operated without any civilian control and had a prescribed block of seats in the parliament.

"But if they're opening up, doesn't that ultimately lead to her being president?" I asked.

"Probably," he said. "Everyone knows that there's only one end to the story, but no one knows how to get there."

Over the course of the day, in giant government buildings, I would sit at the far end of rooms as large as football fields opposite a Burmese official. It seemed as if there were three types of public figures in Burma—dissidents turned politicians, who had no experience governing; military men who had turned into reformers but didn't know how to operate in a democracy; and hard-liners resisting change. The one meeting that was different was with the president's chief of staff, an older man named U Soe Thein. Instead of a ceremonial room, we met in his small, working office. His desk was piled with papers, and he greeted us as if taking a break from nonstop work. He spoke English, and every time I raised an issue he squinted and nodded, a slightly pained look on his face, as if to say *I know, but we can go only so fast.* "We have the citizenship action plan," he said about the Rohingya. "Already, we are granting citizenship cards for those who apply."

"But only if they don't identify themselves as Rohingya," Derek interjected. The Burmese denied that the Rohingya were a distinct ethnic group, referring to them as Bengalis—illegal immigrants from neighboring Bangladesh. For the next three and a half years, we'd have to constantly press the government, often working with other countries, to prevent the situation from spiraling out of control.

"The situation is very complicated," Soe Thein said. "We aren't going to change the views of the local Rakhine or the people in Burma. But we are moving forward." He lamented that he was so busy, saying that he'd prefer the life of a writer. He kept ticking off to-do lists, giving the appearance of doing everything at once.

Aung San Suu Kyi greeted me at the entrance of the parliament building and guided me to a corner of a room, where we sat on couches. She seemed different outside her Yangon home, where she had the air of an icon, sitting under her framed portrait of Gandhi. There, she was the hero who'd spent a huge chunk of her life sacrificing in principled opposition to autocracy, missing the death of her husband and the lives of her children who remained in England. Here, she was a politician, taking a break from parliamentary maneuvers. The only nod to her icon status was the characteristic flower in her hair.

I handed her a letter from Obama and said that he wanted me to check in with her. "Well, what is it you want to say?" she asked. She seemed curt, distracted. I expressed our support for Burma's transition to democracy, falling into the points that had been prepared for me. I encouraged her to support efforts to promote reconciliation with Burma's ethnic groups and better conditions for the Rohingya. "We will get to those things," she said. "But first must come constitutional reform. The military could change the constitution in a moment." Everything she said indicated that she cared mostly about the upcoming 2015 election, in which she was barred from seeking the presidency by a provision that disqualified people with foreign-born children—known informally as the Aung San Suu Kyi provision. "It won't be a free and fair election without constitutional reform."

Every time I returned to different issues, she kept turning the conversation back to the election and the constitution. "Of course we care about human rights," she said, "for all our people. But we cannot have human rights without democracy." She'd spent decades imprisoned and could now envision actually becoming president of the nation her father had founded before he was assassinated. *I'm so close,* her body language seemed to suggest.

THAT NIGHT, ON THE BALCONY of my hotel room in Yangon, I watched as feral dogs circled each other down below, darting through short bursts of traffic. Parking attendants, newly employed at this luxury hotel, shouted instructions at cars as they maneuvered through an undersized lot. I thought about the distance from the street scene to the cartoonish capital where decisions were made, and the even greater distances to places like Washington and Beijing that set the course for the wider world.

The next day, Derek arranged for me to see a sampling of the many different facets of Yangon society adapting to change. Former political prisoners ate sparingly at a luncheon and spoke with single-minded focus about their efforts to free the remaining prisoners. One writer told me in a matter-of-fact way that she had nearly died in prison because she shrank to under eighty pounds. Rohingya brought me large volumes of documentation proving that they had lived in Burma for generations, as if I were the one who would judge this fact. Rakhine Buddhists were unabashed in their bigotry, speaking of the "Bengalis" as illegal immigrants who needed to be deported. At the Myanmar Peace Center, we talked to a small group of men trying to negotiate a cease-fire with more than a dozen ethnic armed groups. I was surprised to see pamphlets that translated the Cairo speech into Burmese. I asked why the speech was of interest to people here. "The people admire Obama," one man said.

"We use this speech to teach them how to be tolerant of people from different religions."

At a roundtable with me, representatives from America's business community were full of complaints about doing business in a country with no experience of it. "I agreed to a contract at a ministry only to find that the terms had changed by the time I got home," one said. Derek told me about the government cronies who still control huge chunks of the economy. One of them offered a several-thousand-dollar bottle of wine at a dinner in his house, which is near a street where people beg for food. The people who were sanctioned by the United States seemed to be doing just fine; it was the rest of the country that was suffering.

Derek was determined to give me a feel for the city, and my last night there we walked out on darkened streets with few lights. We were joined by three young women—one Burmese, one American, one French—who led an NGO dedicated to preserving the old city. We walked into dilapidated buildings, smelling of urine with trash filling the hallways, wires hanging from the ceilings, squatters in the empty apartments. The women took out flashlights and pointed them down to the floors where, under layers of dust, you could see Art Deco tiles from the 1920s.

The tour ended at an old movie theater. We entered by walking across wooden doors that covered open sewage drains, then climbed a flight of musty stairs. A kitschy soap-opera-style Burmese film was playing on an enormous curved screen. A handful of people were sitting in the darkness. The women lit their flashlights to reveal an impossible glamour—balcony seats like an aged opera house, empty of human beings. It was like standing in some forgotten past. Then we headed outside, back across the wooden doorway, into an uncertain future.

Burma, in the minds of Americans like me, was a place where Aung San Suu Kyi suffered imprisonment to promote democracy— a recognizable concept, a commendable struggle. Years of U.S. sanctions had been put in place to support her struggle. But the actual country was a mystery that eluded easy understanding, with a cosmopolitan capital ready for change, a sprawling countryside where people's lives unfolded out of sight, and a violent periphery where the government held little writ. The only thing that united all of these elements was Suu Kyi herself, an icon of democracy, the daughter of the national hero, a politician who did not control the levers of power.

CHAPTER 18

RED LINE

———

On Wednesday, August 21, 2013, Ann and I were sitting on a flight waiting to take off when I saw a news story on my BlackBerry reporting a potentially catastrophic chemical weapons attack in Syria. The plane took off and I had several hours without Internet. We were going to spend a few days with Ann's family in Portland, Oregon, before heading down to Orange County to her mother's house. It was her sister's fiftieth birthday and the anniversary of her father's death. It was my first vacation in more than a year.

On the plane, I thought about the news. Chemical weapons had been a concern in Syria for the last year. In July 2012, we received reports that the regime was preparing to use them against the opposition or transfer them to the terrorist organization Hizbollah. Assad had huge stockpiles of sarin gas. There were concerns in Israel that any sarin passed to Hizbollah could be used against Israelis. As soon as we received those initial reports in July 2012, McDonough convened a task force that developed a plan to issue private warnings to Russia, Iran, and the Syrian government. We prepared some carefully worded language that Obama used in a speech to the Veterans of Foreign Wars on July 23, 2012: "Given the regime's stockpiles of chemical weapons, we will continue to make it clear to Assad and those around him that the world is watching, and that they will be held accountable by the international community and the United States should they make the tragic mistake of using those weapons."

At first, it seemed that the warnings worked. Weeks and months went by with no sign of chemical attacks. In August 2012, Obama was asked about what could lead him to use military force in Syria: "We have been very clear to the Assad regime," he said, "that a red line for us is we start seeing a whole bunch of chemical weapons moving around or being utilized. That would change my calculus."

In the course of a presidency, a U.S. president says millions of words in public. You never know which of those words end up cementing a certain impression. For Obama, one of those phrases would be "red line."

Late in 2012, we received reports of small-scale chemical weapons use. These reports were difficult to verify in a place as chaotic as Syria, where many horrifying weapons were being used against civilians, from tear gas to napalm to barrel bombs. The U.S. intelligence community was resistant to snap judgments, particularly after the experience of the inaccurate statements made about weapons of mass destruction in Iraq before the 2003 U.S. invasion. So it took a period of months before the intelligence community formally determined that the Assad regime had in fact used chemical weapons. When this assessment was released in April 2013, the question became what we were going to do about it. To show Assad and the world that there would be consequences, Obama decided to publicize a decision to provide military support to the Syrian opposition—the latest iteration of the plan that Petraeus had first presented in 2012.

It was an unsatisfying response, and there weren't any volunteers to announce the plan publicly. Almost by default, the responsibility fell to me. Even though I had misgivings about our Syria policy, I was glad that we were doing *something*. I had also internalized a certain ethos: If there was an issue that no one wanted to talk about publicly, I would do it. I thought it was a form of leadership, given my responsibility for communications across the government. I thought it was part of my job, as Obama deserved to have someone willing to defend him. I sensed, though, that it would cost me, allowing me to be blamed for decisions I didn't make but that others didn't want to defend.

And defend it I did: on conference calls, in televised briefings, and in long conversations with reporters. I fought with lawyers to get clearance to say that Obama had decided to provide "direct military support" to the Syrian opposition, as we were in the impossible position of not being able to discuss details about a key element of our policy. Legally, we couldn't say what the support was; all I could say were things like "This is going to be different—in both scope and scale—in terms of what we are providing to the opposition." I was giving partial answers about an incremental response and felt as though whatever stockpile of credibility I had built up over four years was being drawn down.

That summer had been thankless in so many other ways. It began with the spectacle of Edward Snowden releasing a devastating cache of classified information in June, fleeing to Hong Kong, and then somehow boarding a plane to Moscow even though he had no passport. There were weeks of drip-drip-drip revelations about U.S. surveillance, the same tactic that would shadow the run-up to our 2016 elections, involving the same people: Russia, Wikileaks. I had to spend my days explaining to our liberal base that Obama wasn't running a surveillance state because of the activities of the NSA, which we couldn't really talk about. Then came the Egypt coup, which we refused to call a coup. Instead of carrying out an affirmative agenda, I felt I spent my days in a defensive crouch.

As our August vacation began, I was wrestling with my own creeping suspicion that Obama was right—maybe we couldn't do much to direct events inside the Middle East; maybe U.S. military intervention in Syria would only make things worse. I wanted to get away from Washington, to stare at the ocean, to get reacquainted with my wife, to read a book. When our plane finally touched down in Portland, I had more than a hundred emails, some with harrowing accounts of how scores of people had been killed by clouds of gas on the outskirts of Damascus.

I HAD A SENSE of foreboding as Ann and I checked into our hotel. As we fell into the rhythm of a family vacation, I sensed Ann keeping a careful eye on how much I was looking at my BlackBerry, silently anticipating the inevitable encroachment of world events. At the same time, I could sense the frantic response building back in Washington through my in-box—invitations to meetings I wouldn't be attending, draft talking points I had to approve, news stories pressing Obama to respond, photos of lifeless children who had choked to death.

I was asked to find a way to attend a meeting that Obama was going to convene with his National Security Council. I drove to an FBI field office out by the airport and parked in an empty lot. A couple of guys who looked annoyed to be working on a weekend set up a secure video link for me so I could be patched in to the Situation Room. I listened as it was reported that there was a "high confidence assessment" that a sarin gas attack had killed more than a thousand people in a suburb of Damascus, and that the Assad regime was responsible. One after another, officials advised Obama to order a military strike. This included the chairman of the Joint Chiefs of Staff, Marty Dempsey, who had internalized the limits of U.S. military action in the Middle East. One time he surprised me in the hallway of the West Wing by recommending that I read Rachel Maddow's book, *Drift: The Unmooring of American Military Power*. Up to this point, he had argued that Syria was a slippery slope where there was little chance of success; now he said that something needed to be done even if we didn't know what would happen after we took action.

When the conversation got around to Obama, he asked about the UN investigators who were going to the scene of the attack to obtain samples. Could something be done to get them out? I thought the tone of the whole meeting suggested an imminent strike. The advisor who urged the most caution against military action was Denis McDonough, who raised questions about the legal basis for it and what would come next. What if we bombed Syria and Assad responded by using more of his chemical weapons? Would we put in ground troops to secure those stockpiles?

At the end of the meeting, Obama said he hadn't yet made a decision but wanted military options prepared. I walked outside and convened a conference call with the lead communicators for the government on national security. Pacing back and forth in an empty parking lot, I started to plan a public campaign to ramp up to a military intervention. John Kerry could make a statement that Monday making the case for action. The intelligence community would have to make its assessment public. DoD needed to prepare for an announcement of strikes. It felt energizing, as though we were finally going to *do something* to shape events in Syria.

I rejoined Ann and her family at a restaurant. I told her there was a chance I'd have to go back early. "Why can't someone else do this?" she asked. McDonough called me and said that I needed to get back as soon as I could. I knew that that would upset Ann; we had plans to visit her father's grave on the anniversary of his death. I asked McDonough if it was possible for Obama to call so he could talk to Ann—something he occasionally did for people who have grown weary of their spouse's work schedule. Instead, I got a short email from Obama telling me to come home as soon as possible.

Sitting in a crowded restaurant among my in-laws, I felt the loneliness of knowing that I'd have to do what the president of the United States was asking me to do, and that on the scale of what was going wrong in the world, my own inconvenience—however dramatic in the context of my family—was not going to be anyone else's concern. I waited a couple of hours before telling Ann, trying to preserve for a little while longer the illusion of normalcy. I flew back to Washington the next morning.

———

As we sat outside the Oval Office waiting for the morning briefing with Obama, the director of national intelligence—Jim Clapper—looked agitated. A Vietnam veteran, former Air Force lieutenant general, and longtime intelligence professional, Clapper was an avuncular older guy with a bald head. He spoke in clipped sentences and had an easy rapport with Obama, who liked to needle him for always dropping paper clips on the rug in the Oval Office. Clapper never put spin on the ball; he told you what he knew and what he didn't know. I respected him as much as anyone in government.

Speaking to me and Susan, who had recently become national security advisor, Clapper said that it wasn't yet a "slam dunk" case that Assad had authorized the chemical weapons attack. The assessment would firm up over time, as samples were gathered and information analyzed. The choice of words was striking—"slam dunk" was the exact phrase that George Tenet, then director of the CIA, had used to assure George W. Bush that Saddam Hussein had weapons of mass destruction. Clapper seemed to be signaling that he wasn't going to put the intelligence community in the position of building another case for another war in the Middle East that could go wrong.

When we entered the Oval Office, we took our usual seats— Obama in his armchair opposite Biden; Clapper at the end of one couch, opposite Rice; Lisa Monaco, Obama's counterterrorism advisor, and Tony Blinken, Rice's deputy, in the other seats on the couches; and Jake Sullivan, now Biden's national security advisor, in a chair next to me, filling out a semicircle. I always took this seat because I liked to face Obama, which made it easy to make eye contact. Obama could signal a lot with his eyes.

Clapper always opened with a summary of key intelligence. On this morning, he indicated that all signs pointed to Assad's ordering a catastrophic sarin attack, but then he paused and repeated his line that the case was not yet a "slam dunk," using air quotes for emphasis. His words hung in the air. Obama made eye contact with me, and I could tell we were both thinking the same thing: This will find its way into the press.

"Jim," Obama said, "no one asked you if it was a slam dunk."

I felt the burden on Obama. He had to respond to this awful event in Syria while bearing the additional weight of the war in Iraq—which caused his own intelligence community to be cautious, his military to be wary of a slippery slope, his closest allies to distrust U.S.-led military adventures in the Middle East, the press to be more skeptical of presidential statements, the public to oppose U.S. wars overseas, and Congress to see matters of war and peace as political issues to be exploited. Later that day, in a Principals Committee meeting, Clapper repeated the slam-dunk formulation. Sure enough, later that week it leaked.

In that same Principals Committee meeting, Clapper said that the intelligence community would not prepare an assessment for public release. Instead, he suggested they share all of their information and judgments with me and I could write a U.S. government assessment, which they would review for accuracy and sign-off. It took me a moment to understand what he was suggesting. In all my time at the White House, I had never written that kind of assessment, and never would again. These were usually technical documents produced by teams of people in the intelligence agencies.

After the meeting, I called Jake Sullivan and Bernadette Meehan into my office. Meehan was a thirty-seven-year-old Foreign Service officer who worked for me. Twice she had nearly been killed during overseas tours. In Colombia, a group of men had kidnapped her and thrown her into the trunk of a car; after driving for some time, they stopped and tossed her out on the side of the highway. A few years later, posted in Baghdad, she was badly wounded by a rocket fired by an Iran-backed militia. Still she kept at it. She spoke Arabic and loved the Middle East.

"He really asked *you* to write it?" she asked me.

"That's what he said. Ask Jake."

She looked over and he nodded, having been in the meeting.

"Are you going to do it?" she asked.

"What choice do I have?" I understood that Clapper was protecting the intelligence community from a repeat of the role it
played before the war in Iraq. But this was different. Our intelligence community had a high-confidence assessment that a weapon
of mass destruction had been *used* by the Assad regime. The evidence was running in a loop on our television screens.

We worked out a plan whereby each of us would write a different piece of what would be a "U.S. government assessment" instead
of an "intelligence assessment." We were given stacks of intelligence
reports about what had happened, as well as volumes of publicly
available information. I sat at my computer and typed out the first
sentence: "The United States Government assesses with high confidence that the Syrian government carried out a chemical weapons
attack in the Damascus suburbs on August 21, 2013." For the next
two days, I sat at my desk poring over the information and turning
it into a short, stark, and simple analysis. I watched publicly available videos of people lying disoriented on the floors of hospitals,
looked at pictures of dead children. I felt waves of anxiety, anticipating how I might be hauled before Congress if things went ter-
ribly wrong after a military intervention. I was responsible for
writing the public document that would justify the United States'
going to war in Syria.

Obama remained focused on the United Nations inspection
team that was on the ground in Syria. That afternoon, he called Ban
Ki-moon, the UN secretary general, and urged him to pull them
out. Ban refused, saying that the team had to finish their work. "I
cannot overstate the importance of not remaining in Syria for a
lengthy time," Obama said. Ban replied that it could take a few
days. Obama pressed again, saying they should be out by the following night. To this day, I wonder if Obama would have launched
a strike early that week if the UN team hadn't been in the way.

Obama's next call was to Angela Merkel. There was no foreign
leader he admired more. Like him, she was a pragmatist, driven by
facts, dedicated to international order, deliberate in her decision

making. She had emerged as the dominant leader in Europe, working closely with Obama to respond to the global economic crisis and the instability in the Eurozone that followed. I'd seen them sit together, sometimes for hours, with notepads in front of them, designing strategies that could keep the global economy crawling forward, or hold Afghanistan together. Now I sat in the Oval Office listening to Obama ask for her support for military action. Even if Germany didn't participate, the United Kingdom and France had indicated that they would. But her public support would show that the United States and Europe were united, and could help bring along the rest of the European Union. Merkel argued that the UN team should have the time to prepare and submit its report, at which point we should pursue a Security Council resolution authorizing action. If the Russians blocked us, then at least we would have tried. This would take several weeks. Obama knew a delay of that length would tie his hands, especially because there wasn't much public support for war in the United States. As the fresh horror of Assad's attack faded, the opposition to a U.S. strike would build. With any additional time, Assad could also put innocent civilians around potential targets as human shields.

I sat on the couch watching him make this case, waiting for Merkel's words in response. *I don't want you to get into a situation where you are left on a limb,* she said. Obama listened intently as he cradled the phone against his ear while the rest of us listened on speaker. She said she wanted to use the time to build agreement among the European countries. *Then,* she said, *we have a situation where you are not exposed to vague allegations. This is what I say as a friend.*

After he hung up the phone, he came over to where we were sitting. It was the first time I saw him look uneasy about acting in Syria. He asked our opinion on the timing for military action. I plunged into the case I'd been making in meetings—that only action by us would change the emerging dynamic, that the biggest concern in the United States and Europe was that we were going to have another Iraq War. Only by acting in a limited way, with air strikes that were over after a period of days, could we demonstrate that we weren't beginning an all-out war. He listened, but I knew he was skeptical that we could contain military action once we'd begun.

Just as things were stalling in Europe, congressional opposition to strikes was building at home. On Wednesday, a large group of Republican members of Congress wrote Obama a letter that threatened him bluntly: "Engaging our military in Syria when no direct threat to the United States exists and without prior congressional authorization would violate the separation of powers that is clearly delineated in the Constitution."

This was followed by a letter from the Speaker of the House, John Boehner. "Even as the United States grapples with the alarming scale of the human suffering," it read, "we are immediately confronted with contemplating the potential scenarios our response might trigger or accelerate. These considerations include the Assad regime potentially losing command and control of its stock of chemical weapons or terrorist organizations—especially those tied to al Qaeda—gaining greater control of and maintaining territory." He listed fourteen detailed questions about various scenarios that could take place in Syria and demanded responses to each of those questions.

Boehner also focused on the need for congressional authorization: "It is essential you address on what basis any use of force would be legally justified and how the justification comports with the exclusive authority of congressional authorization under Article I of the Constitution."

After deriding Obama's response to Syria as weak, Republicans were now making the same warnings about action that we had used to publicly defend our inaction in the past. In doing so, they were signaling that Obama would be held accountable if these scenarios were realized, while seeking impossible guarantees that they wouldn't be. More ominously, a message was being delivered: Acting without going to Congress would be unconstitutional.

Our lawyers also had concerns. There was no firm international legal basis for bombing Syria—no argument of self-defense, which justified our actions against al Qaeda; no UN resolution such as we had had in Libya. Nor was there any domestic legal basis beyond the assertion that the president had the inherent power to take military action that did not constitute a "war" under the Constitution, which the Republicans were disputing. Some argued that the Republicans could even try to impeach Obama if he acted without congressional authorization—hardly a wild thought, given their posture toward Obama.

On Thursday afternoon, Denis convened the national security team for a call with congressional leaders. One after the other, nearly all expressed some degree of support for strikes but demanded that Obama seek authorization. Some were quoting a candidate questionnaire that Obama had filled out for *The Boston Globe* in 2007, in which he had said, "The president does not have power under the Constitution to unilaterally authorize a military attack in a situation that does not involve stopping an actual or imminent threat to the nation"—an argument that had also been mounted against Obama after we intervened in Libya.

I sat listening to all this, exhausted from staying up late the last two nights working on the assessment, getting angrier and angrier. It felt as if I was trapped within a system fueled by hypocrisy and opportunism. For eight years, Republicans had defended Bush's ability to do whatever he pleased as commander in chief; now they were suddenly devoted to constitutional limits on the commander in chief? I was used to the relentless style of politics from Obama's opponents—the effort to find any piece of information that could embarrass him, put him on the defensive, wound him politically. But I'd spent two days reading detailed descriptions of people being gassed to death, watching video of children with vacant eyes lying on the floor of a makeshift hospital. Faced with this harsh reality, Congress was focused on creating a political trap.

During the meeting, we got word that the British Parliament had voted 285–272 against joining U.S.-led strikes on Syria after a debate filled with demands that the United Kingdom not follow the United States down the path to war as Tony Blair had followed

George W. Bush. A shell-shocked David Cameron called Obama to apologize, explaining that he could no longer offer his support. When I got back to my desk, I had distraught emails from Cameron's aides in which they worried about the damage to Britain's role in the world. The hangover from the Iraq War had left us staggering toward military intervention with next to no international support, and a Congress demanding that we go through the same divisive process of seeking authorization that had just failed in London.

On Friday morning, I sat at my desk rereading the assessment, which I had reread more times than I could remember. I had checked every word with the deputy director of national intelligence, Robert Cardillo, who stepped up to help us out—getting information declassified, editing the document, giving us maps to release, and offering to join the press briefing I would give when it was released. That morning, we released "The United States Government Assessment of the Syrian Government's Use of Chemical Weapons on August 21, 2013." Shortly after, Kerry delivered his final case against Assad at the State Department. "My friends," he thundered, "it matters here if nothing is done. It matters if the world speaks out in condemnation and then nothing happens."

We had a final National Security Council meeting that morning. Kerry suggested that we wait another week to bring other countries into a coalition. I argued that we had to act as soon as possible—time was not our friend, and our military action was likely to change the public dynamic. Obama, who seemed increasingly focused on the factors aligning against us, pressed for the domestic and international legal basis that we could cite for taking action. In short, there was no good answer, other than to point back to when NATO had acted without an international mandate in Kosovo. Still, throughout the day, the drama of Kerry's speech and the horrific details in the public assessment seemed to tilt things back in the direction of action. It felt as if all of the week's setbacks and preemptive criticisms were part of an unfolding drama that would inevitably conclude in cruise missiles hitting Syria.

Later that afternoon, I went to a meeting in Denis's office where all the participants were slated to review their role in the event of a strike. We were discussing whether Obama had to address the nation in prime time as soon as the bombing began. Denis, the sole voice against military action, got a note at the beginning of the meeting that Obama wanted to see him; he left and never returned. An hour later, I was back in the Situation Room when I got a note asking me to come to the Oval Office.

I went upstairs and walked into Obama's office. He was alone and looked more relaxed than he had all week. Gone was the grave look that had been frozen on his face. He was looser, standing up from behind his desk and directing me to sit down on the couch.

"I've got a big idea," he said.

"Well," I replied, "you're the big idea guy." Sometimes, the more intense the moment, the more casual I would be with Obama in my comments.

A handful of aides trickled in. Obama laid out his thinking: He had decided to seek congressional authorization for strikes on Syria. At some point, he said, a president alone couldn't keep the United States on a perpetual war footing, moving from one Middle Eastern conflict to the next. In the decade since 9/11, we'd gone to war in Afghanistan, Iraq, Yemen, Somalia, and Libya. Now there was a demand that we go into Syria; next it would be Iran. "It is too easy for a president to go to war," he said. "That quote from me in 2007—I agree with that guy. That's who I am. And sometimes the least obvious thing to do is the right thing." If he attacked Syria without congressional authorization, the Republicans would come after him, and it would be impossible to sustain any military engagement in Syria. If we got congressional authorization for an attack on Syria, everyone would be in on the action, and we'd have more credibility—legally, politically, and internationally. If we couldn't, we shouldn't act.

I sat slouched over on the couch across from him. I couldn't argue with anything he was saying, even though everything I'd been doing for the last few days—and everything I'd been arguing for for the last two years—had been building up to a cruise missile strike on Syria the following day. It was as if Obama was finally forcing me to let go of a part of who I was—the person who looked at Syria and felt that we had to *do something*, who had spent two years searching for hope amid the chaos engulfing the Arab world and the political dysfunction at home.

Obama had not put forward more than one option—it was clear that his mind was made up. Still, as always, he went around the room. One after the other, people voiced agreement with his direction. The only exception was Susan Rice. "We needed to hold Assad accountable," she said. "Congress is never going to give you this authority," she said—the only person to offer that prediction. "It gives away too much of your power as commander in chief." In the years to come, when nearly everyone involved in this drama decided to absolve themselves by saying that Obama should have bombed Assad without going to Congress, Susan never did.

When it was my turn, I found myself almost speaking my thought process out loud. I told Obama I agreed with him. The downside of getting congressional authorization was, ironically, that we'd then have even more ownership over Syria; we'd be raising expectations around the world about what we were prepared to do and what we could achieve. But then I conceded that we had to, at some point, show that we meant what we said about not being on a permanent war footing. "We keep saying that," I said, "and I guess we have to show that we mean what we say." Speaking from my experience defending national security actions that we couldn't talk about—from drone strikes to supporting the Syrian opposition—I said I thought it was time to make decisions in the open.

Then I gave voice to the building frustrations I'd been feeling, the sense of being trapped in systems that don't work. "In this Syria debate," I said, "we've seen a convergence of two dysfunctions in our foreign policy—Congress and the international community. They both press for action but want to avoid any share of the responsibility." All week, I had been thinking the answer to that problem was to go ahead and do something; now I saw Obama's reasoning for

Ann and me on election night in Chicago, 2008. My OBAMA STAFF T-shirt shows through my sweater.
(PHOTO BY SAMANTHA POWER)

Obama and Reggie Love taking a private tour of the Pyramids in Giza shortly after the Cairo speech, June 4, 2009.

With fellow speechwriters Jon Favreau and Cody Keenan and communications director Dan Pfeiffer on the Truman Balcony after the Affordable Care Act passed Congress, March 21, 2010. (PHOTO BY CODY KEENAN)

The spot in Hawaii where Obama's mother used to come and sit when she was pregnant. He attributed his calm demeanor in part to this place.

With campaign spokeswoman Jen Psaki in Iowa on the eve of Election Day 2012. Jen and I joined the Obama team at the same time in 2007.

Crowds lining our motorcade route during Obama's first visit to Burma, November 19, 2012.

The Beast—the heavily armored presidential limousine—parked outside the Church of the Holy Sepulchre in Jerusalem.

Ann holds up six-day-old Ella, our first child, while Obama announces the Cuba opening on December 17, 2014.

(PHOTO BY ANN NORRIS)

Obama and Pope Francis, who had played an indispensable role in our secret negotiations with Cuba.

Obama and Anthony Bourdain during our trip to Hanoi, filming an episode of *Parts Unknown.*

With Japanese prime minister Shinzo Abe looking on, Obama greets a survivor of the atomic bomb in Hiroshima after his speech on May 27, 2016.

Meeting with victims of unexploded U.S. ordnance in Laos, the most heavily bombed country in history—one of the toughest meetings I had in eight years.

(PHOTO BY RUMANA AHMED)

The view from the dais at Fidel Castro's funeral in Havana, with the image of Che hovering over us in the distance.

An example of the hate messages I received constantly on social media.

President Obama holds a newborn Chloe while Ella looks on. (PHOTO BY PETE SOUZA)

With Ricardo Zuniga and Bernadette Meehan, the two Foreign Service officers who carried me through the second term, playing instrumental roles in our dealings with Cuba and Iran.
(PHOTO BY SUZY GEORGE)

With Alejandro Castro, my negotiating counterpart, in Ernest Hemingway's house in Havana.
(PHOTO BY RUMANA AHMED)

On the last night of his presidency, Obama showed me an original copy of the Gettysburg Address in Lincoln's handwriting, which was displayed in the White House residence.

THE GETTYSBURG ADDRESS

President Abraham Lincoln delivered this address on November 19, 1863 at the dedication of the Gettysburg National Cemetery. In March 1864 he prepared this fifth and final copy, the only one to be titled, signed and dated for reproduction for a war charity.

BEQUEST OF OSCAR B. CINTAS
1959

My office in the West Wing from 2011 to 2016. The space wasn't great, but the real estate was good.

On the morning Donald Trump was inaugurated, White House staff cleaned out the Oval Office. On my final walk-through, I spotted Obama's couch and rug (embroidered with Martin Luther King's "arc of the moral universe" quote) sitting on the walkway outside the Oval Office.

The view from the plane: the Obamas preparing to take their final flight on Air Force One after Trump's inauguration, bound for a vacation in Palm Springs. When I asked Obama what he intended to do the next morning, now that he was no longer president, he said, "Sleep in."

why that wouldn't work. "At some point, we have to address that dysfunction head-on."

The meeting ended with Obama saying he would call each member of the national security cabinet that night and let them know his decision. The next morning, he would make a statement in the Rose Garden. The only caveat was the insistence by Susan and Obama's lawyers that we reserve the right to take action even if Congress didn't approve strikes—a point that made sense, in terms of preserving flexibility, but which undercut the moral, ethical, and legal clarity of the stance Obama was taking. Obama called a couple of foreign leaders, including Netanyahu. *Your decision was right,* he said, *and history will be kinder than public opinion.*

OVER THE NEXT FEW days, we pivoted to seeking congressional support. In a meeting in the Cabinet Room between Obama and congressional leaders, Boehner pledged his support but said he would do nothing to help Obama get votes from within the Republican caucus. McConnell, who would end up criticizing Obama for not launching a strike, refused to offer his support. "Real profiles in courage," Obama said to us afterward.

Foreign policy luminaries endorsed authorization; Clinton announced her support; AIPAC lobbied in support of our position; so did the Saudi government—but none of it mattered. No wave of support materialized in Congress or in public polls. One after another, members of Congress in both parties—including people who had demanded that we take action in Syria—announced that they would vote against authorizing it.

On Thursday, we flew to Russia, where the G20 was being held at a lavish Tsarist palace on the outskirts of Saint Petersburg. Putin, recently returned to the presidency, had spared no expense in his preparations. Enormous gardens had been meticulously restored and guesthouses set aside for each of the leaders. As we wandered the grounds, updates continued to pour in from Washington. A resolution authorizing the use of force had limped out of the Senate

Foreign Relations Committee but looked increasingly uncertain; the picture in the House was worse. Denis was quarterbacking a frantic communications and legislative operation despite a creeping sense of inevitable failure in Congress.

Up to that point, I had generally avoided doing television interviews. The thought of them made me nervous, and I didn't want to enlarge the target on my back by diving into the cable news scrum. But Denis was insisting that everyone get out there, so I trudged what seemed like more than a mile through nineteenth-century gardens, along a lake with a floating bar filled with drinking Russians and journalists, across a field, and up a staircase where an enormous black scaffoldlike structure provided places for different international networks to hold interviews. I stood there in the slight chill of dusk, an earpiece playing questions in my ear, a microphone attached to my lapel, and dutifully answered questions—a disembodied head explaining why we needed to go into Syria.

The next morning, I had to get up at five to catch a van back to the palace where the summit was taking place. I was dropped off at the villa where Obama was staying, which looked like a newly built and neatly appointed condominium that you might find alongside a golf course in Arizona. We still had a couple of hours until the meetings began, and I was told Obama was working out. I was rummaging through the fridge looking for a soda or something to eat when Obama popped his head in and asked me to join him in the other room.

He sat at a table, wearing a gray T-shirt and black sweatpants. The television was playing the opening night game of the NFL season, a reminder of the time difference and just how far we were from home. The Broncos were running away with it. The game was on mute, and I started to update him on how support was slipping away, how even hawks on Syria—people like Marco Rubio—were tying themselves in knots to justify opposing authorization. "Maybe they just want to oppose you," I said. "Or maybe no one wants to be on the record in support of another war." I left unspoken the fact that the war could take a bad turn—like Afghanistan, Iraq, and Libya.

"Maybe we never would have done Rwanda," Obama said. The comment was jarring. Obama had written about how we should have intervened in Rwanda, and people like me had been deeply influenced by that inaction. But he also frequently pointed out that the people urging intervention in Syria had been silent when millions of people were killed in the Democratic Republic of Congo. "There's no way there would have been any appetite for that in Congress."

"You could have done things short of war," I said.

"Like what?"

"Like jamming the radio signals they were using to incite people."

He waved his hand at me dismissively. "That's wishful thinking. You can't stop people from killing each other like that." He let the thought hang in the air. "I'm just saying, maybe there's never a time when the American people are going to support this kind of thing. In Libya, everything went right—we saved thousands of lives, we didn't have a single casualty, and we took out a dictator who killed hundreds of Americans. And at home, it was a negative."

His eyes shifted to the football game, a slow-motion replay of a Broncos player making a move. I saw what he had been doing—testing Congress, testing public opinion, to see what the real maneuvering room was for his office when it came to intervention in Syria. It was the same thing he'd done in Situation Room meetings on Syria and in his mind, testing whether anything we did could make things better there or whether it would turn out to be like Afghanistan and Iraq, if not worse. It wasn't just politics he was wrestling with. It was something more fundamental about America, our willingness to take on another war, a war whose primary justification would be humanitarian, a war likely to end badly. "People always say never again," he said. "But they never want to do anything."

At that point, Susan Rice walked in, and the conversation shifted to the events of the day as a breakfast of bacon and eggs was served. Susan and I would spend all day trying to get a group of allies to issue a statement endorsing our position on Syria. It wasn't easy. The Germans preferred to wait for an upcoming European Union meeting. The Saudis, who had spent so much time telling whoever would listen that Obama was weak on Syria, tried to avoid us—Obama finally had to intercept the leader of their delegation in a parking lot to lock in his support. "I wasn't going to let him leave," he told us later, "without looking me in the eye."

On the flight home, Obama mentioned that he'd had a private conversation with Putin on the margins of the summit. For years, Obama had proposed that the United States and Russia work together to address the threat from Syria's chemical weapons stockpile; for years, Russia had resisted. This time, Obama again suggested working together to remove and destroy Syria's chemical weapons. Putin agreed and suggested that John Kerry follow up with his Russian counterpart.

After we landed in Washington, Obama talked about the different ways in which the debate could play out. "The thing is," he said, "if we lose this vote, it will drive a stake through the heart of neoconservatism—everyone will see they have no votes." I realized then that he was comfortable with either outcome. If we won authorization, he'd be in a strong position to act in Syria. If we didn't, then we would potentially end the cycle of American wars of regime change in the Middle East.

Kerry worked quickly to turn Putin's overture into an agreement that could be implemented in a country—Syria—that had never even acknowledged having chemical weapons. Four days after we got back to Washington, the Syrian government announced they would give them up. Five days later, on September 10, Obama addressed the nation and announced that we would pursue this diplomatic opportunity. The congressional vote never took place. Thousands of tons of chemical weapons would be removed from Syria and destroyed, far more than could have been destroyed through military action. The war would continue. Barack Obama would continue to keep the United States out of it.

CHAPTER 19

BECOMING A
RIGHT-WING VILLAIN

T HE MORE COMFORTABLE I BECAME WORKING IN THE WHITE House, the more uncomfortable I became with the way the world looked at me from outside of it.

Over time, the White House complex becomes familiar, just the place where you happen to work. The recognition of the building appearing in the distance, the tourists taking selfies in front of the gate, the bomb-sniffing dogs that greet your car when you drive in—it all becomes the backdrop to your life, the setting where you attend daily meetings and have hallway conversations about sports and television shows. A bust of Abraham Lincoln sits outside the men's restroom. A panel of drawings by Norman Rockwell in the West Wing lobby depicts what it was like to wait in that very spot to see Franklin Roosevelt. You find the smoking area next to the place where a wall is still discolored from when the British tried to burn the place down during the War of 1812.

But it can also be a dangerous place to work. During my first year in the job, I was hanging out in my friend Alyssa Mastromonaco's office when Pete Rouse walked in—a senior advisor to Obama who had been such an institution on Capitol Hill that he was referred to as the 101st senator. He asked us if we had federal liability insurance. I didn't even know what that was or why I'd need it. "Look it up," he said. "This is not optional." I did what I was told and ended up spending a couple hundred dollars a year to cover legal expenses that might come from investigations. This ended up saving me around $100,000.

My initiation into the ritual of being investigated began in the spring of 2012, when two national security leaks to the press took place within a matter of days. David Sanger of *The New York Times* published a book that included details about an alleged cyber-weapon that had sabotaged parts of the Iranian nuclear program, and the Associated Press reported that the United States had a source inside the al Qaeda affiliate in Yemen who helped thwart a terrorist attack. Leaks aren't all that unusual. These two were different because they were detailed and took place in the spring of a presidential election year. Republicans demanded investigations. "They're intentionally leaking information to enhance President Obama's image as a tough guy for the election," John McCain declared. "That is unconscionable!" Attorney General Eric Holder assigned U.S. attorneys to investigate.

Anyone who works in national security communications hates leaks because, inevitably, you have to respond to information that you aren't allowed to discuss publicly. Given that part of my job involved talking to the press about national security, I was on the list of people who would be ensnared in both investigations. That fall, I received a subpoena and ended up having a couple of lengthy sessions with the FBI and the U.S. attorney from Maryland, Rod Rosenstein. I had to leave work at an appointed time, enter the FBI building in downtown Washington, and sit in a Spartan conference room for hours explaining emails and conversations that I'd had. I was told not to talk to my colleagues about this experience; I suspected, and later learned, that my friend Tommy Vietor—who sat right outside my office—was going through the same thing. To cement the absurdity of our situation, Tommy and I also had to answer angry criticisms from journalists and progressives who felt that our administration was too eager to pursue leak investigations.

Over the course of 2012, I also saw my name pop up with increasing frequency in right-wing media, cast as Obama's political hack on the NSC. Early in the administration, I'd become a target for occasional right-wing ridicule for a few reasons: (1) I worked for Barack Obama; (2) I wrote the Cairo speech; (3) I received a master's degree in fiction writing from New York University when I was twenty-four years old. The MFA alone was enough to make me a minor villain: "Ben Rhodes, Obama's Failed Fiction Writer . . ." One time, in 2009, I was surprised to find a colleague of mine—a kind, soft-spoken young woman named Cindy Chang—sobbing at her desk because she was so upset by one of these pieces. "How can they say these things about you?" she cried. I told her not to worry, I was proud of my enemies. Then I went into my office, closed the door, and felt a fluttering in my stomach—reading the piece, unsettled by how unhinged it was, by how much the person who wrote it seemed to hate me.

WHEN I TRAVELED WITH OBAMA in the final weeks of the 2012 campaign, I started to notice scattered protesters holding up signs along the motorcade route with words like BENGHAZI/MURDERER and TRAITOR on them. Conspiracy theories were emerging like mushrooms from the dirt: It was alleged that the U.S. military had been ordered to stand down, intentionally leaving Americans to die in Benghazi, or that the Obama administration was using the facility where Chris Stevens was killed to run guns to jihadists in Syria. To cover this up, the conspiracy theory went, we had invented the ruse of the Internet video insulting Islam.

Part of what was so disorienting was that we had no idea where these theories were coming from. We could track what was on a cable television channel like Fox News or a website like *Breitbart*, but we had no idea what was being discussed in the darker corners of the Internet. Clearly, whatever people were consuming went well beyond a complaint that Hillary Clinton didn't provide enough funding for diplomatic security, or Barack Obama didn't plan for the postrevolution period in Libya. "Benghazi" was an accusation that seemed to mean everything and nothing at the same time, shifting from one conspiracy theory to the next.

I figured this was just part of the end of a presidential campaign. But after the election, this darkness migrated from the Internet and talk radio to Congress. Republicans started investigating the Benghazi attacks in every committee with any possible jurisdiction over the event. The best way to put the whole thing behind us would have been to release all of the information we had about Benghazi. But institutionally the White House counsel needs to avoid setting a precedent that the inner workings of the government are easily obtained so that the president can receive unvarnished advice. And so we were going to face the drip, drip, drip of a story coming out in bits through the drama of congressional committees forcing information out of the White House, information that reached the public only after being filtered through the faux outrage of the Republicans who obtained it.

As 2012 drew to a close, Susan Rice took the brunt of the attacks because she was the front-runner to replace Hillary Clinton as secretary of state. As outwardly composed as she was, she was shocked by the vitriol. Her aging mother couldn't look at the news; her young daughter didn't understand what was happening. Stories were popping up about her finances, her work history, her temperament; columns were written about everything from her Africa policy decisions in the 1990s to the fact that she'd once—decades ago—given Richard Holbrooke the finger. A picture was drawn of an unethical, incompetent careerist who'd gone on television to lie about the deaths of four Americans.

I knew better than anyone else how false that was—Susan had merely used the CIA talking points I'd forwarded her before her appearances. And yet I had to watch her character being assassinated, her chances of achieving a dream job slipping away. She never blamed me. Instead, she'd call and ask for advice. "Do you think it's better for me to get out there, or keep my head down?" I'd sit holding the phone, not knowing what to say. "Let us get out there on your behalf," I'd respond. But the reality is that nothing we did made a difference—the people attacking her weren't going to change their minds; reporters would tell you privately that they knew Benghazi was a bogus scandal, but they would still report on the allegations against her in print and on TV. The Republicans were talking about it incessantly, so it was news. In December, Susan told Obama she was taking her name out of the running for secretary of state. The next time I saw her, she looked as if a weight had been lifted off her shoulders—maybe this would make it go away—and Obama had told her she was likely to be his next national security advisor. She told me that she loved me, and that I was one of the only people who defended her.

At some other point in the past, perhaps a story like Benghazi would have petered out—facts might have mattered. But in 2013, the partisanship in our politics merged with new media platforms and allowed "Benghazi" to survive the long stretches when it wasn't dominating the news cycle. During those gaps in attention, new conspiracy theories expanded their reach on fringe right-wing media outlets, like a creature that grows larger in the depths of the ocean. Social media also gave someone like me the ability to open a window onto this world through the comments people made about me. One day I was part of a global Jewish conspiracy, working with my brother to fix the news. The next I was a virulent anti-Semite, covering for the Muslim Brotherhood. Most days I'd get a trickle of such comments. But every now and then, there would be an enormous spike—dozens or hundreds coming in bursts of a few minutes—people calling me a traitor, a fascist, a Nazi, an Islamist; people who wanted me to be imprisoned, brutalized, even killed; people who seemed unable to contain their rage. When those spikes happened, I knew somewhere in America, a talk radio segment had just aired, or someone had just posted something about me on some website I'd probably never heard of before. It felt like a malevolent force in America that I couldn't comprehend, an anger attached to something bigger than Benghazi, the same blindness to reason that led people to believe that Barack Obama wasn't born in the United States.

Things boiled over for me on a Friday in May, when an ABC reporter named Jon Karl published an "exclusive" revealing that I'd written an email the Friday night before Susan's Sunday show appearances that said, "We must make sure that the talking points reflect all agency equities, including those of the State Department." To Benghazi aficionados, this confirmed a theory that the White House sided with Hillary's State Department in rewriting the talking points. And with this, the vitriol for me no longer came in short bursts; it became a permanent, angry shriek.

On Monday morning, I gave in to an impulse to search for the offending email—ironically, it was located in a folder labeled PROTESTS on my computer, which I'd created in the midst of chaos, back when I had no idea if Benghazi was a violent protest or a terrorist attack. There it was, dated September 14, a relic from an evening eight months ago, something I probably spent thirty seconds writing: "We need to resolve this in a way that respects all of the relevant equities, particularly the investigation." Then I read the Karl story again, quoting my email: "We must make sure that the talking points reflect all agency equities, including those of the State Department."

I stared at the words. I figured that if an email of mine was quoted by ABC News, the reporter must have had it. Clearly, he didn't. What he had was my email translated into Benghazi-speak. "We need to resolve this" became "We must make sure that the talking points"—because our focus on these relatively obscure talking points as the fulcrum of a cover-up was essential. "All of the relevant equities, particularly the investigation" became "all agency equities, including those of the State Department"—because we must have cared more about Clinton than about the FBI investigation. The fake was close enough to be recognizable, but its meaning was transformed to support a conspiracy theory. I brought it to the press team, and they gave it to a reporter.

Like a condemned man who thinks he's going to be exonerated, I walked the hallways with a lighter step, telling anyone I could about what I'd found. Perhaps like Susan after she withdrew from consideration for State, I thought the thing would be over. I was wrong. No one who was already inclined to insist that we had perpetrated a cover-up on Benghazi was moved by facts that told a different story. The vitriol directed at me only intensified, becoming sufficient to prompt the Secret Service to patrol the streets around my apartment building in northwest D.C. because of the threats of physical violence.

It was a new feeling, to have so many people hate me. Worse was the realization that this was never going to be cleared up. At no point would some movie judge step forward to declare me innocent of the charges. I had strange thought patterns while lying awake at night or in breaks during the day. I wished, for instance, that I was being attacked over something I had actually done wrong. No matter how many investigations found no wrongdoing, there would be another one. No matter how clearly mainstream reporters saw it was a sham, they'd cover it anyway—it was a story, and I was one of the characters.

I started to change—the kind of change that is imperceptible day to day but builds visibly over time. I withdrew into myself, growing distant from friends and colleagues. I couldn't fall asleep unless I listened to an interview program, *Fresh Air*, which could distract my mind from worry. I was less joyful at working in the White House, more burdened by it. Without discussing it with others, I nursed a ball of anger deep within me that I kept pushed down—anger at Republicans, anger at the media, anger at the realization that I had no control over what people thought of me. I sensed that some of my colleagues held similar feelings. We worked in the most powerful building in the world yet felt powerless to change the environment around us.

But the one thing I wouldn't do was hide. To disappear would mean defeat. That's what *they* wanted, whoever they were. If I was going to be turned into a cartoon villain, then at least I was going to get something done.

On June 14, 2013, Hassan Rouhani was elected president of the Islamic Republic of Iran, representing the more moderate faction of Iranian politics. He was not the preferred candidate of Iran's hard-line Supreme Leader, Ayatollah Ali Khamenei. This fact alone was an extraordinary contrast to the 2009 election, when Khamenei had thrown his support behind the incumbent, Mahmoud Ahmadinejad, placing opposition leaders under house arrest and launching a sustained crackdown on the opposition. Rouhani had campaigned on a platform of seeking improved relations with the West, linking progress on the nuclear issue to the goal of improving the Iranian economy. His election indicated that Iranian public opinion could apply pressure on the country's leadership from the bottom up. If that pressure was sufficient to get Rouhani elected, perhaps it could compel Iran to make concessions on its nuclear program.

During a morning meeting shortly after the election, Obama proposed taking advantage of this opening. "Why don't I send Rouhani a letter?" he asked. "It's worth testing." Susan agreed. In the past, he had sent letters to the Supreme Leader that led nowhere, and he'd never reached out to Ahmadinejad—a disempowered and polarizing figure. At Obama's direction, a letter was drafted to Rouhani proposing discussions on the nuclear issue. Within weeks, we received a positive response—the Iranians wanted to get a diplomatic process under way.

Over the course of that summer, we went back to the government of Oman, which in the past had offered a venue for meetings between the United States and Iran, to see if they could host such a meeting. And so, that August, at the same time that I was pursuing secret diplomacy with Cuba, we initiated a secret diplomatic channel with the Iranians in Oman, which would be led by Jake Sullivan and Bill Burns, the deputy secretary of state. A routine was established: Jake would get Obama's input before his trips to Oman and then brief us upon his return. Sitting in those meetings, I felt I was seeing what it must have been like in those early stages of the bin Laden hunt. Obama would probe what elements of their nuclear program the Iranians would put on the table and how much they were asking for in return, delving into arcane details of nuclear infrastructure and sanctions policy like an explorer who has spotted some destination in the distance that he is intent on bringing into focus.

After a few weeks, Bill and Jake developed a framework for an interim agreement: The Iranians would, essentially, freeze their nuclear program in return for some limited relief from sanctions. To achieve it, we would have to shift our diplomacy into the so-called P5+1 process, in which the five permanent members of the UN Security Council—the United States, Russia, China, France, and the UK—plus Germany negotiate with the Iranians. The obvious time to do this was during the meeting of the United Nations General Assembly, in late September. John Kerry would join a meeting with the other P5+1 countries and Iran to kick off the formal negotiation, which would be the highest-level contact between the United States and Iran in decades. As those meetings approached, another question emerged: Would Obama meet with Rouhani, who was also coming to New York? Overruling his political advisors, who thought the last thing Obama needed was a photo with the Iranian president, Obama told us that he'd do the meeting. I took it as a signal that he was prepared to take on a lot of political risk if it meant achieving a nuclear agreement.

Our first night in New York, Jake left the Waldorf to go meet with the Iranian delegation in the lobby of a hotel. At first, he was worried about so public a venue, but we agreed that he was relatively anonymous, and who would think he was meeting with a group of Iranians? The Iranians told him that Rouhani was interested in a meeting, but they were noncommittal. What seemed clear is that they wanted the meeting to take place but were worried about how it would play with the hard-liners back home.

The only window where Obama and Rouhani would be in the United Nations building at the same time was after Obama's speech to the General Assembly. We told the UN that Obama needed someplace to wait between meetings, and they offered him some offices adjacent to the Security Council. So he sat there, in a UN office suite, scanning his iPad, while Jake paced outside in a hallway talking on his cellphone with an Iranian. Occasionally, he'd come in to report that they were going back and forth. "Just tell them I'm happy to meet up with him," Obama said. He was, I saw, demonstrating the absurdity of some taboos. It should not be politically impossible for the leaders of two nations on a collision course involving nuclear weapons and war to meet at the United Nations.

The Iranians couldn't get to yes, and so we left without meeting. Walking through the hallways of the UN building, I asked Obama what we should say publicly. "Just tell it straight," he said. "We were willing to meet, but for their own reasons, they couldn't." I gathered a group of reporters and delivered this message, which was sure to make the Iranians uncomfortable. Rouhani had been trying to portray himself, at home and around the world, as a reasonable man, committed to dialogue. We were undercutting that narrative, which was its own form of pressure. After we were back in Washington, the Iranians reached out to Jake and floated different ideas. Would Obama come back to the UN for a meeting of the P5+1? No, we said, most of the leaders weren't even there. Would we do a phone call? Yes.

On Rouhani's last day in New York, I sat on the couch in the Oval Office while we dialed a cellphone that was handed to Rouhani, who was driving to the airport. I then watched as Obama became the first U.S. president to speak to an Iranian president since the Islamic Revolution of 1979. The fifteen-minute conversation was cordial. Obama joked about the traffic in New York. Both of them stressed the need to pursue dialogue and to reach an agreement over the nuclear program, and they said it should be pursued with urgency. Their words weren't particularly remarkable, even if the fact of the conversation was. Returning to my desk afterward, I ran into my former assistant, Ferial Govashiri, a kind and proud Iranian American who had been born in Tehran and exiled since her family left in 1980. She was in tears at this small gesture of reconciliation.

LATER THAT FALL, John Kerry and Wendy Sherman, State's point person on the negotiations, held a series of meetings in Geneva to finalize the interim agreement. While there was a seeming inevitability about it, there were still huge swings in the negotiations, in part because of the drama surrounding them.

In my eight years in the White House, I worked for a government overseeing multiple wars in which thousands of people were killed, and yet nothing in our foreign policy was as fiercely contested as the nuclear deal with Iran. Part of this was rooted in history: Iran evokes images of dark-eyed ayatollahs and blindfolded American hostages in 1979—images of humiliation that still held power over the American mindset. Iran has been central to the backdrop of terrorism and conflict that has endured in the Middle East ever since, unfailingly hostile toward America, our interests, and our friends—particularly Israel and Saudi Arabia. We spend less time examining our own support for Saddam Hussein, who used chemical weapons against Iran, or the fact that our subsequent removal of Saddam did more to empower Iran than anything else that has happened in the Middle East since 1979. Indeed, the fact that mistakes in American policy have helped Iran only increased antipathy toward it among the people responsible for those mistakes.

The advocacy of Israel and the Gulf States is perhaps an even more important factor. In Washington, where support for Israel is an imperative for members of Congress, there was a natural deference to the views of the Israeli government on issues related to Iran, and Netanyahu was unfailingly confrontational, casting himself as an Israeli Churchill standing up to the ayatollahs, except that instead of taking on Iran himself, he wanted the United States to do it. AIPAC and other organizations exist to make sure that the views of the Israeli government are effectively disseminated and opposing views discredited in Washington, and this dynamic was a permanent part of the landscape of the Obama presidency. Iran's other biggest antagonists are the Gulf States, principally Saudi Arabia and the UAE, which don't recognize Israel's existence but made common cause with Netanyahu's government in pressuring us. In addition to being the key producer of oil for the American-led global economy, the Saudis and Emiratis have poured money into the U.S. national security establishment—investing in think tanks, universities, corporate positions, lavish parties, and paid speaking opportunities for opinion journalists and people in the revolving door between the private sector and high-ranking government positions. Taken together, the Israeli and Gulf advocacy ensured a steady flood of well-funded commentary advocating a harsh stance against Iran and, ultimately, the Obama foreign policy.

That fall, these governments knew that an interim agreement would increase the odds of a more comprehensive long-term deal; and if there was a comprehensive long-term deal, the odds of the United States going to war with Iran would plummet. Obama's phone calls with Netanyahu became more acrimonious, as Netanyahu's objections to an agreement became more strident, even as Israeli technical experts were in constant contact with our negotiating team so that we could prioritize their concerns. AIPAC became more unsubtle in raising questions about the agreement before it was even reached. Criticisms of our Iran policy from unnamed "Arab diplomats" reached a fever pitch. Everybody from junior congressional staffers to political journalists to cable television pundits was an expert on nuclear physics, armed with talking points.

I knew this debate was going to be rough, and that it was a dress rehearsal for a longer, harder fight to come if we reached a comprehensive nuclear deal. I started to host regular meetings of staffers from across the government who worked on the Iran negotiations as well as public affairs and congressional relations. Our approach was to produce a steady flow of facts about what was in the potential deal, to arm supporters with the case for diplomacy, and to pre-rebut the barrage of criticism that was going to come. I threw myself into this mission, meeting with anyone who wanted to be briefed—journalists and experts, progressive groups and congressional skeptics, Quakers and arms control advocates. We had a chance to avoid a war and a nuclear-armed Iran, but diplomacy wouldn't succeed if we couldn't keep Congress from killing it with new sanctions legislation.

There was a final flurry of meetings in late November 2013. As Kerry negotiated in Geneva with the Iranians and the other P5+1 countries, he'd call back with different formulations on the remaining issues. One of the most contentious was an Iranian insistence that we recognize their "right to enrich uranium"—the process necessary for a civil nuclear program (and a nuclear weapons program); we didn't want to recognize a right to enrich, and we wanted to assert that any Iranian enrichment had to be negotiated with the P5+1. We had conference call after call, arguing over the most minute language, with Susan demanding changes in wording. Kerry reached a breaking point, shouting into the phone—"Susan, this is a goddamn good deal!" I was a little worried, but Susan assured me that she was just bucking him up. "I want John to be as worried about us as the Iranians," she said. Kerry got the final language and asked to speak to Obama. Tony Blinken, the deputy national security advisor, who had capably helped guide the negotiations, sat with me on the couches in the Oval Office as Kerry read the agreement to Obama. On all the outstanding issues, Kerry had secured what we needed. We held our thumbs up. Obama stood up from his desk, holding the phone to his ear, and congratulated Kerry.

Late that night, in the East Room of the White House, Obama made a televised statement about the deal while I watched off to the side. After six years of sanctions, diplomacy, and political fights, here we were. "As president and commander in chief," he said, "I will do what is necessary to prevent Iran from obtaining a nuclear weapon. But I have a profound responsibility to try to resolve our differences peacefully."

When he was done, I walked with him back to the residence. The familiar hallways were quiet; the discord over the deal felt a great distance from the stoic portraits that lined the walls. "You know," I said, "right when I went to work for you we had this fight in the primary, about whether to talk to Iran." I reminded him of the scene in that small campaign office on Massachusetts Avenue: *It. Is. Not. A. Reward. To. Talk. To. Folks.*

He stopped at the base of the stairs that led up to his living quarters and smiled. "We were right then," he said, "and we're right now."

CHAPTER 20

RACE, MANDELA, AND CASTRO

———

A COUPLE OF WEEKS AFTER THE INTERIM NUCLEAR DEAL was announced, I walked into the Oval Office to find Obama reading alone at his desk. "What do you want to say about Mandela?" I asked.

He looked up at me. "What about him?"

"You haven't seen?" I said. I suddenly felt unequal to the task of telling him this news. "He's passed. Zuma is making a statement." The fact of reporting that Jacob Zuma, the South African president, was making a statement seemed insignificant, the type of detail that would occur to a White House communications official already calculating how long Obama's statement would come after Zuma's, how soon his words would appear in the obituaries—the quotable line, the voice for the rest of us. Behind me, a bust of Martin Luther King, Jr., sat on a pedestal; in the adjacent room, a large framed photograph showed Mandela seated on a chaise, hand reaching up to greet a younger Barack Obama, who sat before me as the first black president of the United States of America, a nation that—like South Africa—had suffered under an apartheid system and its aftermath.

"Why don't you draft something short and simple," he said. "I assume there's going to have to be something longer for the memorial."

———

WE HAD GONE TO South Africa earlier that summer, but Mandela had been too sick to receive visitors. Instead, we visited Robben Island—the piece of rock off the coast of Cape Town where he was imprisoned for decades. We flew there by helicopter, with an awe-inspiring view of the coastal city from the air—mountains ringed around a glistening harbor, birds squawking overhead.

Jay Carney and I toured the quarry where prisoners used to work, while the Obama family set off on their own tour, some thirty feet ahead of us. Our tour guide, a former prisoner, was an older man with an elegant manner and a belly protruding over his belt. He referred to himself as being from "the rank and file" of the African National Congress. He described fourteen years of work that he did in the same sunshine that beat down on us, how Mandela would set the pace for the other prisoners. Then he pointed to a small, dark cave on the other end of the quarry where they were allowed to eat lunch and occasionally use the toilet. "That," he said, "was the best university in the world. That is where Mandela and others would debate political theory and all manner of topics. Then their discussions would filter out to the rank and file."

Occasionally, our guide would stop talking and just stare at the Obamas, as if needing to confirm again with his own eyes that this family was the First Family of the United States, and that they were here. He told us about a guard who once smuggled an eight-month-old baby into the arms of Mandela so he could be reminded of what it felt like to hold a child. In the prison courtyard, he told us how they used to communicate by putting messages into tennis balls and hitting them over the wall to the others. Then, in the cellblock, he walked us through the ways in which the prisoners smuggled things in and out. The Obamas lingered in Mandela's cell. When we went inside after them, I felt the smallness of the space. Our guide spoke of Mandela's refusing a bed if the other prisoners couldn't have one. I asked him what they could see from Robben Island. "The top of the mountain," he replied. When he got out of prison, he told me, he climbed it.

That afternoon, I rode alone in the limousine with Obama after he made a speech at the University of Cape Town, the car winding through hills occasionally dotted with crowds. As we compared our experiences of Robben Island, Obama told me that the one time he teared up was when he asked his tour guide what had been most difficult for Mandela, and he responded, "the absence of children." Mandela had not seen his own children for decades. "When you have kids," Obama told me, "you'll understand in a different way."

I told him the story that my own tour guide had mentioned, about Mandela holding the smuggled baby. Obama just stared out the window at the passing countryside, lush green hills that resembled the coastline of northern California. I took his silence as a signal that he was done with the subject.

NOW, SEVERAL MONTHS LATER, Mandela was gone. A few hours after his initial statement, Obama called me back into the Oval Office to talk about the speech he would give on our return trip to South Africa for Mandela's memorial. "We should remind people that he wasn't a saint," he said. "He was a man. You can't appreciate what he did without that."

For the next couple of days, I didn't work on the speech—it hung there, impossible to focus on while I was living the day-to-day reality of American politics in 2013. Instead, I read the words of the young man who had been sentenced to live the rest of his life in prison in 1964: *"I have fought against white domination, and I have fought against black domination. I have cherished the ideal of a democratic and free society in which all persons live together in harmony and with equal opportunities. It is an ideal which I hope to live for and to achieve. But if needs be, it is an ideal for which I am prepared to die."* I went jogging along the Potomac River listening to recordings of Mandela's later speeches—the melodious accent, the hard-earned wisdom in the voice of an older man. Running past memorials to

white men, some of them slave owners, I began to see glimpses of
something more clearly—not the saint played by Morgan Freeman
in the movies and celebrated in Western capitals, but the man who
struggled, who turned to violence, who was labeled a terrorist by
large swaths of white society, the man who was willing to die for
what he believed with no idea that he would become a global icon
for happy endings.

Racism was a constant presence and absence in the Obama
White House. We didn't talk about it much. We didn't need to—it
was always there, everywhere, like white noise. It was there when
Obama said that it was stupid for a black professor to be arrested in
his own home and got criticized for days while the white police officer was turned into a victim. It was there when a white Southern
member of Congress yelled "You lie!" at Obama while he addressed
a joint session of Congress. It was there when a New York reality
show star built an entire political brand on the idea that Obama
wasn't born in the United States, an idea that was covered as national news for months and is still believed by a majority of Republicans. It was there in the way Obama was talked about in the
right-wing media, which spent eight years insisting that he hated
America, disparaging his every move, inventing scandals where
there were none, attacking him for any time that he took off from
work. It was there in the social media messages I got that called him
a Kenyan monkey, a boy, a Muslim. And it was there in the refusal
of Republicans in Congress to work with him for eight full years,
something that Obama was also blamed for no matter what he did.
One time, Obama invited congressional Republicans to attend a
screening of *Lincoln* in the White House movie theater—a Steven
Spielberg film about how Abraham Lincoln worked with Congress
to pass the Thirteenth Amendment abolishing slavery. Not one of
them came.

Obama didn't talk about it much. Every now and then, he'd
show flashes of dark humor in practicing the answer he could give
on a particular topic. *What do you think it will take for these protests to
stop?* "Cops need to stop shooting unarmed black folks." *Why do you*

think you have failed to bring the country together? "Because my being president appears to have literally driven some white people insane." *Do you think some of the opposition you face is about race?* "Yes! Of course! Next question." But he was guarded in public. When he was asked if racism informed the strident opposition to his presidency, he'd carefully ascribe it to other factors.

I came to realize that this was about more than not offering up what some of his opponents craved—the picture of the angry black man, or the lectures on race that fuel a sense of grievance among white voters. Obama also didn't want to offer up gauzy words to make well-meaning white people feel better. The fact that he was a black president wasn't going to bring life back to an unarmed black kid who was shot, or alter structural inequities in housing, education, and incarceration in our states and cities. It wasn't going to change the investment of powerful interests in a system that sought to deny voting rights, or to cast people on food stamps working minimum wage jobs as "takers," incapable of making it on their own. The last person who ever thought that Barack Obama's election was going to bring racial reconciliation and some "end of race" in America was Barack Obama. That was a white person's concept imposed upon his campaign. I know because I was once one of them, taking delight in writing words about American progress, concluding in the applause line "And that is why I can stand before you as president of the United States." But he couldn't offer up absolution for America's racial sins, or transform American society in four or eight years.

I was one of those well-meaning white people looking forward to seeing Barack Obama eulogize Nelson Mandela so that I could feel better about the world, only I was the person tasked with writing the eulogy. After putting it off for a few days, I came in early one Saturday morning and wrote a first draft in one sitting. By the time we got on the plane for South Africa, I still had no idea what Obama thought of it. He called me up to his office in the front of Air Force One, which was carrying a delegation that included George W. and Laura Bush, and told me that he liked what I'd written, that it was a "safety net" because he could deliver it if nothing else came to him on the flight over. "Are you happy with it?" he asked me.

"I am," I said. "I'm sure you can make it much better."

A few hours later, Obama came back and gave me several handwritten pages on a yellow legal pad. It was an entirely new draft. "See what you can do with this," he said. He had made it into a study of Mandela the leader.

We stopped in Senegal to refuel, and as we idled on the tarmac I got into a long conversation with George W. Bush about Texas football. I knew a bit about the subject because of my father's Texas background—he'd been in the high school band at football games, wearing the gray uniform of Confederate soldiers for Robert E. Lee High School. Bush was pleasant, and he knew everything there is to know about Texas football, the Southwest Conference that my dad grew up with. It was hard to attach the genial man in front of me to the catastrophe of the war in Iraq. Obama stumbled upon us as he was walking back to give me his latest revisions. He mentioned that I'd gone to Rice, which was home to the Baker Institute.

"They'll give anyone an institute these days," Bush joked.

"Maybe they'll give Ben one someday," Obama replied.

"Nah," Bush said. "He's already got them scholarships named after him."

As I returned to the computers to finish editing the speech, something was missing—it was fuller of wisdom than my draft, but it felt impersonal. Susan wandered back and read it over my shoulder. She agreed. "He's not there," she said, referring to Obama. She offered to go talk to him with me—it was going to be an awkward conversation, as Obama didn't like to be told to be more revealing, particularly on matters that intersected with race.

We found him playing spades at the conference room table. I could tell from the look on his face that he was pleased with what he'd written. "How're you feeling about it?" he asked.

"It's great," I replied. "There's just one thing. We think it needs to be more personal."

"I've already done that," he said. "Remember that speech in Cape Town?" I did—a speech that began with a reminiscence of how Obama had first become politically active in the antiapartheid movement when he was at Occidental College. But this was different. This was Mandela's memorial.

"Yes, it doesn't have to be the same," I said, "but you need to put more in here about what Mandela meant to you personally."

He flashed a little anger, a look I'd learned to read, a narrowing of the eyes. "I don't want to claim him or put myself in his company."

"But *they* want to hear that," I said. "People want to see you as part of that legacy, and they can do that without your comparing yourself to Mandela."

Susan chimed in. "They do," she said. "Folks want to hear from you on this."

He complained again that South Africans had heard him talk about that before, but he agreed to take another stab at it. What came back an hour later was some of the most personal writing I'd ever seen him do. In small, careful script, he had written: *"We know that, like South Africa, the United States had to overcome centuries of racial subjugation. As was true here, it took sacrifice—the sacrifice of countless people, known and unknown, to see the dawn of a new day. Michelle and I are beneficiaries of that struggle. . . . Over 30 years ago, while still a student, I learned of Nelson Mandela and the struggles taking place in this beautiful land, and it stirred something in me. It woke me up to my responsibilities to others and to myself, and it set me on an improbable journey that finds me here today. And while I will always fall short of Madiba's example, he makes me want to be a better man."*

WHEN WE LANDED IN South Africa, it was raining in sheets. Shortly before Obama had to leave for the memorial, I went to check in with him. The Secret Service was explaining that he'd have to wear a bulletproof vest while speaking; the memorial service was outside in a soccer stadium, and there wasn't going to be any partition.

"I forgot to go over one thing," I said. "Raúl Castro is going to be up there on the dais with you."

"So?" he asked.

"So the question is, what do you do if you see him?" Some press had started asking about this—no U.S. president had greeted a Cuban president since the revolution. Their interaction would be a matter of intense scrutiny.

"I'll shake his hand, of course," Obama replied. "The Cubans were on the right side of apartheid. We were on the wrong side." In the 1980s, while Reagan was backing the apartheid government in South Africa, Cuba was fighting a war against its right-wing proxies in Angola. Their decisive 1988 victory in a battle against that racist government at Cuito Cuanavale was, in the words of Mandela, a "turning point for the liberation of our continent—and of my people—from the scourge of apartheid." With his short reply, Obama had casually recognized a history that no other president before would have dared to speak aloud. After trying on the bulletproof vest, Obama refused to wear it—its bulk would be obvious under his suit and the message would be disrespectful. No one in that stadium was going to harm Obama anyway.

I stayed behind at the hotel and watched on television as Obama approached the lectern and warmly shook Raúl Castro's hand. Seeing Obama speaking about the antiapartheid struggle and the importance of Mandela, I felt I was watching him in a separate role from his status as president of the United States—here, in South Africa, he was more appreciated and more intuitively understood than he would have been saying these same things at home. When Obama got back to the hotel, he called me into his suite, where he was decompressing with Michelle. He was sitting in his bedroom, a muted television on in the background, looking energized. "That was one of my favorite speeches we've ever done," he said.

"It looked like the crowd loved it," I said.

"Yeah. It was kind of awkward, though," he said. "Whenever they showed Zuma on the big screen, they booed."

I asked him about his interaction with Castro. "It's funny," he said. "He seemed taken aback that I actually shook his hand."

"It's getting a ton of attention in our press," I said. Already, there were vigorous debates about whether it was right to shake Raúl's hand.

"What am I supposed to do? Snub the guy at a funeral?" His voice was rising a bit. I had taken him out of the moment he'd been in, honoring Mandela, and put him back into the reality of American politics.

Obama started talking about how he'd gone out of his way to talk to F. W. de Klerk, the white leader who had released Mandela from prison and handed power over to him after an election. I mentioned that Desmond Tutu had closed the event. Obama was surprised—Tutu, no longer in the best graces of the ANC, had been left off the official printed program. "I feel bad I didn't see him," he said.

"Let's give him a call," Michelle said. I stood off to the side as they both spoke to him, Michelle going on about how much she enjoyed their time together on her last visit to South Africa, and ending the conversation by telling Tutu that she loved him.

On the flight home, I scanned the American press. There was almost no coverage of the first African American president eulogizing the most iconic African of the last century. Instead, the lead story back home was a selfie that the Danish prime minister had taken with Obama. Everywhere, the picture was splashed across websites, on social media, on cable news: Obama grinning next to an attractive blond woman. The thought and care Obama had put into honoring Mandela, and his efforts to reveal himself in doing so, were subsumed by the opportunity to talk about this photograph. Before we landed, Obama told me he'd never been so annoyed by the U.S. media. He didn't have to explain why.

THAT SUMMER AND FALL before the funeral, we had more secret meetings with the Cubans in Ottawa. I'd wake up at dawn, take a cab to Dulles Airport, and board a small regional jet for the short flight. Since almost no one at work knew what I was doing, it was easier to offer no explanation, acting as if it was perfectly normal to be gone for a day here or there. The Cubans always insisted that phones be left in an adjacent room, mindful that a good hacker could turn a phone into a listening device. I'd step out of several hours of discussions to find hundreds of emails backed up, from people who just assumed I was at my desk, within reach.

In our second meeting, the Cubans remained fixated on getting their four guys out of prison in exchange for Alan Gross, something we would never agree to. We did make some progress, however. When two adversaries are just beginning diplomacy, it's necessary to build confidence, a process of showing that small steps can lead to bigger ones. With help from Senator Patrick Leahy, we allowed the wife of one of the prisoners to pursue artificial insemination. The Cubans allowed for improvements in Alan Gross's confinement: moving him into a different room, allowing him to take Spanish lessons, giving him access to a printer.

There was one other, more important signal. Around the time of our second meeting, Edward Snowden was stuck in the Moscow airport, trying to find someone who would take him in. Reportedly, he wanted to go to Venezuela, transiting through Havana, but I knew that if the Cubans aided Snowden, any rapprochement between our countries would prove impossible. I pulled Alejandro Castro aside and said I had a message that came from President Obama. I reminded him that the Cubans had said they wanted to give Obama "political space" so that he could take steps to improve relations. "If you take in Snowden," I said, "that political space will be gone." I never spoke to the Cubans about this issue again. A few days later, back in Washington, I woke up to a news report: "Former U.S. spy agency contractor Edward Snowden got stuck in the transit zone of a Moscow airport because Havana said it would not let him fly from Russia to Cuba, a Russian newspaper reported." I took it as a message: The Cubans were serious about improving relations.

In October, before our third meeting, Ricardo Zuniga and I

considered three options: a smaller swap of some of the four Cubans for Gross; proceeding without Gross's release; or insisting on some kind of swap that went along with a broader transformation of the relationship between our two countries. We went to Susan for guidance, and she urged us to go for what she called "the big bang." Obama agreed, saying, "If I'm going to do this, I want to do as much as we can all at once."

When we sat down for our third meeting, I listened again to Alejandro's insistence on getting their four prisoners back. When it was my turn to speak, I tried to move past the prisoner discussion and put the entire relationship on the table. "We have a channel where we can be candid," I said. "Given our shared interest in prisoners, we'll keep discussing that issue. But President Obama wants us to discuss bigger issues as well. He wants to change the relationship in fundamental ways while in office. We won't resolve this all in one meeting, but we want to discuss this in this channel." I then went through a long list of nearly every aspect in the U.S.-Cuba relationship that we wanted to change. The State Sponsor of Terrorism list; unwinding the U.S. embargo; restoring diplomatic relations; the reform of Cuba's economy and political system, including Internet access, labor rights, and political freedoms. During the pauses for translation, I looked at Alejandro and thought about how he was processing this in a different language, informed by a different history, focused primarily on getting these Cubans out of prison. I ended by reiterating that Alan Gross's release was essential for any of this to happen and noting that we would respect Cuban sovereignty—our policy was not to change the regime.

When I was done, Alejandro put aside his talking points. "Thus far," he said, "we had the perception that the U.S. side had the political will to advance. Your intervention confirms my view. Talking candidly is the only way for us to advance on the road established by the two presidents." He paused for a moment. "President Obama wants to advance these, correct?"

He was still uncertain that I was really speaking on Obama's behalf. "Yes," I answered.

"You discussed these options with him?"

"Yes."

We spent the rest of the meeting going through the list of everything that each side wanted the other to do. Whereas we wanted Cuba to reform its economy and political system, Cuba wanted the embargo lifted, the naval base at Guantanamo Bay returned, and our funding for democracy programs and Radio and TV Martí to end. We wouldn't be able to get all of this done; there were things that neither side was ready to do, and we were going to have our ideological differences. But our task was becoming clearer. We needed to find some solution on prisoners, and we needed to figure out what each side could do to transform the relationship and whether that added up to a deal.

Our fourth meeting was a few weeks after Obama shook Castro's hand at the Mandela memorial. We were concerned about overstaying our welcome in Canada, so we agreed to meet in an alternative location: the Caribbean nation of Trinidad and Tobago. Their first comment was about the Mandela funeral. They noted, with pride, that the Obama-Castro handshake was the biggest news to come out of the event. "Our assessment is the reaction was favorable."

In response, I tried to mute things a bit, noting that congressional criticism of Obama had been severe. "There are still many people who would oppose changes in our Cuba policy, and not all the reaction was favorable," I said. "But it was an indication that we are open to change. Also, Obama mentioned to me that Cuba had earned the right to be there."

"He said that?" Alejandro asked.

"Yes," I said. I had mentioned it as an aside, but could tell that what I said registered. "He understands the history."

We had a new proposal to put on the table: The intelligence community had come to us and said they had an agent in Cuba whom they wanted to get out of prison, someone who had been valuable to them in the past, who had helped provide information that led to the arrest of the Cuban Five. If the Cubans would release this agent, we could swap three of the remaining Cubans for him, but not Gerardo Hernández—the ringleader of the group, and the only one convicted of murder. They'd also have to release Alan Gross.

Alejandro balked. He went on a lengthy diatribe about how Gross was an intelligence agent and they had information to prove it, and then reiterated what he had been saying since the first meeting: Gerardo Hernández needed to be released. "A solution that does not include Gerardo is not a solution for us." On the other hand, he guaranteed that there would be a solution for Gross if there was a solution for Gerardo. Finally, he said Cuba was open to a spy swap, but they didn't want to release the person that the intelligence community wanted. "He is a traitor," Alejandro said.

We had to insist they weren't going to get Gerardo, and they had to insist we weren't going to get this U.S. asset. We would both have to decide whether to compromise. Neither of us wanted to go first, and neither of us was empowered to make that offer right now. More important, though, was the fact that we both agreed that we were now talking about a transformation in the U.S.-Cuba relationship, not just a prisoner swap. Toward the end of the discussion, after hours of arguing about prisoners, I reiterated that we wanted to keep our eye on the bigger picture, this potential to transform U.S.-Cuba relations.

"We understand that in Obama's circle you are the ones looking for a new relationship," Alejandro said. His language was carefully chosen. The U.S. government, and the U.S. Congress, had plenty of people who were *not* looking for a new relationship. The Cubans had been burned in the past by people who met with them without being fully empowered by the president. The difference this time, he said, was the fact that "we have the political will of our leaders, Raúl Castro and Obama."

CHAPTER 21

RUSSIANS AND INTERVENTION

ONE MORNING IN EARLY FEBRUARY 2014, LAURA LUCAS—
a spokeswoman who worked for me on the National Security
Council—sat in my morning staff meeting and asked how we
should respond to an intercepted phone call that had been released
on YouTube.

"What phone call?" I asked.

"You haven't seen?" she said. "It's Toria."

I Googled it on my computer. At that point, a crisis was boiling
over in Ukraine. In November 2013, the corrupt, pro-Russian leader,
Viktor Yanukovych, had announced that he was suspending preparations to enter into an "association agreement" with the European
Union, a step that would have helped cement Ukraine's ties with
the West. Over the next several weeks, hundreds of thousands of
people held demonstrations in Kiev's central square, the Maidan.
Calls for Yanukovych's resignation began as he pursued talks with
Vladimir Putin on a "strategic partnership," an obvious ploy to pull
Ukraine away from Europe. There were clashes in the streets, a new
law banning antigovernment protests, and mounting violence. The
Arab Spring pattern was playing out in a European capital, on Russia's border: Putin's worst nightmare.

The intercepted call was between Toria Nuland, our assistant
secretary of state for Europe, and Geoff Pyatt, our ambassador in

Kiev. Nuland was a hawkish Foreign Service officer, anti-Russian, a savvy veteran of Dick Cheney's staff who served as Hillary Clinton's spokeswoman at State. In the recording, she and Pyatt sounded as if they were picking a new government as they evaluated different Ukrainian leaders. "I don't think Klitsch should go into government," she said about one Ukrainian politician. "I think Yats is the guy who's got the economic experience, the governing experience," she said about another Ukrainian, who soon became prime minister. At the end of the call, complaining about a lack of European pressure to resolve the crisis, Nuland said, "Fuck the EU."

I was stunned. The Russians had almost certainly intercepted the phone call. That was hardly surprising—in these jobs, you have to assume that any number of governments could be listening in if you're on a nonsecure phone. What was new was the act of releasing the intercepted call and doing it so brazenly, on social media—the Russian government had even tweeted out a link to the YouTube account. Doing so violated the unspoken understanding among major powers—we collect intelligence on one another, but we use it privately, for our own purposes. A Rubicon had been crossed—the Russians no longer stopped at hacking information; now, triggered by the threat of Ukraine sliding out of their sphere of influence, they were willing to hack information and put it into the public domain.

"I don't know what we can say about this," I said. "What have we said so far?"

"State hasn't commented."

We ended up noting that the Russians were the ones who had published the video and calling it "a new low in Russian tradecraft."

OUR RELATIONSHIP WITH RUSSIA had steadily deteriorated since the reemergence of Vladimir Putin as president. We had assumed, perhaps wrongly, that Putin had supported all of the progress made through the "reset" of the first term—the New START treaty, Iran sanctions, Russia joining the World Trade Organization. Medvedev had gone out of his way to signal a better relationship with the United States. When he visited in 2010, he gave a speech in Silicon Valley, wearing jeans and reading the text off an iPad, trying to strike a picture of a future-oriented, forward-looking Russia. When he came to Washington, we arranged for Obama and him to eat lunch together at Ray's Hell Burger, a casual place where Medvedev oddly ate his burger without the top part of the bun, gripping the bare patty with his fingers.

I think of Medvedev now as a tragic figure—the guy who seemed to know better, who wanted Russia to step more firmly into the Western world. If life took a different turn, he'd be the kind of Russian who'd end up living in London and going back to Moscow on occasion to look after business interests. Instead, he was put in his place by Putin, a man who runs Russia as a personal fiefdom, a source of his own wealth and prestige. In retrospect, Putin must have been watching with growing concern as protests driven by corruption toppled long-standing dictators, and oil prices began to drop. His own election in 2012 was marked by large street demonstrations and a healthy opposition. Once he was restored to power, the momentum in the U.S.-Russia relationship ground to a halt. The first time Obama met with Putin after he became president again, Putin showed up forty-five minutes late. Putin rebuffed further discussions on arms control and missile defense. Russia continued its blank check of support for Assad. In August of 2013, Russia granted Edward Snowden asylum in Moscow.

As a former spy, Putin surely understood the gravity of someone making off with the blueprints for how a nation conducts surveillance. In response, Obama canceled a planned state visit to Moscow. He didn't want to navigate the sideshow of Snowden being in the same city, but he also saw no point in attending a summit where nothing was going to be accomplished. I also noticed an unusual coziness among the Russians, Snowden, and Wikileaks—the way in which Wikileaks connected with Snowden, who was clearly being monitored by the Russians; the way in which the disclosures coincided largely with Russian interests, including the leaks from

Snowden's stolen cache that seemed focused on sabotaging America's relationships abroad—particularly our alliance with Germany. Whoever was behind the disclosures was intent on driving a wedge between the United States and Europe, which also happened to be a key goal of Putin's, who deeply resented the expansion of NATO and the European Union into former Soviet states like the Baltic countries.

While tensions had been building, Ukraine was a tipping point. To Putin, it was an existential threat to his rule and a part of Russia. It was the kind of crisis that creeps up on you in the rearview mirror when you work in the White House, a distant activity that comes further into focus until suddenly it is right on top of you. This happened in February, when more protesters started getting killed in the streets. Obama was wary. He didn't see the protests as a chance to transform Ukraine because he was skeptical that such a transformation could take place. He had inherited the Bush administration's policy that offered the prospect of NATO membership to Georgia and Ukraine. Russia had already invaded Georgia in 2008. The last time there was a protest-driven revolution in Ukraine, the so-called Orange Revolution of 2004, the leader ended up poisoned by the kinds of toxins that Russia uses against enemies abroad.

Obama's outlook was closer to the European Union's. Change should be gradual. Ukraine should be able to draw incrementally closer to Europe. Over time, standards of living would improve, and a less corrupt politics could evolve. "If I'm living in Kiev," Obama told us during one meeting, "I can see how much better people have it in Warsaw. *That's* what's going to pull them closer to the EU."

In late February, Obama and Putin agreed upon a formula that included a schedule for expedited elections in Ukraine. European leaders formalized the deal, and it seemed that the issue might be resolved. But Yanukovych fled the country and protesters took control of Kiev. The scenes were reminiscent of the early days of the Arab Spring: a corrupt leader abandoning ship; jubilant young people cheering in the streets; images of exotic birds and a classic car collection inside Yanukovych's estate, confirming the worst allegations that he was on the take. But this was not the place or time for a revolution to succeed.

The familiar rhythm of crisis: Weekend meetings in the Situation Room chaired by Tony Blinken, email chains with updates, hastily scheduled press briefings. Russia was moving special forces into Crimea. These men didn't wear traditional uniforms, but they occupied buildings, controlled airports, and raised a Russian flag over the Crimean parliament. Just as Crimea evoked a nineteenth-century war, the names in play—Tartars, Cossacks—spoke to a rough part of the world where history was never far away. The Russians no longer bothered to calibrate their denials about what they were doing, they just lied about it.

For the next few weeks, something approaching a routine developed. Obama would have a long conversation with Putin, trying to find some common interest we could work toward. These calls would last more than an hour, and Putin would always steer the conversation back to what he saw as the original sin—in his view, the protests that overthrew Yanukovych were initiated by the United States because some of its leaders received grants from U.S. democracy promotion programs. The people who took power, he told Obama on March 6, made a coup d'état.

Obama argued back at length, stressing that we had no interest in controlling Ukraine and that we respected Russia's historic bonds with that country. "Our consistent interest," Obama insisted, "has been in upholding basic international principles that sovereign states should be able to make their own decisions about their policies internally and externally." He'd get exasperated, but he never seemed surprised. He didn't think Putin was a grand strategist because he was acting on impulse—responding to Assad's opposition in Syria, or Yanukovych fleeing Ukraine. He neither liked nor loathed Putin, nor did he subscribe to the view that Putin was all that tough. "If he was that sure of himself," Obama said, "he wouldn't have his picture taken riding around with his shirt off."

On March 18, Crimea was annexed. We began to ratchet up sanctions on Russia—targeting individuals and entities, oligarchs seen as close to Putin or involved in Ukraine. The value of the ruble plummeted. Massive aid packages were prepared for Ukraine. Obama was in the weeds, speaking regularly with Angela Merkel, designing a response that sought to thread a needle: Hold together a Europe wary of conflict with Russia; pursue coordinated economic pressure through sanctions; and stabilize the Ukrainian government. "Aim first, then shoot," he told us.

Our response went far beyond anything that the Bush administration had done to Russia after it invaded Georgia in 2008, but Republicans still castigated Obama as weak. Some even praised Putin as a strong leader, someone to be admired. Watching this, Obama told me that it represented something of a turning point for a Republican Party that had been rooted in opposition to Russia for decades. In Obama's view, the praise for Putin that you could see on Fox News went beyond partisanship, though that was part of it; Putin was a white man standing up for a politics rooted in patriarchy, tribe, and religion, the antiglobalist. "Some of these folks," he said of the more right-wing elements in the United States, "have more in common with Putin than with me."

Publicly, my job was to make our response look as tough as I could. But nothing we could do was going to make Putin give back Crimea, nor would Obama go as far as the hawks in Washington who wanted us to send arms to Ukraine—even if we would never be willing to escalate as much as Putin. John Podesta, Bill Clinton's former chief of staff, had come on board as a senior advisor. Podesta was a brilliant guy, pencil-thin, with close-cropped hair, a strategist who could anticipate the turn that events would take in Washington. But he also brought something of the Clinton-era ethos. Obama should make his statements on Ukraine standing in front of Marine One, Podesta suggested, so he'd look tougher. McDonough described this kind of posturing as necessary to impress the "Russian judges"—his term for the Washington commentariat. But even as I agreed that Marine One made for a great backdrop, it made me cringe a little: Standing in front of a helicopter was only a degree removed from posing with your shirt off.

Obama's real strength was in his ability to hold Europe together while Biden took the lead in bucking up the Ukrainian government. In late March, we set out for emergency summits on Ukraine. Working hand in glove with Merkel, Obama kept Europe together behind sanctions and secured a multi-billion-dollar IMF package that ended up saving the Ukrainian economy. Instead of sending weapons to Ukraine, he focused on deploying troops and military assets to the NATO members that bordered Russia. He started talking more and more about how he wanted to hand things off to the next president. "I don't want to leave the next president in a position where there's not some kind of trip wires in the Baltics and those NATO front line states," he told us. "Putin needs to understand that even if we won't go to war in Ukraine, we will if it's NATO."

After our trip, the crisis ground on as Russian-backed separatists started to occupy government buildings in the eastern Ukrainian cities of Donetsk and Luhansk. The Ukrainian military was trying to hold on to their territories with force. When Obama called Putin, he again pivoted back to Yanukovych's removal, telling Obama that protesters in the Maidan had also occupied government buildings; what was happening in eastern Ukraine, he said, was no different.

There was something awkward about sitting in the Oval Office for these sessions. One leader, Putin, was lying about what he was doing and flouting international law; the other leader, Obama, was imposing sweeping sanctions on Russia. It never felt like a conversation. Putin would go on for fifteen to twenty minutes at a time, then Obama would do the same. Obama ended with a warning: Despite the break in our relations, we still had time to resolve things in a way that could respect Russia's interests. On the other hand, Obama said he'd impose much stronger sanctions if Russia contin-

ued moving into eastern Ukraine. In that scenario, he said, "relations between Russia and the West will be strained for many years
to come. There is no need for that."

INCREASINGLY, OBAMA VENTED TO us about the constant demands that he *do more*—bomb Assad, arm Ukrainians—even
though there was little evidence it would work. By his sixth year in
office, he had used military force in Iraq, Afghanistan, Yemen, Somalia, and Libya while escalating our use of armed drones against
al Qaeda. He saw the necessity of drones, but he spent an extraordinary amount of time trying to impose restrictions on when they
could be used, setting standards for whom we could target and how
to avoid civilian casualties. I also saw the need for drone strikes and
couldn't argue with their effectiveness in removing al Qaeda leaders.
But I felt it was impossible to know whether every strike was justified. Obama once spoke to this mixture of support and ambivalence: "If someone wrote a novel about us," he told me in the Oval
Office, "it'd be about two guys who got into this to end a misguided
war in Iraq, right about the time that the U.S. government was per-
fecting the technology to use drones."

What bothered both of us the most about the debates in Washington was the sense that there had been no correction after
Iraq—no acknowledgment of the limits to what the United States
could achieve militarily inside other countries. In one session that I
went to with a group of foreign policy experts, we faced a litany of
criticism for not doing more in the Middle East. After I patiently
explained our approach, one of the participants—who'd been silent
up to that point—interjected with an edge in his voice, "You have
to bomb something."

"What?" I asked, taken aback.

"It doesn't matter. You have to use military force somewhere to
show that you will bomb something."

I saw the reasons why these arguments gained traction. Advocating intervention gets attention. And there's something innately

American about believing that there *must* be a solution. Many of the people who work in American foreign policy today were shaped by the experience of the 1990s, when the United States was ascendant. The Berlin Wall had come down. Democracy was spreading across Eastern Europe, Latin America, and East Asia. Russia was on its back foot, and China had not yet risen. We really *could* shape events in much of the world. NATO could expand into the former Soviet Union without fear that Russia would invade one of those countries. We could bring together the whole world to kick Saddam Hussein out of Kuwait.

Obama occasionally pointed out that the post–Cold War moment was always going to be transitory. The rest of the world will accede to American leadership, but not dominance. I remember a snippet from a column around 9/11: *America bestrides the world like a colossus.* Did we? It was a story we told ourselves. Shock and awe. Regime change. Freedom on the march. A trillion dollars later, we couldn't keep the electricity running in Baghdad. The Iraq War disturbed other countries—including U.S. allies—in its illogic and destruction, and accelerated a realignment of power and influence that was further advanced by the global financial crisis. By the time Obama took office, a global correction had already taken place. Russia was resisting American influence. China was throwing its weight around. Europeans were untangling a crisis in the Eurozone.

Obama didn't want to disengage from the world; he wanted to engage more. By limiting our military involvement in the Middle East, we'd be in a better position to husband our own resources and assert ourselves in more places, on more issues. To rebuild our economy at home. To help shape the future of the Asia Pacific and manage China's rise. To open up places like Cuba and expand American influence in Africa and Latin America. To mobilize the world to deal with truly existential threats such as climate change, which is almost never discussed in debates about American national security.

Yet American politics pushes military interventionism, even as public opinion is wary. In the aftermath of 9/11, it became an imperative for politicians to demonstrate that they were tough on terrorism, with the measure of toughness being a willingness to use military force or flout the rule of law. Democrats were deeply scarred by elections in 2002 and 2004, when they were tarred as weak, untrustworthy, or even unpatriotic if they dared question the so-called Global War on Terror. With the public turning against the Iraq War and the election of Barack Obama, it seemed that this dynamic might change. It didn't, at least not in Washington.

The very first debate answer I wrote for Obama in the 2007 primary season dealt with a hypothetical terrorist attack on the United States. I had been asked to prepare an answer on what steps a president should take in response, and he'd delivered it largely as I'd written it: "The first thing we'd have to do is make sure that we've got an effective emergency response . . . the second thing is to make sure that we've got good intelligence, (a) to find out that we don't have other threats . . . and (b) to find out whether we have any intelligence on who might have carried it out so that we can potentially take some action to dismantle that network." John Edwards and Hillary Clinton pounced, making clear that the first thing they would do is go after the people responsible and take them out. Obama's response was treated as a gaffe.

For many years, the phrase "Vietnam syndrome" was used to describe the reluctance of Americans to get back into wars after the catastrophe of Vietnam; but it was often used as a term of derision, as if it was wrong to learn those lessons. In early 2014, with the recent example of the Iraq War still shaping the world in which we operated, Obama was already being roundly accused of "overlearning the lessons of Iraq." So even as the Syria red line episode demonstrated that public opinion was skeptical of war, the political frame for national security debates remained the same: Doing more was tough, anything else was weak.

OBAMA'S FRUSTRATION WITH HIS critics boiled over during a lengthy trip to Asia in the spring of 2014. In the region, the trip was seen as another carefully designed U.S. effort to counter China. We'd go to Japan, to bring them into the Trans-Pacific Partnership (TPP)—weaving together twelve Asia Pacific economies into one framework of trade rules, environmental protections, and labor rights. We'd go to South Korea and discuss ways to increase pressure on North Korea. We'd go to Malaysia, something of a swing state in Southeast Asia, which we were bringing closer through TPP. And we'd end in the Philippines, a U.S. ally that was mired in territorial disputes with China over maritime boundaries in the South China Sea.

Before leaving, we had a meeting in which a guy who focused on strategic planning at the NSC reminded us that the most important foreign policy work often involved incremental advances— hitting singles and doubles, as he put it. Obama leaned forward in agreement. "After I was reelected," he said, "I pulled together a group of presidential historians that I have in from time to time." People like Doris Kearns Goodwin, David McCullough, Douglas Brinkley. "It's interesting: They made the point that the most important thing a president can do on foreign policy is avoid a costly error." He ticked through the list of presidents who had seen their tenures defined by such mistakes: Johnson in Vietnam, Carter with Desert One, Bush in Iraq. The lesson? "Don't do stupid shit," he told us, tapping on the table in front of him.

On Air Force One, Obama sometimes liked to walk back to where the press sat, and he did this in the middle of our Asia trip. Usually this was planned in advance, but on occasion, we'd just see him walking down the aisle of the plane. These sessions were off the record, but the reporters sent detailed notes back to their news bureaus, and the substance of the comments would ricochet around newsrooms, ultimately making their way into news analysis and Washington gossip.

Obama complained about the recent negative coverage of his foreign policy, airing grievances that I'd heard him express privately— about how the press ignored the steady work of American leadership and legitimized every demand that he do more to escalate conflicts.

He went on a long tangent about how the failures of American foreign policy were ones of overreach, complaining about the lack of
accountability for Iraq War supporters who were still the tribunes
of conventional wisdom. Finally, he reached the end of his lecture.
"What's the Obama doctrine?" he asked aloud. The silence was
charged, as we'd always avoided that label. He answered his own
question: "Don't do stupid shit." There were some chuckles. Then, to
be sure that he got his point across, he asked the press to repeat after
him: "Don't do stupid shit."

At the press conference wrapping up his last stop in the Philippines, one reporter asked about "the Obama doctrine," trying to
elicit some less vulgar version. Obama didn't bite. Instead, he gave a
measured description, saying that we needed to avoid errors, and
that in foreign policy, "you hit singles, you hit doubles; every once in
a while we may be able to hit a home run."

As we loaded the motorcade to head back to Air Force One for
the flight home, I got a nervous email from Jake Sullivan—the reference to singles and doubles wasn't going to play well with the
foreign policy crowd. I knew that was true, but I had grown as frustrated as Obama with the odd intersection of the triviality of our
politics and the heavy-handed nature of our foreign policy critics.
"Don't do stupid shit" would be panned, held up as a sign of negli-
gence, but who is *for* doing stupid shit? "Singles and doubles" would
be similarly derided, but what is wrong with hitting singles and
doubles? And, as Obama complained to me, "they keep forgetting
that I said we're also going to hit some home runs."

CHAPTER 22

DIVINE INTERVENTION

———

WE WERE ON THE LONG FLIGHT HOME FROM MANILA WHEN I started to get messages about the fact that another email I'd sent more than a year and a half ago was being made public by Congress. PREP CALL WITH SUSAN was the headline of the email, which I'd quickly drafted for Susan Rice's Sunday show appearances. On a list of goals that I'd written was the line "Underscore these protests are rooted in an Internet video and not a broader failure of policy."

I closed my laptop and felt a wave of dread. In the context of September 14, 2012, the email I'd written was not remarkable. That day, protests were erupting across the Arab world that were rooted in an anti-Muslim Internet video. In the context of April 2014, however, the email was explosive. Nineteen months of investigations, hundreds of segments on Fox News, and thousands of talk radio rants had established the idea that something nefarious had taken place after the attacks in Benghazi. The talking points embedded in the document headed PREP CALL WITH SUSAN had already been litigated in public by multiple congressional investigations. Those investigations had found no wrongdoing. But that only increased the appetite in some quarters for proof that the conspiracy theory was right, that we had invented this excuse of an Internet video. Here, shouted a thousand angry voices, was "the smoking gun."

The destruction of any objective truth over those previous nine-

teen months was one of the strangest aspects of my experience.
Toward the end of 2013, a reporter who was deeply sourced in Libya
reached out to me. He was writing a long reconstruction of the
events in Benghazi, including documenting the ebb and flow of the
crowd, the way in which a large, angry mob ultimately turned into
a smaller group of heavily armed men waging a military-style assault. People he'd spoken to—people who had been there in Benghazi that night—said that some people had gone to the American
facility out of anger over the video. To protest, to loot, to kill—it
depended upon whom you asked. "You're not in Washington," I
said. "If I went out and said that it was actually because of the video,
they'd burn me in effigy."

Benghazi followed me around like an unseen shadow. When I
met strangers, I wondered if they went home to Google me, only to
find a litany of conspiracy theories. I was embarrassed by the idea
that my friends might have to defend me when talking to other
people. I was doing more television, and the guy who arranged
those interviews and followed me, camera to camera, advised me to
smile more. "You have a natural frown," he told me. I had never
thought of myself as unhappy before.

In the days after we returned from Manila, the outrage over my
email began to build. One weekday morning, I woke up around
seven to get my dry cleaning. Mets hat on, plastic-wrapped shirts
draped over my shoulder, this was the most normal I could feel during the course of a day. I came up the stairs of my stoop, pulling my
keys out of my pocket, when I was suddenly surrounded by a camera crew. They were from Fox News, shouting questions about "the
talking points" as I hurried into my apartment building.

Ann, who was pregnant with our first child, could tell something
was wrong when I came through the door. "What's going on?" she
asked.

"There's a Fox News camera crew outside," I said.

"What?" she said. Her face started to dissolve in some kind of
fear. "Oh, no, Ben. Oh, no, no, no." There was panic in her voice,
and I could see how much this was impacting her as well. We crept

over to the window, pulling the blinds to the side, and looked out the window at a car that was parked illegally by the hydrant in front of our window. "What will the neighbors think?" she said.

I ended up leaving through a set of basement stairs that spat me out into an alley. Any sense of cleverness I felt at shaking a tail was undercut by my shame at having to sneak out of my own apartment building through the back door where we deposit our trash.

The White House Correspondents' Dinner was just a few days later. My brother was in town, and we went on our usual run. We ran along the Potomac, Northern Virginia on one side, the Kennedy Center and Lincoln Memorial on the other. He went on about how annoyed he was by the conspiracy theory that he and I fixed the news. He mentioned that he'd met with Lindsey Graham that weekend—a man who had recently called me a "scumbag." When the run ended, we stopped a couple of blocks from my apartment. In past years, my brother had stayed with me; this year he didn't. In past years, I'd gone to the CBS News party before the dinner—my parents had a photo of the two of us, with our wives, smiling at this event on their mantel in New York; I was still out of breath when he said, "It's probably a good idea if you don't come by the CBS party this year."

"Sure," I said.

"See you," he said, jogging in the other direction.

I stood there for a moment, catching my breath, trying to reckon with the realization that my brother didn't want to be seen with me in public.

Around the same time, John Boehner announced a new select committee to investigate Benghazi, and my email was cited as a leading justification. There was a video that went along with the announcement. It resembled a slick but cheap movie trailer, with each Republican member of the committee announced like a professional wrestler. "Trey Gowdy . . . Mike Pompeo . . ." Republicans sent out fundraising appeals citing the new committee. It was clear that the goal was to extend this charade into the presidential election in order to damage Hillary. It was the most politically motivated rollout imaginable, all founded on a theory that we had been the ones to politicize the deaths of four Americans. I felt I was living in an alternate reality that was in some way insane, unable to recognize hypocrisy or to separate facts from politics. The world around me seemed to have come unmoored. The truth had become irrelevant.

That Friday afternoon, my deputy at the time, Caitlin Hayden, asked me to come to a meeting in the Executive Office Building. It was actually a surprise party. I walked in to find a room full of people who'd worked alongside me for years. We drank Scotch at a large oval table and talked ruefully about the controversy. At some point, everyone went around the room and told their own story about how much I meant to them. It was perhaps the nicest thing anyone has ever done for me—that sense of a family closing in around you, protecting you, no matter how bad it was outside. Each person spoke about something I'd done to boost their career, or a time when I'd done something funny or foolish; a younger guy said he decided to go into communications because of me; a former staffer sent a photo of her baby daughter wearing a shirt that read TEAM BEN. In a perfect snapshot of how incapable I was of handling what was happening to me, I had so much to drink that I don't remember most of these tributes.

I somehow made it home and slept in my clothes on a bare mattress in our guest bedroom, soon to be used by our unborn child. The next morning, Ann tried to shake me out of my sense of self-pity. "This isn't a tragedy," she said. "My dad's scan was a tragedy." She was right, but I didn't know how to put that perspective into my daily life.

A few days later, I got a call that Obama wanted to see me. I made the familiar walk down the hallway and up the stairs, a walk I'd made thousands of times, but this time I was filled with dread. I had a feeling this was about Benghazi. I walked into the Oval, where he was standing behind his desk.

"I hear you've been a little upset about everything that's going on," he said, "this whole thing." He gestured with his hand, not even saying the word "Benghazi."

"Yes," I said. "I'm sorry. I know it's a fraction of what you put up with on a daily basis. It's just an out-of-body experience, watching yourself be convicted publicly of a crime you didn't commit."

"Did you do anything wrong?" he asked.

It was, I realized, the first time anyone had ever bothered to ask me that question. "No," I said.

"Then don't worry about it," he said. "All you have is your integrity. And you have as much integrity as anyone I know."

THE DEEPER I SLIPPED into the abyss of Benghazi, the more focused I became on our discussions with the Cubans, determined to ensure that something positive came out of what felt more and more like an ordeal. But to get something done, we'd need some help. That spring, we found it.

On a sunny morning in March, a group of White House staff trailed Obama as he made his way into the Vatican and stood in a large space with little furniture and huge paintings while he met alone with Pope Francis. For months, Ricardo and I had discussed involving the Vatican in our negotiations. It was an institution that had credibility with both the American and Cuban people, was neutral in foreign affairs, and supported a rapprochement. Our basic concept was that the Vatican could be a guarantor for any agreement, since it was hard for the governments of the United States and Cuba to trust each other. But we weren't sure how to enlist the Vatican's help, so we suggested to Obama that he discuss Cuba with the pope.

As the time ticked on, there was a slight stirring among the Vatican officials present. "The Holy Father never meets with people for this long," one of the priests said to me.

After we were back at the U.S. ambassador's residence in Rome, I pulled Obama aside. "Did you talk about Cuba?" I asked.

"Yes," he said. "As long as we talked about any other issue. He was very interested, coming from Latin America. I told him we'd established a channel."

"What did he say?" I asked.

"He was very supportive. He said he'd be helpful in any way he could. He seemed familiar with the fact that there is a dispute over prisoners."

When I asked if they'd discussed any other details—about our negotiations, or what the Vatican could do—he looked surprised. "He's the pope," Obama said. "He approaches things from a pretty high level." Before I left, he told me how much he liked the pope, but also sympathized with him, given how much attention Francis had attracted since his accession. "I know a thing or two about high expectations."

IN MAY, AT OUR next meeting with the Cubans, we proposed a formal role for the Vatican. They reacted a little cautiously—the Church had a complicated history in a country that had embraced Communism and restricted religious freedom. But when I mentioned that Obama and the pope had discussed it, they warmed a bit.

"Papa Francisco?" Alejandro asked.

"Yes," I responded. "He and Obama spoke about how he could be personally involved in supporting what we're trying to accomplish. His involvement could also help with the politics in the United States."

"Papa Francisco is a son of Latin America," Alejandro explained. He was therefore viewed differently in Cuba from other popes, just as Obama was viewed differently from other presidents. With his involvement, they were open to it.

The actual negotiations had reached an impasse. The Cubans still had not agreed to release the intelligence asset we had requested, and we had not agreed to release Gerardo Hernández. It didn't help that we were meeting shortly after Obama had authorized a prisoner swap in which five Taliban inmates from Gitmo were exchanged for Bowe Bergdahl, a U.S. soldier who had been held in brutal conditions by the Taliban in Pakistan for five years. On the day that Bergdahl was released, we'd been elated—he was the only remaining U.S. prisoner of war, and safely completing the exchange with the Taliban suggested that some future effort at peace talks might be possible. By coincidence, Bergdahl's parents were in Washington and were invited to come see Obama a few hours after the exchange was done. A few of us suggested that Obama make a statement in the Rose Garden with the parents. Pfeiffer and Podesta were skeptical, given that the exchange was with the Taliban. "The Republicans won't go after a prisoner of war, will they?" I said.

Podesta grimaced. "I don't share your optimism."

I had rarely been more wrong. I knew that Bergdahl had walked off his base, but I didn't know about the allegations that members of his unit had been killed looking for him. In the high of the moment, I'd failed to do my homework. Hostility toward Bergdahl from fellow servicemembers boiled over, and there were days of heated criticism of the swap, and of our decision to celebrate Bergdahl's release. The Cubans read the Bergdahl episode the wrong way. "We have noted Obama's determination to leave no man behind," Alejandro told me. I had to explain that the Bergdahl swap actually made things harder.

To DESIGN THE VATICAN ROLE, Denis McDonough suggested we work through Cardinal Theodore McCarrick, who had once led the archdiocese in Washington. McCarrick was eighty-three and retired from his official duties, but he was still something of a troubleshooter around the world for the Vatican. He met us early one morning for breakfast in the White House mess—a dining room on the ground floor of the West Wing decorated like a 1950s country club, with large wooden chairs, wood paneling, and paintings of old wood-hulled Navy ships on the walls. As we sat picking at our eggs, I explained to McCarrick the outlines of what we'd been doing with the

Cubans and how we wanted the Vatican's help. I could see him turning the problem over in his head as I spoke, a kindly man with youthful Irish eyes. "The Holy Father," he suggested, with traces of a Bronx accent, "would want to work through the cardinal in Havana," Jaime Lucas Ortega y Alamino. I nodded—if the Holy Father wanted to work through Cardinal Ortega, then that's what we were going to do.

The way to initiate a formal role for the Vatican, McCarrick said, would be through a letter from the Holy Father to Raúl Castro and Barack Obama. The Vatican conducted diplomacy like this only in person, however, so the question was how do we get Cardinal Ortega to Washington to deliver it? Denis and I sat there without ideas while McCarrick thought this over, testing a couple of different ideas out loud, before arriving at a solution: "I can invite him to deliver a speech at Georgetown," he said, "if you can assure him that Obama would be available for a meeting."

A few weeks later, Cardinal Ortega arrived in Washington. We arranged for him to enter the White House through a side entrance so he wouldn't be seen by the press. Denis, Ricardo, and I met with him and McCarrick on the back patio of the Chief of Staff's Office. He clung tightly to an oversized envelope that contained a formal letter from the Holy Father. He was eager, almost giddy, smiling broadly and making small talk until Obama arrived and sat down with us. At that point, Ortega shifted to formality. Holding up the envelope, he told us, "I have recently delivered the exact same letter to president Raúl Castro Ruz in Havana." He paused to let that fact sink in. Then, instead of handing us the letter, he took it out and—with a sense of ceremony—read it aloud in Spanish, pausing so that Ricardo could translate.

It was a simple message: an offer to help resolve issues related to prisoners and to improve the relationship between the United States and Cuba. When Ortega was done, he handed the letter to Obama like a sacred relic. Obama gave me the letter and I took it down to my office. I looked at the text and there at the bottom, in the tiniest handwriting I had ever seen—as if the signature itself conveyed humility—it read FRANCIS.

Perhaps not coincidentally, the Cubans had just sent us a message that they would be willing to hand over the intelligence asset we wanted if we released Gerardo. Suddenly it felt as if the pieces were aligning. Ricardo and I asked for a meeting with Obama to see if we could get guidance on the final package we should pursue. Up to this point, he hadn't been in the weeds. When I'd brief him after my sessions with the Cubans, he'd sit there with a look of mild amusement. "The report from our man in Havana!" he'd say. "Are you going to bring a Panama hat to the next session?" His instructions were always the same: "Go big."

Now, with a deal imminent and the Vatican involved, Obama got serious. He began our meeting by saying that we should set aside politics: "Politics is not something I worry about on this one," he said. "The politics will catch up to what we're doing." His concern was making clear to the Cubans that if we released Gerardo, we'd have to get more than just Alan Gross and the intelligence asset in return. We suggested that the Cubans could release a large number of political prisoners and commit to expanding Internet access on the island. Beyond that, I explained, the mere fact that the Cubans were agreeing to restore diplomatic relations was a big deal—we would get the new beginning, even though the embargo remained in place.

The Bergdahl debacle hung heavy over the room. Denis and others wanted us to press for the return of high-profile fugitives who were living in Cuba, including Joanne Chesimard. Chesimard is one of many bizarre subplots in the U.S.-Cuba relationship. A prominent Black Panther, she was riding in the back of a car on the New Jersey Turnpike in 1973 when the police pulled it over. In an ensuing shootout, a state trooper was killed. Chesimard escaped from prison and made her way to Cuba, where she was granted asylum. The FBI declared her a "domestic terrorist" and a $1 million bounty was offered for her return. She also happened to be Tupac

Shakur's godmother, and had deep pockets of support in the African American community.

"We can try for Chesimard," I said, "but I don't think the Cubans will give her back."

A FEW DAYS LATER, Ricardo and I flew up to Toronto to meet the Cubans at an airport hotel. When we walked into the lobby, we noticed a conspicuous couple sitting at the center of the bar area staring at us—a tattooed man and a woman dressed like an extra in a 1980s Madonna music video. As we checked in, they walked over to where we were standing and stopped a few feet away; the man took out an iPhone, held it out in front of him, and took pictures of us. Then they walked off toward the elevators without saying a word.

"Russians," Ricardo said.

"Why would they do that?" I asked.

"They want us to know they're watching," he said. "They don't like this."

In the meeting, we laid out the proposed package, noting that we still needed final approval from Obama on Gerardo Hernández. I urged the Cubans to release a list of political prisoners that Ricardo had given them; to agree to increased access to the Internet; and to announce additional steps related to human rights and economic reform. I also went through a list of fugitives we wanted back that included Chesimard. I noted that we weren't trying to bury all our differences. "The day after we announce this," I said, "Raúl Castro will still defend the revolution and the United States will continue to support multiparty democracy. We'll have different views, but we'll address them through dialogue."

It was a tough meeting. We argued around several issues. But the Cubans agreed to release almost all of the political prisoners, or—in the language they preferred—"individuals who had been arrested for nonviolent political offenses." We hit a dead end on fugitives because it reintroduced the subject of Luis Posada Carilles, the

Cuban who had blown up a plane flying to Cuba. But we were now just testing what additional items could be added to a transformative agreement. When we took a break in the late afternoon, Ricardo and I walked across a parking lot to get takeout from a cheap Mexican restaurant, then bought a few bottles of wine at a nearby gas station. We laid out trays of food in our hotel room and set a table with plastic utensils. When the Cubans arrived, they were in a jovial mood, as if it was a social occasion.

"So, when can you come to Cuba?" were Alejandro's first words to me.

"Not yet," I answered. "First we have to go to Rome."

We talked over a process whereby we would draft papers that memorialized our agreements and share them with the Vatican at a secret meeting in Rome—neither side could go back once their commitment had been deposited with the pope. The Cubans also insisted that we draft papers describing where each side continued to have differences, which was an interesting way to protect our political flanks—they wanted to note their opposition to the embargo, the U.S. Naval Base at Guantanamo, and other American policies; we could note our continued support for human rights and reforms in Cuba.

The conversation gradually drifted to other things—baseball, Hemingway, Cuban music. Ricardo went into the other room, where we had left our phones for security reasons, and came back with his iPhone playing his favorite Cuban songs. The Cubans reacted excitedly, dancing in place at the table. Politics felt far away. Benghazi felt far away. In that moment, sitting there with five other human beings, eating Mexican food at a cheap airport hotel in Canada, listening to Cuban music playing on an iPhone, I felt a sense of grace.

CHAPTER 23

PERMANENT WAR

———

OBAMA WANTED TO EXTRICATE THE UNITED STATES FROM the permanent war that had begun on 9/11. On the day he took office, there were roughly 180,000 troops in Iraq and Afghanistan. By late 2014, the number of troops in Afghanistan was down to 15,000. All U.S. troops were out of Iraq. These were meaningful achievements; they saved American lives, as casualty numbers fell from nearly a hundred Americans killed each month to nearly zero, and the cost of war shrank by tens of billions of dollars. Most controversially, he had kept the U.S. military out of Syria.

By 2014, just about every negative force in the Middle East had converged in Syria: a murderous autocrat backed by Russia and Iran; al Qaeda–affiliated extremists; sectarian conflict and a Saudi-Iranian proxy war; and ISIL, the rebranded version of al Qaeda in Iraq. As Iraq's Shia prime minister, Nouri al-Maliki, isolated Iraq's Sunnis—and as the civil war in Syria left huge swaths of territory across Iraq's western border ungovernable—ISIL had turned into a mix of terrorist group, insurgency, and local government. In January, ISIL declared the Syrian city of Raqqa as its capital and started a steady advance eastward, back into Iraq. In June, it took over Mosul, one of Iraq's largest cities, overrunning the Iraqi Security Forces who had been trained and armed by the United States. It then announced it was establishing a new caliphate, and changed its name to the more ominously universal Islamic State.

It was becoming apparent that we would have to intervene again in Iraq to stop ISIL's advance. The tipping point came in early August, when ISIL took control of a dam near Mosul that, if breached, could have flooded huge swaths of Iraq. The Kurdish capital of Erbil, normally an island of calm, was under threat from ISIL. And most immediately, ISIL had driven tens of thousands of Yazidis onto Mount Sinjar. The Yazidis were a sect inside Iraq who believed in an ancient brand of monotheism, with roots in Zoroastrianism, and had preserved their tradition for well over a thousand years. Yet ISIL saw them as infidels, and in early August they started to massacre Yazidi men and enslave the women, and declared their intent to wipe the Yazidis from the face of the earth.

For a couple of days, a sense of crisis enveloped the White House. Obama was angry that he didn't have good information. "We didn't get a warning that the Iraqis were going to melt away" in Mosul, he complained to a group of us. "And now we can't even get a read on how many Peshmerga"—the Kurdish security forces—"are in Erbil. I'm not happy with the information I'm getting." It was quiet for a moment. "I'm aggravated," he added, for emphasis.

I was again in a chorus of advisors arguing for air strikes. Obama agreed, though he told us he would impose limits on how aggressively we'd go after ISIL until Maliki was replaced by a less sectarian leader. So on August 7, he announced that we would begin dropping food, water, and other supplies to the Yazidis trapped on Mount Sinjar, and targeted air strikes would break the siege at the base of the mountain.

The next day, I met in the Roosevelt Room with a group of Yazidis who had come to Washington to plead for military action to save their community from extermination. Many had recently emigrated to America; some had been interpreters for the U.S. military during the Iraq War. They were not the polished diaspora representatives I was accustomed to meeting. Many wore T-shirts and jeans.

One after another, they told me of dashed hopes after the U.S. invasion in 2003, of having to flee their communities after helping the U.S. military, and now of ISIL's campaign of terror. A patriarch with a white handlebar mustache sat across from me at the middle of the table, a huge painting of an idyllic American West behind him. When it was his turn to talk, he spoke in Arabic. He described women being taken from their homes and raped, family members being killed. Tears began to roll down his face. "No one will help us!" he shouted. "Not Maliki. Not Barzani. Only you, the most powerful nation in the world, can help us."

Once everyone had spoken, they sat and waited for my response. I urged them to share information with our government about what the needs were on Mount Sinjar, and where ISIL was so that we could target them effectively. I began to tear up. "The Yazidi people are a resilient people," I said, feeling slightly ridiculous but certain of what I was saying. "You have endured for thousands of years, and you will endure this." I walked down to my office and collapsed into my chair.

THE NEXT DAY, I was drafted to go with Obama on his two-week vacation to Martha's Vineyard. Ann was now a senior advisor at the State Department working on global women's issues. She was also five months pregnant and coming with me. These trips could go either way—a paid vacation with the president, or a nightmare of nonstop work with a skeleton staff. On the Saturday that we boarded Air Force One for the Vineyard, the United States began air strikes on ISIL targets, and a young African American named Michael Brown was killed by a police officer in Ferguson, Missouri. This was not going to be a vacation.

Obama was staying at a large rental house on the other side of the island, an hour's drive from the staff. When we got to our hotel, Ann and I were shown to a small, dark room on the ground floor with twin beds. "I'm not staying here," she said. She didn't even sit down. I tried to block off time we could spend together, hoping to schedule something of a vacation within the confines of my job, but I had to spend hours sitting in a dark NSC office, wearing headphones, patched into meetings by secure videoconference so that I could update Obama. I had to draft statements on ISIL and Ferguson. I had to brief the press. When I didn't, reporters would wait in the lobby to intercept me coming and going.

For the first few days, Ann veered between being patient and disappointed, but after seeing the direction things were going, she decided to go home. As in the previous summer, I didn't know what to do. I wanted her to stay, but I knew that I'd only be working. So I drove my pregnant wife to the airport so she could fly home to D.C., ending our last attempt at a vacation before becoming parents.

I slogged through the days. Driving to the nearby school, where our press was camped out, to answer questions about ISIL. Driving out to Obama's rental to staff phone calls, give him updates, or draft statements. He tried to cluster his work in the morning so that he could play golf or relax in the afternoon, and when I showed up, he always seemed a little annoyed—as if I were the stand-in for a world that was ruining his vacation. Nights, I drove to a cheap Chinese takeout place and returned to my room. There I'd sit on the couch, eating lo mein out of a plastic container and watching cable news split-screen the unraveling of two of the loftier aspirations of the 2008 campaign—an end to the permanent war, and a bridging of the racial divide.

We flew back to D.C. for a couple of days in the middle of the vacation. Shortly after we took off for the flight back to the Vineyard for week two, Lisa Monaco called me. "Do you have a few minutes?" she asked.

Lisa is a hypercompetent lawyer who had steadily worked herself up the ladder through a series of positions: congressional staffer, prosecutor, chief of staff to Bob Mueller at the FBI, head of the National Security Division at the Justice Department, and now Obama's chief counterterrorism advisor. She sat across the hall from me in John Brennan's old office, which she had renamed the Lady

Cave. She met repeatedly with the families of Americans held hostage abroad, including the four Americans held by ISIL in Syria. One of those Americans was a forty-year-old journalist named Jim Foley, who had been taken in northwestern Syria in late 2012.

As I sat on the plane with a phone pressed to my ear, Lisa's voice kept cutting in and out. Finally, as the plane reached higher altitude, she came through clearly. There was emotion in her voice: "ISIL has posted a video of Jim Foley," she said.

"A video?"

"On YouTube. I'm watching it. Jim's kneeling in an orange jumpsuit. There's a guy reading a statement behind him." She started to give snippets from the statement. "'This is a message to America. This is a message to President Obama.'" She described the man holding "a small knife."

It was quiet for a moment, then I heard her voice crack. "Oh my God," she said. "Oh my God." Then she started to cry. I sat there staring at the beige wall in front of me.

"Was he beheaded?" I asked.

"Yes," she said.

"I'll go tell POTUS."

I walked into Obama's office at the front of the plane. He was sitting behind his desk, and Malia was on the couch reading something. I leaned over the desk and he saw the look on my face and his eyes opened wider with concern. He asked Malia to give us a minute.

"They've released a video," I said.

"Foley?" he asked.

"Yes," I said. "He's been beheaded." I started to explain what I knew about the video. I hesitated a moment before saying, "They described it as a message to America and to you, in response to the bombing."

Obama chose not to react to that part. "Foley the journalist?" He seemed to want to ground this human being in a vocation, not in his violent end.

"Yeah," I said. "The stringer who was taken in 2012."

"I should call his family," Obama said. "And make some kind of statement." I looked at the clock. It was a short flight to the Vineyard; we'd be landing soon, so I'd have to draft something. "Are we trying to take the video down?"

"Yes," I said. "I think our media will cooperate, but they'll find some ways to get it around."

He left to go find Malia, and I went back to my seat and got on a conference call.

When we landed, I rode in the motorcade to Obama's place instead of the staff hotel. The house had an enormous, high-ceilinged living room that was larger than my entire apartment. The Obamas went into an adjacent room to eat dinner with a small group of friends, and I went into an office where there were a couple of laptops and a printer. It was the kind of house where the sound system played in every room at the same volume. I sat there mustering every ounce of outrage to write a statement that would channel our national disgust toward ISIL, learning as much as I could about Jim Foley so I could compose a tribute to his life. I was sitting in a home that someone else had rented, listening to R&B that was playing for people in other rooms. I felt I could step out of myself and see myself sitting there—the effort it took to inhabit an awful moment like this, the absurdity of the setting, the question in my head that Ann would ask: *Why does it always have to be you?*

By the time I was done and Obama had finished dinner, a collective judgment had been reached to make the statement in the morning—it was getting late, and we'd know more tomorrow. Before I left for the car ride back to the hotel, I met briefly with Obama. I called Denis McDonough and put the phone on speaker on the coffee table in front of us. Clearly, whatever conversation had taken place at dinner included a discussion of whether Obama was entitled to a break. "What difference does it make whether I deliver the statement or we just put it out on paper tonight?" he asked.

"People need to hear from you on this one, Mr. President," Denis said.

Obama looked at me. "They do," I added. "It's a big moment."

Obama paused. He knew as well as we did that he needed to deliver the statement, but he felt his own—more pronounced—version of the exhaustion I was feeling. It also went against his instinct to not inflate a terrorist group. "Okay," he said, standing up. "But I think this just elevates ISIL."

"We understand, sir," McDonough said.

The next morning, I heard nothing from Obama, but he showed up at the school where the press was assembled. Jen Palmieri had come up for the second week, and we spent a minute with him in an anteroom. He complained again about having to give the statement, a feeling that seemed to have hardened overnight. "It just elevates ISIL," he said. "It's exactly what they want." Still, he delivered the statement forcefully, but would end up being heavily criticized for playing golf that same afternoon.

I DIDN'T KNOW HOW I could keep this up for two more years. By the end of 2014, I would have a new baby, and we would be done with our Cuba negotiation. It'd be a natural point to leave. I just didn't know if I could convince myself to go through with it. I told Ann, but despite all the sacrifices she'd made, she surprised me by encouraging me to stay. "If you leave," she said, "you'll regret it."

My father had just undergone knee replacement surgery, and I took the train up to see him one day at the outpatient rehabilitation center where he was staying in White Plains. The place had the appearance of an early-twentieth-century retreat—a stately campus of red brick buildings with an internal courtyard. We sat there making small talk, eating sandwiches. My dad told me about the steps he was planning to take to improve his diet and exercise. He was sixty-eight years old when I went to work for Obama; he was now seventy-four and figuring out what the rest of his life would look like. I could tell he had missed seeing me—his first question when we were together was usually about the next time I could visit. But he also always asked, with pride in his voice, "How's Barack?"

On the train back to New York City, I took out my BlackBerry and saw a series of email chains debating whether Obama should hold a press conference that day. Some of the communications staff thought it was premature—we lacked good answers on ISIL or Ukraine—but McDonough and Palmieri were in a mode where they felt it was always better for him to be out there. Fresh off his vacation, he showed up in the White House briefing room wearing a tan suit, looking like a dapper game show host, which caused a stir. Peppered with questions about ISIL, he responded to one by saying, "We don't have a strategy yet"—the kind of honest answer that gets a president into trouble. Six years into my job, I didn't need to read the cycle of criticism popping up on my BlackBerry to know what it said.

As if to rediscover some part of myself from an earlier time, when I read novels and wanted to write one, I was reading a new book by Haruki Murakami. The main character was exactly my age—thirty-six. In the book, he finds himself paralyzed in his own life and looking to his past for answers. I thought about this short trip I was on: the setting was familiar, the New York streets, trying to make plans with old friends, sleeping in my old bedroom. But everything else was different—the things that I was thinking about, the world coming to me through my BlackBerry, the fact that my father was in a rehab center talking about aging. I could see myself in the present circumstance of the narrator, but not in any rediscovery of the past that I didn't know how to find. I was in the middle of a different story, and if I left my job, I wouldn't see it through to the end.

A FEW DAYS LATER, we flew to Estonia in an effort to show Russia that we would stand up for our easternmost NATO allies. When we landed in the early morning hours, I took a walk through the old part of Tallinn. The streets were empty—just the occasional person going to work, biking, selling flowers. Nestled on the Baltic Sea, Tallinn is a hybrid, with neatly arranged streets and an orderly lifestyle, but with hints of its giant neighbor evident in the Russian orthodox churches that looked like mini-Kremlins. There was a lingering unease, a palpable sense that the place was under threat.

In a meeting, the Estonian president, Toomas Ilves, insisted to Obama that we had to take Putin at his word if he said he would take Kiev. Ilves had an academic manner, and he described methodically how Russia was using fake news and disinformation to turn Estonia's Russian-speaking minority against Europe. Speaking in paragraphs, he tied together Putin, the emergence of right-wing political parties in Europe, and ISIL. *These are people,* he said, *who fundamentally reject the legitimacy of the liberal order. They are looking for another form of legitimacy—one that is counter to our notion of progress.*

After the meeting, I joined Obama for lunch and told him I thought Ilves did the best job I'd heard of tying these disparate threads together, explaining a theory of the forces at work in the world without having to rely on a construct that roots them all in American foreign policy. Without missing a beat, Obama said, "That's the same dynamic as with the Tea Party. I know those forces because my presidency has bumped up against them." He paused. "It's obviously manifest in different ways, but people always look to tear down an 'other' when they need legitimacy—immigrants, gays, minorities, other countries."

Obama was more sanguine about the forces at play in the world not because he was late in recognizing them, but because he'd seen them earlier. As an African American, he had an ingrained skepticism about powerful structural forces that I lacked when I went to work for him. After years of Mitch McConnell's obstructionism, Fox News's vilification, and growing tribalism at home and abroad, he had priced in the shortcomings of the world as it is, picking the issues and moments when he could press for the world that ought to be. This illuminated for me his almost monkish, and at times frustrating, discipline in trying to avoid overreach in a roiling world while focusing on a set of clearly defined priorities. Core interests and allies defended. Old accounts like Cuba closed. New agreements forged. Stupid shit avoided. Our values advanced by how we lived them. Change that is incremental, but real.

A few days after we got back to Washington, I went up to the Oval Office to go over a proposed outline of his upcoming speech at the United Nations. He went on at length, speaking with more passion than he had in a while, woken from his August funk. I heard Marine One landing on the South Lawn in the distance. I asked where he was going. He said he was going to an event in Baltimore to celebrate the bicentennial of the writing of "The Star-Spangled Banner."

"I've always been more of an 'America the Beautiful' guy," I said.

"Yes," he said, "but only if it's the Ray Charles version."

That triggered a memory of 9/11. I told him about how my Queens neighborhood was filled with the funerals of cops and firefighters for days, widows sitting in lawn chairs surrounded by men in uniform; how I went to a small railroad bar near my apartment a few days later, and a burly guy stood next to me at the urinal before looking at me, his eyes welling up, and saying, "I can't even fucking piss." I told Obama, "I went home and sat on my bed and listened to Ray Charles singing 'America the Beautiful,' and it was the first time after 9/11 that I cried."

"You know," he said, "that should be the national anthem."

I laughed. "They should play it before every game."

"Seriously, think about it," he said, as if I had a say in the matter. "It's beautiful in a uniquely American way. It's all there. Black and white. Religious and secular. Glory and pain." With that, he started to sing the first notes, *"O beautiful, for heroes proved,"* swaying—like Ray—from side to side. With that, he made the walk out onto the South Lawn toward Marine One, leaving me alone in the Oval Office. I stood there, in the middle of the carpet ringed with the quote from Martin Luther King about the arc of the moral universe, Ray Charles's voice pulsing in my head: There was no way that I was going to leave this job.

CHAPTER 24

NEW BEGINNINGS

———

RICARDO AND I ARRIVED IN ROME AROUND NOON, TIME ENOUGH for us to get to the Vatican early and walk around the block a few times to process what we were about to do. Over the previous few weeks, Obama gave us clearance to authorize an exchange of the remaining three Cubans imprisoned in the United States for our intelligence asset and Alan Gross. We and the Cubans had agreed to announce the beginning of a process to normalize relations, including the establishment of diplomatic relations. The Cubans had agreed to release fifty-three political prisoners and expand access to the Internet. We had agreed to take steps to ease restrictions on travel and commerce with Cuba, within the confines of the embargo, which we could not lift without Congress.

The Vatican does not do business on email, so all they knew was that we were coming with the Cubans to have a meeting. That afternoon, surrounded by pilgrims, tourists, and Romans, we tried to find the entrance where we were supposed to meet a man named Monsignor Murphy—an aide to Cardinal Pietro Parolin, the Vatican secretary of state.

Murphy found us at one of the gates. He was plainly dressed and spoke with a slight English accent—he was an English Murphy, he told us, not Irish, though many people made that mistake. As he walked us through the Vatican complex, he paused inside a stone courtyard and gestured toward a simple door. "That," he said, "used to be the pope's front door." He had since moved to different living quarters.

When we got to the meeting room, Alejandro surprised Murphy by greeting me with a characteristic bear hug. He asked about a story in *Politico* that said I was leaving the administration. I replied that he shouldn't make too much of it. "But it named three who are leaving," he insisted, "and you are one of the three!"

"I'm not leaving anytime soon," I said. "People like to gossip."

We had a lengthy conversation about kids and the name Ann and I had chosen for our unborn daughter, Ella, which didn't translate easily into Spanish. It clicked when Juana, the Cuban interpreter, said excitedly, "Oh, like Ella Fitzgerald!"

We sat there making small talk, waiting to be summoned. The Cubans went in first, leaving Ricardo and me waiting. We chatted with Parolin's deputy, a kind, soft-spoken man named Monsignor Camilleri, who explained that he'd lived in Cuba for some years and was now working on improving the conditions for Christians in the Middle East. After about forty-five minutes, it was our turn. Parolin was a Vatican diplomat with extensive experience in Latin America, and his face showed a degree of shock. "Normalizing relations?" He kept asking us to clarify. The purpose of these separate meetings, I realized, was to enable him to independently verify our respective commitments.

He also seemed surprised at the role I played. At first, he addressed Ricardo—who looks a little older than I do—by my name. To clarify why we were the representatives there, Ricardo explained the role of the National Security Council in our system. I chimed in that we could be more discreet than the State Department. This seemed to trigger a question that was gnawing at him. "Does John Kerry know about this?" he asked.

"Yes," I said. Earlier that summer, Susan Rice had given Kerry an overview of what we were doing. I assured him that Kerry was supportive.

After about thirty minutes, we moved back into the larger room so that the American, Cuban, and Vatican representatives could be seated around an enormous wooden table in large red-backed chairs that felt as if they were made for some kind of Vatican council from the seventeenth century. Parolin sat at the head, with Alejandro and me flanking him, and read a statement that had clearly been prepared before he knew the full purpose of our meeting, alternating between Spanish and English. He welcomed us to Vatican City, saying it was just a small state in the community of nations, but one that held spiritual power. He thanked us for expressing confidence in the moral authority of Pope Francis, emphasized the Church's neutrality in affairs between states and its commitment to seek peace among peoples. Then he seemed to go off the text in front of him. He looked at each of us intently. "Seeing you here generates hope, especially in the heart of the pope, and he asked me to convey his greetings."

I spoke first. To address any lingering concerns from Parolin, I said that we were there because our presidents had authorized this dialogue and that these commitments reflected their decisions. Then I read the first, short document aloud—stating our mutual commitment to begin normalizing relations. I felt no nerves, just the satisfaction of having nothing left to do other than read what was printed in front of me. When it was Alejandro's turn, I let my eyes wander over his shoulder as he read the same words in Spanish. Behind him was a giant mural of the crucified Christ surrounded by attending angels. On another wall hung an imposing portrait of Benedict XVI, the conservative former pope who was living in self-imposed retirement. The image of the living Benedict seemed a reminder that there were more reactionary forces nearby—in Cuba, the United States, and around the world—forces that were still in the picture.

We read several more documents in turn, memorializing our commitments and noting where we still differed. As we finished, we all agreed formally—in the presence of Parolin—to honor them. Alejandro then made a long speech. He said that this was a first step toward normalizing relations, and that as neighbors the United

States and Cuba should pursue dialogue. He noted irreconcilable differences between our systems of government but said that they shouldn't stand in the way of cooperation that benefits our people. "Ben's daughter, Ella, and my children should be the immediate beneficiaries," he said, "along with other children in Cuba and the United States."

"We have a difficult history," I replied. "We felt the full weight of that history in our talks. Our work together doesn't erase that history or our differences, but we recognize that we're neighbors and we're also family, given how many Cubans live in the United States. We're here today because our leaders have chosen to look forward." Despite our differences, I said, "we can agree on a basic commitment to human dignity—something that is central to the pope's message and the mission of the Church."

At that point, we were both out of speeches, but it seemed that neither of us wanted the meeting to end. Sitting there, as Parolin waited to see if there was anything else from either side, it felt so rare to inhabit a moment of purely good news. In front of me, the faces of angels on the giant mural held serene smiles.

"I enjoy this moment," Parolin said, breaking the silence with a smile. "I thank God to be here able to do this. . . . What you are doing is going to give people hope." Alejandro led us all in a standing ovation. Parolin went around the table shaking hands with each of us. He pulled me close and said, almost conspiratorially, that when we made the announcement publicly, there should be champagne.

When we were led back outside by Murphy, it felt as if we had been inside for days. Ricardo and I walked out on our own, through the crowds, then out the gates and anonymously into the eternal city of Rome, somewhat drunk with wonderment at what had just taken place. We held this secret, a happy thing. This was no longer just some project we were pursuing, flying to Canada, haggling with the Cubans, working to get people's attention and approval back home. This was now something that was going to *happen*, that was going to exist in the world, and the emotions of the Vatican officials seemed to foreshadow the impact that could be unleashed by the announcement itself. We knew something that was going to send out ripples around the world.

We went in search of the perfect, simple Italian meal. We walked for blocks and blocks, looking at restaurants and dismissing them as not quite perfect enough. Finally, we found a place near the river, with a table in the back, where we had buffalo mozzarella, prosciutto, artichokes drenched in olive oil, pasta with ragout, and a bottle of Chianti. For once, Ricardo didn't have his spiral notebook out. "For someone like me," he said, "this is as good as it gets." Sitting there, I felt a thousand years removed from the anxieties that awaited me back in Washington. We had done something big and right for its own reasons. I had never felt so at home so far away from where I lived.

A FEW WEEKS LATER, the Democrats were beaten in the midterm elections, losing thirteen House seats and eight Senate seats. Unlike in 2010, when the losses cast a depressive weight on the White House, the feeling was different this time. Obama made a comment a few days after the election that would end up becoming our mantra for the next two years: "My presidency is entering the fourth quarter; interesting stuff happens in the fourth quarter." Yes, it was a cheesy sports metaphor, but Denis—who has something of the Midwestern high school football coach in him—embraced it. He had stickers made with Obama's mantra on them and started handing them out. This elicited some eye rolling, but also a sense that perhaps we were going to spend the last two years of the presidency doing big things, unencumbered by the caution and exhaustion that had crept in at points over the last few years.

Almost immediately, this shift became a reality. Obama expanded protections for undocumented immigrants who had come to the United States as children, and their families. He flew to Beijing and announced a bilateral agreement to combat climate change. He had spent many months quietly coaxing the Chinese to make

this announcement, aided by John Podesta and our climate nego-
tiator, Todd Stern, appealing to the ambitions of the new Chinese
president, Xi Jinping. On the plane leaving Beijing, Obama—who
had spent six years methodically investing in clean energy, changing
fuel efficiency standards and enhancing environmental protections
without congressional support—took note of China's ability to
make a snap decision that could transform their economy. "They
can send a signal and remake their energy sector," he said. "We can't
even build an airport."

He seemed looser and less burdened by the opposition he faced
at home. At our next stop after China—an East Asian summit in
Myanmar—Susan and I climbed into the Beast after another long
day. Obama took out his iPad. "I've got a song stuck in my head," he
said, and started playing it at top volume—something I'd never seen
him do in hundreds of these limo rides. "Thrift Shop," by Mack-
lemore. He and Susan started dancing in their seats, bobbing and
weaving from side to side—*"I'm gonna pop some tags, only got twenty
dollars in my pocket"*—as I sat there uncomfortably, the stiff white
guy listening to the white rapper, a smile frozen on my face, wondering what the two Secret Service agents sitting in the front of the
limo were thinking. *This,* I thought, *is a guy who is out of fucks.*

BACK IN WASHINGTON, ON December 10 I went into Obama's office to get his guidance for the remarks he'd give on his upcoming
Cuba announcement. "Start at the Cold War," he said, "and hook the
duration of this conflict to the duration of my own life." I went back
to my office, where I was supposed to meet with a Yazidi member of
the Iraqi parliament. Beyond the routine of meetings, speeches, and
press briefings, it felt as if my job was shrinking to a collection of
long shots and lost causes. I was taking a brief break in my office
when Ann called to say she'd gone to the hospital with high blood
pressure. "Don't come right away," she said. "I'll call you if it's time."

I hung up the phone and told Bernadette Meehan, who sat right
outside my office, what she'd said. "Are you crazy? Get out of here."

I drove to the hospital and jogged up to the maternity ward, where I found Ann lying in bed and beginning to go into labor. I sat on a couch with a plastic cover as one of the best-looking men I've ever seen came in to give Ann an epidural. We called him McDreamy. The nurse suggested we take a nap. For a couple of hours, I dozed, glanced at Ann—who was asleep—and texted updates to family and friends to make myself useful, people whom I'd barely been able to keep in touch with for years who were full of congratulations and pressed for updates in a way that felt, to me, like forgiveness. A little after one in the morning, things picked up as Ann and the nurse and doctor went through the pattern of labor while I sat there, feeling as though I was watching something that was at the same time transformative for us and totally routine in the workings of a hospital. After what felt like an eternity, Ella was suddenly there—all four limbs moving at once, full of life and motion in the nurse's hands.

In less than a minute, Ella was cleaned and swaddled and deposited in my arms. It was just before four in the morning as I looked down at her closed eyes and felt the warmth of her body pulsing through the blanket. The nurses' shift changed and we were alone. Ann and I took turns holding her, fighting to stay awake, now a different type of unit, three people living in the world. After we were moved to a private room, the nurse came in around ten, and she and Ann were changing Ella's first diaper when my phone rang. I answered and it was Obama's voice on the phone, the first I'd heard from outside the hospital. "She looks like you," he said. "Hopefully she'll end up looking more like Ann." I laughed. "Your life will never be the same."

Ann asked who it was, and when I said, "The president," it seemed almost normal.

THREE DAYS LATER, I had to go back into the office to meet the team working on the Cuba announcement. Because the circle was so small, I was the only person who could write the remarks, brief the press, and make sure the various pieces fit together. When I walked through the gate and into the West Wing, it felt like visiting a place from my distant past—a high school or college reunion—and not the place I'd been going every day for the last six years. That night, I sat at the table in my apartment and wrote the speech in a few hours. "Today, the United States of America is changing its relationship with the people of Cuba." The words came easily; this was something I'd done, not just something I was writing about.

The day before the announcement, I came in to join Obama's phone call with Raúl Castro—the first such communication between U.S. and Cuban leaders since the Cuban Revolution. As we sat in the Oval Office waiting for the call to be connected, Obama looked at me, Susan, and Ricardo. "As Joe Biden would say, this is a big fucking deal," he said.

"Señor presidente!" Castro declared, coming on the line. I recognized Juana's voice on the phone interpreting. After the greetings, Obama went through all the points we'd given him to make, which took nearly twenty minutes. When it was Castro's turn to speak, he joked that Obama hadn't come close to Fidel's record for speaking uninterrupted.

Castro started reviewing the commitments of both sides. Then he went on a long tangent about efforts to sabotage the Cuban government over the years. As I sat on the couch, my forehead began to sweat as I watched the hands on the antique grandfather clock mark time—ten minutes, twenty minutes, thirty minutes. I passed Obama a note saying that he could cut this off. He shook his head, covering the receiver with his hand. "It's been a long time since they've talked to a U.S. president," he told me. "He's got a lot to say." The call wrapped up with Castro inviting Obama to come to Cuba to go hunting—the thought of Obama hunting, anywhere, seemed far more improbable than a U.S. president visiting Cuba.

There was one final thing that could have derailed what we were doing. The communications team had been planning to set up a lectern in the Roosevelt Room—a location that would put Obama in front of a giant portrait of Teddy Roosevelt charging up San

Juan Hill—the moment, symbolically, when the United States initiated its de facto colonization of Cuba. We had them move it instead to the Cabinet Room.

The next day, I went to work early. It was cold and I had barely slept in days, but the secret had held. I awoke to a clutter of messages—separate planes had taken off for Cuba to pick up Alan Gross and the intelligence asset; notification had begun for different members of Congress and our administration. All of the pieces were now in motion. I sat at my desk and made some final tweaks to the statement that Obama would give when I got word that the plane with Alan Gross on board had taken off from Cuba, a corned beef sandwich—his favorite—ready in the galley, his wife, Judy, who had endured more than five years of separation, waiting for him. News started to break and we did a press call. I'd done hundreds of these over the years, but now I was telling a story of the last year and a half of my life. When that was done, I walked back out into the cold to get some air and take a break by myself, before reentering a world that now knew my secret.

I went back inside and watched Obama speak on the small television mounted on the wall in my office. I'd attend no celebration, no victory party; I wanted to take care of business so I could go home to my daughter, who was still not a week old. Before Obama was even finished speaking, Ann gave me the greatest gift that I could have received when she sent me a photo her sister, Teresa, took of Ann holding Ella in front of the image of Obama speaking on television, the chyron below him reading "OBAMA ANNOUNCES NEW CUBA POLICY: Obama: normalizing relations between our two countries, most sweeping change to U.S.-Cuba policy since 1961." This was, as Ricardo had told me in Rome, as good as it gets.

PART FOUR

WHAT
MAKES
AMERICA
GREAT

2015–2017

CHAPTER 25

TAPPING THE BRAKES

———

As we started the fourth quarter, Obama had the national security team that he wanted in place: Susan Rice, Lisa Monaco, and Susan's principal deputy, Avril Haines, a smart, diligent, and eccentric woman who combined the experience of having been the NSC's top lawyer, insisting on fidelity to the rule of law, with the operational background of having been deputy director of the CIA. Together, this team had constructed a counter-ISIL strategy and an emergency global effort that would stamp out the Ebola epidemic that had spawned fears of millions being killed around the world.

Toward the end of 2014, the Senate Intelligence Committee released the summary of a 6,700-page report on the Bush administration's use of torture and rendition, detailing in stark terms the moral collapse of the United States government after 9/11. There had been a lengthy period of declassification, with our White House put in the position of mediating between a CIA reluctant to see information go public and a Senate committee that wanted as few redactions as possible.

The day after the report was released, McDonough asked Obama if he felt the rollout of the report had gone okay. "Yeah," he said. "I thought it went fine. What did you think?"

"I thought it went fine, too," McDonough said. "I just wanted to make sure you were good."

"You know," Obama said, "I think it's a chance for all of us to reflect on what fear can do to this place. We're not so different from the people who came before us, though I think we're right about more things." His tone was unusually formal. "If you want to know why sometimes I tap the brakes, that's why. We can't make decisions based on fear."

"You're goddamn right," Biden said. "And we're lucky to have you." He reached out like an old pol and grabbed Obama's wrist.

After the ISIL beheadings, there had been a limitless demand for Obama to take military action, to obtain some measure of vengeance. Fear, bordering on hysteria, seemed to project from cable television. At one event, a businessman pulled me aside, as if in confidence, and told me he'd hired a private security detail so that he wouldn't be beheaded on the streets of New York. At one point in the midst of it all, Obama called me up to the Oval Office, as he did sometimes when he wanted to unburden his mind. We chatted a bit about the current state of our public line on ISIL. "You know," he said, "I can see how the Iraq War happened."

"What do you mean?"

"People are so scared right now," he said. "It'd be easy for me as president to get on that wave and do whatever I want."

Instead, that fall, he had been more deliberate, commencing a limited bombing campaign in Iraq and Syria and putting small teams of U.S. advisors on the ground to help organize the Iraqi and Syrian Kurdish forces who were going to start steadily retaking territory from ISIL. He placed strict caps on the numbers of these troops, and on what they could do, prompting another series of complaints about Obama "micromanaging" the Pentagon. He didn't care. ISIL was a serious enough threat to warrant launching thousands of airstrikes, but he cringed when he heard the threat described as "existential." ISIL had killed four Americans, a tiny fraction of those lost in Iraq and Afghanistan. It wasn't, as some of our critics roared, analogous to Nazi Germany—the same rhetoric

Bush used after 9/11 when the government was authorizing torture.

BY THE WINTER OF 2015, a principal Republican attack on Obama was that he didn't refer to our enemy as "radical Islam." Early in the administration, we decided to move away from the phrase "Global War on Terror," believing that you can't wage war against a tactic, nor could you ever defeat it. We also generally avoided using the word "Islam" in describing the enemy because terrorist groups like al Qaeda wanted to cast themselves as a religious movement. After bin Laden was killed, communications were found in his compound in which he lamented that the absence of a religious name for al Qaeda allowed the West to "claim deceptively that they are not at war with Islam." ISIL—"the Islamic State"—was addressing that challenge in their name and their declaration of a caliphate.

Since most Republicans didn't want to call for more troops in places like Syria, their strategies often began with the assertion that they would identify the enemy as "radical Islam," as if the clarity of this rhetoric would cause ISIL to crumble. The media constantly asked us about our refusal to do so. That February, we were hosting a Summit on Countering Violent Extremism, which would bring together experts and leaders from communities (largely Muslim ones) where there was a threat of radicalization. The absence of the word "Islamic" from the conference name kicked the issue up yet again in the press, and Obama called me up to his office.

"Hey," he said, sitting behind his desk. "I didn't realize that we were being so politically correct in talking about Islamic extremism. I thought it was just some Fox News bullshit." He had just read a column by Thomas Friedman entitled "Say It Like It Is," lambasting us for not saying we were at war with radical Islam.

I stood there, feeling a weakness in my legs. Had we spent months defending a position that Obama didn't care that much about? "I think it's the phrase 'radical Islam,'" I said. "That makes it sound . . ."

"Like all of Islam is radical," he said, nodding. "I get that. But I don't have any problem saying this ideology is a problem in the Islamic world."

"We've pointed to all the times you've said that." I tried to think of an alternative phrase, and then realized that that was the problem. "I think the issue that comes to Josh," I said, referring to our press secretary's daily press briefings, "is why we don't say that we're at war with radical Islam."

I saw Obama registering the absurdity of the debate. It was often the case that these controversies—which migrated from fringe websites, to Fox News, to the White House briefing room, and then finally to columns by people like Tom Friedman—did not reach him until later in that process than the rest of us. "So anything we do now would be a shift in our position."

"Exactly," I said.

"And attract more attention."

"Yes," I said. "Here and around the world."

We were both silent for a moment. "So it's not on the level," he said.

"It's not on the level."

"Okay," he said, realizing that it was a domestic political issue, and not really a matter of national security. "I'll talk to Josh and Denis about it."

We went ahead with the Summit on Countering Violent Extremism, announcing a series of measures to work with communities to combat the threat from ISIL, as well as other extremist groups—such as white supremacists. We announced commonsense, technocratic things to do—build ties between law enforcement and Muslim communities targeted by ISIL; recognize that violent extremism can take different forms. But politically, that only raised the temperature. Ted Cruz, gearing up for a presidential run, denounced Obama—who had waged war as commander in chief every day of his presidency—as "an apologist for radical Islamic terrorists."

———

I FINALLY CONFIRMED TO Obama that I would stick it out through
the end of the administration. I was standing in the Oval Office
when he asked me, as he had two years ago after the election on Air
Force One, if I wanted to take on an additional project—something
like Cuba.

"No," I said, "but I would like some things to change."

"What?" he asked.

"I'd like to work less," I said, "and see my family more." To give
him a sense of what I meant, I added, "I'd like to get out of the day-
to-day communications where I can. I don't want to be coming to
work in late 2016 and still answering some criticism about why
you're weak on ISIL."

He laughed. "Neither do I," he said. "But I'm going to need you
for Iran."

We were entering the homestretch of negotiations with the Iranians, and the ferocity of opposition to the agreement—which
didn't even exist—was building. In late January, Speaker Boehner
put out a press release announcing that Netanyahu would be traveling to the United States at his invitation to address a joint session
of Congress. We received no advance notice of this visit from either
Boehner or the Israeli government. This type of interference in
American foreign policy—a foreign leader invited to lobby the U.S.
Congress against the policy of a sitting president—would have
been unthinkable in 2009. But by 2015, Netanyahu had become almost a de facto member of the Republican caucus, and Republicans
had abandoned any norms about working with a foreign government to undermine the policies of a sitting president.

Congress was debating yet another Iran sanctions bill, a short-
sighted and unnecessary piece of legislation that would have blown
up the negotiations. Obama went before the Democratic caucus
and gave a lengthy defense of the need to give John Kerry time and
space to negotiate a nuclear deal. "This vote," Obama said, "is not a

freebie. I need you on this." He told them, again, that he'd veto anything that put the negotiations in danger. I was meeting regularly with Democratic members of Congress to try to convince them that we were pursuing a good deal, one that would roll back the Iranian nuclear program and avert a war. This included a standing meeting with the Jewish Democrats in the House. These were occasionally raucous meetings, as we all talked over one another and debated the various intricacies of the Iranian nuclear program: how many centrifuges they'd have operating; what facilities they could use; what would happen to their heavy water reactor, which was on track to produce plutonium—hours and hours talking about a deal that hadn't even been reached.

Usually, I was on permanent defense, responding to various lines of criticism circulating on the Hill. After Netanyahu's speech was announced, the dynamic shifted; suddenly, the Democrats were more annoyed at Netanyahu for interfering in our politics than at anything we were doing. I'd have these meetings in the Capitol, often right before or after the Israeli ambassador, Ron Dermer—a close Netanyahu confidant—was meeting with the same group. It felt as if we were sparring, getting ready for a bigger fight to come.

A TEN-DAY STRETCH IN June encapsulated both the events that ensured Obama's presidency would be a historic success and the clouds that would hover over his legacy.

On June 16, Donald Trump announced his candidacy for the presidency. I watched as he rode down an escalator in the gold-plated lobby at Trump Tower, waving to an assembled crowd. He launched into a rambling, semicoherent rant that sounded like a greatest-hits version of Fox News opposition to Obama, and called Mexicans rapists. We didn't take it all that seriously. Trump was just a cruder expression of what we'd heard from Republicans for years, and it seemed he had little chance of becoming president.

The next day, June 17, a young white supremacist named Dylann Roof walked into a black church in Charleston, joined a Bible study group, and then opened fire—killing nine people in a matter of minutes. At that time, Roof had killed more Americans than ISIL and added a particularly vile act of terror to the long list of mass shootings that had taken place during the Obama presidency— shootings that we felt powerless to stop with a Congress that opposed any gun restrictions. Privately, Obama lamented that he was out of words to express outrage at another shooting. "Maybe I'll just go and attend the memorial service," he said, "and not say anything."

Then, on June 25, we filed into the Oval Office for the morning meeting. While Obama was getting briefed, he was interrupted, which was unusual, and told that "the Supreme Court upheld the ACA." Then he held his hand over his head and closed his eyes tightly, as if to say, *Give me a minute.* We all applauded, stood up, shook his hand. After less than a minute, he sat down and asked us to continue the briefing. It seemed that a weight had been removed from his shoulders.

On the twenty-sixth, more good news; the Supreme Court ruled in favor of same-sex marriage. The White House became a celebratory place, people embracing in the hallways, gay colleagues in tears at the news. Plans were made to light the White House that night in rainbow colors. Coupled with healthcare, it felt as if the outlines of a successful presidency were coming into focus.

Obama had been up late the night before, rewriting the speech that he was slated to give in Charleston at a memorial service for the nine people who'd been killed. Cody Keenan had done the first draft, but told me that Obama had rewritten much of it himself, choosing to anchor the speech in the concept of grace. In raw, handwritten prose, he addressed squarely the racial taboos that he often shied away from—the racism of the Confederate flag and the criminal justice system; the scourge of gun violence and the casual bias that leads people to "call Johnny back for a job interview but not Jamal"; the need to "examine what we're doing to cause some of our children to hate." As Cody took off on Marine One, he sent me a note that Obama had said something unusual: Perhaps, if the spirit moved him, he would sing "Amazing Grace" during his speech.

That afternoon, I was working at my desk when the speech came on the White House television channel that played whenever the president was speaking. Over the course of the speech, I stopped to watch as he delved deeper into these subjects. As was often the case in black churches, he fell into a more rhythmic style, feeding off the crowd, a man far more welcome there than he had ever been in Congress. "God has visited grace upon us, for he has allowed us to see where we've been blind," Obama said. "He has given us the chance, where we've been lost, to find our best selves. We may not have earned it, this grace, with our rancor and complacency and shortsightedness and fear of each other—but we got it all the same."

It felt as though he was speaking directly to all of the conflicting emotions about America that I'd come to feel—the disappointment in the reality around me, but also the redemptive nature of the project that we were all a part of. As Obama neared the end of the prepared text, he described the dignity of the victims, the grace in their lives that could heal the hate in America. "If we can tap that grace," he said, "*everything can change.* Amazing grace. Amazing grace." I froze.

Obama stopped talking and put his head down. I stared at the television. He paused for what felt like an eternity. The African American clergy behind him sat in prayerful silence, draped in purple vestments. It felt as though he'd reached the end of one kind of speech, a particularly good one, but something was not yet fully expressed. Then something changed in his face—a face I had stared at and studied across a thousand meetings, a face I had learned to read so I could understand what he was thinking, or what he wanted me to do. I saw the faintest hint of a smile and a slight shake of the head as he looked down at the lectern, a letting go, a man who looked unburdened. *He's going to sing,* I thought.

"Amazing grace, how sweet the sound . . ."

The pastor behind him let out a joyful laugh. The audience began to cheer, springing to their feet, released from some more passive form of mourning.

"that saved a wretch like me . . ."

The voices of the other congregants started to rise in unison with his. One of the preachers behind him opened up into the largest smile that you could ever have at a memorial service, a wistful smile. Obama's body relaxed into the moment, his imperfect singing voice mining the depths of the hymn.

"I once was lost, but now I'm found . . ."

I started to feel everything at once—the hurt and anger at the murder of those nine people, another thing that I'd kept pressed down in the constant compartmentation of emotions that allowed me to do my job; the stress that came from doing a job that had steadily swallowed who I thought I was over the last eight years; the more pure motivations, to do something that felt right, buried deep within me; the sense that maybe we were all going to be okay even if the world wasn't.

"was blind, but now I see."

An organ was playing, people were giving praise in the audience, and in that instant I was reminded that there were people, good people, kind people out there in the world who were more important than any of the petty controversies that enveloped us every day, people who understood who Obama was and what he had been trying to do, people whose support could allow him to stand there, in the middle of his seventh year as president, and be totally open in a way that I had almost never seen him be in public before. It was always hard to explain what it was that I most admired about this complicated man. Watching him, I felt that I would never have to explain it to anyone again.

He then started reciting the list, punctuated by organ chords, of the names of every one of the victims, a stratagem that managed to do something I had never seen before, as the entire life of each person was celebrated, vindicated, and elevated by the short, declarative words that he spoke:

Clementa Pinckney found that grace.

Cynthia Hurd found that grace.

Susie Jackson found that grace.

Ethel Lance found that grace.

DePayne Middleton-Doctor found that grace.

Tywanza Sanders found that grace.

Daniel L. Simmons, Senior, found that grace.

Sharonda Coleman-Singleton found that grace.

Myra Thompson found that grace.

Then it was over, this moment that had opened up a window into something—into Obama; into a better America than the one I lived in every day, into a purer sense of what we were all doing, as people who worked for him, what we were a part of, what kept me coming back to work all these years. I sat at my desk, the White House feed on my television now an empty blue screen, and for the first time in many years, I sobbed.

A FEW DAYS AFTER the Charleston speech, I went up to the Oval Office. It was the last meeting of the day, and Obama wanted to talk to me, Denis, and Anita Decker Breckenridge, now his deputy chief of staff, about the potential rollout of an Iran deal. When the three of us walked in, instead of getting up and walking over to his chair as he normally would, Obama sat at his desk, lingering over a letter. He didn't offer his customary "Have a seat" or acknowledge our presence, so the three of us stood over the couches awkwardly—

people who saw Obama as much as anyone, but still deferential to the protocols of his office.

"'Dear Mr. President,'" he began to read aloud. "'I used to not like you because of the color of your skin. My whole life I have hated people because of the color of their skin. I have thought about things since those nine people were killed and I realize I was wrong. I want to thank you for everything you are trying to do to help people.'"

He finished, and put the letter down. None of us knew what to say. It felt as if the whole presidency was for the purpose of receiving this single letter.

He looked at the letter on his desk, as though it were another person in the room. "Grace," he said. Then he got up and walked over to his chair. "It's a shame," he said, sitting down, "that those nine people had to die for that to happen."

CHAPTER 26

THE ANTIWAR ROOM

———

BARACK OBAMA TOOK OFFICE AFTER IRAN HAD THE SCIEN-
tific knowledge and infrastructure necessary to build a nuclear
weapon. By the time we reached the interim agreement in 2013,
they were less than a year from producing enough of the raw materials for the purpose if they chose to break out and pursue it.
Therefore, the negotiations became an extended effort to solve a
pressing scientific problem: How can we impose enough restrictions on Iran's nuclear program to prevent them from approaching
that tipping point? Given the nature of the challenge, in addition to
John Kerry, an increasingly important member of our negotiating
team was Ernie Moniz—the nuclear physicist who served as our
secretary of energy, a brilliant, unusually plainspoken scientist with
unkempt gray hair combed back in a style that made him resemble
one of America's Founding Fathers.

As the negotiations intensified into the spring of 2016, we inched
closer to a deal. That is when my role became more pronounced.
Because I was responsible for leading the effort to secure the congressional support necessary for an agreement to survive, I became
a kind of barometer. In meetings or videoconferences with Kerry
and the negotiating team, Obama would glance at me as they reported the latest progress or backsliding, looking to see if I cringed

or lit up at the latest report. I was familiar with the attacks that would come our way, in part because I was already hearing them.

Obama had to balance security, science, and politics. For example, we had consistently opposed Iran having any centrifuges at Fordow, a site buried deep underground, and therefore a harder military target. The Iranians wanted to keep some centrifuges there, but disconnected, with electronic seals in place to make sure they were off. In exchange, they'd make additional concessions on other issues.

"Ernie, what do you think?" Obama asked.

"Substantively, it makes no difference," he replied, adding that he'd rather have other Iranian commitments on their stockpile and ability to build new reactors.

Satisfied, Obama would ask me if we could make that shift. As long as we can say there's no enrichment at Fordow, I said.

Kerry and Moniz flew to Vienna in late June to see if they could close the deal. Obama told Kerry that he had to be willing to walk away. "John," he said, referring to the victories on healthcare and same-sex marriage, "I've already got my legacy. I don't need this." Kerry said he understood, but he was also after his own legacy—he'd spent hundreds of hours in negotiations with the Iranians, and built a close relationship with the Iranian foreign minister, Javad Zarif. Moniz had also developed a close relationship with his Iranian counterpart, who had attended MIT while Moniz was teaching there, before the Iranian Revolution opened up the chasm between our two countries. These were the two relationships that were going to have to get us over the finish line.

Kerry and Moniz ended up spending seventeen days in Vienna, capping off years of work—there is simply no way the Iran deal would have gotten done without both of them. Most of the final questions had to do with how long the different restrictions on Iran would last. It was a complicated process—with some restrictions lasting eight years, some ten, some fifteen, some forever. Every day, Obama was updated. Multiple times a day, I'd check in via videoconference with the team in Vienna, who had barely slept for weeks. We were holding out in Washington for things that often made little substantive difference but could help us defend the deal against the barrage of criticism that was coming.

Complicating matters was the fact that Congress had passed the Iran Nuclear Agreement Review Act, which required a congressional vote on a final deal within thirty days of its being submitted to Congress. We initially resisted this, but Democrats had grown weary of blocking Iran sanctions bills and thought it would be awkward to block an effort to call a vote. Here is what this meant in practice: Republicans needed a majority in the House, and sixty votes in the Senate, to formally reject the Iran deal. If we had enough votes to sustain a presidential veto in either the House or Senate, then they wouldn't be able to kill the deal. If we could secure forty-one votes in the Senate, then Congress wouldn't even be able to reject it at all. Everyone knew that the review period would offer a forum for Republicans, the Israeli government, and AIPAC to attack the deal.

Given the protracted negotiations, we missed a July 9 deadline that Congress had set in the legislation, which meant that the review period before a vote would be *sixty* days instead of thirty. This would make it harder to secure congressional support, as the review period would now run through the August congressional recess, making it possible for critics of the deal to run advertisements in districts and states to pressure members of Congress. The Iranians thought we would cave on the remaining issues to avoid the longer congressional period, but Obama wanted to show that we were willing to live without a deal.

Day after day, on little to no sleep, Kerry and Moniz haggled over the remaining issues. On July 12, the pieces started coming together. On the thirteenth, Susan and I went into the Oval Office for Obama's final call with Kerry. The deal was basically done, but Obama needed to give his approval. We watched as Obama listened on the phone. "John, you should be very proud," he said. With that, he hung up the phone and smiled. "Looks like we have a deal."

"That took eight years," I said.

"We should call that YouTube guy," he said, referring to the 2007 debate question about engaging adversaries.

Obama turned to the statement he'd give the next morning. "Make sure we frame this as a nuclear issue," he told me. Ever since Netanyahu's speech to Congress, critics had been using Iran's non-nuclear behavior—its support for terrorism, its belligerence in the Middle East—to delegitimize the deal. "We don't want to let the critics muddy the nuclear issue with the other issues."

A FEW DAYS BEFORE the deal was finalized, I sat at my desk reading a story in my press clips. "This is insane," I said.

Ned Price, a former CIA analyst who had recently become the NSC spokesperson sitting right outside my office, came in and asked what I was talking about. "Check out this *Breitbart* story," I said. Ned read the beginning of the story over my shoulder: "Deputy national security advisor Ben Rhodes—who lacks any prior qualifications for the post—has explained to the Atlantic's Jeffrey Goldberg at the Aspen Ideas Festival on Monday that the administration believes that a bad Iran deal is worth doing because political reform inside the Iranian regime is more likely with the deal than without. Or, to use Rhodes's own words: 'We believe that the kiss of the nuke deal will turn the Iranian frog into a handsome prince.'"

"That's insane," Ned said.

Unlike my doctored Benghazi email, this didn't sound anything like something that I—or any human being—would say. We checked the transcript. As it turned out, this is what I had actually said: "We believe that an agreement is necessary and has to be good enough to be worth doing even if Iran doesn't change. If ten or fifteen years from now Iran is the same as it is today, in terms of its government, the deal has to be good enough that it can exist on those merits." This was central to our whole argument: We needed a deal to prevent Iran from obtaining a nuclear weapon precisely because it was a bad actor; that, of course, is why critics were trying to turn the argument inside out.

I reached out to Goldberg, who publicly disputed the story. But fact checks weren't going to reach the readers of *Breitbart*, which had already published more than one story, spawning an unknowable number of follow-on Internet stories, talk radio segments, and tweets. *We believe that the kiss of the nuke deal will turn the Iranian frog into a handsome prince.* Millions of people would consume this information in a matter of hours, far more than the readership of *The New York Times*. It was fake news, and there was no way to dissuade people who chose to believe things that validated their established convictions.

Breitbart had already run a story about an NSC staffer on Iran named Sahar Nowrouzzadeh, because she was Iranian American and once interned for an organization that advocated for diplomacy with Iran. Sahar was a career civil servant for a decade, starting out in George W. Bush's Pentagon. The stories made her out to be a Manchurian candidate, advocating for Iran's interests within the Obama White House. Afterward, Obama invited her into the Oval Office. "Don't let them get you down," he said, posing for a picture with her in front of his desk. She kept a huge smile frozen on her face, fighting off tears.

Later, in my office, I gave her my own pep talk. "We just can't let them win." It was the type of thing I had been telling myself for years, and I knew it was cold comfort—enough to motivate you through the day but not to make the nature of our opposition any less disconcerting.

Dozens of people—diplomats, lawyers, sanctions experts, nuclear scientists, intelligence analysts—had worked on Wendy Sherman's team for years to get the Iran deal done. I felt as though they had handed off a baton to me and my team, and we had sixty days to make sure Congress wouldn't undo their work. There was no doubt we'd confront a well-financed and relentless effort to undermine the deal. The last time we raised concerns before an actual vote on a piece of Iran sanctions legislation—a 2011 sanctions bill strongly supported by AIPAC—it ended up passing 100–0 in the Senate.

I sat at the table in my apartment, reviewing different pieces of a plan of congressional briefings and public outreach that would carry us through the next two months. "I've never been this stressed before," I said to Ann, who was in the kitchen.

"What do you mean?" she asked.

"I feel like this is all on me."

"That's crazy," she said. "There are lots of people in this." She started ticking off the State Department's leadership: "Kerry, Wendy, Tony . . ."

"It's not the same," I said.

"Why?" she asked. "This is what John Kerry has worked for his whole life."

"It just isn't the same," I said. I took a deep breath and stared at the computer screen. "I can't explain." Kerry, at least, was also able to focus on diplomacy; I was about to spend two months down in the muck, doing the part of my job that I enjoyed the least, and it felt like the most important thing I was ever going to do.

THE NEXT MORNING, I pitched Denis McDonough on my concept: I wanted to take the Iran team I'd already built and turn it into a standing working group of people who would focus entirely on securing congressional support for the deal. "You still have a job," he said. "You'll need someone else to run the war room."

I turned to a guy named Chad Kreikemeier, an amiable Nebraskan and former Hill staffer who worked on legislative affairs at the White House. Together, we'd put together a collection of combative personalities and eccentric experts who would cover policy, communications, digital outreach, engagement with the Jewish community, liaison with progressive organizations, and—above all—constant communication with members of Congress and their offices. I made the offer and Chad said he'd think about it; unspoken was the fact that whoever took on a prominent role defending the Iran deal was going to put a target on his own back. Less than an hour after leaving my office, he came back. "Okay," he said. "There's no way I'm not doing this."

"Congratulations," I said. "I think. You just took command of the war room."

We ended up calling it the Antiwar Room. Obama charged us with making sure we mobilized the constellation of progressive groups who had joined together during the Bush administration to oppose the Iraq War. "Democrats are going to be feeling a lot of pressure from the AIPAC folks," he said. "We need to make sure they hear from folks on the other side, especially over August recess."

Our case was straightforward: The deal prevented Iran from getting a nuclear weapon. The Iranians had to remove two-thirds of their centrifuges, couldn't use their more advanced centrifuges, and had to get rid of 98 percent of their stockpile. They had to convert a heavy water reactor so it couldn't produce plutonium. Inspectors would have 24/7 access to Iran's nuclear facilities, and the ability to access Iran's entire nuclear supply chain—from uranium mines and mills to centrifuge manufacturing and storage facilities. To cheat, Iran wouldn't just need a nuclear facility like Natanz or Fordow—they'd have to run an entirely secret supply chain. If they cheated, sanctions would snap back into place.

Then there were the consequences of not having the deal. Without it, Iran could quickly advance its nuclear program to the point of having enough material for a bomb. That would leave us with a choice between bombing their facilities and acquiescing to a nuclear-armed Iran. Holding out for a better deal was not going to work. It was diplomacy or war.

The press reported that AIPAC and other opposition groups were planning to spend up to $40 million on advertisements and other efforts to kill the deal, which would intimidate members of Congress, several of whom called me to express concerns that we had no similar resources to spend. They sent out long anti–Iran deal documents that would shape the arguments we'd hear made back at us from deal opponents on the Hill or in the media. Every morning, we'd convene the twenty or so people who comprised our Antiwar Room to map out what arguments needed to be countered, what Hill meetings needed to be scheduled, what briefings had to take place—of scientists, experts, journalists, or advocates. Matt Nosanchuk, the permanently smiling man in charge of our Jewish outreach, asked what his objective should be. "I want you to talk to every Jewish person in America," I said.

"Every Jew in America," he repeated. "Okay."

Chad set up an office in a closet-sized room in the basement of the West Wing where he listed every Democratic senator on a whiteboard to track where they were on the issue and what needed to be done to win their vote. Every question that was raised about the deal would be fact-checked, both publicly and in materials sent to Congress. To make sure that people would see our fact checks in real time, we set up a Twitter account, @theIranDeal.

If the opposition's advantage was the fact that the Israeli government and AIPAC were focused on lawmakers who dreaded taking a position against them, our advantage was the fact that we needed only Democratic votes. When Scott Walker, a Republican presidential candidate, said he might take military action against Iran on the first day of his presidency, we made sure that got around to Democratic offices. When Scooter Libby, an intellectual architect of the Iraq War, wrote an op-ed attacking the deal, we pointed out that the same people who got us into Iraq wanted to take us to war in Iran. "Wrong then, wrong now" became our mantra.

Obama made a point of being the chief salesman himself. He had the entire Democratic caucus to the White House. He did interviews and made speeches. Toward the end of July, he went on *The Daily Show* to reach the younger audience that we'd need to buck up Democrats. "If people are engaged, eventually the political system responds," Obama said. "Despite the money, despite the lobbyists, it still responds." Later, on a conference call with antiwar activists, he noted that the same people who supported the Iraq

War were now opposing the Iran deal. That's when things began to take an ugly turn.

These were anodyne and accurate statements. Yet some deal opponents started to make a new charge: that Obama and his team were anti-Semites, conjuring up stereotypes of moneyed Jewish interests propelling us into a war. This put us into an impossible position. Even to acknowledge the fact that AIPAC was spending tens of millions to defeat the Iran deal was anti-Semitic. To observe that the same people who supported the war in Iraq also opposed the Iran deal was similarly off limits. It was an offensive way for people to avoid accountability for their own positions.

Obama wasn't going to be intimidated. In a short meeting with a group of us before he spoke to American Jewish community leaders in early August, I explained that people were accusing him of using anti-Semitic dog whistles.

"Dog whistles?" he asked. "How, exactly?"

"By saying that the same people who got us into the war in Iraq want to take us to war with Iran."

"How is that a dog whistle?" He was incredulous, and—as was often the case when I was the messenger for this type of thing—he talked to me as if I was the one making the criticism.

"They're saying that's us calling Jews warmongers."

"Oh, come on," he said. "John Bolton wants to bomb Iran, right?"

"Yes," I said. Bolton had written an op-ed for *The New York Times* entitled "To Stop Iran's Bomb, Bomb Iran."

"Is he Jewish?"

"No."

"Dick Cheney?"

"No."

"I'm black," he said. "I think I know when folks are using dog whistles. I hear them all the time." His voice was raised a bit, which almost never happened. "Come on." He paused, returning to his even temperament. "This is aggravating."

"I know," I said. "I'm the self-hating Jew. Or half self-hating."

He laughed, then turned more serious. "This isn't about anti-

Semitism," he said. "They're trying to take away our best argument, that it's this or war."

Before going on his own August vacation, he gave a speech at American University. In it he made a case for the deal that he wanted Democrats to take home with them over recess. "I know it's easy to play on people's fears, to magnify threats, to compare any attempt at diplomacy to Munich, but none of these arguments hold up," he said. "They didn't back in 2002, in 2003, they shouldn't now. That same mindset, in many cases offered by the same people, who seem to have no compunction about being repeatedly wrong, led to a war that did more to strengthen Iran, more to isolate the United States, than anything we have done in the decades before or since."

The reaction was fierce. In one of the harsher responses, an editorial in *Tablet* magazine lamented, "The use of anti-Jewish incitement as a political tool is a sickening new development in American political discourse, and we have heard too much of it lately—some coming, ominously, from our own White House and its representatives." I cringed when I read these things. Support for Israel had been central to my own sense of identity as I was coming of age, a way for a child of mixed religious background to find an anchor in culture and history. Now that kind of attachment was being cynically manipulated to discredit a profoundly unbiased president, destroy a diplomatic agreement, and once again avoid any reckoning with the actual legacy of Iraq.

I SPENT MY AUGUST vacation calling senators and comparing vote counts with Dick Durbin, who was leading the effort in the Senate and reporting every shred of gossip to Obama. Unlike the previous year, Obama relished working in Martha's Vineyard, calling more than thirty members of Congress from his vacation home. After each call, he'd send me a note about something we could do to help a Democrat get to yes—a letter from him, a surrogate in their district, a particular argument that needed to be made.

Gradually, things started to break our way. People other than us

started to shoot down the anti-Semitism charge. Twenty-nine leading physicists came out for the deal. European ambassadors lobbied
on behalf of the agreement. Retired national security officials and
ambassadors to Israel wrote letters of support. Dozens of retired
Israeli generals signed a petition contradicting Netanyahu and supporting the deal; so did the former head of Mossad. Three hundred
forty rabbis wrote an open letter. Several dozen Iranian dissidents
signed a letter indicating that supporters of human rights in Iran
supported the deal. A majority of American Jews supported the
deal in public opinion surveys, a higher percentage than in the
broader public. A steady drumbeat of Democrats started to come
out in support.

As Congress came back to town, it was clear we'd have enough
support in the House and Senate to uphold a presidential veto if
Congress voted to reject the deal. Our efforts narrowed to a handful
of Democratic senators who could get us to the forty-one votes
necessary to prevent Congress from even passing a rejection of the
deal. We also wanted to secure a healthy majority of Jewish Democrats in the House so the deal would be less polarizing. The key vote
remained Debbie Wasserman Schultz, the congresswoman from
Florida—and head of the Democratic National Committee—
whom I had spent many hours talking to about Iran over the years.

I was up in New York City when she called and said she needed
to speak to Obama. Around the same time, a reporter emailed me
to say he'd heard Debbie was coming out against the deal. All day, I
was in a bad mood, worried that the head of the DNC was announcing her opposition. Obama couldn't call her until late at night,
and so it was midnight when I got a note that they'd connected.
When Debbie finally called me, my mother was speaking in Yid-
dish in the background, saying she'd go down to Debbie's district to
give a piece of her mind to any of the *meshugganahs* who gave her
grief. Debbie told me she was a yes, and we both ended up in tears.
"Tell your mother she's welcome down here anytime!" she said.

By the time Congress voted on the deal, we had logged more
than twelve hundred engagements with members of Congress. For

many of them, the decision was wrenching, politically and personally. But in the end, nearly all of the final votes broke our way. Forty-
two senators supported the deal, ensuring that Congress would not
be able to express disapproval.

On the day that we secured our final votes, Dick Cheney gave a
speech at the American Enterprise Institute, the heart of neoconservatism, which he'd scheduled before our success was a foregone
conclusion. We watched gleefully from the Antiwar Room as
Cheney reinforced our contention that the same people who got us
into war in Iraq wanted to do the same thing in Iran. One moment
in particular seemed to encapsulate all that had happened over two
months: Antiwar protesters disrupted the speech, shouting, "He
was wrong on Iraq, he is wrong on Iran," which prompted an older
white guy to get up and try to rip a sign from a young woman's
hand; after a few awkward moments, he gave up and fell back into
his chair.

I took Chad up to the Oval Office. Obama smiled. "That was
actually kind of fun," he told us.

"I'll never do anything like that again in government," Chad
said.

CHAPTER 27

BOMBS AND CHILDREN

———

A BOUT FIFTEEN OF US BOARDED A WEATHERED, CANOPIED motorboat from Luang Prabang, the ancient Buddhist capital of Laos, for a ninety-minute ride up the Mekong River. The water was brown and slow-moving, and as the wooden hotels and temples faded in the distance, the riverbank became overwhelmed by thick, green forest at the base of rolling hills. The boat was filled with embassy staff and some local Lao contacts who chatted leisurely and kept a slight distance from me. I had the sense that they were all trying to figure out what I was doing there.

We arrived at a beach where several dozen young children were assembled under a tarp tied to some wooden poles, singing songs. Our boat was full of school supplies. The kids were arranged into rows for some kind of performance while I stood in front of them next to our ambassador, Dan Clune. I noticed a particularly sassy girl of about five in the front row, wearing an oversized T-shirt decorated with a huge picture of Elsa from *Frozen*. After the kids danced and sang a couple of songs, Dan, my assistant, Rumana Ahmed, and I climbed into a Toyota Land Cruiser with a large stamp on it stamped FROM THE GOVERNMENT OF JAPAN for a short drive to a clearance site for unexploded ordnance. "They'll give you a briefing," Dan said, "and then there will be a demonstration."

Laos is the most heavily bombed country in the history of the world. From 1964 to 1973, the United States dropped more than two million tons of ordnance on Laos to disrupt the Ho Chi Minh Trail and try to stanch a Communist insurgency—more than was dropped on all of Germany and Japan during World War II. There were 580,000 bombing missions, which averages out to one every eight minutes for nine years. Sometimes, U.S. planes returning to Thailand from missions over Vietnam indiscriminately dropped their remaining bombs on Laos. More than 270 million cluster munitions—"bombies"—were used, and 80 million of them failed to detonate. In the four decades since the end of the war, only 1 percent have been cleared. More than fifty thousand people have been killed or injured in UXO accidents; over the last decade, nearly half of those casualties have been children.

We stopped and got out of the Land Cruiser. A white tent was set up on a hill overlooking a field, where a team of women wearing khaki uniforms had been searching for bombies with rudimentary metal detectors in the tall grass of a rice paddy. Under the tent, a briefing space was set up where a group of men huddled around U.S. military maps from the war that showed the location of bombing runs. This was an eclectic group of briefers: a man from UXO Lao—the agency responsible for clearance efforts; a Laotian in a drab military uniform who looked old enough to have fought in the war; an excited French contractor; a farmer who had found the ordnance in the adjacent field. He smiled when they gestured to him, showing only a couple of teeth.

"With additional resources," said the man from UXO Lao, "we can conduct a survey of the whole country. Then we can clear areas needed for farming. UXO is not just a humanitarian issue. For us, it's also development."

The man paused, measuring my reaction. Everyone seemed a bit on edge, as if I represented their best shot at securing an infusion of funding. There was no mention of the fact that I represented the government that had dropped hundreds of millions of cluster munitions on this country for no reason that could possibly be rationalized.

"This is actually one of the most heavily bombed areas," he said to me, gesturing at the hills in the distance. "The Plain of Jars."

We crossed over the field to where a woman with a smiling face showed me how the metal detectors work, leading me over to where they'd found a bombie earlier that day. We stood in a circle around it, looking down. It resembled a metallic baseball.

"The children, they see it," said the head of UXO Lao. "They think it's a toy and pick it up and then . . ." he broke off into the sound of an explosion.

We moved back across the field. They had tied a long wire to this bombie and attached it to an orange device under our tent. I thought of the time and effort that went into finding and exploding this single bombie, with eighty million still buried out there in the vast country. They asked me to turn a handle several times to blow it up. I expected something akin to a large firecracker; instead, an enormous blast shook the ground underneath my feet, echoing across the river valley, sending a towering plume of smoke into the air. It was possible, in that moment, to envision the river valley filled with explosions, smoke covering the Mekong, planes overhead.

In one of my meetings with the Lao government that day, I had pressed for more cooperation in identifying the remains of American servicemen who'd gone missing in Laos. To date, we had found the remains of 273 Americans. Extraordinary efforts were put into finding even the most minimal traces of life—a tooth, for instance. It was hard to square the extent to which we admirably valued every American life with the bombs that we'd dropped. The briefing team stood waiting for me to say something. "Every morning," I had said, "I meet with President Obama. We want to do everything that we can to help. When I get home, I will tell him about the work that you are doing here." Tears welled up in the eyes of one of the men, even though he was much more hardened by life than I am.

We drove back to where the children were, less than a mile away. I stood at the front of a line, handing out books, pencils, and M&M's that Rumana had brought in her luggage. Rumana, a Muslim

American covered in a hijab, smiled and played with one of the girls, who shook the box of M&M's, thinking it was a rattle. An embassy staffer next to me asked how the UXO demonstration had gone. "It was a much bigger explosion than I expected," I said.

"Yeah," he said. "None of the kids even looked up."

I KNOW HOW THIS is going to sound, but Anthony Bourdain was the one who hooked me on Laos. Over the previous year, I had slipped further into insomnia—the accumulated effect of Benghazi stress and a hungry newborn keeping me awake for long stretches of each night. I'd fill that time lying on my couch in a darkened living room plowing through every episode of Bourdain's various travel shows, over and over. I felt a sense of recognition in this guy wandering around the world, trying to find some temporary connection with other human beings living within their own histories. I'd been vaguely familiar with the story of Laos. Hillary had visited in 2012, and I remembered that we cobbled together some money for UXO clearance—a few numbers on a budget sheet. But the Bourdain episode that showed human beings on a television screen in the middle of the night, struggling in a place that was still a war zone, forty years after a war that I'd never learned about in school, woke my interest. I added two items to the bucket list for my final year in the job: Get more money for Laos, and get Obama to tape an episode of *Parts Unknown* with Anthony Bourdain.

Obama was scheduled to visit Laos in the fall of 2016 for a summit, so I had resolved to go myself, a year in advance, to create the basis to come back to Washington and find more money to clean up bombs. Now, here I was, in a hotel in Luang Prabang, having just seen one of those bombs with my own eyes.

I lay in bed, replaying the day's events in my head. We'd boarded the boat for the ride back to the city, heading back down the river as the light drew down to near complete darkness, and I'd thought about what it'd be like to leave the world behind to run some small hotel on the riverbank, catering to backpackers and European tourists. At dinner that night with Dan Clune, I had talked about how the longer I served in government, the more war of any kind made less sense to me, rife as it was with unintended consequences. We were in our fifteenth year of war in Afghanistan, and it was hard to see what positive difference we were making. A rounding error of the money we spent each year in Afghanistan could alter the trajectory of a country like Laos—feeding children, sending them to school, cleaning up the bombs that they stumbled upon.

As I finally started to drift to sleep, a loud group of people returned to the hotel room next to me, laughing drunkenly and playing music. I gave up on sleep, and my efforts to shut down my thoughts. My mind ran over the six weeks that had passed since we secured the Iran deal. There had been the United Nations General Assembly in September, where Putin seized the spotlight by escalating Russia's military intervention in Syria and beginning to bomb Assad's opposition. As usual, the issue had been framed as a showdown between Putin and Obama. As usual, Obama's case depended upon a much longer view of history. Ultimately, he argued, the bill would come due for Putin's interventions—the money spent on wars abroad, the impact of sanctions on his economy, the rot of a corrupt system in which Putin and his cronies ran Russia as a cartel. But in the reality of politics in 2015, Putin was better than Obama at putting himself at the center of events that captured attention. We ended up looking as if we were reacting to Putin, and not the other way around.

I couldn't escape a gnawing sense of futility about our ability to change things in Syria. More civilians were being killed and displaced. Refugees were streaming into Europe. A brutal dictator, backed by brutal regimes in Iran and Russia, was winning the war, even if it was hard to see how what he was doing amounted to victory. At the same time, I couldn't summon the optimism I'd had in 2011 and 2012, the belief that America could make things better in the Middle East.

It was far easier for me to see how the war in Syria was in part an unintended consequence of other American wars, no matter how well-meaning they might have been. The toppling of Saddam Hussein had strengthened Iran, provoked Putin, opened up a Pandora's box of sectarian conflict that now raged in Iraq and Syria, and led to an insurgency that had given birth to ISIL. The toppling of Muammar Gaddafi had made plain to dictators that you either cling to power or end up dead in a sewer. Syria looked more and more like a moral morass—a place where our inaction was a tragedy, and our intervention would only compound the tragedy. Obama kept probing for options that could make a positive difference, finding none.

It was approaching two in the morning, and the party next door raged on. I reached up and banged on the wall. Muffled voices quieted. After a few minutes, I heard a door close as people left.

I could imagine the staff for Johnson and Nixon, people who worked in the same offices that I spent my day in back in Washington. People just like me, with the same titles and similar pressures. One of the reasons we had bombed Laos was to preserve our credibility, to show that even if America was defeated in neighboring Vietnam, we would make the victory a costly one for our adversaries. In our post-9/11 chapter, I knew there would be no victory in Afghanistan or Iraq, or in any other new war that we might start in that part of the world. I thought of how Obama chafed at the argument that he needed to bomb Syria to preserve his own credibility. "That's the worst reason to go to war," he'd say.

As I drifted to sleep, the quiet in the next room was interrupted as the couple remaining began to make love. Sleep was going to be hard to come by.

A FEW WEEKS LATER, Obama slid into the backseat of the Beast after finishing a press conference at the conclusion of the G20 in Turkey. It was only a few days after a horrifying terrorist attack in Paris, which killed more than a hundred people and sent waves of panic around the world. "Can you believe that?" he said. "Every one of them asked the same question."

"One hundred and twenty-nine people were killed in Paris on Friday night. ISIL claimed responsibility for that massacre, sending the message that they could now target civilians all over the world. The equation has clearly changed. Isn't it time for your strategy to change?"

"A more than year-long bombing campaign in Iraq and in Syria has failed to contain the ambition and the ability of ISIL to launch attacks in the West. Have you underestimated their abilities?"

"In the days and weeks before the Paris attacks, did you receive warning in your daily intelligence briefing that an attack was imminent? If not, does that not call into question the current assessment that there is no immediate, specific, credible threat to the United States?"

"I think a lot of Americans have this frustration that they see that the United States has the greatest military in the world, it has the backing of nearly every other country in the world when it comes to taking on ISIS. I guess the question is—and if you'll forgive the language—is why can't we take out these bastards?"

Obama popped a piece of Nicorette into his mouth and took out his iPad. "Why don't you get the bastards?" he said, laughing ruefully. He looked at Susan. "Susan, why don't you get the bastards?"

"I still think we should just put them in the terror dome," I said. For a few weeks, we'd fantasized about creating a kind of Hunger Games with ISIL, al Qaeda, the Iranian Revolutionary Guard, the Russian special forces in eastern Ukraine; we'd just gather up all of the world's most nihilistic forces and put them under one dome.

"Put 'em in the terror dome," Obama said. He noticed that I was reading some of the initial coverage of the press conference on my BlackBerry. "What is it?" he asked.

"Nothing," I said, knowing it would bother him.

"No, what is it?"

"Some people think you were most passionate in talking about refugees," I said.

In his last answer, Obama had attacked some of the refugee proposals being made in the Republican primary, including one from Jeb Bush to admit only Christians fleeing persecution. "When I hear political leaders suggesting that there would be a religious test for which a person who's fleeing from a war-torn country is admitted," Obama had said, "that's shameful. That's not American. That's not who we are. We don't have religious tests to our compassion." That statement was being held up as a sign that he was out of touch.

"So?" he asked.

"They're saying you were angrier at the Republicans than at ISIL."

"What do I have to do to convince these people that I hate ISIL?" he asked. "I've called them a death cult. I've promised to destroy them. We're bombing them. We're arming people fighting them." His voice trailed off. It was silent for a few moments. "You know why I do that?" he said, returning to the criticism he'd leveled against Republicans. "Because it's my job to calm folks down, not to scare them. I expect it from Trump. But someone like Jeb Bush should know better. He *does* know better. And I've got Angela taking in hundreds of thousands of refugees. I've got to have her back. I can't leave her hanging." He looked down at his iPad, scanning the coverage. "Why don't you get the bastards?" he said again, shaking his head.

On the flight to our next stop, Manila, Obama called Paul Ryan, who had just become Speaker of the House. There were proposals in Congress to ban refugees from coming to the United States, and Obama wanted to slow them down. He argued that we could put in place stricter vetting for people coming from certain countries, and that it'd be harder to get other countries to take in refugees if the United States didn't. I watched as he listened to Ryan's response, his face betraying growing annoyance. "Paul," he said. "Paul, I understand the problems you have in your caucus, but you're Speaker now. This isn't something to play politics with. This is about who we are as a country."

A few moments later he hung up and looked at us. "I'm going to miss Boehner," he said, and walked out of the room.

ELIZABETH PHU WAS THE NSC staffer traveling with us, responsible for Southeast Asia. She was also a refugee. Her Vietnamese father had worked for the U.S. Army during the war. After America pulled out of South Vietnam, Phu was sent to a reeducation camp for several months. She was three years old. Her grandparents sold all of their possessions to get them out and put Phu and her parents on a small boat with more than 250 people on it. When the boat's engines died, pirates seized it, demanding any possessions of value. Phu's father made a deal: In exchange for the wedding rings of those on board, the pirates would tow the boat to a nearby Malaysian island. Once ashore, Phu and her family waited in a refugee processing center.

The last stop of our trip was Malaysia, and we were going to visit the Dignity for Children Foundation, where refugees similarly await permanent resettlement in other countries, including the United States. That morning, I invited Phu to ride with us in the Beast, and she told Obama about her journey—from being one of the "boat people," to an upbringing in California, to working for the U.S. government. It made me proud to be American. When we pulled up at the refugee center, she sat next to Obama and had her picture taken.

Inside, there was a group of small children seated at low, round tables in a classroom. Each of them had fled their own pocket of the world's wars, famine, and suffering—Rohingya and South Sudanese, Kachins and Pakistanis. Just as Phu had made it out of Vietnam, and hundreds of thousands of refugees had escaped Laos at the end of that war, some of these kids were making the journey to America.

For the last few days, each time Obama had a media availability, there was a mini-intervention beforehand as people tried to help him find the right tone on ISIL. Show more anger. Speak to people's fears. "As a mother," Susan Rice told him in one of these sessions, "I can see why people are afraid. You have to meet them where they are."

"I get that. But more people die slipping in the bathtub than from terrorist attacks," Obama said.

"But folks back home think that ISIL is going to come behead them," Susan said.

"That's because there's a bunch of folks on television telling them that," Obama shot back. "I'm trying not to do that."

Obama made his way around the room, asking the children what they wanted to be when they grew up. An engineer, one said. An artist, said another. He knelt for some time next to a Rohingya girl with a white headscarf. She was painting something, smiling shyly while averting her eyes. I stood against the wall, looking at the different kids, most of whom had been rescued from human traffickers.

When we were done, Obama took a few pictures with the kids, and then made his way to an adjacent room. "That's who we need to keep out of the country," he said to me, mimicking his Republican critics with a sharp edge in his voice. "That little girl with the headscarf."

WE FLEW TO PARIS a couple of weeks after the terrorist attack to join the world in pursuing a global accord to combat climate change. Republicans disparaged the effort; reporters asked us what we thought was the bigger threat, ISIL or climate change. It was a trap. Of course climate change is a bigger threat. Now that I had a young daughter, I shuddered to think of a world—ravaged by conflict and disruption—that awaited her if we failed to take the threat half as seriously as terrorism, which we'd spent trillions of dollars fighting. But if we said that out loud, we'd only fuel another controversy—

one more thing for Donald Trump to attack—a couple more days of oxygen for cable news debates.

"Think about it," Obama said to us on the flight over. "The Republican Party is the only major party in the world that doesn't even acknowledge that climate change is happening." He was leaning over the seats where Susan and I sat. We chuckled.

"Even the National Front believes in climate change," I said, referring to the far-right party in France.

"No, think about it," he said. "That's where it all began. Once you convince yourself that something like that isn't true, then . . ." His voice trailed off, and he walked out of the room.

For six years, Obama had been working to build what would become the Paris agreement, piece by piece. Because Congress wouldn't act, he had to promote clean energy, and regulate fuel efficiency and emissions through executive action. With dozens of other nations, he made climate change an issue in our bilateral relationship, helping design their commitments. At international conferences, U.S. diplomats filled in the details of a framework. Since the breakthrough with China, and throughout 2015, things had been falling into place. When we got to Paris, the main holdout was India.

We were scheduled to meet with India's prime minister, Narendra Modi. Obama and a group of us waited outside the meeting room, when the Indian delegation showed up in advance of Modi. By all accounts, the Indian negotiators had been the most difficult. Obama asked to talk to them, and for the next twenty minutes, he stood in a hallway having an animated argument with two Indian men. I stood off to the side, glancing at my BlackBerry, while he went on about solar power. One guy from our climate team came over to me. "I can't believe he's doing this," he whispered. "These guys are impossible."

"Are you kidding?" I said. "It's an argument about science. He loves this."

Modi came around the corner with a look of concern on his face, wondering what his negotiators were arguing with Obama about.

We moved into the meeting room, and a dynamic became clear. Modi's team, which represented the institutional perspective of the Indian government, did not want to do what is necessary to reach an agreement. Modi, who had ambitions to be a transformative leader of India, and a person of global stature, was torn. This is one reason why we had done the deal with China; if India was alone, it was going to be hard for Modi to stay out.

For nearly an hour, Modi kept underscoring the fact that he had three hundred million people with no electricity, and coal was the cheapest way to grow the Indian economy; he cared about the environment, but he had to worry about a lot of people mired in poverty. Obama went through arguments about a solar initiative we were building, the market shifts that would lower the price of clean energy. But he still hadn't addressed a lingering sense of unfairness, the fact that nations like the United States had developed with coal, and were now demanding that India avoid doing the same thing.

"Look," Obama finally said, "I get that it's unfair. I'm African American."

Modi smiled knowingly and looked down at his hands. He looked genuinely pained.

"I know what it's like to be in a system that's unfair," he went on. "I know what it's like to start behind and to be asked to do more, to act like the injustice didn't happen. But I can't let that shape my choices, and neither should you." I'd never heard him talk to another leader in quite that way. Modi seemed to appreciate it. He looked up and nodded.

CHAPTER 28

HAVANA

———

A S WE HEADED INTO THE FINAL YEAR OF THE OBAMA PRES-
idency, we inhabited two distinct worlds. In one, we'd achieved a
global climate change agreement, the Iran deal was being implemented, the economy was growing, twenty million people had
signed up for healthcare, and Obama's approval rating was rising. In
another, Republican presidential candidates were painting a picture
of a dystopian nightmare of crime, rampant immigration, ISIL terrorism, and wage stagnation in America. Because the two realities
were so far removed from each other, and because Obama wasn't
running, it was hard to do anything but put our heads down and
focus on what we could get done.

My issue of focus continued to be Cuba and, increasingly, the
trip Obama would make to Havana in 2016—the first for a U.S.
president since Calvin Coolidge. Over the last year, I'd learned that
my work in Cuba was far from done. We wanted to push as far as
we could to open a door for American travel and business and promote reform in Cuba. The Cubans wanted to make as much progress as possible to build a bilateral relationship during the last two
years Obama was in office. I assured them that any Democrat who
succeeded Obama would continue our approach, but I couldn't say
the same about a Republican. The Cubans understood this.

Each time I'd go, I stayed at a guesthouse that seemed transported from the 1970s, with white floors, modernist furniture that went out of style so long ago that it'd be trendy in Brooklyn, and long balconies from which I could see security guys dressed in guayaberas. Fidel, I was told, had convened an all-night meeting at the building next door, where he had made a pivotal decision about a military operation in Africa. Cuba, it seemed to me, was a layered society—an inner core that grasped onto its revolutionary legitimacy, the old stories of Fidel; and a broader outer ring comprising millions of people, whose opportunities were embalmed by politics—a government focused on sustaining its own power, U.S. policies that walled them off from the wider world. We were trying to breathe new life into Cuba by opening things up.

My first night in Havana, we piled into a van to tour the city. We stopped to get out in Old Havana. A small enclave of Europe in the Americas, nineteenth-century facades and cobblestoned squares, a place frozen in time by the absence of American engagement, like a ruin preserved deep underground. We passed the national assembly, a smaller replica of the U.S. Capitol. Old American cars filled the streets. We were shown a spot where Batista's troops surrendered to Che Guevara's unit during the revolution. Nearby, Ricardo mentioned to me under his breath, was a spot where firing squads had purged political opponents.

We stopped at a statue of Christ, something sponsored—I was told—by Batista's wife in the final days before the revolution. I stood at the base of it until I noticed what appeared to be a few tourists nearby. Not unlike the people who had photographed Ricardo and me in the lobby of a hotel in Toronto, they approached us conspicuously. They spoke accented English at first, and then switched to Russian, speaking loud enough to ensure we could hear. None of us acknowledged it. I thought, again, about what kind of message the Russians were trying to send. In 2017, months after leaving government, I learned that some Americans at our embassy were harmed in mysterious attacks—from a sonic weapon or some kind of toxin. I knew that the Cuban government had never done something that brazen, even at the height of conflict with the

United States. Whoever harmed those Americans clearly wanted to sabotage the opening between our countries, and I wondered whether the Russians who took such an apparent interest in my efforts had played a role.

Late that night, we arrived at an enormous parade ground. On the large concrete building in front of me, there was a huge illuminated image of Che over the slogan HASTA LA VICTORIA SIEMPRE, the same image that adorns the walls of thousands of college dorm rooms across America. We stood at the base of a soaring statue of José Martí, the independence hero of Cuba, who is claimed by both Cubans and Cuban Americans. This, I was told, is where Fidel gave his speeches. I looked out at the vast, empty expanse in front of me; if you closed your eyes, you could see the crowds that would stand there for hours and hours, extras in an endless duel between the Cuban state and its massive neighbor to the north, chanting slogans. The entire night seemed to be, inadvertently, a demonstration of how the United States and Cuba have been locked in an embrace, like two exhausted boxers who become tangled up in each other's arms, at odds with each other yet needing each other as foils.

"This is where heads of state lay wreaths," Alejandro said. Before I could respond, someone appeared at my side holding a wreath. It was now after midnight. I would be photographed by the Cuban government laying a wreath here, in the middle of Cuba's revolutionary square. It was not an image that would go down well in Florida, or parts of Capitol Hill. To reject it, though, would have been playing the part of the ugly American, pressed into an insult of Cuban dignity. I took the wreath and looked up at Martí, the one figure in Cuba's history revered on both sides of the Florida Straits. "To the memory of José Martí," I said, "who is beloved in both the United States and Cuba."

OBAMA'S TRIP TO HAVANA would be in March, because he wanted it to coincide with Sasha and Malia's spring break. Every detail of the trip—from the policy changes we were both pursuing, to supporting the American businesses trying to get into Cuba, to the intricacies of Obama's schedule—was a subject for painstaking negotiation, in endless Skype sessions and multiple trips to Havana.

At the end of one of our meetings, Alejandro asked to see me alone. They had one dramatic proposal that they wanted me to explore. "We are very interested in Guantanamo," he told me. "We know of President Obama's interest in closing the prison. And so we would propose to take custody of Guantanamo."

I started to say, as I had many times, that Obama's priority was closing the prison, that we couldn't even talk about the naval base. He cut in. "We take note of your difficulty in removing prisoners." We were still haggling with other countries to take one or two detainees who were cleared for transfer. "Cuba is prepared to make the security requirements to hold them."

It dawned on me what he was proposing—that Cuba would take all of the prisoners if we gave them back the naval base, a piece of Cuban territory that had been occupied by the United States for more than a century. Each year, the United States gives Cuba a check for a few thousand dollars to pay for the facility; the Cubans never cash it. "I just want to be clear here," I said. "You are offering to take all of the prisoners?" There were, at that time, nearly a hundred.

"Cuba is very good at holding people securely," he said.

"There are some that we'd need to remove," I said, thinking of Khalid Sheikh Mohammed, the 9/11 mastermind. We'd been prevented from transferring him and others to prisons in the United States because of laws passed by Congress. Teams of lawyers had looked at other possibilities, including holding them in U.S. territories such as Guam or Puerto Rico.

"Whatever you need to do," he said.

For the rest of my time in government, there wasn't a meeting when he didn't revisit this idea. Even as I knew it was unlikely to happen, I came to like the idea, and I told Obama so. We could have some negotiated transition period, where the United States and Cuba jointly administered the facility. In meeting after meeting on Gitmo, I'd hold up my hand and say, "I'm the only one with a Plan B." Obama dismissed it as a bridge too far, even for the fourth quarter. But I couldn't help but see the unintentional genius in the idea—righting two historical wrongs, ending two chapters at once.

DURING ONE LENGTHY DINNER in Havana a few days before Obama was scheduled to arrive, Alejandro abruptly left the table to take a phone call. When he returned, he announced that he and I would now go to visit the president. He never once referred to him as his father. We left abruptly, piling into the back of a black BMW for the short drive to a large government building. A few plain-clothes security guys stood in the lobby, as I was ushered into an underfurnished room where Raúl was sitting wearing a guayabera. We sat down, Oval Office style, with me in a chair adjacent to Raúl.

Raúl did most of the talking. A few minutes into the meeting, he took out a foldout map of Cuba and made me hold one end of it as we leaned over like two generals assessing a campaign. He began by tracing the progress of the revolution, from the Sierra Maestra mountains to Havana. He showed me various military airstrips that could be turned into civilian airports, and described their proximity to beaches and other attractive sites. Pointing to Cuba's perimeter, he welcomed the Paris agreement, talking about the risk of climate change to Cuba's outer ring of islands and keys. In his own way, he was showing me the outlines of a tourist economy that Cuba was building, an economy that depended upon an eclectic mix of state-run hotels and individually owned small businesses such as restau-rants, shops, and taxis.

He pointed to a tiny speck of land south of Cuba. "There, I have allowed an Italian businessman to park a houseboat with five beds where he feeds sharks all day." I nodded, not sure what to make of this anecdote.

"Caroline Kennedy was in my office the other day," I said. "She noted that it wasn't her father who had closed the embassy. That he'd inherited Eisenhower's Cuba policy."

Castro nodded. "Robert Kennedy's son recently came to Cuba," he said. "And even though his father tried to kill my brother, I let him stay on these beaches. I even let him stay with the Italian who feeds the sharks." Somehow this anecdote seemed to reveal something essential about Cuba.

He returned again and again to the revolution, to the stories of how poorly the landing of the *Granma* had gone, and of how he and Fidel greeted each other: "I had five rifles," he said. "When we came together he grabbed me and put his forehead to mine and said, how many rifles do you have? I said five. He said, I have two." Raúl sat back and slapped his knees. "That makes seven rifles. So we will have to take them from the enemy. And that is what we did."

I also knew that this talk of the revolution wasn't just posturing, it was intended to show that he wasn't going to compromise the revolution's legitimacy. The talk of the evolving economy was intended to show that there was a streak of pragmatism to Raúl, one that his brother didn't share.

I tried—again and again—to steer the conversation back to our demands. We wanted Cuba to expand its nascent private sector. We wanted Cuba to reform its economy, to allow foreign businesses to hire Cubans directly, and to show more restraint in its treatment of protesters. I began to enjoy playing this part, friendly but persistent.

"You know," Raúl said to me, "a thought has occurred to me that I have never shared. The Americans like to give people candy." He looked around the room, finding nodding agreement on his side. "They like to give people candy for doing whatever they want in Latin America. But Cuba is not interested in candy."

After more than two hours of this, Raúl announced he would send me a copy of his own biography. "It's by a Russian," he said. "It's good, but it also shows my flaws."

"None of us is innocent," I said, and he laughed.

I went through some of the remaining issues for our trip, including Obama's planned meeting with dissidents. "Obama is welcome to meet whoever he wants in Cuba," he said, waving his hand in front of him. "Obama is welcome in Cuba."

As we neared the three-hour mark, we wound down the meeting. "It is hard for us," he said, "being your closest neighbor."

I corrected him. The Mexicans were our closest neighbor, and they liked to say of themselves, "So close to America, so far from God."

He laughed, but in turn corrected me. "Look," he said, pointing down at Guantanamo Bay Naval Base on the map in front of us. "*We* are your closest neighbor."

As Air Force One began its descent into Havana, Obama knelt next to me on the couch peering out the windows. I was nervous about everything, including some rain that had begun to fall, as if any blemish on the trip would be a personal failure. This felt like the capstone of my eight years in government; I wanted everything to go perfectly. As the outskirts of Havana came into view—thatched houses and corrugated shacks—Obama said, "That doesn't look like a threat to our national security to me."

By the time we touched down in Cuba, we'd announced the farthest-reaching changes in U.S. policy that the law would allow— enabling Americans to travel there for people-to-people engagement and authorizing more financial transactions in Cuba. We'd initiated direct mail service between the United States and Cuba for the first time in decades, with Obama himself responding to a letter from an elderly Cuban woman who had written to the White House. We'd arranged for a Major League Baseball exhibition game to be played during our visit, between the Tampa Bay Rays and the Cuban national team. We'd reached a slew of agreements to get U.S. businesses in the door in Cuba. We'd even had Obama tape a segment with a Cuban comedian named Luis Silva, whose character Pánfilo featured on one of the most popular shows in Cuba.

As the trip approached, it had become clear that for all our focus on using the trip to maximize changes in policies, the symbolism and story of Obama's visit were going to matter more. I had taken a trip down to Miami to do a series of meetings with leaders in the

Cuban American community. It spoke to the raw feelings of some Cuban exiles that when I exited my commercial flight, I had a sizable police escort waiting for me that followed me throughout the day. In Miami, history was a present thing, and there were people who saw any rapprochement with the Castro government as an act of betrayal.

But over the course of the day, I heard a different message. To younger Cuban Americans, Obama's policy was long overdue. The children and grandchildren of exiles didn't carry the same baggage, didn't see the future of Cuba as a competition between Castros and exiles. Some of the old hard-liners were changing, too. Carlos Gutierrez, who had been George W. Bush's commerce secretary, had been transformed from a hard-liner into an enthusiastic proponent of engagement. "I just got tired of using the same talking points," he told me.

What I heard in Miami, though, was a single message: The most important element of the trip was the speech Obama would give in Havana. Cuban Americans wanted to hear him make the case for democracy, for openness, and to include them in whatever story he told about Cuba. More than any other diaspora community I'd engaged with, Cuban Americans saw themselves as a people in exile. I asked them to share stories and cultural touchstones that would be meaningful for Obama to talk about, and for days afterward my in-box was filled with stories: people whose parents had put them alone on planes to America, people who had been separated from family for decades, people who opposed the government in Havana but clung to their connections with Cuba.

Cuba also seemed to attract a unique assortment of personalities that represented powerful threads from America's own story. Ernest Hemingway had lived there for more than twenty years, and his grandsons reached out to me before our trip. José Andrés, the prominent Spanish American chef, came with us, as he had supported Cuba's self-employed cooks. Jimmy Buffett made plans to play a concert. Jackie Robinson had played baseball in Havana, and we were joined on Air Force One by his daughter and ninety-three-year-old widow, Rachel. It felt as if we were traveling to Havana with a cast of American underdogs and overachievers: Cuban exiles and the offspring of cultural icons; baseball players and singers; civil rights heroes; and, of course, an African American First Family. The delegation itself spoke for America.

As we rode in from the airport, the ambivalence of the Cuban government was on display. The government had apparently warned people not to line the route of the motorcade, to avoid too enthusiastic a greeting for an American president, but they had also repaired and refurbished the streets we drove on. As we passed cement block apartment complexes, I saw clusters of faces pressed against the rain-swept windows, peering out at something they'd never expected to see.

The rain built to a downpour as we pulled in to Old Havana. Obama went into the Catholic cathedral and was greeted by Cardinal Ortega, the man who had carried the pope's personal message to the White House a year before. "I delayed my retirement for this," Ortega said, clutching Obama's hand in greeting. As we walked through the secured streets, people clustered in the windows of shops, smiling and waving, some holding miniature American flags.

THE NEXT MORNING, ALEJANDRO was a mix of nerves and confidence. We met in the same government building where I'd spent dozens of hours over the past year, but this time I was traveling with a thousand Americans: staffers, security personnel, Cuban Americans, athletes, journalists, and assorted celebrities. Still, I had the feeling we'd be negotiating every aspect of the trip until the moment our plane took off. Sensing my own mix of fatigue and annoyance at having to meet so early, Alejandro declared that he had good news. They had agreed to our two remaining asks: that Obama and Castro do a press conference after their meeting, and that Obama's speech be broadcast—uncensored—to the Cuban people. Neither thing had ever happened before in Cuba.

On the motorcade over to the Plaza de la Revolución, it seemed that the Cuban government had either relaxed its restrictions or lost some degree of control, as huge crowds greeted the motorcade.

After a lengthy meeting with Raúl, the press conference was a circuslike atmosphere. The Cuban journalists, all employees of state-run media, seemed astonished to see their own leader taking questions. Jim Acosta, the same reporter who had asked Obama why he didn't get the bastards, stood up and said, "My father is Cuban. He left for the United States when he was young. Do you see a new and democratic direction for your country? And why do you have Cuban political prisoners?"

When it was his turn to answer, Castro looked momentarily confused. His grandson came over and whispered something in his ear. "Give me the list of political prisoners and I will release them immediately," he then thundered. "Just mention a list. What political prisoners? Give me a name or names." It was, in a way, great theater—the Cuban president forced to answer for his repressive policies—but I knew we were pushing the Cuban system hard, and that there would inevitably be blowback. This was the tension in our policy. The imperative back home was to push the Cubans on human rights, but that could backfire. We got fifty-three political prisoners out through quiet talks, not through denunciations. Pushing them publicly was not always the best way to get results.

After the press conference ended, the Cuban reporters all applauded. Castro shook hands with Obama and then tried to raise their hands together in triumph. Obama, not wanting to have that image plastered on front pages all over the world, let his hand dangle limply in Castro's. It seemed an apt metaphor for our approach—engaging without embracing.

That night, I went to the house where the Obamas were staying. The Obama family was hanging out in the living room while he pulled me aside to review the speech. He'd barely edited it, deferring to me. "Do we have enough in here for the Cuban Americans?" he asked.

"I think I've talked to just about every Cuban in the United States," I joked.

"Well, maybe punch up the point on reconciliation. People are people. Cubans are Cubans. Give it some lift."

I went back to the quiet of my empty hotel room. I'd put everything I had learned about Cuba over the last three years into the speech Obama would give the next day, and I was happy with it. Usually, the night before a big speech, I'd sit on my balcony and read the words over to myself. Instead, I invited the team who had worked on Cuba with me—Ricardo, Bernadette, and Siobhan Sheils, a young staffer on Cuba—to my room. For a couple of hours, we drank Havana Club rum, read the speech out loud to one another, and told stories of our endless talks with the Cubans.

"Sometimes I think we underestimate how hard they are pushing inside this system," I said to Ricardo. I knew that even if the Cubans weren't making changes in exchange for candy, they had opened the door to America: our travelers, our businesses, the giant neighbor to the north, with our different ideology and way of doing things, and now our president.

"Yeah," Ricardo said. "Hey, thanks for including me in this." A few months earlier, he'd left the NSC for a posting in São Paulo. Before leaving, he told me something that he never had before about his father. I knew he had been a Honduran military officer who ended up on the wrong end of an internal struggle and was eventually killed, which led to Ricardo's growing up in America and going to work for the State Department because he saw America as a force for good in a chaotic world. But the story was more complicated. Even though he came from a right-wing family, Ricardo's father had become something of a reformer and whistleblower on corruption. He was pushed out of the military over his opposition to Honduran support for the Contra program, and he was killed by the type of reactionary forces who had battled Cuban proxies across Latin America, a victim of the poisoned politics that we had set out to bury.

From my balcony, we looked out at the darkened Florida Straits that separated Cuba from the southern tip of America. Being there, in Havana, with this group of people who'd become like a second family, I felt better than I ever had before in my job. This is why you put up with everything.

THE SPEECH TOOK PLACE at a grand theater that had been restored for the occasion. Raúl Castro sat in a balcony. The famous blind Cuban ballerina Alicia Alonso, for whom the theater is named, entered to thunderous applause. We'd fought hard to invite dozens of guests, including many Cuban Americans. Obama walked to the lectern and began with the words of Martí's most famous poem, "Cultivo una rosa blanca." From there, the speech broadened out to track both the story of sixty years, and my own feelings working on Cuba for the last three. "Havana is only ninety miles from Florida," Obama said, "but to get here we had to travel a great distance— over barriers of history and ideology, barriers of pain and separation." Covering the period from the revolution to the missile crisis to today, Obama said, "I have come here to bury the last remnant of the Cold War in the Americas. I have come here to extend the hand of friendship to the Cuban people." The audience erupted in applause.

It was too much for me. I slipped out a back door to a side street, smoking, staring at dilapidated facades and old cars, the empty street frozen in time outside a theater where history was happening. I knew the notes he was hitting, having nearly memorized the speech myself. The tributes that Cubans would appreciate—to their education and healthcare systems, their stance against apartheid in South Africa. I knew the cultural touchstones that would unite people across the Straits—the music and dances and athletes. I knew the language that would resonate to the north: "In America, we have a clear monument to what the Cuban people can build. It's called Miami."

I went back inside just as Obama was making the case for engagement. "This is not just a policy of normalizing relations with the Cuban government," he said. "The United States of America is normalizing relations with the Cuban people." And then came the careful balancing act. An extended tribute to Cuban small business owners, something that Cubans never heard from their own government. A call to end the embargo, which drew thunderous applause. But then the onus was put on the Cubans: "But even if we lifted the embargo tomorrow, Cubans would not realize their potential without continued change here in Cuba."

I had set up the language about democracy by acknowledging the past. "Before 1959," Obama said, "some Americans saw Cuba as something to exploit, ignored poverty, enabled corruption. And since 1959, we've been shadow boxers in this battle of geopolitics and personalities. I know the history, but I refuse to be trapped by it." It was the same thing I had said to Alejandro in our very first meeting.

And then Obama said what he believed: that people should be equal under the law; that citizens should be free to criticize their government and protest peacefully; that voters should have the freedom to choose their government in open elections. "I believe those human rights are universal," Obama said. "I believe they are the rights of the American people, the Cuban people, and people around the world." The Americans in the audience applauded. Raúl Castro sat in his seat with a thin smile. We were pushing, I knew, too far, too fast. But we were saying what we believed, and sometimes that is all that you can do.

The speech ended on Obama's note about reconciliation between Cubans and Cuban Americans, drawing on stories I'd been told over the last few weeks—a woman meeting her sister for the first time in sixty years; another woman who went back to her family's old home and was recognized by a neighbor she hadn't seen in decades. "We can make this journey," Obama concluded, "as friends, and as neighbors, and as family—together. *Si se puede.*"

The speech had said everything I believed and had stirred a pot. Every Cuban would hear it a different way. I had tried to paint a picture of a future in which there was a place for everyone's story—

for the story of the revolution and the dignity of a Cuba that stood up to the United States; for the story of the dissidents who protested that government and the entrepreneurs building a new Cuban economy; for the story of the exiles who'd fled or been forced to flee to the United States; for the story of the nameless Cubans who didn't have a voice in the conflict between our countries but simply wanted a better life. But that's what touched a nerve among hard-liners. A sympathetic speech about the Cuban Revolution would have been easy to dismiss as an apology for tyranny in Miami. A boorish speech about democracy would have been easy to dismiss as imperialism in Havana. This was something different; sure, a speech I wrote, but a speech that only Obama could give. I've never gotten more positive feedback on one of his speeches, but it also ended up provoking a rebuke from Fidel Castro, and pushback from opponents of the rapprochement in both countries.

Our final stop was the baseball game. I walked out into the sunshine of a baseball stadium with tens of thousands of cheering fans. I was seated next to Alejandro, who passed me his young daughter, just a year or two older than Ella. A few seats away from me, Obama was introducing Rachel Robinson to Raúl Castro while Derek Jeter looked on. And then the game began, my favorite sport, the one I'd played as a child in Central Park with my father, finding my own confidence in the ability to catch a ball and throw it back to him. For a few moments, politics disappeared; there was just a game on a sun-splashed field, and it was easy to feel that the future didn't belong to missile crises or ISIL attacks, ideological disputes or geopolitical competition, demagogues in Cuba, America, or anyplace else. I was just one person in a large crowd watching a game on a perfect afternoon, comforted by the sound of so many human beings responding to the direction of the ball in front of us, feeling that finally I could just relax in the midst of something that was real, that was true.

CHAPTER 29

THE STORIES PEOPLE
TELL ABOUT YOU

———

E ARLY ONE AFTERNOON IN FEBRUARY, I WALKED OUT OF THE entrance of the West Wing, climbed into the backseat of a black car, and was driven a single block to the underground parking garage of the New Executive Office Building, a characterless government building across Lafayette Park, to appear before the House Select Committee on Benghazi.

Every aspect of my and Susan Rice's appearance had been subject to a months-long negotiation. No White House likes to allow staff to appear before Congress, because it wants to avoid setting a precedent by which staff who give advice to the president can be summarily hauled up to Capitol Hill. I just wanted to get the whole thing over with, but I was caught in the middle of powerful interests: Republicans who wanted to perpetuate their Benghazi show; a presidential campaign that had been shaped in part by the Select Committee's discovery that Hillary Clinton had used a private email server as secretary of state; and a White House protecting the institution of the presidency. My own story, what had actually happened during the few days around the Benghazi attacks, seemed to have become irrelevant.

To avoid the spectacle of Susan's and my going to the Hill amid a cluster of reporters, the White House counsel agreed to this alternative venue. Susan appeared in the morning, and I passed her in the parking garage as she left, making eye contact and saying very little. It was now forty months since the Benghazi attacks. Ever since, we'd both been living as figures of controversy, convicted of a charge that neither of us understood. How had we hatched some kind of cover-up? And what exactly were we alleged to have covered up? At Susan's fiftieth birthday party, I'd kept my eyes on her aging mother, who had taken the villainizing of her daughter particularly hard, as she stared at a slide show of Susan's life that was playing on a loop, her eyes filled with tears that never seemed to fall.

The meeting took place around a large table in a conference room, with a handful of members of Congress and staff on one side. I sat flanked by White House lawyers and my own personal attorney. For the first few minutes, there were conversations back and forth about the agreed-upon process and parameters. I sat there silently, feeling more like a prop than a human being. The day before, I'd had a stomach flu, and I had two large Gatorades to sustain me.

I spent the next four hours being questioned about the minutiae of my experience on the day of the attacks, and the week after. Emails I had little memory of writing or receiving were placed in front of me. I had to be mindful that anything I said could be taken out of context and used to suggest a meaning I didn't intend. The questioning was split between staffers who seemed to have only a slight understanding of how government works, and congressional representatives who enjoyed playing the role of prosecutor. It wasn't hard to navigate, as there was nothing for them to discover, no hidden truth that could justify the time, expense, and outrage that they had dedicated to this charade. The chief antagonist on the Republican side was the committee chairman, Trey Gowdy, a former assistant U.S. attorney whose small, beady eyes opened wide when he feigned incredulity, and whose stiff shock of gray hair looked like a Tyrolean hat.

The absurdity of the exercise hit home for me about halfway through, when Gowdy grilled me about a printed-out email chain that was handed to me. "What is that subject line?" he asked.

I read it aloud. "The U.S. public response to events in Libya and Egypt." On the list of recipients were many of the various people who worked on national security communications in September 2012.

"In Libya and Egypt," he said, as if circling some essential truth. "And the very first item discussed are [sic] talking points on what?"

I stared at the email, which included talking points about the Internet video, the stock language we'd circulated so that people could condemn it while stressing that it didn't justify violence. The email chain was the kind of basic communications channel we always established so that we could share public talking points and draft Q&As. "Mr. Chairman," I said, "the subject line was originated on September 12 in reference to statements that the U.S. government was going to make in response to events in Libya and Egypt. The contents with respect to the movie were in an email I wrote the following day."

"Mr. Rhodes, I'm asking you who told you the movie was the catalyst for the attacks in Benghazi. Who told you that?"

I looked at the email, trying to understand what he was getting at; I hadn't even written the subject line. "Again," I said, "I'm not suggesting that the movie is the catalyst for the attacks in Benghazi."

"Well, can you see how a reader might think that maybe you were? Since the—since the first country mentioned in the subject line is Libya?"

"But the subject line was created the day before I wrote the content of my email, regarding a different set of circumstances," I said, and that's when the cynicism of what he was doing hit home. We had started the email chain after the violence in Libya and Egypt and used it for days because the right people were on the distribution list, including people at the State Department who had to find the right words to answer questions and try to put out the fires burning across the region because of this offensive video. Gowdy was using the subject line to turn everything that followed into a conspiracy theory. To believe we'd done something wrong, you'd have to believe that we were all pretending to be concerned about the video all week, or that we were using something as innocuous as a subject line—"The U.S. public response to events in Libya and Egypt"—to signal some grand conspiracy theory to people working across the government.

Gowdy isn't dumb. He had to know that wasn't the case. He was simply using whatever shred of language he could to keep his conspiracy theory alive, just as the Republican Party had been doing for the last forty months. He stared at me evenly, as though I wasn't a real person whose own life and reputation had already been ravaged by this farce. The Republicans loved, especially, to point out that I'd received a master's degree in fiction when I was twenty-four years old, as if—like the subject line of an email—that fact confirmed I was a liar, an inventor of stories. "So you never intended anyone to believe that the video was in any way connected with the attacks in Benghazi? Is that what you are testifying to?"

I stared at him across the table, suppressing an urge to shout. Instead, I just said calmly, "I intended at every juncture to provide the best information I had from the intelligence community about what took place in Benghazi. I also had to try to mitigate the fallout from this video."

"Those are two separate things," he said.

I could have said: *No, Mr. Chairman, they weren't two separate things! This offensive video—probably fueled by the crass Islamophobia that characterized the right wing's nativist response to the 9/11 attacks and Obama's election—lit a spark in the Middle East. It led people to attack our embassy in Cairo. People in Benghazi saw that happening and went to our facility—to protest, to loot, to attack, to commit acts of terror—and four Americans were tragically killed. Violent protests burned for days in dozens of places. What we said all week, what Susan Rice said on those stupid Sunday shows, was what we believed at the time, what the intelligence community told us we could say, and was far closer to the truth of what actually happened than anything you, Trey Gowdy, and the Republican Party and Fox News and* Breitbart *and thousands of talk radio segments and Donald Trump have alleged in an effort to destroy people's careers and delegitimize Barack Obama and Hillary Clinton. Your entire theory rests upon knowing the motivations of every individual who showed up at our facility in Benghazi that night, on knowing that they weren't motivated by a video that coincidentally motivated other people to attack other U.S. facilities in other Muslim-majority countries at the same time, and on knowing that all of us in the White House and the State Department and the intelligence community decided to pretend to care about that video—which we were also being asked about all week, because it was the dominant news story in the world—to cover up . . . something. You have relentlessly politicized the terrible loss of four Americans and constructed your own pyramid of conspiracy theories to further pollute American discourse and polarize the American people, a dynamic that has led to Donald Trump's being the front-runner for the nomination of your party.*

But that would have been pointless. In that room, at that moment, I wasn't a human being, I was a character in a political drama, one in which truth was meaningless. I looked at Gowdy with an empty expression; he'd already fulfilled his mission long before I showed up in this conference room. I gave a much shorter answer: "I was," I said, "dealing with both those things."

AT THE SAME TIME that we were negotiating the terms of my Benghazi appearance, a writer named David Samuels sent me an email. He wanted to write a profile of me for *The New York Times Magazine* and wanted to know if I would agree to some interviews and let him follow me around for a few days. I'd never dealt with Samuels before; he wasn't someone on the White House beat. A cursory Google search showed that he'd written for the type of magazines I liked to read—*The New Yorker, The Atlantic, Harper's.* Underneath all that, there surely was a mix of vanity and approval seeking as well. I'd spent seven years in a basement office. I was proud of what I'd done over the last year, with the Cuba opening and the Iran deal. I was frustrated at being transformed into a one-dimensional right-wing villain. Maybe this could be different. I said yes.

Over the holidays, I traveled to Hawaii with Obama. While I was there, I started to hear from people whom Samuels was interviewing about me. Samantha Power reached out to say she was slightly disturbed by her conversation. "He seems to really like you," she said, "but I'd be a little careful. I can't tell what his angle is."

When I finally sat down with Samuels in January, I had no idea what to expect. He was an intense guy, wide-eyed, probing, with glasses and slightly unkempt brown hair. We spent an hour or two talking about my life without even reaching the point at which I went to work for Obama. He asked questions about my parents, my religious background, my 9/11 experience, what authors I liked to read. He was eccentric, and there was a cynical edge to some of his questions. But if anything, the conversation seemed to confirm my hopes: This guy was going to have a different perspective; he seemed actually interested in who I was.

Over the next few weeks, I did a few more interviews and let him follow me around to some meetings and appearances. One afternoon in my office, we had a long conversation about the decline of the news media. I lamented the fact that so many news organizations had been forced to close their foreign bureaus, leaving it to young political reporters to cover foreign policy, which caused complex issues to be covered through the distorted prism of Washington's political reality show. I complained about a foreign policy establishment that couldn't shake the groupthink around military intervention in the Middle East that had gotten us into Iraq. As I spoke, he urged me on, often in vigorous agreement. I was enjoying the back-and-forth, letting myself get worked up, dispensing with the Washington tradition of distinguishing between being on the record and off the record as we went along, a practice that always felt a bit slippery, to me anyway.

I never could figure out his angle. He interviewed Favreau about speechwriting, Ricardo about Cuba; he asked to speak to some of the people I'd worked with on Burma and Iran. Each time, I heard similar things from the people he talked to: Be careful, he's an unusual guy, not sure what he's getting at. Favreau forwarded me a several-thousand-word email that Samuels had sent him in the middle of the night, filled with questions about narrative, storytelling, and the practice of political rhetoric. Something wasn't right. Then one day, I heard from a journalist I knew. "You're doing a profile with David Samuels?" he asked, as if I had lost my mind. Samuels had opposed the Iran deal, he said. His wife was the editor of *Tablet* magazine, the publication that had accused us of the worst kind of anti-Semitism at the height of the Iran debate the previous summer.

It was now February. My interviews with Samuels were done, and he was writing the piece. It would be almost three months before the article came out. I spent that whole time with a knot in my stomach, sensing that I'd had a terrible lapse in judgment, that this wasn't going to turn out well. I just didn't know how bad it would be.

One morning in early May, I woke up to find that the story had been posted online. Before Ann was awake, I slipped out to the couch and began reading it on my iPhone.

Picture him as a young man, standing on the waterfront in North Williamsburg, at a polling site, on Sept. 11, 2001, which was Election Day in New York City.

There I was, on the day that had changed everything for me, and I could remember the person I had once been, before everything began.

He interspersed personal observations with glimpses of me at work, where he cast me as much better at my job than I actually was. At a time when I felt I had little control of how our foreign policy was portrayed, he described me as a master of communications, deftly navigating a balkanized media and taking on the president's critics.

He referred to the American foreign-policy establishment as the Blob. According to Rhodes, the Blob includes Hillary

Clinton, Robert Gates and other Iraq-war promoters from both parties who now whine incessantly about the collapse of the American security order in Europe and the Middle East.

I remembered using the phrase "the Blob" with Samuels, trying to capture that sense of groupthink that always seemed to lead inexorably to more military intervention in the Middle East, to "bomb something." I didn't know that I'd affixed the label to Clinton. She was going to be the Democratic nominee for president, so I immediately braced for angry calls I'd get from her advisors, friends of mine like Jake Sullivan. Then I reached the part about the media:

> "All these newspapers used to have foreign bureaus," he said. "Now they don't. They call us to explain to them what's happening in Moscow and Cairo. Most of the outlets are reporting on world events from Washington. The average reporter we talk to is 27 years old, and their only reporting experience consists of being around political campaigns. That's a sea change. They literally know nothing."

I remembered the conversation, the vigorous agreement we'd had over the effect of closing bureaus. I sounded mean, arrogant, and dismissive. I was twenty-nine when I went to work on the Obama campaign. Many of the journalists who I had become friends with were around twenty-seven when they went to work covering the campaign. I assumed it would be the worst thing in the story. But then came the section on Iran.

> The way in which most Americans have heard the story of the Iran deal presented—that the Obama administration began seriously engaging with Iranian officials in 2013 in order to take advantage of a new political reality in Iran, which came about because of elections that brought moderates to power in that country—was largely manufactured for the purpose of

selling the deal. Even where the particulars of that story are true, the implications that readers and viewers are encouraged to take away from those particulars are often misleading or false. Obama's closest advisers always understood him to be eager to do a deal with Iran as far back as 2012.

This was far worse than anything I feared, and it was patently untrue. First, because we'd never concealed our interest in an Iran deal; it was the defining fight of the 2008 primary. Second, because we never had serious negotiations with Iran before the election of Rouhani. And third, because we hadn't sold the deal as dependent upon a "new political reality in Iran"—we'd sold it on how the deal prevented Iran from getting a nuclear weapon. I remembered Obama's first instructions to me after the deal was reached—"We don't want to let the critics muddy the nuclear issue with the other issues." That's exactly what Samuels was doing, the trap I'd walked into.

By eliminating the fuss about Iran's nuclear program, the administration hoped to eliminate a source of structural tension between the two countries, which would create the space for America to disentangle itself from its established system of alliances with countries like Saudi Arabia, Egypt, Israel and Turkey. With one bold move, the administration would effectively begin the process of a large-scale disengagement from the Middle East.

I felt that I was seeing stated more clearly what the deal's critics thought about our motives. But it was Samuels's view, his narrative, his story of the Iran deal. We were trying to avoid a war and a nuclear-armed Iran. Samuels had turned the deal into a massive realignment of American foreign policy, one that positioned the United States in some kind of partnership with Iran.

"We created an echo chamber," he admitted, when I asked him to explain the onslaught of freshly minted experts cheerleading for the deal. "They were saying things that validated what we had given them to say."

It sounded diabolical, but all I was describing was the most routine aspect of communications work. Briefing people. Disseminating fact sheets. Hoping that others who share your view will make the same arguments as you in public. This was no different from what any White House communications official does to support the rollout of a new policy.

Sitting there on my couch, I read the story over two or three times. It was a clever and, in places, intelligent piece of writing. It made me sound smart, powerful, and ahead of my time. It also made me sound dishonest, bitter, and cynical. It took multiple readings to see how Samuels had used my criticism of the media to set up what he'd written about Iran, suggesting a connection that I'd never drawn—that a media that knows nothing can be fooled into supporting the Iran deal. It also alluded to my own background as a fiction writer, suggesting that someone who told stories was primed for this dirty work.

I went to the White House nervous, embarrassed to face my colleagues. I felt as if I had a new target affixed to me, a laser dot on my forehead. But on first read, most of the people I heard from thought that the article was great for me, and so I allowed myself to think that for most of the day. Then the backlash started to build.

The rest of that week was a blur. I had, with my own words, managed to pick fights with some of the most powerful interests in Washington: the media, the foreign policy establishment, the organized Jewish community, opponents of Iran. It was a combustible mix, and it seemed to explode, releasing some pent-up anger about things that ran far deeper than my words in a profile piece. The media was sensitive to charges that it'd become more trivial, because that was true. The foreign policy establishment was tired of being blamed for Iraq. Opponents of the Iran deal who'd lost the 2015 fight saw an opportunity to win in a rematch framed on their terms. I'd made myself an easy mark.

The pile-on was worse than anything I'd experienced. At one point, I went to the *Washington Post* homepage and there were seven pieces about me, all negative. I scrolled through Twitter, and almost everyone in my feed was trashing me. Articles were written about the shallowness of the books on the shelves of my office, which Samuels had described. A line of attack emerged that I must have invented an anecdote I'd told Samuels, about seeing an Arab man in tears on the subway on the day of 9/11. I heard a podcast in which a *New York Times* reporter dismissed my negotiations with Cuba as just a few meetings in Canada. I had now been fully erased and replaced with a different person—a liar, an egoist, an asshole.

Samuels wrote me long emails expressing surprise at how things were spiraling, even offering to have me come up to Brooklyn to stay with him. But one of the strangest things, in the eye of the storm, is that I wasn't angry at him. He probably believed the things he wrote about Iran, even the ones I knew to be untrue. I was angry at myself. He had caught me at a moment when I was too high on myself, coming off the successes of 2015, and too embittered at the nature of the political and media world that I'd been at the center of for seven years. When I dropped my daughter off at daycare, and made small talk with the other parents, I wondered if they now saw me as some shady character.

I scrambled to cling to pieces of a life that I felt drifting away from me. I wrote lengthy apologies to the groups of people with whom I'd had the most meaningful collaborations over the last year—the Jewish Democrats in the House; the outside groups who'd helped us advocate for the Iran deal; the Cuban American community in Miami, who proved to be the most supportive. People at work rallied around me, as they had before. I heard from dozens of people I'd worked with over the years, which made me feel as if I was dying—if not dead. Susan hosted a surprise party for me, the second such gathering in a year.

Obama was more muted. A few days after the story, he called me back to his private dining area, behind the Oval Office. "Why were you so eager to talk about how the sausage gets made?" he asked, with a note of irritation. "You've got to be more careful. We've still got nine more months."

Most people told me it would pass, but that wasn't true. My involvement with one of the things I was proudest of, the Iran deal, was now permanently tainted. A label would forever be attached to me: "Ben Rhodes, who boasted of creating an echo chamber to sell the Iran deal . . ." The right-wing critics now had fresh meat for the balance of the Obama years and beyond. All the dots in their drawing of me had been connected—fiction writer, leaker, liar, Benghazi, Iran deal. People tell you those things pass, but they don't. You live your life knowing that the story out there about who you are is different from the person you think you are, and want to be.

CHAPTER 30

THE STORIES
WE TELL

———

"**Y**OU KNOW WHAT THAT *NEW YORK TIMES* STORY GOT WRONG?"
Obama was sitting opposite me in the Beast, staring down at his
iPad. Three weeks had passed but the fire was still not out. We were
in Vietnam, yet another trip, yet another piece of our effort to extend American influence in Asia and turn the page on the past. The
motorcade was winding through the streets of Hanoi, and enormous crowds lined the streets, a powerful sight in a country where
millions of people had been killed only two generations ago, something that lent a little perspective to my own predicament.

"That Iran section?" I said. It made me nervous that he was
bringing up the story at all. Susan shot a protective look my way.

"No, forget about that," Obama said. "That's just a pimple on the
ass of progress." He flipped the cover of his iPad closed. "The notion
that there's something wrong with storytelling—I mean, that's our
job. To tell a really good story about who we are."

For a moment, we all just stared out the window at the crowds.
"I'm reading a good book now," Obama said. "It reminds you, the
ability to tell stories about who we are is what makes us different
from animals. We're just chimps without it." He described how all
civilization, religion, nations were rooted in stories, which could be
harnessed for good or bad. Obama's tendency to take the long view
was getting even more pronounced in his last year in office. But in

his own way, he was also telling me that everything was okay, that this was now just one more subject in our endless conversation about everything.

"What's the book?" I asked, looking for something to grab on to.

"It's called *Sapiens*. You should check it out." Perhaps sensing that this was sensitive terrain, he changed the subject. "Now, what's with this thing I'm doing tonight with Anthony Bourdain?"

That night, we'd arranged for Obama to have dinner with Bourdain at a small local restaurant that wasn't getting advance notice, so it would be filled with whoever showed up there on a random weeknight. "He's the guy who wrote that book, right?" he asked.

"Yeah, *Kitchen Confidential*." I explained to Obama about how much I'd come to like Bourdain's shows. "His philosophy isn't that different from yours. If people would just sit down and eat together, and understand something about each other, maybe they could figure things out."

"So we're doing this for you?" He laughed.

At the restaurant that night, I sat with a small number of staff and Secret Service in a room adjacent to where Obama and Bourdain ate bowls of bun cha and spring rolls. I had headphones that allowed me to listen to their conversation. Sitting in this tiny room with colleagues who'd become close friends, sipping broth, beer, and noodles, thousands of miles from home, I felt a sense of peace. It was an apt metaphor for my experience of the presidency itself—just offstage, eating the same things, hearing the words but not the principal participant.

When the meal was done, I met Bourdain. He looked a little shell-shocked, as if still trying to understand how his own life had led him to interview the president of the United States in this small noodle shop. I rushed through the story of my own experience with Laos, beginning with his show. "You should know," I said to him, "that later this year we're going to Laos, and I think we're going to be able to get a hundred million dollars to clean up UXO." He looked at me as if I was crazy, a bemused grin on his face.

——

THE HELICOPTER TOOK OFF for Hiroshima, the final stop on our trip. I was sitting next to Caroline Kennedy, our ambassador to Japan, who had politely but persistently insisted that we make this visit in calls, emails, and visits to the White House for many months. When Obama took office, no U.S. ambassador had even traveled to Hiroshima for the annual commemoration of the bomb dropping. Obama was going to break an enormous taboo in our relationship with Japan and our own history; he was going to become the first sitting president to visit Hiroshima.

It would be a short stop where Obama would give a speech that he and I had been working on over the course of the trip, something that grappled with the enormity of dropping the atomic bomb. He had rewritten my first draft entirely in his small, careful handwriting. Reflecting each of our strange moods in his last year in office, the speech had turned into a meditation on the meaning of war and whether it can be stopped.

As we left behind a military hangar filled with U.S. troops, Obama returned to talking about the book he'd been reading, and I could tell that it was his way of indirectly addressing the discomfort of flying in a United States military helicopter to a city that the United States had once destroyed. "It's interesting," he said, "that individual human beings didn't benefit much from the agricultural revolution. Life was actually better for hunters and gatherers."

Some of the people in the helicopter looked a little confused, but I knew that he'd rewritten the speech to pose questions about whether the march of technology would inexorably lead to the destruction of humankind. His tangent made a certain kind of sense. "Why?" I asked, knowing I had to keep this conversation going. "Because of feudalism?"

"No," he said. "That was part of it, but it was also because for most of the early agricultural revolution, people focused on grain. Grain is not as nutritious and balanced as eating a diet with pro-

teins, fruits, and nuts. Hunters and gatherers lived in small units—
ten to twelve people—and agriculture required people to have more
children, which led to disease and infant mortality. Life actually got
worse." He looked out the window at the blue water below. It was a
gorgeous, sunny afternoon. "It's interesting, most of human history
is unrecorded. We were around for millions of years and don't know
much about how people lived. Recorded history didn't begin until
eight or nine thousand years ago." Then he went on to talk about
the Neanderthals, and how they were more developed than was
commonly believed relative to *Homo sapiens*. "Humans," he said,
"just developed a slight advantage in terms of language and social-
ization. That allowed them to develop the capacity to overrun the
Neanderthals, who lived in relatively small groups."

"Like the opening scene in *2001*," I said. Everyone laughed. I
looked at Caroline, whose father was president during the Cuban
Missile Crisis, the time we came the closest to nuclear destruction,
and wondered what she was thinking.

It was quiet for a moment. Then Obama said, "It's kind of eerie,
flying into Hiroshima." Down below, fishermen worked with nets
in the water. "What are they doing down there, Caroline?"

"Oysters," she said. She then described the process of harvesting
pearls. From up above, it looked like a peaceful way to make a living.

"Why did we pick Hiroshima?" Obama asked.

"This came up in my research for the speech," I said. "We decided fairly early to preserve Hiroshima from other bombing runs
so that we could demonstrate the impact of the bomb on a city that
was intact."

"We wanted to show the Japanese what we could do," Caroline
added.

"People were so accustomed to the air raid sirens that they didn't
go into the shelters when they heard them," I said. "Especially because there weren't many planes."

"They gave an all-clear," Caroline said.

"I don't know if I'd second-guess Truman's decision to drop the bomb," Obama said, the only person in the helicopter who could put himself in Truman's shoes. "But there's something about the way we did it."

The helicopter landed and I got into one of the support vans in the motorcade. As we turned out of the airport, there was an enormous mass of people, smiling and waving. It was an awesome sight. As the cars rolled by, I tried to make out individuals in the crowds. I fixed on one small boy holding a sign that said WELCOME TO HIROSHIMA and in that moment I felt the flash of responsibility, the fact that we'd killed thousands of boys just like him, even if the brutality of the Japanese Empire compelled it. Going from Hanoi to Saigon to Hiroshima on a single trip was something that I couldn't entirely get my mind around, as was the fact that in these places, we'd been greeted by some of the largest crowds of Obama's presidency.

The whole scene put the unpleasantness of the last few weeks into some perspective, but it also fed a sense of anger at the story I was caught up in back in Washington. The notion that there is no room for complexity: *Ho Chi Minh was a Communist, not a nationalist. We could not have dropped the atomic bomb on something other than a large city. There are no Iranian moderates.* It was as if simply recognizing complexities and context was tantamount to pulling a thread that could cause some American narrative to unravel. The faces of the people lining these streets told a different story. Surely what made America great to them was not the fact that we'd dropped the bomb; it was the ideal associated with who we were, the fact that we had a president who was willing to acknowledge difficult histories and show respect for different people. Our constant struggle to improve ourselves and our country while seeking guidance from the story of our founding values—that is what makes America great.

When we got to the center of the city, thousands of people stretched back from the Peace Park, the site of Obama's speech, right near Ground Zero. My seat was directly in front of the podium, only a few feet from where Obama would be speaking. A young Japanese girl handed Obama a wreath, which he laid at the base of the memorial. Then he stepped up to the lectern to deliver

his speech. I've never heard such a large crowd so quiet as he
began.

Seventy-one years ago, on a bright cloudless morning,
death fell from the sky and the world was changed. A flash of
light and a wall of fire destroyed a city and demonstrated that
mankind possessed the means to destroy itself.

The weather was clear and it was approaching the same time of
year that we'd dropped the bomb, putting an end to a horrific war
and cementing our status as a superpower. I looked at the buildings
all around us; every one of them had been built since that day.

Artifacts tell us that violent conflict appeared with the
very first man. Our early ancestors, having learned to make
blades from flint and spears from wood, used these tools not
just for hunting but against their own kind.

He was, I knew, grasping for the largest possible context in
which to make sense of not just this historical event, but of a world
that he'd interacted with as its most powerful inhabitant for nearly
eight years. The stubborn duality of humanity's capacity for ingenu-
ity and its capacity to do harm. I had a hard time looking at Obama
as he spoke. Normally I'd be pacing somewhere backstage, watching
the lines scroll on a teleprompter. My eyes kept being drawn toward
the eternal flame and dome in the distance. I thought about his own
constant struggle to constrain our own warmaking, his fear—at the
height of the ISIL fever—at how he could have ridden that wave to
even greater destruction. "Civilization," he liked to tell us, "is just a
thin veneer." We like to think that we, as Americans, are different.
But we're just human beings.

Nations arise telling a story that binds people together in
sacrifice and cooperation, allowing for remarkable feats. But
those same stories have so often been used to oppress and

dehumanize those who are different. The wars of the modern age teach us this truth. Hiroshima teaches this truth. Technological progress without an equivalent progress in human institutions can doom us. The scientific revolution that led to the splitting of an atom requires a moral revolution as well.

I thought of Obama's line about storytelling: "That's our job," he'd said. Back home, in our campaign, Trump was telling a story that dehumanized others, those who are different. The stakes of that campaign, of any campaign that concludes in giving a human being the power to destroy whole cities, seemed entirely divorced from its conduct.

My own nation's story began with simple words: All men are created equal and endowed by our creator with certain unalienable rights including life, liberty and the pursuit of happiness. Realizing that ideal has never been easy, even within our own borders, even among our own citizens. But staying true to that story is worth the effort. It is an ideal to be strived for, an ideal that extends across continents and across oceans. The irreducible worth of every person, the insistence that every life is precious, the radical and necessary notion that we are part of a single human family—that is the story that we all must tell.

These were words he'd written. For nearly eight years, Obama had been telling this story. Were people at home listening? I stared down at the concrete in front of me and closed my eyes tightly for a brief moment.

Those who died, they are like us. Ordinary people understand this, I think. They do not want more war. They would rather that the wonders of science be focused on improving life and not eliminating it. When the choices made by nations, when the choices made by leaders, reflect this simple wisdom, then the lesson of Hiroshima is done.

These were words I'd written. For nearly eight years, I had seen how ordinary people often seemed to understand Obama better than the people who had the largest platforms to render judgment on him. That was the thing that gave me hope.

When he was done, Obama went over and greeted the atomic bomb survivors. An elderly man with discolored skin and an enormous smile wept and Obama pulled him into a half embrace, patting his back. It was silent except for the clicks of hundreds of camera shutters being released at once, sounding like the striking of typewriter keys.

We got back into the Beast for the drive back to the helicopter. "You should send a link of that speech to Assad and ISIL and Putin," he told me.

"And Xi," I said.

"No," Obama replied, "the Chinese have not generally been about expansion, they've been focused on consolidating control. And they're fragile." Then he returned to ancient history. The expansionists, he said, were not the Chinese but the Mongols. "Genghis Khan is a reminder of what people can do to each other," he said. "He came from nothing and conquered half the world. His people would get to the edge of a town and give two choices: Surrender and you'll be killed immediately. Don't surrender, and you'll be boiled alive in oil, your daughters will be raped in front of you. He only had to do that in a few places."

"The word got around," I said.

It was, again, his way of talking about Hiroshima. "They had an edge," he said. "In their case it wasn't an atomic bomb, it was good horsemanship."

On the helicopter ride, the weight of the moment had lifted a bit, and we talked about random things—the upcoming schedule, the next markers we had to hit with the time remaining. "I'm going to miss UNGA this year," Susan said. "I'm going to fly with my son out to Stanford, where he's starting in September."

"That's exactly where you should be," Obama said. "We're going to miss them a lot." He looked out the window. Malia was about to graduate from high school. As we made our descent to the tarmac next to Air Force One, Obama more directly conveyed how much he'd begun thinking about the end of his time in office. "I'm not certain of many things," he said, "but I am certain of one. On my deathbed, I won't be thinking about a bill I passed or an election I won or a speech I gave. I'll be thinking about my daughters, and moments involving them."

CHAPTER 31

INFORMATION WARS

———

On July 17, 2014, Malaysia Airlines Flight 17 from Amsterdam to Kuala Lumpur was shot down over eastern Ukraine, killing all 298 people on board. The plane had been flying over territory controlled by Russian-backed separatists, armed by Russia, where Russian advisors were present.

A few days later, the Russian Foreign Ministry held a press conference in Moscow and put forward several different, and contradictory, theories for how the plane was shot down. A Ukrainian combat aircraft did it. Ukrainian surface-to-air missiles were in the area. The missile that shot down the plane was actually in territory controlled by the Ukrainian government. These theories were repeated by Russia's major state-run news outlets—RT and Sputnik—and flooded social media feeds in Russia and Europe. It didn't matter much that the shifting Russian explanations could be debunked. The investigation was going to take years; with their media capabilities and willingness to lie, the Russians could fill that space with all manner of false narratives.

Since the protests had ousted Russia's client leader in Ukraine in 2014, we'd grown accustomed to Russian disinformation. Sometimes it could be thuggishly personal. Jen Psaki, who was then our State Department spokeswoman, was a target. Russian media outlets—amplified by Russian bots—invented quotes from her to

discredit our policies. In social media campaigns, her head was su-
perimposed on the body of a model in a provocative pose to suggest
that she was a crude, unserious person. Then there were the lies
about policy: There are no Russian advisors in Ukraine. There is no
Russian military equipment crossing into Ukraine. Russia had no
responsibility for the shoot-down of MH-17.

Those of us who had to fight it out in the information space with
the Russians on a daily basis started pressing our government to
move faster in debunking Russian narratives and building our capabilities to counter disinformation. A little over a week after MH-17,
we got the intelligence community to declassify overhead imagery
that showed Russian military equipment pouring over the Ukrainian border, but it was still framed by objective international media
outlets as a "he said, she said" story, and Russia just issued more
denials in response. We were like traditional newspapers trying to
keep up with the Internet. Because we had to be fact-based, because
we had to be mindful of sensitive intelligence, we were slower than
the Russians, and couldn't be as definitive in our statements or as
far-reaching in our social media presence.

I felt this asymmetry acutely. Whoever did my job in Russia was
sitting on top of billion-dollar investments in television stations,
marshaled an army of Internet trolls who populated social media,
and was empowered to lie with impunity. I had five people working
in the NSC press office and my own official Twitter feed. U.S. government broadcasting has a legal firewall against editorial direction
from the White House. It took lengthy meetings and email chains
to declassify information to debunk Russian narratives.

Obama occasionally asked me to think about how we could re-
vamp our international broadcasting to make it more relevant, more
responsive, to find ways to compete with the Russian juggernaut. In
a 2014 meeting, we showed him what, hypothetically, it would take
to replicate something like RT—hundreds of millions of dollars,
hundreds of people, and greater White House supervision. He
laughed. "I'm sure the Republicans are going to sign off on giving
me a billion-dollar propaganda channel." The idea was quickly

abandoned. Instead we worked for more incremental advances. We launched a new Russian-language broadcasting channel and prioritized media markets in Eastern Europe and Russia's periphery. But this was a drop in the ocean compared to the Russian effort.

At the same time that we confronted the danger of Russian disinformation in 2014 and 2015, we had a parallel effort to combat ISIL's social media campaign to recruit and radicalize Americans. A team of outside experts from the technology sector recommended changes that led to the creation of a new unit at the State Department—the Global Engagement Center (GEC)—which could serve as a hub to coordinate efforts across the U.S. government, mapping and spotlighting ISIL propaganda, lifting up credible voices against ISIL, and producing content that pushed back on ISIL messaging. Recognizing that Russia now posed a bigger challenge, we added the mission of countering Russian disinformation to the GEC, and formally stood it up in April 2016. The budget was in the low tens of millions of dollars.

To understand what ended up happening in the 2016 presidential election, you have to understand this: When protests toppled the Ukrainian government, Putin interpreted that as the United States coming into Russia, akin to an act of war; when he launched his counterattack—annexing Crimea, creeping into eastern Ukraine— he weaponized information and showed a willingness to lie, using traditional media like television, and new media platforms like Twitter, Facebook, and YouTube, to spread disinformation into open, Western societies like a virus. Eventually, the Russians would come into America, as they believed we'd gone into Ukraine. They took advantage of the fact that we were worn down by decades of political polarization and the balkanization of our media. America's antibodies to the sickness of Russian disinformation were weak, if they were there at all.

IN APRIL 2016, WE landed in London for a hastily arranged trip to help David Cameron fight off a Brexit referendum. Cameron's chief of staff, Ed Llewellyn, had emailed me a couple of months earlier urging the visit; they were barely ahead in the polls and fearful, and Obama polled at more than 70 percent in the United Kingdom. A strong expression of support from him might be enough to inch them over the finish line. On the flight over, I emailed back and forth with Cameron's staff about an op-ed that Obama was publishing in *The Daily Telegraph* making the case for Britain to stay in the European Union. It was unusual to coordinate so closely with a foreign government, but the Brits were different, and Brexit would be calamitous, a crucial piece of the post–World War II order drifting off into the sea.

After we landed, I showed Obama a dueling op-ed that had been written by Boris Johnson, the bombastic mayor of London and a chief proponent of Brexit. To counterprogram our trip and appeal to nationalist sentiment in the UK, the whole lead-in was an indictment of Obama for swapping out a bust of Winston Churchill in the Oval Office. "Some said," Johnson wrote, "it was a symbol of the part-Kenyan president's ancestral dislike of the British Empire—of which Churchill had been such a fervent defender."

"Really?" Obama said. "The black guy doesn't like the British?" We were standing in the U.S. ambassador's house in London, a stately mansion with a lawn so big, with grass so carefully cut that it resembled a football field without lines.

"They're more subtle back home," I said.

"Not really," he said. "Boris is their Trump."

"With better hair."

Obama chuckled. "Talk to Cameron's folks," he said. "Get me the best arguments for and against Brexit."

I talked to Llewellyn and got a thick briefing packet with the key arguments on both sides. The problem, for those who wanted to stay in the EU, was that many of the arguments for Brexit were built on lies: about how much the UK paid into the European Union; about how Brexit wouldn't hurt the British economy. Another problem was that the Brexit campaign was tapping into the same sense of nationalism and nostalgia that the Trump campaign was promoting back home: the days of Churchill, the absence of immigrants and intrusive international institutions. The arguments for staying in the EU were grounded in facts, not emotion: The EU was Britain's largest market. The EU offered Britain a stronger voice in global affairs. Even the name of the campaign—Remain— sounded like a concession that life wasn't going to be all that you hoped it would be.

We had a long, friendly meeting with Cameron at 10 Downing Street. Cameron explained to Obama that one of the claims from the Brexit crowd was that the UK could quickly negotiate a trade deal with the United States if they left.

"What? There's no way that could happen. Isn't that right, Froman?" he called out to our trade advisor.

The Brits laughed. "We'd be at the back of the queue," one of them said.

It'd be great, Cameron said, *if you could make that point publicly.*

At the press conference, Obama and Cameron spoke in front of clusters of flags. "My understanding," Obama said, "is that some of the folks on the other side have been ascribing to the United States certain actions we'll take if the UK does leave the EU." He repeated the formulation that the UK would be "at the back of the queue" for a trade agreement. And he went out of his way to talk about his admiration for Churchill: "I don't know if people are aware of this, but in the residence, on the second floor, my office, my private office is called the Treaty Room. And right outside the door of the Treaty Room, so that I see it every day, including on weekends, when I'm going into that office to watch a basketball game, the primary image I see is a bust of Winston Churchill. It's there voluntarily, because I can do anything on the second floor. I love Winston Churchill." The British press laughed.

Then he turned the knife into Johnson. "Now, when I was elected as president of the United States, my predecessor had kept a Churchill bust in the Oval Office. There are only so many tables where you can put busts—otherwise it starts looking a little cluttered. And I thought it was appropriate, and I suspect most people here in the United Kingdom might agree, that as the first African American president, it might be appropriate to have a bust of Dr. Martin Luther King in my office to remind me of all the hard work of a lot of people who would somehow allow me to have the privilege of holding this office." I looked over at Cameron's people on the other side of the room, and they were congratulating one another.

That night, I went out to dinner with Cameron's team to celebrate a visit that had accomplished everything they had asked. But Llewellyn, a man who usually had a wide, genuine smile affixed to his face, looked uneasy. "It's going to be close, I'm afraid," he said. "We just need people to break, in the end, for the safer choice."

The wine flowed. We laughed at seven years of stories: Cameron and Obama playing Ping-Pong, and losing to some kids; Cameron flying out to Dayton, Ohio, to watch a basketball game with Obama in 2012 and having no idea what the rules of the game were. In a world that led to different outcomes, the dinner would have been a memorable valedictory, a group of people satisfied that they had done their best with the time they had occupying places of leadership in the free world. But this was an uncertain moment. "How are you feeling about Trump?" Llewellyn asked, toward the end of dinner.

"He's probably the Republican that Hillary has the best chance to beat," I said.

"You're not worried that he can win? Putin would like nothing more. Some of our people," he said, referring to conservatives who support Brexit, "say that he's tapped into something with this immigration issue. From Central America."

"Unaccompanied children," I said.

"Yes, that's right. The same way people are feeling about immigration here, a loss of control."

"That's true," I said. "When I watch his rallies, I think how potent his message would be from a more skilled politician." I took a sip of red wine, enjoying the easy chatter of voices from a Saturday night crowd at a comfortable London restaurant. "But, you know," I said, "like you, we need people to break for the safer choice."

———

BACK HOME, AN ANTSY Obama had to wait until the end of a bit-ter Democratic primary before he could get out and start campaigning—like a basketball player waiting by the scorer's table to check into a game. Bernie Sanders had come to meet him after Clinton clinched the race, and I got some inkling of the challenge she had faced: The steps of the EEOB were filled with young Obama White House staffers, craning their necks, trying to get a glimpse of their populist hero.

Our first rally with Clinton was in Charlotte, and the crowd was familiar: Obama people, thousands of them, a sea of white, black, and brown faces, waiting to erupt into applause when he walked on stage.

Just a few hours earlier, the director of the FBI—James Comey—had given a press conference in which he announced that he wouldn't pursue charges against Clinton, but harshly criticized her use of a private email server. We'd gotten no heads-up that this an-nouncement was coming. We were in a staff meeting in McDon-ough's office when Comey came on television, and we watched in silence—nervous as he assailed her, then relieved when he said there'd be no charges. McDonough steered us back to the business at hand.

On the flight down to Charlotte, I had joined a lengthy conver-sation with Obama, Clinton, and Jake Sullivan about Syria policy. She sat and listened closely as Obama described the latest effort to negotiate some kind of cease-fire with the Russians—an effort that was likely to fail. I could see her turning the issue over in her head, absorbing the complexity of the different forces fighting on the ground, with the support of different foreign powers. The Middle East was going to be a difficult inheritance. But, as Obama liked to remind me, he'd be leaving his successor a healthy economy, an ISIL campaign on the road to success, and no American war in Syria.

While Obama launched into a ringing endorsement of Clinton

in Charlotte, I was pacing backstage on a conference call with Jake and John Podesta about how the Democratic Party would handle the issue of trade generally, and the Trans-Pacific Partnership (TPP) specifically, in the party platform. Clinton had tacked left because of Bernie in the primaries, disavowing an agreement she had helped to negotiate, but Obama wanted to get it through Congress. We agreed on a formula that welcomed differences of view in the party.

When the rally was over, our motorcade stopped off at a nearby barbecue joint. It was the kind of thing that Obama did at nearly every campaign stop in 2012—you do a rally, then you go to some local restaurant, order a bunch of food, and shake everyone's hand. I sat in a black SUV outside the restaurant while Obama and Clinton went inside. A few minutes later, I saw Clinton come out and get into a car, and I figured we were leaving. Another thirty minutes or so went by before Obama came out. After we boarded the plane, he walked down the long hallway of Air Force One to where a few of us were clustered. "Did you guys see Hillary leave?" he asked.

"Yeah," I said, "she came out after a few minutes."

His jacket was off and his sleeves rolled up; he had his campaign swagger, a looseness in his body language, like an athlete who'd just finished a game. "We went in, ordered some food, took pictures with the staff, and then she left," he said. "I ended up shaking every hand in there. Most of the folks in these places have been watching Fox News and think I'm the Antichrist. But if you show up, shake their hand, and look them in the eye, it's harder for them to turn you into a caricature. You might even pick up a few votes."

We all stood there, not knowing what to say. Unspoken was the fact that everything was riding on this campaign, and yet he wasn't the one running. Clinton had a lead, and she would have to make it stick. "Well," he said, "go get some barbecue." A pile of takeout bags awaited in the conference room.

A few weeks later, I flew up to Philadelphia with Obama for the Democratic convention. In 2008, I'd sat in the middle of a stadium of a hundred thousand people watching Obama speak; this time, I was standing on the stage as he spoke—running through the accomplishments of the last eight years, offering an endorsement of Clinton, and turning Trump's slogan around: "America is already great. America is already strong. And I promise you, our strength, our greatness, does not depend on Donald Trump." I felt a tug of nostalgia. Obama was receding as a figure; soon he—and I—would exit the stage. At the end, Clinton walked out and the two of them stood there, arms around each other, an African American and a woman, waving to a roaring, diverse crowd. It was the opposite tableau from Trump's angry and almost entirely white convention; it felt like a different country.

When they were done, I found myself in the small group of people backstage with them. After a few minutes of small talk, Obama left to go tape some ads, so I was left alone with Clinton in an empty hold room. Jake had asked me to give her some last-minute advice on her acceptance speech. "Remember," I said, "that you'll already have the audience in the room. They're going to love whatever you say. That's not who you're talking to. You're talking to the people at home." She nodded, a smile on her face.

The conversation quickly turned to a recent trip I'd taken to Burma. She came alive, peppering me with questions. "How is Daw Suu?" she asked, using Aung San Suu Kyi's honorific name. I gave a lengthy explanation of how she was adjusting to being a politician—balancing her quiet power struggle with the military, an ethnic reconciliation process, and a combustible situation in Rakhine State.

"She has to worry about the Chinese in all this, doesn't she?" Clinton asked.

"Yes," I said. "Especially with the Wa and the Kokang," naming two obscure ethnic groups along the Chinese border. She nodded, intently. This was her greatest strength and her greatest challenge. Here we were, fifteen minutes after perhaps the high point of her political career, and she wanted to discuss the intricacies of Burma policy. She was kind, curious, and ready to be president, but she had less instinct for the mechanics of how to get there.

As the room slowly filled with people, I saw Obama and Bill

Clinton off to the side, in an animated conversation about some recent political news. I felt a little awkward, monopolizing the most important person in the room. Obama shot me a few quizzical looks. Finally he came over and broke up the conversation. "What are you guys talking about?" he asked.

"Burma," I said, and he looked at me as if I was crazy. He'd come to care a lot about Burma over the years, joining me in trying to prod that distant country in the right direction. A year later, when the Burmese military escalated a campaign to cleanse Rakhine State of the Rohingya, Hillary's attention to the details of this distant land could have made a difference, but in this political moment, it didn't. *Ben, no one in Ohio cares about Burma.*

IT HARDLY CAME AS a surprise that the Russians hacked into the DNC. From my first day at work, I'd been told to assume that any unclassified email I sent, any nonsecure phone call I made, could be intercepted by the Russians. They'd already hacked into U.S. government servers. But just before the Democratic convention, Wikileaks dumped thousands of DNC emails into the public domain in an effort to sow discord within the Democratic Party. This was new, something of far greater scale and consequence than releasing intercepted phone calls in Ukraine. Debbie Wasserman Schultz had resigned as chair in the face of outrage from Bernie Sanders supporters who saw, in the emails, that she'd shown favoritism for the Clinton campaign.

The leaks continued throughout the summer, a steady release of the kind of gossipy emails designed to draw attention from the political press, popping up on platforms with names such as DC Leaks and Guccifer 2.0. It was all painfully familiar, the same brand of disruption that the Russians pursued in Ukraine and across Europe. The Clinton campaign was already fingering the Russians, but when the White House and NSC press shops would ask what we could say about it publicly, we'd be given little running room by the intelligence community. It took us weeks to be authorized to say even that the FBI was investigating the DNC hack. On the subject of Russian complicity, we could only cite past statements by U.S. officials expressing concern about Russian hacking.

That summer, I noticed that Situation Room meetings were being held that weren't marked on the calendar. It was the same pattern that prefaced the bin Laden raid—cabinet-level officials showing up for meetings that weren't on the books. I knew enough not to ask questions. I hoped it was a sign of some special operation—maybe we were going to nab Zarqawi, the leader of al Qaeda, or Baghdadi, the leader of ISIL. Whatever it was, there was a premium being put on secrecy, and the group meeting was very small.

At the beginning of September, we flew to China for the G20 summit, where Obama would have his final meeting with Putin before the election. They met in a large conference room. I sat on one side of the table with Obama, Susan Rice, and John Kerry. Putin sat on the other side, flanked by three stoic, fleshy men. There was always a charge when you were in the room with Obama and Putin, a sense that you were witnessing an exchange that the whole world would want to see. But whatever privileged access I might have felt was undercut by the difference in our positions. Obama would be gone in a few months, and I would disappear along with him. Putin wasn't going anywhere.

The two of them debated the same topics that had driven us further apart over the past three years. On Ukraine, they had the same tense, legalistic debate that had characterized their every exchange since 2014. Implementation of a peace plan had stalled, and Putin blamed Ukraine's president, Petro Poroshenko. *When Poroshenko opens his mouth,* Putin said, *he lies.* On Syria, they discussed a cease-fire plan in which Russia would stop the bombardment of opposition areas and allow humanitarian access; in exchange, we'd separate out the opposition we supported from the al Qaeda affiliate, al Nusrah. Putin expressed support, but mocked the possibility of separating al Nusrah from the opposition. By trying to provide support to moderates without backing al Nusrah, he said smugly, we were trying to climb a spruce tree naked without scratching our ass.

Obama never lost his patience with Putin. As the meeting dragged on, I stared at him—a short man, with thin hair combed across his head, who always had the same half smirk and level gaze frozen on his face, whether he was telling a joke or getting angry. So many of the things that clouded our second term—Assad's brutal war, the permanent crisis in Ukraine, Edward Snowden living in a Moscow apartment, relentless hacking—were tied directly to the decisions of this one man.

Rather than erupt in frustration, Obama piled up the logic. You should end the Syrian civil war, he told Putin, or else the jihadists are going to come after you, and you're going to bleed more money and men in Syria. You should end the crisis in Ukraine and get out from under sanctions, because the next president is not going to be in a position to lift them. In response, Putin did what he'd done for years: He expressed an interest in cooperation, while his body language suggested no such interest. He'd priced out the consequences of his actions, and he didn't care.

After about an hour, I was asked to leave the room, and Obama stayed behind with Susan Rice. Later, we all came together before Obama's press conference, and went through the questions he was likely to get asked. Josh Earnest and I raised the issue of Russian hacking. Obama waved his Styrofoam teacup at us: "I know how I'm going to handle that," he said. He and Susan looked at each other, and I realized this must have been one of the subjects that was covered when I was out of the room.

When he was asked about it in the press conference, Obama said, "I'm not going to comment on specific investigations that are still live and active. But I will tell you that we've had problems with cyber intrusions from Russia in the past, from other countries in the past. And, look, we're moving into a new era here where a number of countries have significant capacities. And, frankly, we've got more capacity than anybody both offensively and defensively." The reference to offensive cyber capacity, I could tell, was a thinly veiled threat.

Shortly after we got back to Washington, I filed into the Oval

Office for the regular morning briefing. Toward the end of his briefing, Jim Clapper said something about plans for a statement on
Russia, and Obama encouraged him to move faster on it. Susan
made eye contact with me, eyebrows arched, glasses down on her
nose. After years, we'd learned to communicate with looks; this one
meant that she wanted to talk with me after.

I followed her down the hall to her office, and she asked me to
close the door. I sat down at the wooden table I'd sat at hundreds—if
not thousands—of times over the last eight years. "Look, we've had
a small group of principals meeting on Russia," she said, referring to
the kind of high-level working group that focuses on a particularly
sensitive issue. "Denis didn't want you to be involved because you
are the one authorized to talk with Jake. For your own protection.
And ours." I stared hard at the books on her shelves. She went on to
explain that we were trying to get Congress to put out a bipartisan
statement on Russian meddling in the election, and then the intelligence community would put out its own.

"Do you want me to draft it?" I asked.

"No," she said. "This is going to be an IC process. But we'll need
you to think through the questions we'll get asked after."

I walked downstairs to my office and sank into my chair. For
eight years, I'd worked my way up to the place where I thought I'd
always be in the room, and now I was being kept out of the most
important conversation of all. My mind raced with a mix of self-
pity and self-blame. Sure, the explanation Susan gave made sense,
but my contacts with Jake Sullivan had all been authorized and
limited to a few calls about TPP. I couldn't help thinking that it was
something else. Benghazi, maybe, or the *New York Times Magazine*
debacle. Damaged goods—an easy Republican target. Someone
who my closest colleagues had determined needed to be kept out of
meetings about the thing we could all see playing out with our own
eyes.

I went to each of our lead communications people to get help
preparing the questions that we anticipated would come up after
the intelligence community put out their statement. Jen Psaki, her-

self a target of Russian meddling. Josh Earnest, who'd gamely fielded questions on the issue for weeks. Ned Price, my deputy. The Q&A we prepared anticipated the questions we were going to get, and also reflected our own frustration at being on the outside of the process. *Why didn't you tell us earlier? Is Russia trying to help Trump win? What are you going to do in response?*

The statement got held up for a couple of weeks for two reasons. First, an effort to secure a strong, bipartisan statement against Russian meddling from the congressional leadership met resistance from the Senate majority leader, Mitch McConnell, who pointedly refused to sign on. Democrats like Dianne Feinstein and Adam Schiff—the ranking members on the Senate and House Intelligence Committees—were alarmed and incensed, and they put out their own statement on September 22: "Based on briefings we have received, we have concluded that the Russian intelligence agencies are making a serious and concerted effort to influence the U.S. election. . . . We hope all Americans will stand together and reject the Russian effort."

McConnell's refusal was staggeringly partisan and unpatriotic in its disregard for a foreign adversary undermining our democracy. But the sad truth is that it wasn't surprising in the context of the Republican Party of 2016, which had spent eight years disbanding norms and had circled the wagons behind a demagogue. Obama reflected this sense of exhaustion. "What else did you expect from McConnell?" he said. "He won't even give us a hearing on Merrick Garland." He was, after eight years, worn down by Republican obstructionism.

Second, there was a debate about who would sign the intelligence community statement. Not all of the leaders of the intelligence community wanted to be named, particularly Comey, which struck us as ironic, considering how talkative he'd been about the Clinton email investigation. Ultimately, Clapper stepped up and agreed to put it in his name, as the leader of the intelligence community. Jeh Johnson, the secretary of homeland security, would attach his name as well, since he was responsible for defending the architecture of the U.S. election from cyberattack.

On October 7, the statement was finally ready for release. It was the most consequential public statement made on national security in my eight years of government that I had no role in preparing. Referring to the release of hacked documents, the statement said that the "thefts and disclosures are intended to interfere with the US election process . . . only Russia's senior-most officials could have authorized these activities." It was a Friday. Josh, Jen, and I asked Denis and Susan if anyone would be doing Sunday shows. The answer was no—the statement would speak for itself. After Benghazi, there were rarely any volunteers to go on the shows. As with McConnell's obstructionism, Republican attacks had worn people down and—perhaps—intimidated them.

The statement went out from the DNI. Ned was prepared to respond to incoming inquiries, working from talking points that hewed closely to the text of the statement. When asked about our response, we'd just say we had a variety of ways to impose consequences on Russia. Feeling like a supporting actor in this drama, I left at a reasonable hour that evening. As the gate of the White House clanged closed behind me, I looked down at my BlackBerry and saw a breaking news clip that there was a new *Access Hollywood* tape of Trump boasting about sexually assaulting women. Our statement wouldn't be the biggest news story of the day after all.

ONE AFTERNOON THAT FALL, I went to the Brookings Institution to meet with a group that could qualify as the heart of the American foreign policy establishment. It was a regular session hosted by Robert Kagan, a prominent neoconservative. Around the table were columnists like Tom Friedman and David Ignatius, along with a host of experts. When we all sat down, they gave me a gift: a movie poster for *The Blob*, embracing the derisive moniker that I'd used in *The New York Times Magazine*. I chuckled gamely and rolled it up, settling in for a bruising hour.

One after the other, they launched into criticisms of Obama's foreign policy, laying the blame for Ukraine, the catastrophe in

Syria, Brexit, and the rise of China at his feet. This reached a cre-
scendo when Leon Wieseltier, an editor at *The New Republic* and
self-appointed moralist, launched into a diatribe in which he declared that Obama was the first American president in history to
betray American values. I sat there seething. Wieseltier had been a
member of the Committee for the Liberation of Iraq, and did as
much as anyone to offer an impression that the liberal intelligentsia
supported the war in Iraq, a moral catastrophe that *had* betrayed
American values. Iraq, a place where our bombs, not someone else's,
had killed children.

I answered patiently. I'd just come back from Laos, I said, where
unexploded American bombs were still killing kids over forty years
after they'd been dropped. Then I repeated my lengthy refrain about
why not going to war in Syria wasn't a betrayal of who we are—that
there were no good options; that we were trying to preserve America's capacity to lead the world rather than fighting an endless series
of wars in the Middle East. Underneath, I felt incredulous. *You guys
are aiming your fire at Obama when we are a few weeks away from an
election in which someone who is a clear and present danger to American
values and international order could win.* When the session was over,
I walked out into a sunny and unseasonably hot afternoon, my shirt
sticking to my back. Friedman followed me out and expressed regret at the tone in the room. "I think we just got to a place where we
were talking past each other," he said of the last couple of years. I
had come to like and respect him over the years and said thank you.
Then I walked back to the White House, dropping my *Blob* poster
into a trash can along the way.

Obama's popularity kept rising in the country and around the
world, but the criticism being leveled at our foreign policy at home
had reached a fever pitch that reinforced Trump's dystopian vision
of an America in free fall. Of course, the world was faced with a
challenging moment. Everything we had tried had failed to stop
the killing in Syria. Refugees were pouring into Europe. Russia was
lashing out, from Ukraine to Syria. But Obama was the most respected leader in the world, and the acknowledgment that there

might also be limits to our capacity to solve all of the world's problems could be easily cast aside by someone like Trump, who simply asserted that he alone could do so.

We were at the center of power, ensconced in the White House. But we had less and less control over the political forces roiling the country—the toxic brand of nationalism on display at Trump rallies; a media that was increasingly broken into hermetically sealed, impenetrable partisan echo chambers; the obvious Russian efforts to influence our election that continued unabated. Even our scandals had moved on—Benghazi was no longer about Susan Rice's Sunday show appearances, it was now about Hillary Clinton's private email server, something to justify chants of "Lock her up."

In a way, I welcomed the chance to retreat into the backdrop of this drama. I walked my daughter to daycare on my shoulders, counting the passing buses. I listened to all 179 episodes of a podcast about the history of Rome, lying in bed contemplating the dreams of emperors long dead. I binge-watched *The Americans* with Ann, sitting on the couch in a darkened room, following American actors playing Russians pretending to be Americans. I began my days eating the foil-wrapped egg and sausage burritos that warmed under a heat lamp in the White House mess. I plodded through my bucket list, which had increasingly intersected with the ghosts of American interventions past—$90 million to clean up bombs in Laos, negotiating agreements with Cuba, implementing the Iran deal. I chaired meetings on our nascent effort to combat Russian disinformation in Europe.

In an October meeting with Obama, the Italian prime minister, Matteo Renzi, raised the issue of Russian meddling. *They are,* he said, *doing the same thing in Italy as they are doing to you here.* The Italians had a referendum coming up in December. If it failed, Renzi would have to stand down as prime minister, opening the door to Putin's friend Silvio Berlusconi. Renzi described how the Russians were creating fake news stories and then steering them to specific regions. It was sophisticated—not just antireferendum, but miniscandals that created clouds around members of Renzi's coalition.

"Ben's been working on this problem," Obama said. "Your people should follow up with him." Renzi looked at me expectantly, as if I had the answers.

By that point, Wikileaks was publishing John Podesta's emails—a drip, drip, drip of gossip that created an aura of scandal and mirrored the themes Trump was sounding on the campaign trail. Hillary was at the center of a corrupt establishment. Hillary took money from Wall Street. Hillary was in poor health. The Clinton Foundation was a criminal enterprise. The leaked documents, the Trump rallies, and a flood of stories—some true, some false, some a blend of fact and fiction—worked in unison like a symphony. Our government had responded to the Russian meddling as a cybersecurity issue. The people who'd been in meetings were largely intelligence and cyber experts; not one person had a communications background, despite the fact that we'd been dealing with fake news in Ukraine for more than two years. That October 7 statement said nothing about fake news or disinformation.

Cybersecurity was something that the government could at least get its mind around: secure systems, issue warnings. Stopping a flood of propaganda from overwhelming people's Facebook feeds and Google searches was not something that the government could do, or something that the tech companies wanted to do. Even if we were more focused on the fake news, Obama couldn't become editor in chief of people's social media feeds. If I scanned the Internet or Twitter, slogging through the cascade of attacks on Hillary, it was impossible to know where the stories came from. *Breitbart*? *InfoWars*? An American? Or a Russian? The content was the same.

I'd raise this with Obama. "I know," he'd say. "They've found the soft spot in our democracy."

In prep sessions for press appearances, we'd raise the criticisms that Obama should speak out more on the issue of Russian meddling. "I talk about it every time I'm asked," he'd say. "What else are we going to do? We've warned folks." Of course, we had no idea—Obama had no idea—at the time that there was an FBI investigation into the Trump campaign's contacts with Russia; that information was walled off from the White House, and I wouldn't even learn about it until long after I left government, in the press. Clinton was further ahead than we had been at the same point in 2012 and it looked as if she was going to win. On the campaign trail, Trump was railing that the election was "rigged" and that the Russia allegations were "fake news." The crowds responded with a bloodlust that would have been comical if it wasn't so frightening. "If I speak out more," Obama said, "he'll just say it's rigged."

A FEW DAYS BEFORE the election, Susan convened a meeting in her office. "Denis wants us to prepare for the possibility that Clinton wins and Trump says the whole thing was rigged."

"What does that have to do with us?" I asked.

"He's worried about the Russia angle. He wants us to think about validators." For the next thirty minutes, we brainstormed a list of Republicans who could come out immediately after the election to help counter the inevitable accusation from a losing Trump that we'd made up the Russia story: people like Condi Rice, Brent Scowcroft, Jim Baker.

We had meetings to plan for the likelihood of a Clinton victory, and what we'd do with Obama's remaining time in office. The confirmation of Merrick Garland, securing a liberal majority on the Supreme Court for a generation. We could line up some concessions from TPP countries, secure Hillary's tacit approval, get the deal through Congress, the final piece of our foreign policy legacy. Perhaps something bold could be done on Middle East peace. At home, we could push for criminal justice reform. Maybe Obama could decriminalize marijuana.

We also assessed the alternative of a Trump victory. We had a gloomy meeting in McDonough's office where we digested the scenario. "Can you imagine how the Russians would respond?" I said. The room was silent.

In the last week before the election, I went on a couple of campaign trips with Obama. He was loose, powerful on the stump, deconstructing Trump, puffing up Clinton. But it felt a bit like a classic rock concert. The crowds roared, the music played. They were there to see Obama, to hear the hits, but they seemed less enthused when he spoke about Clinton, who was counting on Obama's coalition—young people, blacks, Hispanics—to turn out for her in similar numbers.

One afternoon, I was sitting on the Marine One flight back to the White House after a campaign swing to Florida. It was just a few days before the election. We got an email from Obama's political director with the last requests for Obama's time from the Clinton campaign: The day before the election, could he go to Michigan and Pennsylvania?

"Michigan?" Obama said, eyes wide. It was a state he'd won by 10 points in 2012. "That's not good."

CHAPTER 32

THE END

———

ELECTION NIGHT, I PICKED UP SOME CHINESE FOOD AND HEADED over to Cody Keenan's house. It was going to be an early night, we thought, given Clinton's lead in the polls. As I walked into his building, I checked my phone to find that Florida appeared to be going for Trump. We sat there for the next few hours as the map showed slowly spreading red. Michigan, Wisconsin, Pennsylvania—states we hadn't worried about in 2012. That was it. I drank warming beer and occasionally walked into the kitchen to eat lo mein, standing at the counter. For long stretches of time, we said nothing to each other, together in a room, alone with our thoughts. So many things I had worked on—from Iran to Cuba to climate change—were now at risk. It was all happening too fast to digest; it seemed as if it couldn't be real, that the country—and world—could turn that abruptly from the story of the last eight years to the brand of racist, mean-spirited, truthless politics that had shadowed us since 2008. Everything was suddenly eclipsed; I felt enveloped in a darkness.

After Trump was declared the victor, Obama emailed Cody to call him through the switchboard so that we could discuss what he was going to say about this the next day. We called him on a Black-Berry, putting the phone on speaker. Both of us had received dozens of calls like this, but the familiarity only made it feel more cruel.

"So, that happened," he said. He sounded surprised but as if he was trying to force himself to be subdued, like a man who just received an unexpected diagnosis and is trying to avoid getting too upset.

"What do you want to say?" Cody asked, laptop out, yet another speech to write.

Obama plowed through a set of boilerplate messages that suddenly seemed radical in contrast to Trump—pay tribute to democracy; congratulate Trump and say nice things about Hillary; pledge an orderly and professional transition. "There should be something at the end for young people," he said. "Don't get discouraged. Don't get cynical."

I had been largely silent. "Do you want to offer any reassurance to the rest of the world?"

"What do you have in mind?" he asked.

"Something for our allies, for NATO. That the United States will continue to be there for them."

There was a pause on the other end of the line. "No," he said. "I don't think that I'm the one to tell them that."

I walked home in the early morning darkness, seven blocks, moving slowly as if delaying getting home and going to bed would forestall the world that was to come. The trees were half-empty of leaves and the half-light of the street lamps cast a ghostly light. Obama sent me a brief note reminding me that there are more stars in the sky than grains of sand on the earth. I sent him one back that progress doesn't move in a straight line. I walked past the apartment on S Street where I'd lived when I was twenty-seven years old. I remembered how I'd planned to move back to New York City. I'd met Ann and stuck it out in my job; we'd moved in together; then I got this job working for Obama.

When I got home, Ann and I talked a bit. "I'm sorry, I don't know what to say," she said. "After all the *work* you guys did ..." She let her thought trail off. She was seven months pregnant with our second child, who would be born in an America that I couldn't yet reconcile.

"I know," I said, sitting on the edge of the bed. "I know."

I slept for three or four hours. When I woke, I had a sensation that I'd known only a few times in my life—the feeling that you don't want the knowledge you'd gone to sleep with to be true. When someone has died. When something like 9/11 has happened. It was a sense of profound anxiety, a shortness of breath, a constriction in the chest; it was all those things at once—an event that would challenge my assumptions about America and alter the course of the world as well as my own life. After all the *work* we'd done, it was going to end like this.

I couldn't shake the feeling that I should have seen it coming. Because when you distilled it, stripped out the racism and misogyny, we'd run against Hillary eight years ago with the same message Trump had used: She's part of a corrupt establishment that can't be trusted to bring change. *Change we can believe in.* How many times had I written those words? Because Trump was a product of the same forces I'd seen aligning against us for ten years. Because Sarah Palin. The Tea Party. Benghazi. The irrelevance of facts. A healthy majority of Republicans *still* did not believe that Obama was born in the United States. The Republicans had ridden this tiger, and we'd all ended up inside.

The morning after the election, I went to work, like any other day. I got my PDB, learned about the progress of our counter-ISIL campaign. I ate an egg and sausage burrito. I fought off the sadness that would have been too overwhelming if I succumbed to it. There was still work to do. When I went upstairs for Obama's morning briefing, the entire communications staff of the White House was gathered in the Oval Office. Obama wanted to speak with us directly. He stood in front of the Resolute Desk and addressed a large semicircle of people, most of whom were younger than I was. I stood, clutching my iPad with the government's most prized intelligence on it, mine for a couple more months. When I looked at the faces of the assembled group, most were crying.

Obama was smiling, and tried to strike an optimistic note. "The sun is shining," he joked. Then he thanked us all for our work. "We are leaving this country indisputably better off than we found it eight years ago, and that's because of you." He urged us to be professional in the transition, just as George W. Bush's team had been with us. "Ben sent me a note last night," he said. "We have to remember—history doesn't move in a straight line, it zigs and zags."

With that, the group filed out of the Oval Office so that we could resume the normal rhythm of the day, the daily briefing. Walking over to my seat, I saw the words stitched into the ring around the carpet on the floor, the quote from Martin Luther King, whose bust watched silently from a table along the wall: THE ARC OF THE MORAL UNIVERSE IS LONG, BUT IT BENDS TOWARD JUSTICE.

OBAMA WENT THROUGH STAGES. That first day, I was in multiple meetings where he tried to lift everyone's spirits. That evening, he interrupted the senior staff meeting in Denis McDonough's office and gave a version of the speech that I'd now heard three times as we all sat there at the table. He was the only one standing. It was both admirable and heartbreaking watching him take everything in stride, working—still—to lift people's spirits. When he was done, I spoke first. "It says a lot about you," I said, "that you've spent the whole day trying to buck the rest of us up." People applauded. Obama looked down.

On the Thursday after the election, he had a long, amiable meeting with Trump. It left him somewhat stupefied. Trump had repeatedly steered the conversation back to the size of his rallies, noting that he and Obama could draw big crowds but Hillary couldn't. He'd expressed openness to Obama's arguments about healthcare, the Iran deal, immigration. He'd asked for recommendations for staff. He'd praised Obama publicly when the press was there.

Afterward, Obama called a few of us up to the Oval Office to recap. "I'm trying to place him," he said, "in American history." He told us Trump had been perfectly cordial, but he'd almost taken pride in not being attached to a firm position on anything.

"He peddles bullshit. That character has always been a part of the American story," I said. "You can see it right back to some of the characters in *Huckleberry Finn*."

Obama chuckled. "Maybe that's the best we can hope for."

In breaks between meetings in the coming days, he expressed disbelief that the election had been lost. With unemployment at 5 percent. With the economy humming. With the Affordable Care Act working. With graduation rates up. With most of our troops back home. But then again, maybe that's why Trump could win. People would never have voted for him in a crisis.

He kept talking it out, trying on different theories. He chalked it up to multiple car crashes at once. There was the letter from Comey shortly before the election, reopening the investigation into Clinton's email server. There was the steady release of Podesta emails from Wikileaks through October. There was a rabid right-wing propaganda machine and a mainstream press that gorged on the story of Hillary's emails, feeding Trump's narrative of corruption.

He talked about what it took to win the presidency. To win, he told us, you have to have a core reason why you're running, and you need to make it clear to everyone how much you want to win. "You have to *want* it," he said, like Michael Jordan demanding the ball in the final moments of a game.

Ten days later, on our final foreign trip, there were flashes of anger. Standing backstage before his press conference with Angela Merkel, I told him that it was probably the last time a U.S. president would defend the liberal international order for a while. "I don't know," he said. "Maybe this is what people want. I've got the economy set up well for him. No facts. No consequences. They can just have a cartoon."

In a way, he was just like the rest of us—trying out different theories for what had happened, trying to figure out what it meant, what it said about us as a country. But of course he was different. He'd seen the country, and the world, from a different perch. And the one thing he kept coming back to was the expanse of time, the fact that we were just "a blip" in human history. In giving advice on how to deal with Trump, he offered a simple maxim: "Find some high ground, and hunker down."

SHORTLY AFTER THE ELECTION, Obama convened a National Security Council meeting on Russia. He opened by saying that he wanted the intelligence community to do a comprehensive review of Russia's meddling in the election that could be presented to him, and to Congress, before he left office. "We need to learn the lessons about what they did, because they're going to do it again," he said. Unspoken was the fact that Trump would never convene such a review. One after the other, the leadership of the intelligence community walked us through what they knew. It was worse than I'd previously known, more expansive, more clearly designed to aid Trump.

In the weeks to come, nearly everything I learned reinforced this dreadful reckoning. In Germany, Merkel's spokesperson told me about how fake news impacted their politics. He gave an example. At the height of Merkel's political vulnerability over the refugee issue, there would be stories about crimes committed by Syrian refugees. A rape, for instance, caused a huge outcry in a community. For days, there were protests, political fallout.

"And then?" I asked.

"And then we investigate this story and learn that it never happened," he said. "And we trace the story, and it started with a social media user with a German-sounding name, but something is not exactly right. The name is a little off. And the server, it is not German."

"It's probably in eastern Ukraine or Moldova," I said.

"Yes, this is right," he answered. "Russians."

I thought about all the made-up stories about Hillary—her ill health, her corruption, her crimes. It seemed impossible to know where they all began; which ones came from the American right wing and which ones came from Russians; how they spread; whether this flood of content was coincident or coordinated with the Trump campaign.

I'd run into different staffers who worked on Russia in the government, and they all had the same message: It's even worse than you think. Always, the suggestion was that there was more to the story. Trump, one told me, is exactly the kind of person that the Russians like to invest in for years. *Invest in how?* I asked. The Russians build relationships—finances, personal ties, associates, compromising information. What those relationships are for, or how they are activated, or whether the Americans involved are witting or not, can be an open question.

I walked around the West Wing feeling a kind of hollowness inside. I pulled Jen Psaki into Josh Earnest's office. "I think this Russia thing is a lot worse than we knew," I said, and went through all the different things I was learning. Josh looked at me with the same frozen smile he used on reporters who asked uncomfortable things in the briefing room.

"Have you talked to POTUS about this?" he asked.

I went to see Obama and told him that I thought we had a problem with Russia. "You think?" he said, sarcastically.

"I mean us. *We* have a problem. There's going to be a narrative," I said, choosing my words carefully, "that we didn't do enough. It's already building."

"What were we supposed to do?" he asked. "We warned people."

"But people will say, why didn't we do more, why didn't you speak about it more."

"When?" he asked. "In the fall? Trump was already saying that the election was rigged."

I told him that I worried about the scale of the fake news effort, the disinformation that went beyond hacking. "And do you think," he asked me, "that the type of people reading that stuff were going to listen to *me?*"

THE LEADERSHIP OF THE Trump transition team was fired shortly after the election. There would be two or three iterations of it before the inauguration. I never met any of them. Our NSC had prepared volumes of briefing papers on every possible subject—from Syria to Ukraine, from China to Cuba, but it was never clear to us who, if anyone, was reading them. Nobody on the Trump transition team wanted to talk to me or interact with me in any way, even though I'd spent eight years in the White House. "You're kind of PNG," our transition director told me. I heard they were collecting lists of people who had worked with me, suggesting that career people could pay a price for having served on my staff. It felt less like a peaceful transition of power than a vindictive extension of the right-wing campaign against Obama and people like me.

During our transition, in 2008, we'd all worked out of a government office space in downtown Washington, using government email accounts. The transition I was watching on television was taking place at Trump Tower, and foreign governments told us they'd chase down Trump officials—and Trump himself—on personal email and cellphones; a clever and capable foreign adversary would have no trouble puncturing that bubble. The Saudis and Emiratis were boasting around town about the access they had to Trump's family, which had much to gain financially from the kind of casual wealth that emanated from the Gulf.

You're never as high as you are after winning an election—everyone is asking for a job, telling you how great you are. You imagine that the political moment will be frozen in time—your congressional majorities, your media coverage, your fawning treatment from foreign governments and domestic constituencies. Almost immediately after assuming real responsibility, however, all of that capital starts to drain. *These guys*, I thought, *are acting as though the rules don't apply to them.*

In mid-November, Mike Flynn was named national security advisor. Flynn was an impetuous, angry former three-star general who had fulminated against Obama ever since he'd been fired by Jim Clapper in 2014 as the head of the Defense Intelligence Agency. Flynn liked to attribute his firing to some ideological dispute with Obama over "radical Islam"; in reality, Obama had no role in it. Clapper had gotten rid of him because he was destroying morale at

the agency. In 2015, he'd been photographed next to Putin at a dinner for RT, the principal propaganda organ for the Kremlin, which
had led the pro-Trump charge. He took a couple of weeks after his
appointment to accept Susan Rice's invitation to meet. His own
transition team volunteered to us that he'd met with Sergei Kislyak,
the Russian ambassador, before meeting with the American official
he was replacing.

Meanwhile, we were still running the government. Around
Christmas, we finalized a package of measures against Russia to
retaliate for their attack on our democracy; we'd delayed this until
after the election, assessing that anything before could have led
them to hack the election itself. The State Department was worried
about retaliation against Americans serving in Russia, but Susan
made clear that we needed to pursue the toughest option. We'd
impose sanctions. We'd close two Russian estates that were used for
intelligence gathering and expel thirty-five Russian agents from the
country.

"What about Putin?" I asked, in the final Situation Room meeting on the topic.

"What *about* him?" Susan asked.

"People are going to ask why we aren't sanctioning Putin."

There was a brief debate. I argued that if we were naming him as
responsible for the interference, he should be included. It was decided that that would be a bridge too far—we rarely sanctioned
heads of governments, and usually only where we favor regime
change.

I did a press call to announce the measures. I chafed at the Russian denials. "There are facts," I said, "and then there are things that
Russia says." In the back of my head, I wondered what I could say
that might trigger the Russians to mount a disinformation campaign against me. I dismissed those worries, but the fact that the
thought even crossed my mind sent a chill through my body: *If I'm
thinking this,* I thought, *every public official in a Western democracy is
going to think twice before criticizing Russia.*

On January 5, the leadership of the intelligence community filed into the Oval Office to brief Obama on the report on Russian meddling. Jim Clapper, James Comey, John Brennan, and Mike Rogers took seats on the couches. I sat in my usual seat facing Obama. One after the other, they painted a stark picture of a methodical and relentless campaign waged by Putin on behalf of Trump. Once again, it went well beyond anything that any of us, including Obama, had heard before. The act of pulling up all the information in the government had clearly connected some dots, corroborated some things, filled in a more disturbing picture. The same report, they told us, would be briefed to Trump the next day. A classified version would then be sent to Congress. A short, unclassified summary would be released to the public.

Obama sat silent and stoic, occasionally asking questions for clarification. Biden was animated, incapable of hiding his incredulity. We sat there looking at one another. The inauguration was in two weeks. We'd already announced our countermeasures. This review was now a body of evidence that would have to be reckoned with by our intelligence community, the FBI, Congress, and the White House. Our time was done, and our government was about to be led by the very people Putin had spent so much effort trying to put there. Sometimes there are no words to say.

Obama's response to Russian meddling had scrupulously adhered to the norms and responsibilities of his office. Establish the facts. Have the intelligence community do the public warning in its own, carefully chosen words. Protect the election infrastructure. Order a review of everything that happened. Stay in the lane of the rule of law and good governance; be impartial; don't stray for a moment into the dirtier political space occupied by everybody else: the Russians, the Trump campaign, Wikileaks. This set limits on what he, or any of us, could do before the election—limits that, in hindsight, did not extend far enough to encompass the scale of the assault on our democracy. Yet that disposition also ensured the painstaking review that established the facts about what happened and raised additional questions about what the Trump campaign had done, which would endure long after we were gone. If Obama's faith in norms and institutions is validated, then the truth will all come out, and consequences will flow from that.

THE DAY AFTER THE ELECTION, in a Skype session with the Cubans from the Situation Room, I apologized for my confidence that Clinton would win, which I had predicted would lead inexorably to the lifting of the embargo. Alejandro Castro showed no irritation. "You are the first person from your country who approached us with a sense of mutual respect and equality," he said. I looked down the table at Bernadette, who was in tears. Alejandro then expressed some hope for the Trump team: As recently as that summer, representatives from the Trump organization had traveled to Cuba to scout hotel opportunities.

I'd planned to fly to Havana one more time along with Caroline Kennedy: another symbolic end to the Cold War. It was another one of those victory laps that would never be run. Just after Thanksgiving, the day before we were set to go, Fidel Castro died. I was invited to attend his funeral as the sole representative of the U.S. government. I'd never met Fidel, and he'd criticized the opening between our countries. Many of the Cuban Americans I was friends with despised him. But given the precarious state of U.S.-Cuba relations after the election, I decided to go.

For the first time, I flew down to Havana by myself. That evening, a black car dropped me off behind the statue of Martí as the sun was setting. I was told to find my own space in rows of chairs that flanked the dais. When I came around the statue, there were hundreds of thousands of people in front of me, filling the square in the way I had imagined it during my first midnight visit. I walked up and down the dais, looking at the names printed out on white sheets of paper, antagonists of America for the last forty years: Robert Mugabe, Daniel Ortega, Nicolás Maduro. Gerhard Schroeder, the former chancellor of Germany, wandered the rows, with the red face of hard living, searching for his name. I found a protocol officer who led me to my seat, next to the French representative and one row in front of Hugo Chávez's daughter.

For the next several hours, the global left was heard from in speech after speech. The message was tired, out of date. Africans talking about the struggle to shake off colonialism. Latin Americans honoring the Cuban people and their resistance to the "empire" to the north. Middle Eastern royals offering tributes that seemed rooted in hotel interests. Russians and Chinese mouthing words of proletarian revolution. I sat on the dais, dozens of international television cameras pointed in my direction from a platform nearby, with a frown frozen on my face—mindful of my critics back home, not wanting to be criticized for smiling. I stared out into the crowd, the occasional Cuban flag waving. Che's face loomed over the square, young in death, the face of ideology not curdled by the passage of decades, or the corruption of power. Up front, a few hundred people clapped and chanted "Viva Fidel!" and other slogans. But the mass of humanity behind them was quiet, only occasionally stirred to life. Who knows why they were there—devotion to Fidel or shock at his finally passing; coercion or curiosity. I was out of place on that dais, just as I was now out of place in Washington. As I sat there, thirty-nine years old, the one American official who could somehow be on the dais at Fidel Castro's funeral, my belief was not in revolutions or the administration preparing to take power back home: I believed in the people standing in the back of the crowd.

I made one last trip to Cuba the week of the inauguration to conclude the last in a flurry of agreements meant to lock in as much of our progress as possible before Trump took over: agreements that overhauled U.S. immigration policy toward Cuba, established deeper business ties, and initiated law enforcement cooperation. The Cubans arranged for me to tour the house that Hemingway lived in for more than two decades. My hero growing up—they'd done their homework. I wandered through the house, browsing his bookshelves. There, in the bathroom, was line after line of tiny, barely legible black ink handwriting on the wall—Hemingway recording his weight day to day, month to month, year to year. People are people.

Raúl hosted me for a long dinner—just him, me, Alejandro, and Juana, sitting in the same room where Obama had attended a meeting earlier that year. We drank rum and talked about hurricanes and weather modeling, liberation struggles in Angola and Namibia, the period after the Soviet Union fell and Cuba's economy, me making my normal pitches for change. Deep into the dinner, and the rum, I asked Raúl whether Cuba would have made itself America's enemy—and the Soviet Union's partner—if America had responded differently to the revolution. "We would not," he said. "We just wanted to survive. It was your choice!"

Before it was over, I tried to reassure Raúl that he should seek a deal with Trump, that the forces in the United States still pointed—inevitably—toward engagement between our countries. As I talked, I thought about how he was into his eighties, that this change he had initiated with the United States might not fully take hold during his lifetime after all. He smiled, driving his eyes to squint. "Ben," he said. "There was once a general from Ossetia who had the authority to launch nuclear missiles from my territory without telling me, even though I was defense minister. I've dealt with harder things than Trump."

ON JANUARY 3, our second daughter, Chloe, was born. She came quickly, as if she was in a hurry. Chloe wouldn't have the Internet fame that Ella had, the pictures of her wearing her elephant Halloween costume in the Oval Office with Obama. But she also wouldn't have the absences of the first two years, the early morning daycare drop-offs and late-afternoon pickups. She had a life to begin, and I did too. Ann and I took some small measure of satisfaction in the fact that she wasn't born while Trump was president.

There was the matter of the rest of our lives. If Hillary had won, Ann would have stayed on in her State Department job for at least a few months. Now she'd be gone with me on January 20. I knew I was going to keep working for Obama. I thought I might write a book. That's about all I knew. I was out of touch with every person and aspect of my life other than the next thing that had to get done. After bringing my new family of four home from the hospital, I went back to the White House to complete the last two weeks of eight years of work.

My days shrank to completing a few final pieces of business, packing up my office, and attending one goodbye party after another, fighting off a sense of desolation at who was taking our places. Outside the White House, the inauguration platform was steadily constructed, day by day, like a coffin for your own funeral. The enormity of what I was saying goodbye to was impossible to measure. The people who'd surrounded me, some for ten years; people who'd been in the middle of the most important events we'd ever experienced, perhaps the most important things we would ever experience. This group of people would never be together again. Some were staying in government, seeking posts overseas. Some were headed out to California to ride the wave of technology that had helped bring Obama and then Trump into office. Some, like me, were going to wake up on January 21 without knowing what they were going to do the next day.

And there was the place. In my first days on the job, I'd marveled at the Oval Office and the fancy rooms; now I roamed the White House complex like a ghost to my own experience. Here was the staircase that led to the Usher's Office in the residence, where I'd meet Obama after hours to get his speech edits, the words he'd speak in Cairo or announcing our opening to Cuba. Here was the bench out behind the kitchen area, where they'd assemble the flowers for an event or cook the meat on grills for a dinner, where I disappeared sometimes to think because no one could find me there. Here was the milk crate I sat on, down a metal staircase in the inner courtyard of the EEOB, one of the few places you could smoke, where I'd turned over in my head the hundreds of thousands of words I wrote for Obama.

On January 19, the last full day of the Obama presidency, I gathered up the items I had to return: multiple laptops that had followed me around the world; a BlackBerry from which I'd sent hundreds of thousands of messages; a diplomatic passport on which I could no longer travel. A group of us walked over to the Executive Office Building, as if it would be easier if we went together, carrying boxes of personal belongings like laid-off workers. After we were done "out-processing," we came back to the West Wing and a few people went into Cody's office to have a beer and watch old speeches.

Instead, I sat alone in my office—my email account would be deactivated within an hour. So I typed out some last messages. My final note was to Obama. We had this debate, over the years, about whether individuals or social movements shape history—the kind of casual, esoteric conversation that filled in downtime in cars, helicopters, airplanes, or the quiet of the Oval Office. I had been on the side of social movements, dating back to the early days of the Arab Spring. "I was wrong," I told him in my message. "You've made a difference in the lives of billions of people."

That night, the Obamas hosted a reception for the remaining staff in the White House, a skeleton group of core staff, as most people had had their last days during the previous week. The table in the State Dining Room was covered in the same snacks that I'd eaten at a hundred White House parties before; the bar in the corner served the same booze. Obama gave a toast. In the middle, he said, "Ben and I have had this debate over the years about what makes history: individuals, or movements." He stopped and looked at me. "But I think the answer is actually that it takes a team of people."

He invited us all up to his private residence, guiding us through the different rooms, a part of the White House I'd been in only a couple of times over the last eight years. He took me over to a frame in the corner of one room. "This is one of five original copies of the Gettysburg Address." I leaned in and examined Lincoln's careful handwriting, larger and more legible than Obama's. The speech barely went onto a third page before it ended with the signature "Abraham Lincoln. November 19, 1863."

"We could never get them this short," I said, peering down at the writing.

He laughed. "I used to come in here sometimes in the middle of the night while I was writing. For inspiration." I thought about him roaming these rooms in the early morning hours, going over some text I'd written, while I was off somewhere staring at a laptop.

We walked out onto the Truman Balcony, which overlooked a darkened South Lawn, the Washington Monument and the Jefferson Memorial in the distance beyond. I thought about something a Secret Service agent had said about the end of the administration—that he'd been relieved to complete two terms with Obama alive. Unspoken were the myriad threats that must have come their way, the pressure of an African American being elected president in a country with its own history of political violence, as Lincoln's handwriting recalled. Obama, unlike Lincoln, was not going to be frozen in time as a young man taken by tragedy; he'd reached the end of the race, which made him more human in the scope of history. As he'd said about Mandela, he wasn't a saint, he was a man.

I went back to my office and stayed until five thirty in the morning. I couldn't seem to get to the end of the paper. I couldn't take any of it with me; it was now the property of the National Archives, and I had to box up what I might want access to in the years ahead. There was a large, heavy metal safe in the corner where I had set aside paper over the years, documents that I might want to look at later. I sat there, in the middle of the night, looking at photographs of bin Laden's emptied compound after the raid; early versions of what became the Iran deal; communications from the Vatican on Cuba. I put aside the things that had to be saved for posterity, stored away someplace to be found at a later date.

ON INAUGURATION DAY, I went out to Andrews Air Force Base for the Obamas' final flight on Air Force One. That morning, I had trouble getting past the Secret Service checkpoints that formed an outward perimeter, like an armed encampment, on Seventeenth Street and then into the White House; an agent recognized me, waved his hand at the one giving me trouble, and told the others, "He's okay." And with that, I walked through the White House gate one final time, eight years to the day since I walked in for the first time.

When I got inside the West Wing, all of the jumbo photographs of Obama had been taken down, the space in the walls now filled with empty frames reserved for photographs of Trump. The Oval Office had already been remodeled—yellow curtains, a new rug. This was Reagan's design, I was told: Make America Great Again. Ferial Govashiri, my old assistant, now Obama's, showed me his things stacked outside on the walkway that led to the colonnade. There was his couch that I'd sat on, the cushions piled up and his rug rolled up on top of it like furniture hastily prepared for a moving van on its way to some warehouse and, ultimately, a museum.

After the inauguration, the Obamas did a farewell with several hundred former staffers in a hangar at Andrews. While they shook one last set of hands along a rope line, I boarded the plane with a small staff cohort who would accompany them on their flight out to Palm Springs, California, where they'd start their vacation. George W. Bush's team had recommended we do this to make the flight less lonely for them after eight years when they were surrounded by dozens of people. When I got on board, I noticed that the place cards that usually read AIR FORCE ONE now simply said ABOARD THE PRESIDENTIAL AIRCRAFT—it wasn't Air Force One since the president wouldn't be on board.

It had been drizzling, and I watched through dampened windows as the Obamas took one last walk down a long red carpet, through a military honor guard, and up the stairs to the plane. Once on board, Michelle Obama sat, as if feeling the full exhaustion of the last eight years, on the first couch down the hallway of the plane. Obama held her closely, whispering something in her ear.

The mood on the flight was subdued. The Obama girls sat with some family and friends in the staff area. They had been so young;

now they were both taller than me. I stood in the hallway of the plane chatting with Obama—for the first time in eight years, I was no longer talking to the president. His face acquired a slight droop when he was tired, and the crevices in his cheeks were deeper and more pronounced than the fresh face, full of confidence, that I'd first looked at in a conference room all those years ago.

"I came to see the presidency like a game of Pac-Man," he told me, moving his hand as if using a joystick in front of him. "Sometimes I felt like I was just outrunning people, trying to avoid getting tripped up before I got to the end of the board." He was nestled between two presidents far less qualified than he was, yet he—the only black person to hold the office—had been held to a higher bar, and he'd cleared it.

"And here you are," I said.

"And here I am." He laughed. He looked profoundly relieved, though it was jarring to hear him talk about the presidency in the past tense, as a job he once had.

I told him about my first thoughts upon boarding the plane. "I always get on this plane," I said, "put down a foldout desk, take out my laptop, and start working. But now I've got nothing to do. No emails to answer, no speech to write, no crisis to deal with. It's . . . strange."

"And I've got no briefings to read," he said. "All the decisions have been made."

I thought about the weight that was lifted, but also all of the information that must have filled his thoughts for eight years, now unoccupied. What must that be like, to suddenly have all of that mental space, all of that time, now open. "What are you going to do tomorrow morning, with all that extra time?" I asked.

"Sleep in," he said, before walking back to his family.

The military aide, who would continue under Trump, the person who would sometimes carry the nuclear football that could end life on earth, warned me I was about to go through "an intense physiological experience. You've been running on stress and adrenaline," he said, "for years." He wasn't wrong. I felt a creeping tiredness coming on, a pending collapse.

When we got to Palm Springs the weather was bad and the plane flew in circles for about an hour. If it had been an urgent presidential trip, we might have just gone for it. Instead, they found a regional airport an hour or so away. They wouldn't need a full presidential motorcade. As we landed, I gave Obama a half hug and slap on the back. "Love you, brother," he said, heading off to get his things.

I got off the plane and walked a hundred feet or so over to an area where I could smoke. It was dark, and there were only a few cars parked on the tarmac: SUVs and a van for the personal staff that was still traveling with them. It felt eerily like all the stops we'd made to refuel Air Force One at U.S. military bases over the years—in Anchorage and Guam, in the Azores and in Germany—short breaks in the middle of long-haul trips around the globe. There was no arrival party, no red carpet. I watched as the Obamas deplaned without waving and climbed into their SUVs, heading off to begin the next chapter of their lives.

Air Force One normally bustles with activity—press, Secret Service, staff—people at the center of a traveling drama. But as we took off for the flight back to Washington, there were fewer than ten passengers on board the enormous plane—the handful of staffers who'd made the trip out with the Obamas out of some combination of sentimentality, indispensability, and moral support. The people who hadn't left. We ate a quiet meal as the plane flew east toward home. I walked up and down the length of the plane—the seats in the back, where I'd briefed the traveling press; the four-top tables, where we'd watched movies; the conference room, where I'd watched Obama make decisions, take briefings, and play a seemingly endless game of spades; the computers, where I'd panicked over speeches that felt like the most important and urgent things imaginable.

I settled into the senior staff cabin, no longer a staffer myself, and sank into the cocoon of the white noise that always marked a long flight home. I lay down on the floor, feeling the slight, cool vibration of the carpeted floor below me. I was too tired to do anything, but there was also no way I could sleep. I looked at a framed star that the Air Force One crew had given me, a memento of having flown more than a million miles on this aircraft.

I thought of the young man I'd been who went to work in Chicago. In those days, I used to walk anonymously through the city streets, scattered skyscrapers and new construction reaching into the sky around me. I would make my way to the campaign office through a series of alleys that cut across to Michigan Avenue. Always, at the opening of a cross street or a break in the buildings, I could see out of the corner of my eye a new, wide glass tower climbing into the sky along the Chicago River. In my mind, the building came to be a symbol of what we were building in the campaign, as it worked its way to completion. It wasn't until after we'd won the Iowa Caucus that put Obama on a path to the presidency that the letters TRUMP were affixed to the side of that building, about a third of the way up. We had no idea of the shadow that the owner of the building would cast over the historic presidency that we were about to claim.

The twenty-four-year-old I'd been, handing out flyers on a Brooklyn street on 9/11, was closer in time to the young man who went to work for the Obama campaign than I was, flying back to Washington on this plane. Trump was impossible without 9/11. The jingoism in the media; the assertion of a new, militaristic American nationalism; the creeping fear of the Other, and the way that it could be manipulated by an ideologue; the wars that sapped America's strength, and unsteadied our place in the world; the recognition that there would be no victory, as promised by Bush, no parade or period on the end of a paragraph in history.

I closed my eyes. Somewhere out there, in the vast expanse of darkness, was the story of the last eight years, the world as it is. Markets once crippled by crisis teemed with optimistic forecasts on computer screens. Iranian centrifuges sat idle in a storage warehouse with electronic seals. Yazidi women and children who had escaped from Mount Sinjar awaited a new life in Turkish refugee camps. A team of women in Laos scoured the rough grass for unexploded bombs. Syrian prisons were filled with human beings suffering untold horror. A refugee went looking for a job in Berlin. An aging survivor of the atomic bomb in Hiroshima went about her day in a tidy apartment. Vladimir Putin presided over a revanchist and rotting Russian regime. Angela Merkel prepared her run for another term as German chancellor. NATO patrolled the skies over Estonia. Mohamed Morsi sat in an Egyptian prison cell. American-backed forces inched closer to Raqqa. A compound once occupied by Osama bin Laden in Abbottabad was no more. American troops guarded the perimeter of Bagram Airfield. Scientists researched new methods to meet the targets set by the Paris climate accord. Colombian guerrillas planned to turn in their weapons. A Cuban shopkeeper took stock of his inventory. A young person in Kenya who had participated in a U.S. exchange program went to work building a community organization back home. The congregants of a black church in Charleston accepted God's grace. Donald Trump watched cable news in the residence of the White House. Barack Obama finished his drive to a vacation home in Palm Springs. All the people who'd worked for him readied themselves for new lives. My own daughters lay sleeping in my small apartment, unaware of the convulsions in the world around them.

Billions of people around the globe had come to know Barack Obama, had heard his words, had watched his speeches, and, in some unknowable but irreducible way, had come to see the world as a place that could—in some incremental way—change. The arc of history. How had his presence altered the direction of these individual human beings and the larger forces they touched; the lives they would lead; the stories they would tell? I was just one human being in this expanse—altered by experience, distorted by forces beyond my control, hurtling through the American darkness on the most iconic aircraft in the world. I would land for the first time at Andrews Air Force Base without a helicopter or collection of vans waiting to escort me back to the White House. I'd touch down, in the predawn hours, another human being whose own story, whose own life, had been changed by Barack Obama. I was a man, no longer young, who—in the zigzag of history—still believed in the truth within the stories of people around the world, a truth that compels me to see the world as it is, and to believe in the world as it ought to be.

ACKNOWLEDGMENTS

———

I COULDN'T HAVE WRITTEN THIS BOOK, OR MADE IT THROUGH the story it tells, without kind, patient, and generous support from many people. My Obama family picked me up when I was down, came of age with me, always stuck together, and continues to give me hope for the future. The incredible team of people who worked for me are responsible for whatever good I did at work—you inspired me with your passion, professionalism, and made coming to work fun . . . most days. The talented career professionals in the United States government are a national treasure. The many people I met, negotiated with, or collaborated with around the world extended my own horizons. Barack Obama made this entire story possible, taught me more than I could ever put into words, and continues to give me faith in the world as it ought to be.

A number of people were indispensable to making this book a reality. Rumana Ahmed did invaluable research with her characteristic good humor and idealism. Kristen Bartoloni and Alex Platkin kept my facts straight. Bernadette Meehan, Charlie Fromstein, Peter Rundlet, and Nimi Uberoi picked up my slack and were patient through my absences. Elyse Cheney was an invaluable guide, editor, and sounding board. Andy Ward made everything I wrote better, as did all of my other readers.

My wife, Ann, traveled this entire journey with me while also doing her own extraordinary and impactful work on behalf of women and girls around the world and becoming an incredible mom. And our girls, Ella and Chloe, who matter more to me than anything else in the world, always fill me with love and hope.

INDEX

healthcare reform, 71, 79, 91, 142
Hemingway, Ernest, vii, 353, 412–13
Hernández, Gerardo, 266, 284, 287,
 288
Hiroshima:
 atomic bombing of, 374, 375
 Obama's visit to, 374–80
Hizbollah, 223
Ho Chi Minh Trail, 335
Holbrooke, Richard:
 diplomatic career of, 64–65
 as Special Representative for
 Afghanistan and Pakistan
 (SRAP), 64–65
 in 2008 Clinton campaign, 17
Holder, Eric, 242
Holocaust, 24, 203
House of Representatives, U.S.,
 Republican control of, 92
House Select Committee on
 Benghazi:
 Rhodes's appearance before,
 360–64
 Susan Rice's appearance before,
 360–61
humans:
 and capacity for doing harm,
 377–78
 storytelling as distinct trait of,
 372–73
 technological advances of, 374–75,
 377, 378
Hungary, 1956 revolution in, 110
Huntington Beach, Calif., 172
Hussain, Rashad, 55
Hussein, Saddam, 5, 7, 44, 50, 251,
 275
 overthrow of, 339
 supposed WMDs of, 50, 224, 228

Ignatius, David, 70, 395
Ilves, Toomas, Obama's meeting
 with, 298
India:
 climate change and, 344–45
 Pakistan and, 73
Indonesia, Obama's childhood in,
 47–48, 165
Innocence of Muslims (video),
 backlash against, 177–79, 181–82,
 183, 279, 362–63
intelligence community, U.S.:
 Obama's speeches reviewed by,
 50–51
 President's Daily Briefing and,
 87–88
 Russian meddling report of, 406,
 409–11
 statement on Russian hacking by,
 393–95
International Criminal Court, 111
Internet, fake news on, 398
Iran:
 American hostages in, 128
 Assad supported by, 156, 197, 198,
 199, 205, 290
 Israel and, 173
 nuclear program of, 173, 242,
 248–49, 322
 Obama's secret outreach to, 55
 Obama's willingness to talk with,
 12, 14, 15, 17
 Rouhani elected president of,
 247–48
 sanctions against, 151, 160, 174, 252,
 268, 315, 326–27
 U.S. relations with, 55–56, 174
Iran-Contra, 215, 216
Iranian Revolution, 250, 323